Science

Based on Latest NCERT

Class 8

Authors

Rahul Kumar *(Physics)*
Er. Abhishek Kumar Gupta *(Chemistry)*
Himanshi Gambhir *(Biology)*

ARIHANT PRAKASHAN

(School Division Series)

卐 **ADMINISTRATIVE & PRODUCTION OFFICES**

Regd. Office

'Ramchhaya' 4577/15, Agarwal Road, Darya Ganj, New Delhi -110002
Tele: 011- 47630600, 43518550; Fax: 011- 23280316

卐 **Head Office**

Kalindi, TP Nagar, Meerut (UP) - 250002, Tel: 0121-7156203, 7156204

卐 **SALES & SUPPORT OFFICES**

Agra, Ahmedabad, Bengaluru, Bareilly, Chennai, Delhi, Guwahati, Hyderabad, Jaipur, Jhansi, Kolkata, Lucknow, Nagpur & Pune.

PO No. : TXT-59-T066245-07-25

Published By Arihant Publications (India) Ltd.

For further information about the books published by Arihant, log on to www.arihantbooks.com or e-mail at info@arihantbooks.com

Follow us on    

卐 **PRICE** ₹285.00

PRODUCTION TEAM

Publishing Managers
Mahendra Singh Rawat &
Keshav Mohan

Project Head
Ashwani

Cover Designer
Bilal Hashmi

Inner Designer
Ankit Tyagi

Page Layouting
Mayank Saini

Proof Readers
Mukul Kaushik
Manish Kumar

Inside the Book

Allinone
COMPLETE STUDY | COMPLETE PRACTICE | COMPLETE ASSESSMENT

All in One
COMPLETE STUDY | COMPLETE PRACTICE | COMPLETE ASSESSMENT

Allinone
COMPLETE STUDY | COMPLETE PRACTICE | COMPLETE ASSESSMENT

Key Features

Science Class 8

Chapter Intro

A quick information about the coverage of the chapter to explain students about what they are going to study.

CHAPTER 04

Combustion and Flame

We use different kinds of fuels for various purposes at home, in industry and for running automobiles. These can be cowdung, wood, coal, charcoal, petrol, diesel, Compressed Natural Gas (CNG), Liquefied Petroleum Gas (LPG), etc. Some materials burn with flame (e.g. candle) whereas some burn without flame (e.g. coal). Let us know the chemical process of burning and the types of flame produced during this process.

Science Insight

Additional but informational matter related to given concept. It helps & motivate students to explore more beyond their books.

(iii) Another way to obtain CO_2 is to release large amount of powdered baking soda (sodium bicarbonate) or potassium bicarbonate over the fire. Heat of the fire releases CO_2 gas from baking soda which cut off the fire.

SCIENCE INSIGHT When a LPG cylinder catchs fire, it is wrapped with a wet cloth. It lowers the temperature of fire and cuts off its contact with oxygen.

Boxed Matter

Information given in the boxes is related to the explanation of daily life phenomena related to the concept given.

History of Matchstick

More than five thousand years ago, small pieces of pinewood dipped in sulphur were used as matches in ancient Egypt. A mixture of antimony tri-sulphide, potassium chlorate and white phosphorus with some glue and starch was applied on the head of a match made of suitable wood. These days the head of the safety match contains only antimony tri-sulphide and potassium chlorate. When the match is struck against the rubbing surface, some red phosphorus gets converted into white phosphorus. This immediately reacts with potassium chlorate in the matchstick head to produce enough heat to ignite antimony trisulphide and start the combustion.

Try These

A set of 3-5 Questions given in between the text, helps students to remain connected with the text while studying. They can instantly assess themselves for their understanding.

Try These 4.1

1. **Is light always given off as flame in combustion process?**
2. **Is it possible to burn a paper in a room where only CO_2 and nitrogen gases are present?**
3. **A heap of dry grass burns easily while a wet one does not. Why?**
4. **Why inflammable substance like petrol, kerosene is used to burn substance having high ignition temperature?**

Illustrative Figures

To make the concepts completely visible, illustrative diagrams have been given at various place.

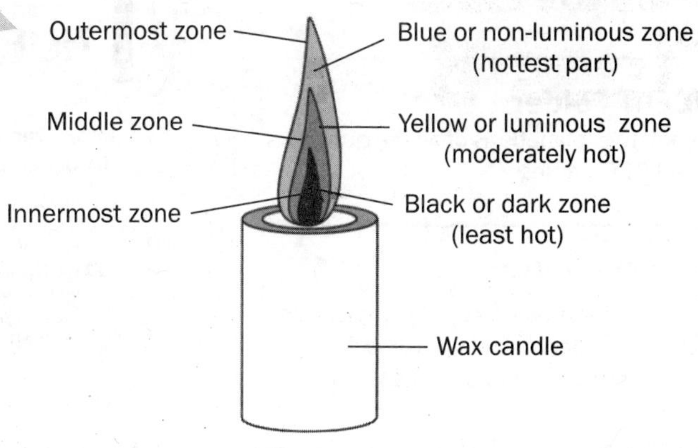

Different zones of a flame

Science Glossary

List of important scientific terms used in the chapter with their definitions.

Science Glossary

Acid rain When oxides of sulphur and nitrogen react with water molecules in the atmosphere, it forms an acid. This acid mixes with rainwater and causes acid rain.

Calorific value It is the amount of heat energy produced on complete combustion of 1 kg of fuel.

Combustion It is a process in which a substance reacts with oxygen and gives off some heat or light.

Deforestation Cutting of trees leads to deforestation which is quite harmful to the environment.

Explosion When a cracker is ignited a sudden reaction takes place. A large amount of gases is evolved in the process along with heat, light and sound. Such a reaction is called explosion.

Flame A flame is a region where combustion of gaseous substances or vapour takes place.

Mind Map

A quick revision visual tool for the complete chapter.

Let's Investigate

To connect the theory to related practical aspects, this section contains scientific activity with complete procedural details.

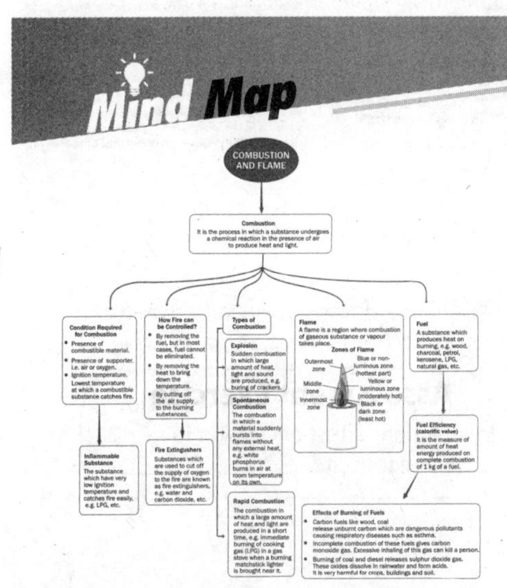

Let's Investigate

ACTIVITY 1 (Page 41)

Aim To show that quality of burning flame depends on the amount of air available around it.

Materials Required A candle, glass chimney, few wooden blocks and a glass plate.

Procedure

1. Fix a lighted candle on a table.
2. Put a glass chimney on the candle.
3. Rest this arrangement of chimney on the wooden blocks .
4. Make sure that air can enter the chimney as shown in the figure (a).
5. Remove the wooden blocks and let the chimney rest on the table as fig. (b).

NCERT Folder

Complete explanations of all the questions of NCERT Exercises.

NCERT FOLDER

Complete Explanations of all NCERT's Questions

Intext Questions

Q.1 We were told that food is a fuel for our body. Why? Page 40

Ans. The food that we eat is broken down in our body by reaction with oxygen and energy is produced, which is utilised by our body as a fuel.

Q.2 We have read that the Sun produces it's own heat and light. Is it also some kind of combustion? Page 42

Ans. No, it is not combustion. The heat and light in the Sun are produced by nuclear reaction.

Q.3 Explain how the use of CNG in automobiles has reduced pollution in our cities.

Ans. CNG has replaced diesel and petrol as fuel in automobiles because petrol and diesel produced a lot of unburnt carbon particles and emitted carbon dioxide, nitrogen oxide and sulphur dioxide. These all gases are poisonous gases and cause various environmental hazards. The main causes of acid rain are nitrogen oxides and sulphur dioxide.

But CNG is safe because it produces these harmful substances in very small amounts. Thus, the use of CNG is reducing pollution in our cities.

REVIEW EXERCISE

Including Competency Based Questions

Part I

Multiple Choice Questions

1. Combustion is a process that
(a) releases light and heat
(b) absorbs light and heat
(c) produces only heat
(d) produces only light

2. Combustion is generally
(a) a physical process (b) a chemical process
(c) Both (a) and (b) (d) None of these

3. The product(s) of combustion is/are
(a) only oxygen (b) oxygen and water
(c) carbon dioxide and water (d) only carbon dioxide

11. The substance expected to have the highest ignition temperature out of the following is
(a) kerosene (b) petrol (c) coal (d) alcohol

12. Water was poured over a large oil fire to extinguish it. What would happen and why?
(a) The fire will be put off since water extinguishers fires
(b) The fire will spread since oil floats on water
(c) The fire will be put off since water dissolves oil
(d) The fire will spread since water contains hydrogen that is a combustible gas

13. In a fire extinguisher, which substance is commonly used for cutting off the oxygen supply to the fire?
(a) Water (b) Sand

Review Exercise

Chapter exercise having all types of questions; MCQs, Assertion-Reason, True-False, Fillers, Matching, Case based, VSA, SA, LA.

NEP 2020 Based Exercise

Questions based on elements/skills given in NEP 2020; Thinking Skills, Experimental Skills, Enquiry Skills etc.

Skill Based Questions as per NEP 2020

1.

Fire triangle

On the basis of fire triangle given above answer the following questions.

(i) Which part of the fire triangle is removed to control fire in the following cases?
(a) Putting a fire blanket on fire.
(b) Removing dead leaves and dead grass in forest fire.

3. In severe cold weather, Mohan's family burnt wood in the room during the night keeping the windows close. After some time, they felt suffocation. Mohan immediately opened the windows and get relief.
(i) What did actually happen?
(ii) What values are associated with Mohan?

Thinking skill

4. A factory was started near a village. Suddenly, villagers started feeling the presence of irritating vapours in the village. Mr. Lalit Jain was school teacher in that village He noted that the cases of

ASSESSMENT EXERCISE

Part I

Multiple Choice Questions

1. Which type of combustion is characterised by a lack of oxygen during the burning process?
(a) Spontaneous combustion (b) Incomplete combustion
(c) Rapid combustion (d) Controlled combustion

2. What is the minimum temperature at which a substance catches fire and burns on it's own?
(a) Boiling point (b) Melting point
(c) Ignition temperature (d) Freezing point

3. Which of the following fire extinguishers is suitable for tackling electrical fires?
(a) Water fire extinguisher
(b) Foam fire extinguisher
(c) Carbon dioxide fire extinguisher
(d) Powder fire extinguisher

Assertion-Reason Questions

The following questions consist of two statements **Assertion** (A) and **Reason** (R). Answer these questions by selecting the appropriate option given below.
(a) Both A and R are true and R is the correct explanation of A
(b) Both A and R are true but R is not the correct explanation of A
(c) A is true, but R is false
(d) A is false, but R is true

9. Assertion (A) Electrical components can catch fire.
Reason (R) Electrical fire can be extinguished using water.

10. Assertion (A) Candle can burn a block of wood.
Reason (R) Ignition temperature of wood is high.

Assessment Exercise

Complete Test of chapter in Exam format.

Crop Production and Management

All living organisms require food for their growth and survival. Plants prepare their food themselves, while animals including humans obtain their food directly or indirectly from plants. In order to provide food for a large population of living beings, regular production, proper management and distribution of food is necessary.

This can be accomplished by proper agricultural practices. Agriculture (Latin word *Ager*–field and *culture*–cultivation) is the applied branch of biology which involves the practice of cultivating crops as well as rearing of animals.

1.1 Crops

When plants of same type are grown and cultivated in a field on a large scale, it is called a crop (fasal in Hindi), e.g. wheat crop, paddy crop, etc.

India is a vast country, where the climatic conditions like temperature, humidity and rainfall vary from one region to another. Accordingly, there is a rich variety of crops grown in different parts of the country.

Despite this diversity, two broad cropping patterns can be identified on the basis of particular season in which they grow.

These are as follows

1. Kharif Crops

The crops which are sown in rainy season are called Kharif crops or summer crops, e.g. paddy (rice), maize, soyabean, cotton, groundnut, millets (bajra), etc.

These crops generally grown from June to September.

2. Rabi Crops

The crops that are grown in winter season are called Rabi crops or winter crops, e.g. wheat, gram, pea, mustard and linseed.

These crops are generally grown from October to March.

Note Paddy or rice crops are grown in rainy season because it requires a lot of water. It cannot be grown in winter season.

1.2 Agricultural Practices

Cultivation of crops involves several activities undertaken by farmers over a period of time. These activities or tasks are referred to as agricultural practices.

The various agricultural practices of crop production involves

(i) Preparation of soil
(ii) Sowing
(iii) Adding manure and fertilisers
(iv) Irrigation
(v) Protecting from weeds
(vi) Harvesting
(vii) Storage

1.3 Preparation of Soil

The first step for the crop production is soil preparation. Soil is the uppermost layer of the Earth where plants are grown. Only a few centimeters of top layer of soil supports plant growth. It provides water, air, minerals, humus, etc. to the plants. Soil is prepared for sowing seeds by three major methods which are as follows

1. Ploughing

The process of loosening and turning the soil is called ploughing or tilling. It is done by using a plough.

The loosening and turning of soil by ploughing is beneficial because of the following reasons

(i) Plant roots can penetrate freely and deeper into the soil and plants are held firmly to the ground.

(ii) Loose soil helps the plant roots to breathe easily.

(iii) Ploughing of soil brings the nutrient-rich soil to the top so that plant can use these nutrients.

(iv) Loosened soil helps in the growth of earthworms and microbes present in the soil. These organisms are friends of the farmers since they further turn and loosen the soil and add humus to it.

2. Levelling

Levelling of soil is done with the help of leveller. The ploughed field may have big pieces of soil called crumbs. Levelling helps to break these crumbs with a planks and prevents loss of moisture from the loose soil. It also helps in the uniform distribution of water in the fields during irrigation.

3. Manuring

Continuous growing of crops makes the soil deprived in certain nutrients. Therefore, farmers have to add manure to the fields to replenish the soil with nutrients. This process is called manuring. Sometimes, manure is added to the soil before tilling. This helps in proper mixing of manure with soil.

Agricultural Implements

The above mentioned practices are done by using various tools. These tools are called agricultural implements. These are discussed below.

(i) **Plough** It is the most ancient tool used for tilling the soil, adding manures and fertilisers, removing weeds and turning the soil. This is made up of wood and is drawn by a pair of bulls and other animals, (horses, camels, etc). It comprises of strong triangular iron strip called **ploughshare**.

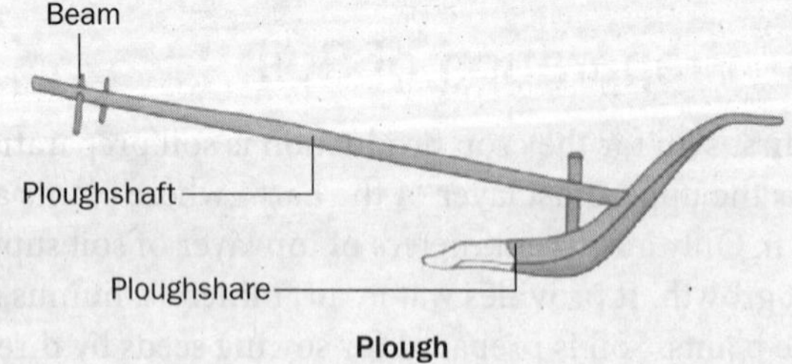

Plough

The main part of the plough is a long log of wood which is called **ploughshaft**. It has a handle at one end and the other end is attached to a beam which is placed on bull's necks. One pair of bulls and a man can easily operate the plough. Now-a-days the indigenous wooden plough is increasingly being replaced by iron ploughs.

(ii) **Hoe** It is used for removing weeds and for loosening the soil. Hoe is simple in structure, with a long rod of wood or iron. A strong, broad and bent iron plate is fixed at one of its ends which works like a blade. It is pulled by the animals.

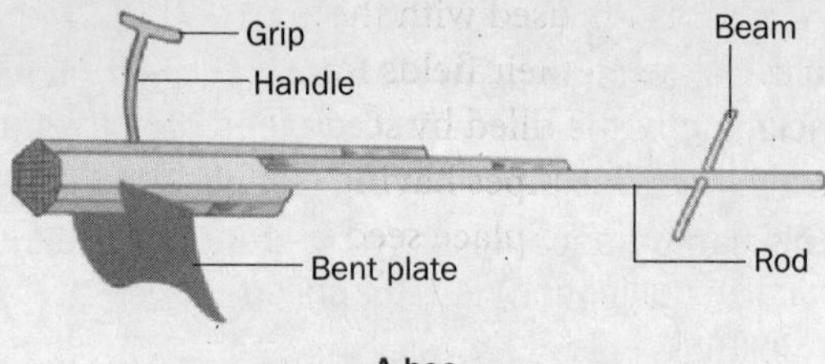

A hoe

(iii) **Cultivator** Now-a-days ploughing is done by tractor-driven cultivator. It is a modern form of plough which can dig into a considerable area of soil at the same time loosen it and turn it. A cultivator saves both labour and time.

Cultivator driven by a tractor

Try These 1.1

1. Crop 'A' was sown during Oct-Nov and harvested by March. Name the crop 'A'.
2. The farmer ploughed and levelled the soil in his field, yet his harvest yielded poor results. What essential step was overlooked?
3. Name the tool which is used for removing weeds and for loosening the soil.
4. Besides plough, what are the other agricultural implements used for loosening and turning soil?

1.4 Sowing

It is the process of scattering or planting seeds into the soil, so as to grow a new crop plant. Sowing is the most important part of crop production. Before sowing, clean, healthy and good quality of seeds are selected to produce healthy plants and high yield of crops.

Methods of Sowing

Sowing is done either manually or by using machines, as described below.

1. Traditional Tools

Traditional tools are used with the help of bulls. It was used by farmers earlier in their fields for sowing seeds. It's upper funnel-shaped part is filled by seeds. The seeds pass down through two or three pipes having sharp ends. These ends pierce into the soil and place seed in that space.

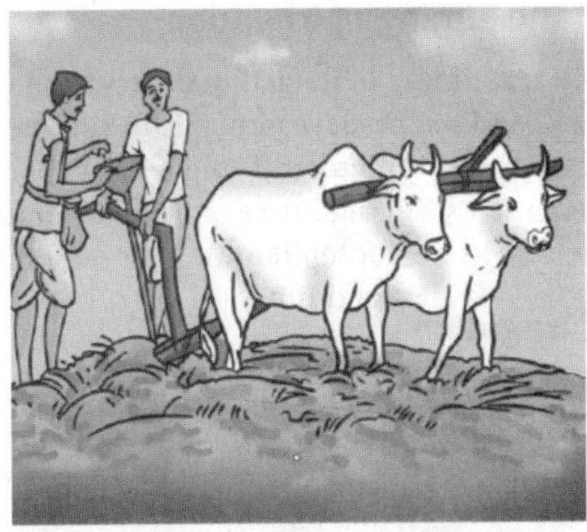

Traditional method of sowing

2. Seed Drill

It is a mechanical method of sowing by using a tractor.The seeds are sown uniformly at equal distance and depth and get covered by the soil after sowing.

A seed drill

This method protects the seeds from the damage caused by birds. It also saves time and labour. The advantage of sowing seeds at an appropriate distance and depth is that, it prevents overcrowding of plants and each plant gets sufficient sunlight, nutrients and water from soil.

SCIENCE INSIGHT The National Seed Corporation (NSC) in India plays a key role in producing high-quality agricultural seeds and has contributed to the establishment of seed-testing laboratories across various regions in the country.

1.5 Adding Manure and Fertilisers

Manure and fertilisers are the substances that are rich in nutrients and are added to the soil for healthy growth of plants. Addition of manure or fertiliser to the soil is called **manuring**. Farmers add manure to the fields to replenish the soil with nutrients. Improper or insufficient manuring makes plants weak. For replenishing soil with nutrients following methods are used.

Manures

These are organic (natural) substances derived from the decomposition of plant and animal wastes, like cow dung, etc. Plant and animal wastes are dumped in pits at open places and allowed to decompose by some microorganisms. The decomposed matter is used as organic manure.

Fertilisers

These are the chemicals which contain the necessary plant nutrients like nitrogen, phosphorus, etc.

Examples– Urea, ammonium sulphate, super phosphate, potash, NPK (Nitrogen, Phosphorus, Potassium). Fertilisers are used to increase soil fertility, that helps farmers to get better yield of crops such as wheat, paddy and maize.

The excessive use of fertiliser is harmful because it makes the soil less fertile and also causes water pollution.

Advantages of Manure Over Fertilisers

The organic manure is considered better than fertilisers because of the following reasons

(i) It enhances the water holding capacity of the soil.
(ii) It makes the soil porous due to which exchange of gases becomes easy.
(iii) It increases the number of friendly microbes.
(iv) It improves the texture of the soil.

Difference between manure and fertilisers

Manure	Fertiliser
Manure is a natural substance obtained by the decomposition of animal wastes like cow dung, human waste and plant residues.	Fertiliser is a man-made inorganic salt which contains necessary plant nutrients.
Manure is relatively less rich in plant nutrients.	Fertiliser contains a rich amount of nutrients like nitrogen, phosphorus and potassium in concentrated form.
Manures are prepared in the field by decomposing wastes.	Fertilisers are prepared in the factories.
Manure provides humus to the soil in large amount.	Fertiliser does not provide any humus to the soil.
Manures are not soluble in soil, therefore absorbed by plants at a very slow rate.	Fertilisers are highly soluble in water and readily absorbed by the plants.

Crop Rotation

The practice in which different types of crops, especially leguminous and non-leguminous crops are grown alternately in the same field is called crop rotation.

This procedure is followed in order to improve the fertility of soil, e.g. crops like cereals, vegetables, etc. deplete the nitrogen from the soil. Therefore, leguminous crops are grown alternatively after these crops, to maintain the nitrogen level of the soil.

The leguminous plants possess nitrogen fixing bacteria called ***Rhizobium*** in their roots which can directly fix the atmospheric nitrogen into soluble nitrogenous compounds. Rotation of crops also save a lot of nitrogenous or chemical fertilisers.

Try These 1.2

1. **A funnel-shaped tool is used for sowing seeds. Name the tool.**
2. **Seeds were sown with the help of machine at equal distance and depth and get covered by the soil after sowing. Name this machine.**
3. **What happens when excess fertiliser is added in the soil?**
4. **The farmer cultivates clover plant in his field, asserting that these plants harbor a nitrogen-fixing bacteria. What is the name of this bacteria?**

1.6 Irrigation

The process of supplying water to crop plants at regular intervals is called irrigation.

Water is important for the proper growth and development of all living organisms including plants. Plant contains nearly 90% of water.

Importance of Water to Crop Plant

(i) Water is absorbed by the plant roots. Along with water, minerals and fertilisers are also absorbed.

(ii) Water is essential because germination of seeds does not take place under dry conditions.

(iii) It also protects the crop from both frost and hot air currents.

(iv) For healthy crop growth, fields have to be watered regularly to maintain moisture of the soil.

Frequency and Timing of Irrigation

The frequency and timing of irrigation differs from crop to crop, soil to soil and season to season, e.g. In summers the frequency of irrigation is required at higher rate than in rainy or winter season. This is because the rate of evaporation of water from soil and leaves is high in summer season.

Sources of Irrigation

Water supplied for irrigation can be taken from different sources, e.g. rain, wells, tubewells, ponds, lakes, rivers, dams and canals.

Traditional Methods of Irrigation

The water from different sources such as wells, lakes and canals is lifted up by different methods for taking it to the fields. Cattle or human labour is used in these methods.

Traditional methods of irrigation

The various traditional ways of irrigation are moat (pulley system), dhekli, chain pump and rahat (lever system). Pumps are commonly used for lifting water. They run on diesel, biogas, electricity and solar energy.

Modern Methods of Irrigation

Traditional methods use manpower and animal power and there is a wastage of water also occur during irrigation. To overcome these problems, modern methods of irrigation are used. The main methods used are as follows

1. Sprinkler System

In this system, there is a main pipeline laid in the field joined with perpendicular pipes, having rotating nozzles on the top.

When water is allowed to flow through main pipe under pressure with the help of pump, it escapes from rotating nozzles and is sprinkled like rain over the crops. Sprinklers are very useful for lawns, coffee plantation and several other crops. This system of irrigation is useful on uneven land where sufficient water is not available.

Sprinkler system

2. Drip System

In this system, water flows through the narrow pipes and falls drop by drop just near the roots of plants.

Drip system

In this method there is no wastage of water as water falls drop by drop, therefore this system of irrigation is very useful in regions where availability of water is poor. It is the best technique for watering fruit plants, gardens and trees.

1.7 Protection from Weeds

The unwanted, wild plants that grow along with the cultivated crops are called **weeds.**

The process of removal of weeds is called **weeding**. It is necessary to remove weeds time to time because

(i) These unwanted plants are harmful because they competes with the crop plant for the nutrient, fertiliser, space, light and water. Thus, they reduce crop yield.

(ii) Some weeds interfere even in harvesting and may be poisonous for animals and humans.

Weeding Methods

Farmers adopt many ways to remove weeds and control their growth. Tilling before sowing of crops helps in uprooting and killing of weeds which may then dry up and get mixed with soil. The best time for the removal of weeds is before they produce flowers and seeds. Weeding can be done either manually or by spraying weedicides as discussed below

Manual Weeding

In this method, the weeds are removed from the crop field by pulling them up by hands and throwing them away. Another method of manual weeding is done by using a **khurpi**. A seed drill is also used to uproot weeds.

Spraying Weedicides

Certain chemicals called weedicides (herbicides) like 2,4-D are sprayed in the fields to kill the weeds. The crops remain unaffected from weedcides.

It should be sprayed during the vegetative growth of weeds before flowering and seed formation, otherwise weeds become difficult to control. Precautionary measures such as covering nose and mouth with cloth should be taken while spraying weedicides, as they impose health hazards.

Try These 1.3

1. **In which season, the frequency of irrigation is required at higher rate?**
2. **Sprinker system, moat, chain pump and drip system are the some methods of irrigation. Which among the following are traditional methods of irrigation?**
3. **In which method of irrigation, there is no wastage of water?**
4. **Name the tool used for manual weeding.**

1.8 Harvesting

The process of cutting and gathering mature (ripened) crop is called harvesting. When crops get mature, they usually turn yellow, golden or brown. In harvesting, crops are pulled out or cut close to the ground. Harvesting in our country is either done manually by **sickle** or by a machine called **harvester**.

To obtain seed grains from harvested crops, following two methods are used

Sickle used for manual harvesting

Threshing

The process by which the grain seeds are separated from the chaff is called threshing. This is carried out with the help of a machine called **combine** which is a combination of a harvester and thresher.

Combine

Winnowing

After threshing, the grains are separated from chaff by a process called winnowing. In this process, the mixture of grain, hay and chaff is dropped from a height into blowing wind. The heavier seed, fall straight to the ground, whereas the chaff and hay are much lighter and are carried away by the wind. The grains form a separate heap and can be collected and packed in gunny bags.

Winnowing machine

> **Harvest Festivals**
>
> After three or four months of hard work there comes the day of the harvest. The sight of golden fields of standing crop, laden with grain, fills the hearts of farmers with joy and a sense of well-being. The period is of great joy and happiness. It is celebrated with great zeal. Special festivals associated with the harvest season are Pongal, Baisakhi, Holi, Diwali, Nabanya and Bihu.

1.9 Storage

The harvested and cleaned grains are dried to evaporate moisture from them before storage. Since the crops/grains have to be kept for longer time, they should be safe from moisture, insects, rats and microorganisms. Also insecticides, rodenticides are sprayed to protect them from rats and insects.

Silos for storage of grains

The grains are stored in **jute bags** or **metallic bins** by farmers. At large scale, grains are stored in **silos** and **granaries** to protect them from pests.

Dried neem leaves are used for storing food grains at home as neem is a natural insecticide.

1.10 Food from Animals

Besides plants, some animals also provide us with different kinds of food. The food obtained by animals is rich in protein.

The food derived from animals and the sources are tabulated below

S.No.	Food	Sources
1.	Milk	Cow, Buffalo, She-goat, She camel.
2.	Egg	Hens and Duck
3.	Meat	Chicken, Fish, Goat
4.	Sea food	Fish, Prawn, Oyester

Animal Husbandry

The process of rearing animals, by providing them proper food, shelter and care is called animal husbandry.

Fishes are an important source of animal food in coastal areas. We get cod liver oil from fish which is rich in vitamin-D.

Try These 1.4

1. **The grain seeds are carried out from the chaff with the help of which machine?**
2. **Where are the seeds stored when present in large quantities?**
3. **Is it possible to acquire food from sources other than plants?**
4. **A patient had rickets and the doctor gave cod liver oil to him. What nutrient does cod liver oil contain in abundance?**

Science Glossary

Animal husbandary Agricultural practise of breeding and raising livestock.

Agriculture practices Tasks carried out by farmers for cultivation of crop.

Crop Plants of same kind, cultivated in a field at a large scale.

Fertilisers Chemical substances used to increase the fertility of soil.

Granaries Places where large amount of grains can be stored.

Harvesting Process of cutting and collecting the mature crop.

Irrigation Water supply to crops at regular intervals.

Kharif Crops grown in rainy season.

Manure Organic substances derived from the decomposition of plant and animal wastes.

Plough Agricultural implement used for tilling or ploughing the soil.

Rabi Crops grown in winter season.

Sowing Planting the seeds in the soil.

Seeds Fertilised and matured ovule.

Storage Process of protecting the grains, by keeping them in closed containers.

Silo Tall and cylindrical structures used for storage of grains.

Threshing Method of separating seed grains from the chaff.

Winnowing Method of separating seed grains from the chaff by blowing air.

Weeds Undesirable plants that grow along with crops.

Weedicide Chemicals used to kill weeds.

Let's Investigate

ACTIVITY 1 (Page 4)

Aim To separate good and healthy seeds of wheat from the damaged ones.

Materials Required Seeds of wheat, beaker and water.

Procedure

1. Take a beaker and fill half of it with water.
2. Now, put some seeds of wheat in it and stir it well.
3. Let it rest for some time.

Observation After some time we observe that most of the seeds will settle down, while some seeds will float on the top.

Conclusion From this activity, we can conclude that the seeds which settle down, at the bottom of the beaker are heavy and healthy seeds. The seeds that float on the top of water are spoiled seeds. These seeds may be damaged due to disease or eaten by pests, causing them to turn hollow and lightweight, allowing them to float on water.

Viva Questions

1. Why are only healthy seeds selected for sowing?
2. Why damaged wheat seeds float on the top of water?

ACTIVITY 2 (Page 6)

Aim To show the effect of manure and fertiliser on the growth of plant (using germinated gram seedlings).

Materials Required Pots, soil, cow dung manure, urea (chemical fertiliser), water and germinated gram seedlings.

Procedure

1. Take three pots and mark them A, B and C.
2. In pot A, add some soil mixed with cow dung manure.
3. In pot B, add soil mixed with urea (chemical fertiliser).
4. In pot C, put some soil only.
5. Pour equal amount of water in each pot and plant the seedlings of gram (already germinated).
6. Keep the pots in sunlight and water them daily, for 7-10 days.

Observation After 7-10 days the growth of seedlings was observed. Plant in pot B shows maximum growth followed by plant in pot A. Plant in pot C shows the least growth among the three.

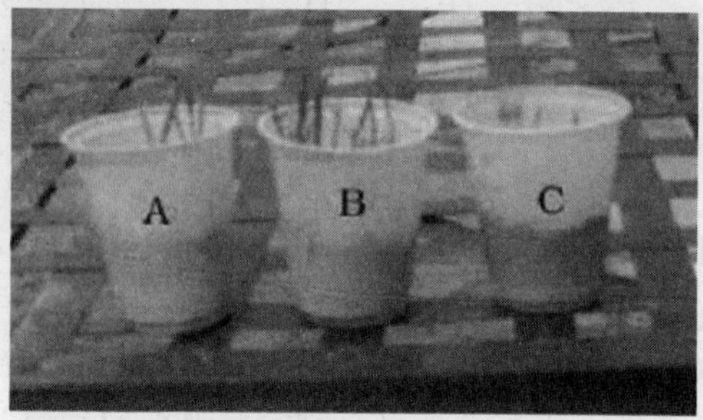

Growth of seedling with manure and fertiliser

Conclusion From this activity, we can conclude that in the soil mixed with fertilisers, plants exhibit maximum growth. The fertilisers are more soluble in water and readily absorbed by plant as compared to manure. It also shows that manure and fertilisers are required for better growth of plants.

Viva Questions

1. Why least growth is observed in seedling of pot C?
2. The plants grow fastest on adding fertilisers. Give reason.

Mind Map

CROP PRODUCTION AND MANAGEMENT

Crops
Same kind of plants are grown and cultivated at one place.

Kharif Crops
Sown in rainy season (June to September).
e.g. paddy, maize, soyabean and groundnut

Rabi Crops
Grown in the winter season (October to March).
e.g. wheat, gram, pea, mustard and linseed.

Basic Practices of Crop Production

Ploughing of Soil
- Loosening and turning of soil.
- Allows root to penetrate deep into the soil.
- Turning and loosening brings nutrient rich soil to the top.

Levelling of Soil
- It breaks the soil crumbs with the help of leveller.
- Beneficial for sowing and irrigation.

Sowing
- Planting seeds in the soil.
- Good quality, clean and healthy seeds of good variety are selected.

Harvesting
- Cutting of crop after maturation. Grains are separated from chaff through threshing .
- Winnowing is also used for separation of grain from chaff.

Adding Manure and Fertiliser
Substances provide nutrients to the plants, gives better yield of crops.

Fertiliser
- Man-made inorganic salt.
- Prepared in factories.
- Rich in nitrogen, phosphorus and potassium.
- Excessive use makes soil less fertile.

Manure
- Organic substance, formed by decomposition of plant and animal wastes.
- Improves soil texture and water retaining capacity.

Storage
- Harvested grains are sun dried before storage to reduce moisture.
- It prevents the attack by insect, pests, bacteria and fungi.
- Farmers store grains in jute bags or metallic bins.
- On large scale grains are stored in silos and granaries.

Irrigation
- Supply of water at regular intervals.
- Sources of irrigation are wells, tubewells, ponds, lakes, dams and canals.

Protection from Weeds
- Weeds are undesirable plants.
- Weeding is removal of weeds.
- Weeds compete with crop for water, nutrients, space and light.

Manual Weeding
- Weeds are removed before flowering.
- Uprooting of weeds is done by khurpi and seed drill.

Spraying Weedicides
Weedicides are chemicals, kills weed, e.g., 2, 4-D.

Agricultural Implements

Tools for Soil Preparation
Used to break soil clumps.

Plough
- Made up of wood.
- Driven by a pair of bulls, horse and camels.

Hoe
- Strong, broad and bent plate of iron is fixed with long rod of wood.
- Pulled by animal.

Cultivator
- Tractor driven
- It can dig into a considerable area of soil at the same time loosen it and turn it.

Tools for Sowing

Traditional tool
- Funnel-shaped.
- Seeds are filled in funnel.
- Seeds passed through pipes having sharp ends.

Modern tool
- Driven by tractor.
- Sows the seeds uniformly at equal distance and depth.

Tools for Irrigation

Modern Methods of Irrigation
Use water economically

Sprinkler System
- Useful on unevenland.
- Rotating nozzles attached on perpendicular pipes.
- Water sprinkled on crop from rotating nozzles.

Drip System
Water falls drop by drop near the roots.

Traditional Methods of Irrigation
- Cattle or human labour is used.
- Cheaper but less efficient e.g. moat (pully system), chain pump, dhekli and rahat (lever system).

Tools for Harvesting

Modern Tool (combine)
- Combination of harvester and thresher.
- Used for winnowing, threshing and reaping.

Traditional tool (sickle)
- Hand-held.
- Curved metal blade.

NCERT FOLDER

Complete Explanations of all NCERT's Questions

Intext Questions

Q.1 Boojho wants to know where we use the tools like khurpi, sickle, shovel, plough, etc? **Page 1**

Ans. We use tools like khurpi, sickle, shovel, plough, etc. in agricultural activities.

Q.2 Boojho wants to know, since we all need food how can we provide food to a large number of people in our country? **Page 1**

Ans. Large scale production of food is essential to meet the needs of a sizable population. It requires regular production, proper management and distribution of food.

Q.3 Boojho wants to know why paddy cannot be grown in the winter season. **Page 2**

Ans. Refer to text on page no. 1.

Q.4 One day Paheli saw her mother put some gram seeds in a vessel and pour some water on them. After a few minutes some seeds started to float on top. She wondered why some seeds floated on water? **Page 4**

Ans. Damaged seeds become hollow and thus lighter. Therefore, they float on top of water.

Q.5 Boojho saw one nursery near his school. He found that little plants were kept in small bags. He wants to know why? **Page 5**

Ans. Seeds of a few plants such as paddy are first grown in a nursery. When they grow into seedlings, they are transplanted to field manually. Some forest plants and flowering plants are also grown in the nursery.

Q.6 Boojho went to a farm and saw a healthy crop growing there. Whereas in the neighbouring farm the plants were weak. He asked Paheli why do some plants grow better than others? **Page 5**

Ans. The plants with proper manuring and care, grow better than others.

Q.7 Boojho asked the farmer that there were other plants growing along with wheat. He wanted to know if they had been purposely grown? **Page 10**

Ans. No, these plants are not purposely grown. In a crop field many other undesirable plants may grow naturally along with crop. These undesirable plants are called weeds.

Q.8 Boojho wants to know whether weedicides have any effect on the person handling the weedicide sprayer?

Ans. Yes, spraying of weedicides may affect the health of farmers. **Page 10**

Q.9 One day Paheli saw her mother putting some dried neem leaves in an iron drum containing wheat. She wondered why? **Page 11**

Ans. Dried neem leaves are used for storing food grains at home. They protect the wheat from insects, pests and fungal growth.

Exercise

Q.1 Select the correct word from the following list and fill in the blanks.

float, water, crop, nutrients, preparation

(a) The same kind of plants grown and cultivated on a large scale at a place is called ....

(b) The first step before growing crops is .... of the soil.

(c) Damaged seeds would .... on top of water.

(d) For growing a crop, sufficient sunlight and.............. and .... from the soil are essential.

Ans. (a) crop (b) preparation

(c) float (d) water, nutrients

Q.2 Match the items in Column A with those in Column B.

	Column A	Column B
(a)	Kharif crops	(i) Food for cattle
(b)	Rabi crops	(ii) Urea and super phosphate
(c)	Chemical fertilisers	(iii) Animal excreta, cow dung urine and plant waste
(d)	Organic manure	(iv) Wheat, gram and pea
		(v) Paddy and maize

Ans. (a)–(v), (b)–(iv), (c)–(ii), (d)–(iii)

Q.3 Give two examples of each.

(a) Kharif crop **(b) Rabi crop**

Ans. (a) Soyabean and groundnut are the two examples of Kharif crops.

(b) Pea and mustard are the two examples of Rabi crops.

Q.4 Write a paragraph in your own words on each of the following.

(a) Preparation of soil (b) Sowing
(c) Weeding (d) Threshing

Ans. (a) **Preparation of soil** It is the first step before sowing the crop. In this, the soil is ploughed to loosen it and make it aerated, which allows the roots to breathe easily. This also helps in the growth of earthworms and microbes in the soil that further turn and loosen the soil. The process of loosening and turning of soil is called tilling or ploughing and is followed by levelling and manuring.

(b) **Sowing** It is the process of planting seeds in the soil for the purpose of growing crops. Traditionally, funnel-like tools were used for sowing. But now-a-days, seeds are sown by a seed drill. It sows the seeds at regular intervals in the soil.

(c) **Weeding** It is the removal of weeds from the field. Weeding is an essential process as weeds are harmful for the growth of crops because they compete with the crop plants for water, nutrients, space and light.

(d) **Threshing** The process in which the grain seeds are separated from chaff is called threshing. This is carried out with the help of a machine called combine which is a combination of a harvester and thresher.

Q.5 Explain how fertilisers are different from manure.

Ans. Refer to text on page no. 4.

Q.6 What is irrigation? Describe two methods of irrigation which conserve water.

Ans. Refer to text on page no. 4 and 5.

Q.7 If wheat is sown in the Kharif season, what would happen? Discuss.

Ans. The seeds of wheat need low temperature and less humidity to grow. If they are sown in Kharif season, (i.e. rainy season), the seeds would get destroyed due to excess of water and would not grow.

Q.8 Explain how soil gets affected by the continuous plantation of crops in a field.

Ans. Soil supplies mineral nutrients to the crop. These mineral nutrients are essential for the growth of plants. If crops are grown continuously in the same field for a long period of time, the soil becomes poorer in nutrients. Thus, soil gets deficient in nutrients and the field becomes infertile.

Q.9 What are weeds? How can we control them?

Ans. Refer to text on page no. 5.

Q.10 Arrange the following boxes in proper order to make a flow chart of sugarcane crop production.

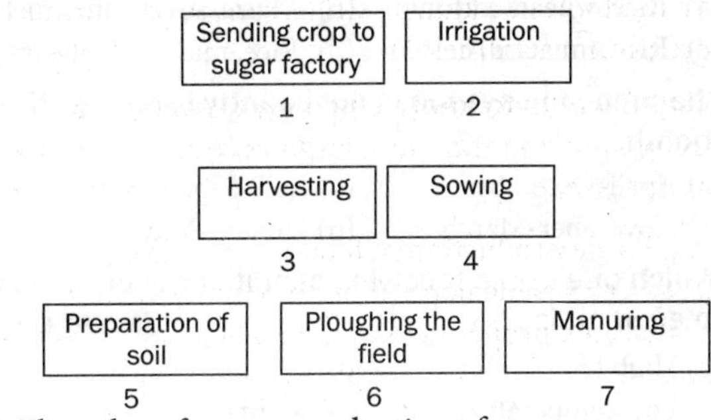

Ans. Flow chart for crop production of sugarcane.

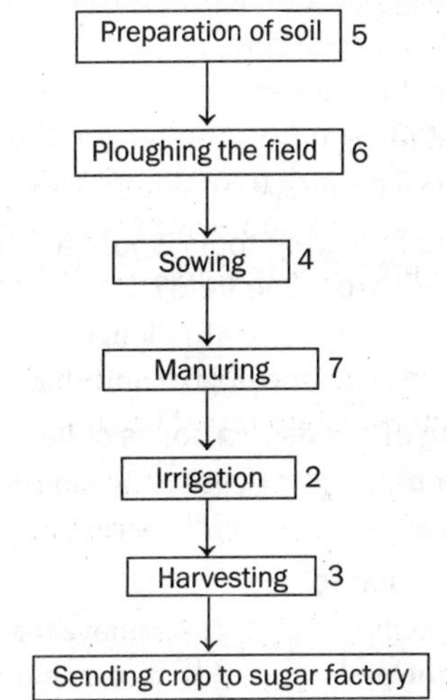

REVIEW EXERCISE

Including Competency Based Questions

Part I

Multiple Choice Questions

1. Which of the following set of crops has Kharif crops?

(a) Rice, wheat, cotton (b) Maize, soyabean, mustard
(c) Rice, mustard, cotton (d) Rice, maize, soyabean

2. The monsoon season in our country is during the months

(a) April-December (b) June-September
(c) November-March (d) January-May

3. Which one of the following conditions is not essential to grow maize? NCERT Exemplar

(a) High temperature (b) Humidity
(c) Low temperature (d) Rainfall

4. The process of loosening and turning of soil is called

(a) irrigation and manuring
(b) digging and winnowing
(c) tilling and ploughing
(d) harvesting and storage

5. Which of the following tools would a farmer use to remove weeds from the field?

(a) Hoe (b) Plough
(c) Axe (d) Cultivator

6. The planting of seeds in a soil is called

(a) cultivation (b) irrigation
(c) harvesting (d) sowing

7. Seed drill is used to

(a) sow the seeds (b) remove the weeds
(c) remove the pest (d) mix manure in the soil

8. A farmer aims to enhance the soil nutrients in his field without using chemical fertilisers. What natural method should he consider for replenishing the soil?

(a) Sowing seeds that are healthy
(b) Growth the same crops every year
(c) Growing different crops alternatively
(d) Supplying water to crops at regular interval

9. Which of the following statements is not true for organic manure? NCERT Exemplar

(a) It enhances water holding capacity of soil
(b) It has a balance of all plant nutrients
(c) It provides humus to soil
(d) It improves texture of soil

10. Which of the following is not true for fertilisers?

(a) They increase the yield
(b) Their excessive use disturbs the balance of nutrients in the soil
(c) They provide a lot of humus to the soil
(d) They are not environment-friendly

11. Read the statement given below.

(i) Seeds requires moisture for germination.
(ii) Plants can absorb nutrients mostly in dissolved form.
(iii) Irrigation protects crops from both frost and hot air currents.
(iv) Irrigation improves soil texture.

Choose the combination of statements which indicate the need to irrigate crops. NCERT Exemplar

(a) (i) and (ii) (b) (i), (ii) and (iii)
(c) (i), (ii), (iii) and (iv) (d) (i) and (iii)

12. Watering the crops at regular intervals is called

(a) sowing (b) manuring
(c) tilling (d) irrigation

13. The system of irrigation, where water is supplied drop by drop near the roots of plants is called

(a) pulley system (b) drip system
(c) sprinkler system (d) lever system

14. The pictures below display, two techniques.

Pulley system

Sprinkler system

What are advantages of choosing sprinkler system over pulley system for irrigation? Competency Based Que.

(a) Sprinkler system reduces wastage of water
(b) Sprinkler system decreases water requirement of the crops
(c) Sprinkler system increases water absorption capacity of the crops
(d) Sprinkler system provides excess water to the crops for high productivity

15. **Weeds are the**
(a) main crop plants
(b) insects and pests
(c) unwanted plants growing along the crop
(d) chemical substances

16. **Given below are statements about the harmful effects of weeds on crop plants.** **Competency Based Que.**
(i) They interfere in harvesting.
(ii) They help crop plants to grow healthy.
(iii) They compete with crop plants for water, nutrients, space and light.
(iv) They affect the plant growth.

Choose the correct combination of statements.
(a) (i), (iii) and (iv) (b) Only (iii)
(c) (iii) and (iv) (d) (i), (ii), (iii) and (iv)

17. **2, 4-D is a**
(a) pesticide (b) insecticide
(c) fungicide (d) weedicide

18. **The term used for the process of separation of grains from chaff is** **NCERT Exemplar**
(a) sieving (b) winnowing
(c) threshing (d) hand picking

19. **Why are the grains dried in the Sun, before storing them?**
(a) To keep the grains warm
(b) To increase the size of the grains
(c) To prepare the grains for germination
(d) To reduce the moisture content of the grains

20. **How can the food items like milk, egg and meat can be produced on large scale?**
(a) By doing animal husbandry
(b) By performing plant harvesting
(c) By providing food to the animals
(d) By storing grains in big godowns

21. **Consider the following list of food items.**

1. Honey 2. Wheat 3. Sunflower oil
4. Eggs 5. Fish oil 6. Beans
7. Pulses 8. Cheese 9. Milk
10. Apple

Which choice categorises sources of the food items correctly.

(a)	Animal source	Sunflower oil, fish oil, eggs, rice, milk
	Plant source	Beans, pulses, apple, honey, cheese
(b)	Animal source	Honey, fish oil, eggs, cheese, milk
	Plant source	Rice, beans, pulses, sunflower oil,apple
(c)	Animal source	Eggs, pulses, fish oil, honey, sunflower oil
	Plant source	Rice, cheese, milk, apple, beans
(d)	Animal source	Rice, beans, pulses, sunflower oil, apple
	Plant source	Honey, fish oil, eggs, cheese, milk

Answers

1. (d)	2. (b)	3. (c)	4. (c)	5. (a)
6. (d)	7. (a)	8. (c)	9. (b)	10. (c)
11. (b)	12. (d)	13. (b)	14. (a)	15. (c)
16. (a)	17. (d)	18. (c)	19. (d)	20. (a)
21. (b)				

Fill in the Blanks

1. The crops grown in rainy season are called ....
2. Cotton cannot be grown in......... season.
3. Pea belongs to the .... crops.
4. Ploughing helps the roots to .... deep in the soil.
5. .... is a process to loosen soil.

Answers

1. Kharif crops 2. winter 3. Rabi
4. penetrate 5. Tilling

True/False

1. Using good quality seed is the only criterion to get high yield.
2. All crop plants are sown as seeds in the field.
3. Growing different crops in different seasons in the same field will deplete the nutrients of soil.
4. Cells of root nodules of leguminous plants fix nitrogen.
5. Freshly harvested grains must be dried before storing. **NCERT Exemplar**

Answers

1. False, apart from good quality seeds, using appropriate agricultural practices are also important for getting higher yield.
2. False, some crop plants need transplantation.
3. False, it actually enriches the soil.
4. False, *Rhizobium* (bacteria) present in the cells of root nodules of leguminous plants fix nitrogen.
5. True

Match the Columns

1. **Match the Column I with Column II.**

	Column I	Column II
A	Silos	1. Fertiliser
B	Combines	2. Storage of grains
C	Urea	3. Sprinklers
D	Irrigation	4. Harvesting and threshing

2. Match the Column I with Column II.

Column I	Column II
A Sickle	1. Ploughing
B Hoe	2. Sowing
C Seed drill	3. Harvesting
D Root	4. Irrigation

Answers

1. A–2, B–4, C–1, D–3
2. A–3, B–1, C–2, D–4

Assertion-Reason Questions

The following questions consist of two statements. Assertion (A) and Reason (R). Answer the following questions by selecting the appropriate option given below

(a) Both A and R are true and R is the correct explanation of A

(b) Both A and R are true, but R is not the correct explanation of A

(c) A is true but R is false

(d) A is false but R is true

1. **Assertion** (A) Paddy is a Rabi crop.

Reason (R) It requires a lot of water and is grown in the rainy season.

2. **Assertion** (A) Farmers add manure to the fields to replenish the soil with nutrients.

Reason (R) Continuous cultivation of crops make the soil poor in nutrients.

3. **Assertion** (A) In drip irrigation system, water is not wasted at all.

Reason (R) In drip irrigation system, water is escaped from rotating nozzles and get sprinkled on the crop as if it is raining.

4. **Assertion** (A) Weeds should not be removed from fields.

Reason (R) They compete with the crop plants for water, nutrients, space and light.

Answers

1. (d) A is false, but R is true. A can be corrected as Paddy is a Kharif crop. It is sown in the rainy season as it requires a lot of water to grow.
2. (a) Both A and R are true and R is the correct explanation of A.
3. (c) A is true, but R is false. R can be corrected as In drip irrigation system ,water falls drop by drop directly near the roots. It is a boon in regions where availability of water is poor.
4. (d) A is false, but R is true. A can be corrected as Weeds should be removed from fields because they compete with the crop plants for water, nutrient, space and light. Thus, they affect the growth of the crop.

Case Based Question

1. **Soham investigates the water holding capacity of four different types of soils. He sets up an experiment for each type of soil as shown in the diagram. Soham records his observation in a table.**

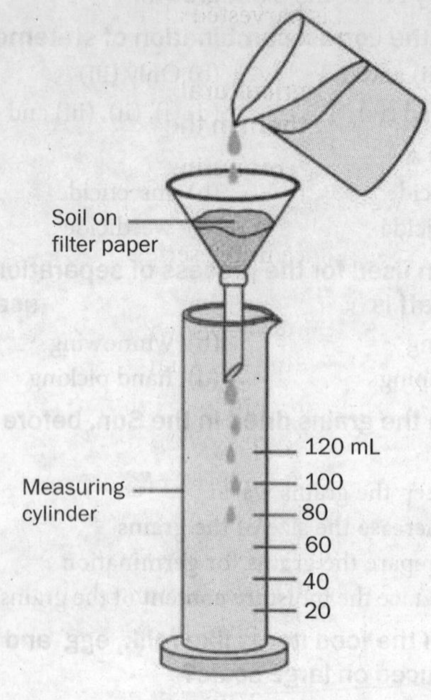

	Soil type			
	Clay	Loam	Sand	Silt
Amount of water added to the soil (mL)	150	150	150	150
Amount of water collected in the measuring cylinder (mL)	30	60	105	50

Competency Based Que.

(i) Which type of soil absorbs the most water?

(a) Clay (b) Loam

(c) Sand (d) Silt

(ii) Soham added the same amount of water to each type of soil. State one more thing that Soham needs to keep the same in his experiment.

Answer

(i) (a) Clay

(ii) The amount of each soil type on the filter paper must remain the same for the experimental setup .

Part II

Very Short Answer Type Questions

1. Explain the meaning of crop.

Ans. The same kind of plants grown and cultivated on a large scale at one place is called a crop.

2. During which months do farmers grow mustard in India? NCERT Exemplar

Ans. Farmers grow mustard during the months from October-March. Mustard is a rabi crop which is sown in beginning of winters (Oct-Nov) as it needs low temperature and is harvested at the end of winter (April-May).

3. Terms related to agricultural practices are given below. Rearrange them in the correct sequence.

harvesting, sowing, manuring, tilling and ploughing, irrigation, weeding. Competency Based Que.

Ans. The correct sequence in the series of agricultural practices is

Tilling and ploughing ⟶ sowing ⟶ manuring ⟶ irrigation ⟶ weeding ⟶ harvesting

4. If you are given a dry piece of land for cultivation, what will you do before sowing the seeds?

Ans. Before sowing on a dry piece of land, can be taken to prepare the soil for cultivation such as soil preparation, irrigation, leveling and seedbed preparation.

5. Which activity of the farmer can promote growth of earthworms and microbes in the field? NCERT Exemplar

Ans. Ploughing of the soil during soil preparation creates aeration and loosen the soil which promotes the growth of earthworms and microbes and release nutrients in the soil.

6. Pick out the odd one from the following words given in the box and give reason for it.

Plough, Seed drill, Hoe, Chain pump, Sickle

Ans. Seed drill is an odd pair in the above given set of tools. It is a modern agricultural tool used to sow seeds at uniform distances and to properly cover them with soil.

7. What are organic foods?

Ans. The crops (foods) that are cultivated using organic substances like manures, are known as organic food. These products are grown and processed without the use of synthetic chemicals including fertilisers, pesticides, weedicides, etc.

8. Is the time and frequency of irrigation same for rice and cotton?

Ans. No, the time and frequency of irrigation is not same for rice and cotton. Rice requires more frequent and continuous flooding, while cotton requires less frequent but deep watering. The specfic irrigation practices may vary depending on the climate, soil and growth stage of the crops.

9. Give names of two traditional methods and two modern methods of irrigation.

Ans. Traditional methods of irrigation are dhekli and moat and modern methods of irrigation are sprinkler system and drip system.

10. Pumps are often used in agriculture. Give its usage.

Ans. Pumps are commonly used to drawn water from a water source and distribute it to fields through irrigation system.

11. Drip irrigation is considered advantageous over other methods of irrigation. Do you agree? Explain.

Ans. Yes, in drip irrigation method, water is released drop by drop near the roots of plants. It is thus considered advantageous over other methods as there is no wastage of water and it is also economical.

12. Some grass is growing in a wheat field. What will it be known as?

Ans. Grass growing in a wheat field is unwanted, thus it will be known as weed.

13. Name the tool used for manual harvesting.

Ans. Sickle is used for manual harvesting. It is hand held tool with a curved blade.

14. Define animal husbandry. Write the names of some food materials provided by animals.

Ans. The process of rearing animals by providing them proper food, shelter and care is called animal husbandry. Some food materials provided by animals are eggs, milk, meat, honey, etc.

15. Fishes are considered good for health. Give reason.

Ans. Fishes are good for health because they are highly nutritious and rich in vitamin-A and vitamin-D. They are an important source of animal food in coastal areas.

Short Answer Type Questions

1. Classify the following crops into Kharif and Rabi crops and write in the tabular column given below.

Maize, paddy, mustard, pea, gram, wheat, groundnut, cotton **NCERT Exemplar**

Kharif	Rabi
....	....
....	....

Ans. From the above given crop list, the Kharif and Rabi crops can be grouped as

Kharif	Rabi
Maize	Mustard
Paddy	Pea
Groundnut	Wheat
Cotton	Gram

2. The levelling of ploughed field is beneficial. Give reasons to support your answer.

Ans. The levelling of ploughed field is beneficial because of the following reasons

(i) It helps in uniform distribution of water in the fields during irrigation.

(ii) It also prevents loss of moisture from the ploughed soil.

(iii) It ensures ever germination and uniform growth of crops.

3. (i) Name the tool used with a tractor for sowing seeds in a field.

(ii) What are the advantages of using this tool?

Ans. Refer to text on page no. 3.

4. Beera wants to practice crop rotation in his field. Suggest a Rabi crop and a Kharif crop which will replenish his field with nitrogen. Which crop replenishes nitrogen and why? **NCERT Exemplar**

Ans. Rabi crops are pea and gram, while Kharif crop is soyabean. These are grown in different seasons and therefore can very well be rotated alternatively.

Pea and soyabean are leguminous plants which harbour bacteria, i.e. *Rhizobium* in their root nodules. These bacteria convert atmospheric nitrogen into usable form for plants. These nitrogen fixing plants can replenish nitrogen in the field and hence Beera can easily practice crop rotation.

5. Leguminous plants do not require nitrogenous fertilisers. Why is it so?

Ans. The planting of a leguminous crop in a field has the same effect as adding nitrogenous fertiliser in the field. They can fix atmospheric nitrogen themselves by using nitrogen-fixing bacteria in their root nodules. Therefore, nitrogenous fertilisers are not required for growing leguminous plants.

6. State two advantages of using chemical fertilisers over manures. What would happen if fertilisers are used in excess?

Ans. Advantages of using chemical fertilisers over manures are

(i) Fertilisers are nutrient specific and provide specific nutrient to soil in desired quantity.

(ii) These being readily soluble in water can be absorbed easily by the crop plants.

If it is used in excess, it causes tremendous changes in the chemical nature of soil and makes it less fertile.

7. Chemical substances are added to the soil. How do they differ from manure on the basis of their formation?

Ans. Fertilisers are chemical substances that have a particular plant nutrient in concentrated form. They differ from manure on the basis of formation, as these are produced in factories while manure can be prepared by the farmer himself on the field.

8. Write the functions of

(i) leveller (ii) hoe (iii) combine (iv) thresher

Ans.

Tools	Functions
(i) Leveller	Smooth out uneven area and create a flat and even surface for sowing and irrigation.
(ii) Hoe	Used for removing weeds and for loosening .
(iii) Combine	Harvesting as well as threshing.
(iv) Thresher	It separates the grain from the chaff.

9. Despite favourable climatic conditions, a farmer's crop failed to give good yield. Give the possible reasons for this. **NCERT Exemplar**

Ans. If despite favourable climatic conditions, farmer's crop failed to give good yield, the possibilities may be

(i) he did not use good quality and healthy seeds.

(ii) his field was not well irrigated.

(iii) manures/fertilisers were not timely and properly applied.

(iv) weeds were not removed.

(v) seeds were not sown at appropriate distance.

(vi) the soil was not ploughed and levelled properly.

10. **(i) Name the practice followed for large scale rearing of farm animals.**

(ii) What facilities are provided to farm animals?

NCERT Exemplar

Ans. (i) The practice of rearing of farm animals on a large scale is called animal husbandry. This practice is used to increase the livestock of animals such as pigs, buffaloes, horses, sheep, etc.

(ii) In animal husbandry, animals are provided with following facilities.

(a) Proper food and water on time.

(b) Appropriate shelter.

(c) Have medical access.

(d) Safe disposal of animal excreta.

Long Answer Type Questions

1. **Paddy is a major cereal crop in our country.**

(i) In which season is paddy cultivated?

(ii) Discuss the method of sowing.

(iii) What measures must be taken to prevent spoilage and insect attack of harvested grains?

NCERT Exemplar

Ans. (i) Paddy is cultivated in rainy season as it is a Kharif crop.

(ii) For sowing paddy, seeds are first grown in a nursery and later seedlings are transplanted in the field. This allows us to select only healthy and better seedlings for cultivation.

(iii) Measures taken to prevent spoilage or damage of harvested crops from insect attack are

(a) Exposing them in sunlight for drying as freshly harvested crops have moisture.

(b) Dried neem leaves are kept with stored grains, so as to prevent damage from pests.

(c) Specific chemical treatments are also available for preventing crops from spoilage and insect attacks.

2. **Explain various agricultural practices in sequential manner.**

Ans. Various agricultural practices are as follows

(i) **Preparation of soil** The first step is preparation of soil. In this the soil is loosened and turned up. It helps the plants to grow and develop. The process of loosening and turning of the soil is called tilling or ploughing. Sometimes manure is also added to soil before tilling.

(ii) **Sowing** After preparation of soil, the second step called sowing takes place. It is the process of scattering or planting seeds into the soil. Before sowing good quality seeds are selected. The seeds should be clean and healthy.

(iii) **Adding manure and fertilisers** Soil supplies minerals and nutrients to the crops. These nutrients are essential for growth of plants. Sometimes these nutrients are lacking, so substances are added to maintain or to replenish the soil. These substances are called manures and fertilisers. Manures and fertilisers are essential to increase the crop production.

(iv) **Irrigation** The process of watering the crop plants at regular interval is called irrigation. Plants take all the nutrients and minerals in dissolved form. So, water is most essential for germination of seeds, growth and development of plants.

(v) **Harvesting** After maturation the crop is cut off. This process is called harvesting. It is done by a sickle or by a machine called harvester.

(vi) **Storage** Storage of product is one of the most important tasks. To keep the grains for longer they should be safe from moisture, pest, insects and other microorganisms.

3. **As a part of eco-club activity, students were asked to raise a kitchen garden in the school premises. They were provided with some materials given in the box. List the other materials you would require. How will you plan the garden? Write the steps.**

Khurpi, water-can, spade, shovel

Competency Based Que.

Ans. Besides the given tools, the other items required for raising a garden are seeds and seedlings of vegetables, plants from nursery, kitchen waste, manure, water, soil, etc.

Steps for raising the garden.

(i) Kitchen waste will be collected and composted in a pit.

(ii) A patch of land will be identified for the garden.

(iii) Soil will be dug up and levelled with the help of a spade.

(iv) Sowing of seeds/ transplanting of seedlings will be done at even distance.

(v) Seeds/seedlings are selected as per the season. Water the plants regularly with a water-can.

(vi) Compost or manure will be applied.

(vii) Weeds will be removed periodically with the help of khurpi.

4. You must have heard farmers talking about soil fertility. What is it? Mention some methods by which soil fertility can be replenished.

Ans. The ability of soil to supply all the essential plant nutrients to a crop in adequate quantity is called soil fertility. Repeated growing of crops in the same soil removes various nutrient elements from the soil due to which the soil loses its fertility.

The soil fertility can be replenished or regained by the following methods

(i) By putting manures and fertilisers in the soil.

(ii) By practising crop rotation.

(iii) By growing leguminous plants or crops like pulses, pea, beans, groundnut, etc.

5. Explain the role of water in the production of crops. Why is it necessary to supply water to the crop plants?

Ans. Refer to text on page no. 4.

6. Given below is a conversation between two farmers Heera and Beera. **NCERT Exemplar**

Heera: Brother Beera, your maize crops look beautiful. They have grown pretty fast.

Beera: Yes, I have sprayed urea this time. What about you?

Heera: Well, I am still relying on good old cow dung. I am saving money for buying a tractor.

Beera: That's good. Tractor saves a lot of time and labour.

Heera: Yes, it's been very labour intensive for me and now these weeds have come up.

Beera: Try weedicides, they are very effective.

Now, answer the following questions.

(i) List the practices which are not environment friendly and why?

(ii) What is the advantage of modern agricultural implements over traditional ones?

(iii) Name one weedicide and the precaution, farmers must take during its application.

Competency Based Que.

Ans. (i) The practices used in field which are not environment friendly are use of fertilisers, pesticides, weedicides and other chemical substances that pose health hazards. Tractor though saves labour and time but contributes to air pollution.

(ii) Modern agricultural implements save both time and labour as compared to traditional equipments.

(iii) An example of a weedicide is 2,4-D. The precaution taken by farmers while spraying it on crops is that they should properly cover their nose and mouth, so as to avoid inhaling these chemicals.

Case Based Questions

1. A farmer wants to grow crops in his field between the months of June and July.

The chart below shows a list of crops and different agricultural practices. **Competency Based Que.**

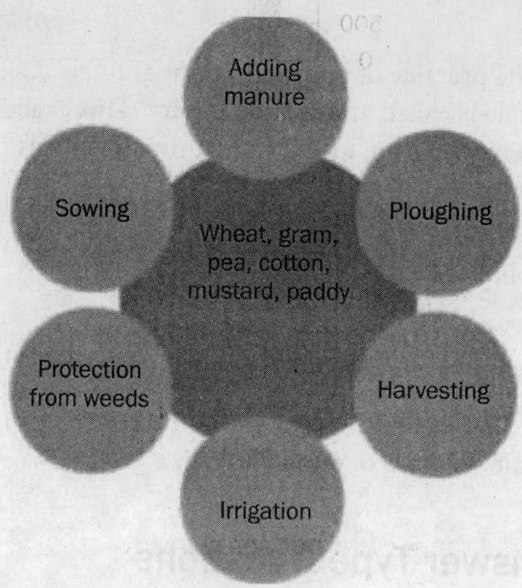

Select two crops from the list that grow best during June and July.

(i) Crop 1......... Crop 2..........

(ii) The farmer prepared the soil in his field by turning and loosening the soil.

How does turning and loosening the soil help in growing plants?

(iii) Farmers follow a sequence of agricultural practices to grow crops. A part of the sequence is shown below.

Choose an appropriate agricultural practice from the chart above to fill in the box.

Irrigation → Protection from weeds → ☐ → Winnowing

2. Weedicides are chemicals that are sprayed on crop fields to remove weeds. **Competency Based Que.**

A farmer wanted to test the effect of two different weedicides on wheat production.He sprayed each weedicide on two different fields. No weedicide was sprayed on field 3.

Field 1 Sprayed with weedicide 1

Field 2 Sprayed with weedicide 2

Field 3 Sprayed with no weedicide

The graph shows the production of wheat crop from each field over two years.

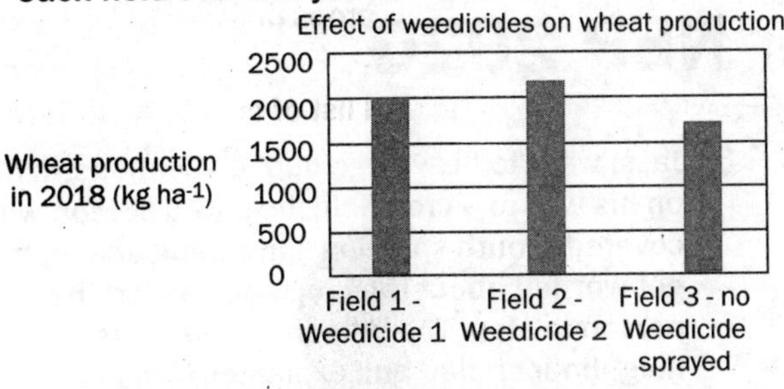

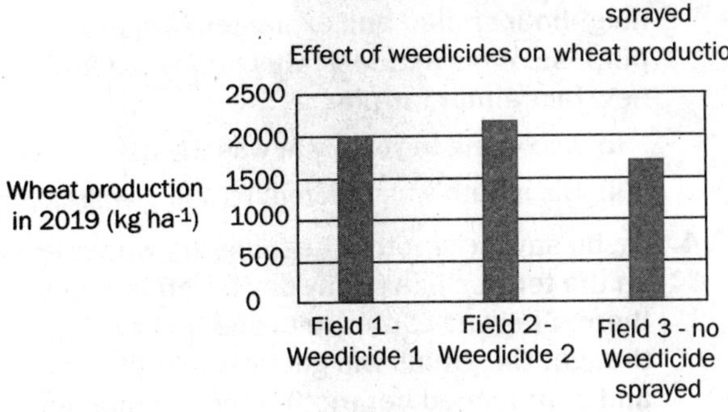

(i) Why did the farmer not spray any weedicide on Field 3?

(ii) What can the farmer conclude from his tests?

(a) Weedicides 1 and 2 were not effective in controlling weeds.

(b) Wheat production was better in fields sprayed with weedicide.

(c) Crop production decreased in Field 3 as the soil was not fertile.

(d) Weedicide 1 was more effective than weedicide 2 in controlling weeds.

(iii) The farmer's friend suggested that the farmer should have tested weedicide 1 on wheat field and weedicide 2 on mustard field. Will this suggestion help improve the experiment? Explain your answer.

(iv) Why are weedicides generally sprayed on weeds before they start producing flowers and seeds?

(a) Weedicides can kill only young weeds.

(b) Weedicides can kill the crops if not sprayed early.

(c) The weeds cannot be killed after they start producing flowers and seeds.

(d) The flowers produce more seeds and the seeds germinate to form more weeds

Ans. 1. (i) Crop 1 → Paddy

Crop 2 → Cotton

(ii) The turning and loosening of the soil helps the plants in following ways.

(a) It allows the plant roots to penetrate deep into the soil.

(b) It brings the nutrient rich soil to the top layer , so that plant can use these nutrients.

(iii) Irrigation → Protection from weeds → Harvesting → Winnowing.

2. (i) The farmer did not spray any weedicides on field 3 because, without field 3 the farmer would not be able to tell if the weedicide was effective or not.

(ii) (b) Wheat production was better in fields sprayed with weedicide.

(iii) No, this will not help to improve the experiment. As we cannot compare production of wheat with production of mustard. To compare the effect of two different weedicides, the crop should remain same.

(iv) (d) The flowers produce more seeds and the seeds germinate to form more weeds.

Skill Based Questions as per NEP 2020

1. Observe the following graphs and answer the questions

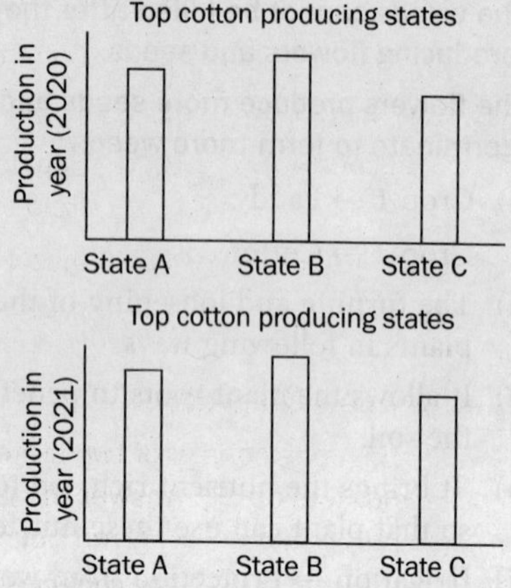

What could be the possible reason behind the varied production of cotton in state 'C' from year 2020 to 2021? **Thinking skill**

2. Take two sets of seeds, label them as A and B, respectively. Treat seeds of set A with insecticide. Do not provide any treatment to seeds of set B. Plant both the set of seeds in the soil. Analyse the growth of seeds of both set. **Observation skill**

3. Jassi went to his village during vacations. While on his way to a crop field, he saw a person with covered mouth spraying something on crops. He got worried about the crops and asked the person to stop. The person who was his neighbour smiled and explained him the purpose of his act. Jassi was happy to learn a new fact about farming.

(i) According to you, what was the person doing?

(ii) His mouth was covered. Why? **Thinking skill**

4. Tashu saw her mother keeping the wheat grains on the terrace in a sunny day before storing them. She was confused to see this as she thought the grains will get dirty if kept in open and approached her mother for clearing her doubts.

Her mother explained Tashu the reason behind her act. Tashu then helped her mother to carry the grains to the terrace happily.

(i) The grains were kept on the terrace. Can you suggest a reason?

(ii) Is it necessary to keep the grains in the Sun? Why or why not? **Thinking skill**

ASSESSMENT EXERCISE

Part I

Multiple Choice Questions

1. Which of the following is not a Rabi crop?
(a) Linseed
(b) Pea
(c) Gram
(d) Groundnut

2. What kind of tool should the farmer select to safeguard seeds from animal consumption while sowing?
(a) Seed drill as it coats a chemical above the seeds
(b) Traditional tool as many seeds are sown together
(c) Seed drill as it covers the seeds with soil after sowing
(d) Traditional tool as seeds passes through a funnel-shape cube

3. Which of the following statement is incorrect?
(a) Freshly harvested grains must be dried before storing.
(b) Organic fertiliser has a balance of all plant nutrients
(c) Weeding is the process of growing weeds
(d) Drip irrigation system is suitable for fruit plants

4. What advantages can the farmer expect from transitioning to using manure after a prolonged period of using fertilisers on his land?
(a) It will improve the texture and water retention capacity of soil.
(b) It will decrease the number of earthworms in the soil
(c) It will make the soil more compact to hold more water in roots
(d) It will increase particular chemicals in the soil to increase the yield

5. Which of the following is not a traditional method of irrigation?
(a) Moat (b) Chain pump
(c) Sprinkler system (d) Dhekli

Fill in the Blanks

6. Growing different crops alternately on the same land is called ....

7. The main part of the plough is a long log of wood which is called a ....

True/False

8. Fertilisers are organic substances obtained from the decomposition of plant and animal wastes.

9. Stubs burning in the fields causes air pollution.

Match the Columns

10. Match the Column I with Column II.

	Column I		Column II
A.	Weedicides	1.	Cotton
B.	Rabi season crop	2.	2, 4-D
C.	Kharif season crop	3.	Separating grains from chaff
D.	Threshing	4.	Insect
E.	Honey	5.	Pea

Assertion-Reason Questions

The following questions consist of two statements **Assertion** (A) and **Reason** (R). Answer these questions by selecting the appropriate option given below.
(a) Both A and R are true and R is the correct explanation of A
(b) Both A and R are true, but R is not the correct explanation of A
(c) A is true, but R is false
(d) A is false, but R is true

11. Assertion (A) Water plays an important role in crop production.

Reason (R) It protects the crop from both frost and hot air current.

12. Assertion (A) Harvested grains should be protected from moisture.

Reason (R) Moisture prevents the growth of moulds.

Part II

Very Short Answer Type Questions

13. What do you mean by transplantation?

14. Name the chemical sprayed in the field to kill the weed.

Short Answer Type Questions

15. Give two advantages of adding manure to crops.

16. Differentiate between sprinkler system and drip system which is more beneficial to rise.

Long Answer Type Question

17. Distinguish between the following
(i) Manure and fertilisers (ii) Kharif and Rabi crops

Answers

1. (d) **2.** (c) **3.** (c) **4.** (a) **5.** (c)
6. crop rotation **7.** plough **8.** False **9.** True
10. A–2, B–5, C–1, D–3, E–4
11. (a) **12.** (c)

Microorganisms: Friend and Foe

CHAPTER 02

There are several kinds of living organisms around us ranging in size from very small to very large. Some extremely small organisms cannot be seen with the unaided eyes. These are called **microorganisms** or microbes. For example, during rainy season, the greyish white patches develop on a moist bread. When we observe these patches through a magnifying glass we see tiny black rounded structures. These structures are called **fungi**. Although, some microorganisms such as fungus can be seen with the help of magnifying glass but some microorganisms others cannot be seen without the help of a microscope.

2.1 Major Groups of Microorganisms

The microorganisms may be unicellular (single-celled) or multicellular (many celled). These are classified into four major groups as described below

(i) **Bacteria** These are the simplest unicellular organisms having rigid cell wall like plant cells, e.g. *Lactobacillus, E. coli,* etc.

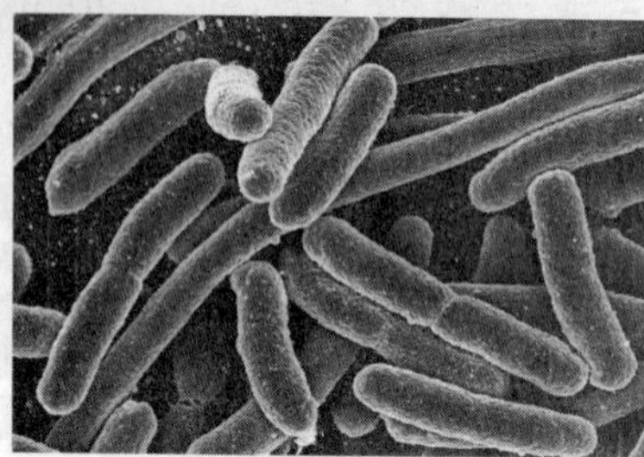

Bacteria

(ii) **Fungi** It is a large group of organisms which do not have chlorophyll and hence, do not photosynthesise. Thus, they are heterotrophs, e.g. yeast, *Penicillium, Aspergillus, Rhizopus* (bread mould). Fungi may be unicellular or multicellular.

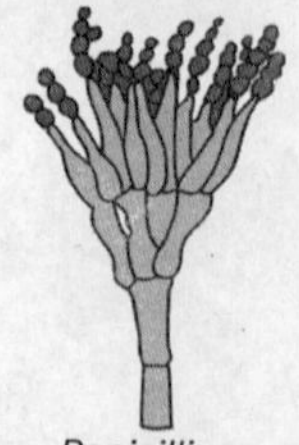

Penicillium

Aspergillus

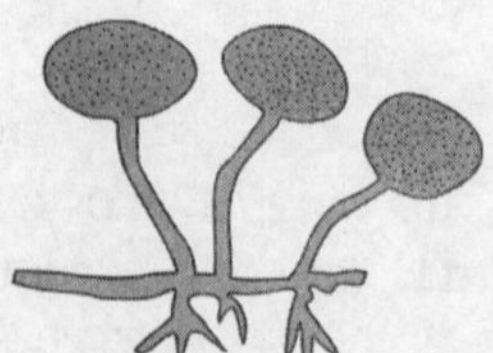

Rhizopus (bread mould)

Fungi

(iii) **Protozoa** It is a group of single-celled microorganisms that have animal like characteristics. They can move from place to place, e.g. *Amoeba* and *Paramecium.* Diseases like dysentery and malaria are caused by protozoans.

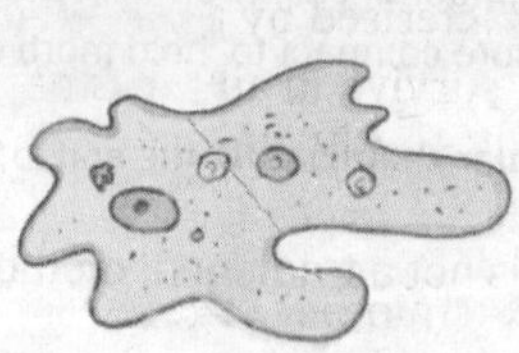

Amoeba

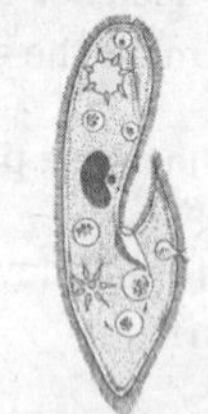

Paramecium

Protozoa

(iv) **Algae** It is a large group of simple, plant-like organisms. They have no true roots, stems or leaves. They can be unicellular or multicellular. Algae are photoautotrophic organisms that carry out photosynthesis, e.g. *Chlamydomonas, Spirogyra*, etc.

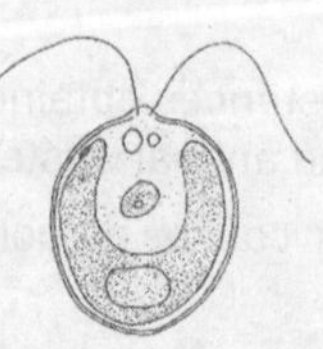

Chlamydomonas

Spirogyra

Algae

Viruses

These are also microscopic organisms but are different from other microorganisms. They reproduce only inside the cells of the host organisms. These host organisms can be a bacterium, plant or animal.

Common ailments like cold, influenza (flu) and most coughs are caused by viruses. Serious diseases like polio and chickenpox are also caused by viruses.

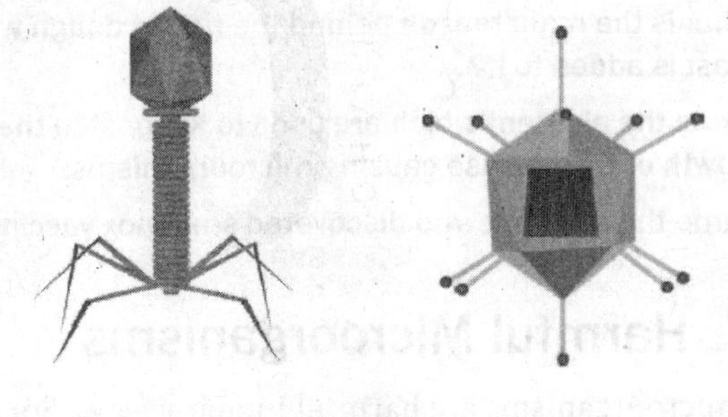

Viruses

Try These 2.1

1. **Do you know why organisms such as fungus on bread, might require a magnifying glass for observation?**
2. **Name the microorganisms that can make their own food by photosynthesis.**
3. **Name a microscopic organism which is different from other microorganisms.**

2.2 Where do Microorganisms Live?

Microorganisms spread over the entire biosphere, e.g. in soil, water, air, inside the bodies of animals, including humans, etc. They are characterised by a very high degree of adaptability, as they can survive in all types of environment, ranging from ice cold climates to hot springs and deserts to marshy lands.

Some microorganisms grow on other organisms, while others exist freely. Microorganisms like *Amoeba* can live alone, while bacteria and fungi may live in colonies.

2.3 Microorganisms and Us

Microorganisms play a dual role in our lives. They not only offer various benefits, but also cause significant number of diseases.

Friendly Microorganisms

Microbes are used for various purposes. Some common beneficial activities of microbes are discussed below

1. Microbes in Household Products

Some of the household products obtained from microbial activities are as follows

(i) **Curd** It contains several microorganisms. Of these, the bacterium, ***Lactobacillus*** promotes the formation of curd. It multiplies in milk and converts milk into curd. The curd is added to rava idlis and bhaturas to make them soft and spongy.

(ii) **Baking industry** The dough for making bread, cakes and pastries is prepared by adding yeast to flour. Yeast reproduces rapidly and produces carbon dioxide (CO_2) during respiration. Bubbles of this gas fill the dough and increase its volume. It adds sponginess to cake and bread.

(iii) Bacteria are also involved in the making of cheese, pickles and the other food items. Bacteria along with yeast are helpful for fermentation of rice idlis and dosa batter.

2. Commercial Use of Microorganisms

Microbes are used for the large scale production of alcohols, wine and acetic acid (vinegar). Yeast is used for commercial production of alcohol and wine. For this purpose yeast is grown on natural sugars present in grains like barley, wheat, rice, crushed fruit juices, etc.

The process of conversion of sugar into alcohol is called **fermentation. Louis Pasteur** discovered fermentation in 1857.

3. Medicinal Use of Microorganisms

When an individual falls ill, the doctors prescribe antibiotics for treatment. The source of these antibiotic medicines and vaccines are microorganisms. The details of antibiotic medicines and vaccines are given below

(i) **Antibiotics** The medicines, which are used to kill or stop the growth of the disease causing microorganisms are known as antibiotics.

These antibiotics in the form of tablets, capsules or injections are products of microorganisms (mainly bacteria and fungi), e.g. penicillin, streptomycin, tetracycline, erythromycin.

The antibiotics are manufactured by growing specific microorganisms and are used to cure a variety of diseases. Antibiotics are even mixed with the feed of livestock and poultry to check microbial infection in animals.

They are also used to control many plant diseases. Antibiotics are not effective against cold and flu as these are caused by viruses.

Certain precautions to be taken for using antibiotics are as follows

(a) It should be taken only on the advice of a qualified doctor in proper dose. In wrong doses (or taken when not needed), it becomes less effective when taken in future.

(b) Person must complete the course as prescribed by the doctor.

(c) It should not be taken unnecessarily as it may kill useful bacteria in the body.

History of Antibiotic: Penicillin

The first antibiotic penicillin which was discovered by **Alexander Fleming** in 1929.

He was working on a culture of disease causing bacteria. During the experiment he observed that the presence of a mould in one of his culture plate prevented the growth of bacteria. Infact it also killed many of these bacteria. From this mould penicillin was prepared.

(ii) **Vaccine** It is a biological preparation that provides immunity (or protection) against a particular disease.

A vaccine consists of dead or weakened microbes which when introduced in a healthy body, produces suitable antibodies to fight and kill the invading bacteria/microbes.

These antibodies remain in the body to protect from disease causing microbes, thus developing **immunity**. The diseases which can be prevented by vaccination are polio, cholera, tetanus, rabies, TB, smallpox, measles and hepatitis.

Vaccination

- **Edward Jenner** discovered the smallpox vaccine in 1798.
- A worldwide campaign against smallpox has finally led to its eradication from most parts of the world.
- Pulse Polio Immunisation Programme was launched in India in 1995 for eradication of polio. Children in the age group of 0 (zero) month to 5 years are administered polio drops (actually vaccine) every year.

4. Increasing Soil Fertility

Some bacteria and cyanobacteria (blue-green algae) are able to fix nitrogen from the atmosphere to enrich soil with nitrogen and increase its fertility.

These microbes are commonly called **biological nitrogen fixers,** e.g. *Rhizobium.*

5. Cleaning the Environment

Microorganisms decompose dead organic waste of plants and animals, converting them into simple substances. These substances are again used by other plants and animals. The microorganisms are used to degrade the waste and smelly substances from our biosphere and thereby clean the environment.

Try These 2.2

1. **Among the following microorganisms, i.e. bacteria, fungi and *Amoeba*, which can live alone?**
2. **What is the main reason behind the rise of dough when yeast is added to it?**
3. **Name the element which are used to kill or stop the growth of the disease causing microorganisms.**
4. **Name the scientist who discovered smallpox vaccine.**

2.4 Harmful Microorganisms

The microorganisms are harmful in many ways. Some of these cause diseases in human beings, plants and animals. Such disease causing microorganisms like bacteria, fungi, virus and protozoans are called **pathogens**. They enter the body by various means, where they multiply and cause harm to the body. Some of their activities are described below.

Disease Causing Microorganisms in Humans

Certain microbial diseases are spread from infected person to a healthy individual through air, water, food or physical contact. Such diseases are called **communicable diseases,** e.g. cholera, common cold, chickenpox and tuberculosis.

Transmission of Communicable Diseases

There are various ways through which communicable diseases can be transmitted. These are as follows

(i) When a person suffering from common cold or flu sneezes, coughs or spits, fine droplets of moisture carrying viruses spread in the air. The virus may enter the body of a healthy person while breathing and cause infections, e.g. tuberculosis.

(ii) Through direct contact with **infected person,** e.g. chickenpox, ringworm.

(iii) Through the food we eat or the water we drink, e.g. cholera, typhoid.

(iv) Through **vectors** or **carriers** like some insects and animals. The organisms that transmit pathogens from an infected individual to a healthy one are known as **carriers.** For example,

- Housefly is one such carrier. The flies sit on the garbage and animal excreta, accumulating pathogens on their bodies. When these flies land on exposed food, they can transfer these pathogens.
- Another example of carrier is female *Anopheles* mosquito which carries the parasite of malaria (*Plasmodium*). Female *Aedes* mosquito acts as a carrier of dengue virus.

Prevention of Communicable Diseases

Some methods of preventing the occurrence and spread of communicable diseases are as follows

(i) Cover mouth and nose with a handkerchief while sneezing.

(ii) Keep your food covered and avoid consuming uncovered food items.

(iii) Drink clean and safe water.

(iv) Use mosquito nets and mosquito repellent creams to protect yourself from mosquito bites.

(v) Take vaccination at proper time.

(vi) Avoid breeding of mosquitoes by not allowing water to collect anywhere, i.e. in coolers, tyres, etc. and by keeping surroundings clean and dry.

Some of the common diseases affecting humans, their mode of transmission and few general methods of prevention are given in table below.

Common human diseases caused by microorganisms

Human diseases	Causative microorganisms	Modes of transmission	Preventive measures (General)
Tuberculosis	Bacteria	Air	Keep the patient in complete isolation. Keep the personal belongings of the patient away from those of others. Vaccination to be given at suitable age.
Measles	Virus	Air	
Chickenpox	Virus	Air/contact	
Polio	Virus	Air/water	
Cholera	Bacteria	Food/wate r	Maintain personal hygiene and good sanitary habits. Consume properly cooked food and boiled drinking water. Vaccination.
Typhoid	Bacteria	Water	
Hepatitis A	Virus	Water	Drink boiled drinking water. Vaccination.
Malaria	Protozoan	Mosquito	Use mosquito net and repellents . Spray insecticides and control breeding of mosquitoes by not allowing water to collect in the surroundings.

Disease Causing Microorganisms in Animals

Several microorganisms not only cause diseases in humans, but also in other animals, e.g. Anthrax is a dangerous human and cattle disease caused by a bacterium. Some of the common animal diseases caused by microorganism are given in table below

Common animal diseases caused by microorganisms

Animal diseases	Microorganisms	Animal affected
Anthrax	Bacteria (*Bacillus anthracis*) discovered by Robert Koch (1876)	Cattle and human
Foot and mouth disease	Virus	Cattle

Disease Causing Microorganisms in Plants

Several microorganisms cause diseases in plants like wheat, rice, potato, sugarcane, orange, apple, etc. These diseases reduce the yield of crops. They can be controlled by the use of certain chemicals which kill the microbes. Some of the common plant diseases caused by microorganisms are tabulated below

Common plant diseases caused by microorganisms

Plant diseases	Microorganisms	Modes of transmission
Citrus canker	Bacteria	Air
Rust of wheat	Fungi	Air, seeds
Yellow vein mosaic of bhindi (okra)	Virus	Insect

Food Poisoning

Microorganisms that grow on food may produce toxic substances, thereby causing spoilage of food. The spoilt food starts giving foul smell, bad taste and its colour may also change. This spoiling of food is a chemical change. Consumption of spoilt food can lead to a condition called **food poisoning.**

The symptoms of food poisoning include vomiting, diarrhoea, headache, fever, etc. It can cause serious illness and even death. So it is very important that we preserve food to prevent it from getting spoilt.

Try These 2.3

1. The female *Aedes* mosquito is a carrier of a particular disease. Name the disease.
2. Viruses can infect humans as well as plants and animals. Give example.
3. Name the condition developed by the consumption of spoilt food.

2.5 Food Preservation

The process by which spoilage of food is prevented using suitable chemical or physical methods is called food preservation. Some of these methods are given below

(i) **Chemical method** The chemicals used to check the growth of microorganisms are called **preservatives. Salts, edible oils** and **acid preservatives** are added to pickles to prevent the attack of microbes. **Sodium benzoate** and **sodium metabisulphite** are common preservatives used to check the growth of microbes. They are added in jams and squashes to check their spoilage.

(ii) **Preservation by common salt** It has been used to preserve meat and fish for ages. Salting is also used to preserve amla, raw mangoes, tamarind, etc.

(iii) **Preservation by sugar** Jams, jellies and squashes are preserved by sugar. It reduces the moisture content which inhibits the growth of bacteria which spoil food.

(iv) **Preservation by oil and vinegar** Use of oil and vinegar prevents spoilage of pickles because bacteria cannot live in such an environment. Vegetables, fruits, fish and meat are preserved by this method.

(v) **Heat and cold treatments** Boiling kills many microorganisms. Similarly, we keep our food in the refrigerator as low temperature inhibits the growth of microbes.

(vi) **Pasteurisation** It is used for the preservation of milk. It involves the process of heating milk to about 70°C for 15 to 30 seconds (killing most of bacteria) and then cooling it quickly at a very low temperature. This milk is then stored in cold temperature. Pasteurised milk can be consumed without boiling as it is free from harmful microbes. The milk that comes in packets does not get spoiled as it is pasteurised. The process of pasteurisation was discovered by **Louis Pasteur.**

(vii) **Storage and packing** These days dry fruits and even vegetables are sold in sealed air tight packets. This helps to preserve food by keeping germs and microbes out. Airtight packets also prevent food from moisture and contamination.

SCIENCE INSIGHT Irradiation is a modern method of food preservation. The food is exposed to high energy gamma rays or X-rays. These powerful radiations completely destroy the harmful microorganisms. The food can be preserved for years without refrigeration.

2.6 Nitrogen Fixation

Plants cannot directly utilise the nitrogen gas present in the atmosphere. It is taken up by plants from the soil only when it is converted to nitrogenous compounds. The process of conversion of atmospheric nitrogen into nitrogenous compounds is called **nitrogen fixation.**

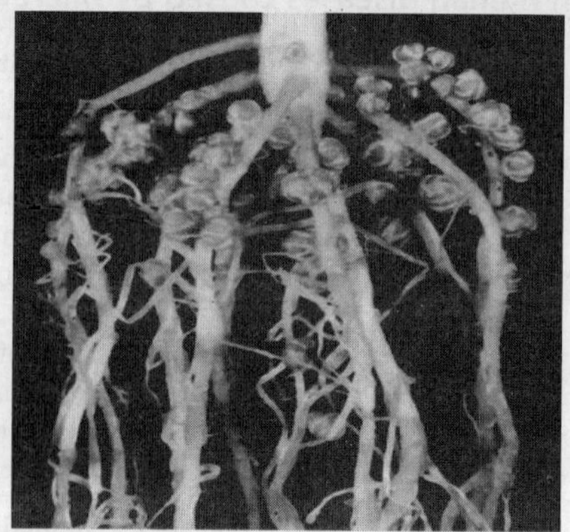

Roots of a leguminous plant with root nodules

Nitrogen can be fixed by

(i) Lightning is a natural process that converts nitrogen into a usable form.

(ii) *Rhizobium* bacteria is involved in the fixation of nitrogen in leguminous plants. These bacteria live in the root nodules of leguminous plants such as beans and peas, with which it has a symbiotic relationship.

(iii) Some of the blue-green algae have capacity to fix nitrogen, e.g. *Anabaena, Nostoc,* etc.

The atmospheric nitrogen although continuously used up by plants and animals, remains constant. This happens through a cycle of processes grouped together called nitrogen cycle.

2.7 Nitrogen Cycle

It is a repeating cycle of processes during which nitrogen in atmosphere is circulated again and again through living and non-living things. Nitrogen is one of the essential constituents of all living organisms. It is a part of proteins, chlorophyll, nucleic acids and vitamins. Our atmosphere contains 78% nitrogen gas. The main steps in this cycle are as follows

(i) The atmospheric nitrogen is fixed through various means and is converted into usable compounds.

(ii) These compounds are utilised by plants from the soil through their root system. This nitrogen is used for synthesis of plant proteins and other compounds.

(iii) Animals taking these plants as food, get these proteins and other nitrogen compounds.

(iv) When these plants and animals die, certain bacteria and fungi convert these complex nitrogenous compounds present in their bodies into simple nitrogenous compounds. These simple nitrogenous compounds are again absorbed by the plants for their growth.

(v) Certain other bacteria convert some of these compounds into nitrogen gas which goes back into the atmosphere. As a result, the percentage of nitrogen in atmosphere remains nearly constant.

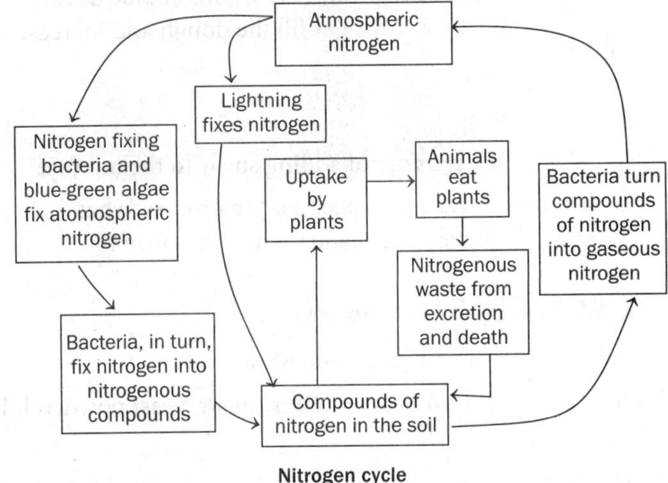

Nitrogen cycle

Try These 2.4

1. **Give the best way to preserve items like meat for longer periods.**

2. **A chemical is added to pickles to check their spoilage. Name it.**

3. **A type of plant roots can fix nitrogen gas from in the air into compounds of nitrogen. Give its name.**

4. **Name an element present in the atmosphere that is essential constituent of living organisms.**

Science Glossary

Algae A type of microorganism that can photosynthesis and form green patches on water.

Antibiotics The medicines that kill or stop the growth of disease causing microorganisms.

Antibodies The substances produced by our body to fight against the invading microorganism.

Bacteria A type of microorganism which can be found in all kinds of environment.

Carrier Animals that carry disease causing microorganisms.

Communicable diseases Microbial disease that can spread from an infected person to a healthy person through air, water, food or physical contact.

Fungi A type of microorganism which cannot photosynthesise.

Fermentation A process of conversion of sugar into alcohol by bacteria and yeast.

Lactobacillus A type of bacteria that promotes the formation of curd.

Microorganism The living organisms which cannot be seen through the unaided eyes.

Nitrogen fixation Process of conversion of free nitrogen gas present in the atmosphere into nitrogenous compounds.

Nitrogen cycle The nitrogen in the atmosphere is circulated again and again in a cyclic manner by the living and the non- living things. This circulation is called as nitrogen cycle.

Protozoa A type of microorganism that have animal like characteristics.

Pathogen Disease causing microorganisms.

Preservatives The chemical substances used to check the growth of microorganism.

Pasteurisation Process of destroying microorganism in food items, e.g. milk. It involves high heating followed by sudden cooling.

Rhizobium Bacteria that lives in the roots of leguminous plants and is involved in the fixation of atmospheric nitrogen.

Virus A type of microorganism which can reproduce only inside the host.

Vaccine Weak or dead microbes that are injected into our body to fight against a disease.

Yeast A unicellular fungi that is used in baking industry.

Let's Investigate

ACTIVITY 1 (Page 17)

Aim To show the presence of microorganisms in soil and in pond water.

Materials Required Soil, water, two beakers, pond water, microscope, dropper and slide.

Procedure

1. Collect some moist soil from the field in a beaker A and add water to it.
2. Take another beaker B, pour some pond water into it.
3. After the soil particles have settled down put drop of water from the beaker A with the help of dropper on a slide and observe under a microscope.
4. Similarly, take a few drops of water from beaker B with the help of dropper, spread them on a glass slide and observe through a microscope.

Observation We will observe tiny organisms moving around in both the slides.

Conclusion From this activity we can conclude that soil and pond water contains many microorganisms.

Viva Questions

1. Why is it important to let the soil particles settle down before observing under the microscope?
2. How would you modify the procedure if you want to investigate the different microorganisms present in different soil types?

ACTIVITY 2 (Page 20)

Aim To show the effect of yeast on dough.

Materials Required 1/2 kg Flour (atta or maida) sugar, warm water and yeast powder and a lid.

Procedure

1. Take 1/2 kg flour (atta or maida), add some sugar and mix with warm water.
2. Add a small amount of yeast powder and knead to make a soft dough.
3. Cover the dough and keep it aside for two hours.

Observation We will observe that the dough has risen and its volume has increased.

(a) Freshly prepared dough with yeast powder

(b) CO_2 produced by yeast caused the dough to rise

Conclusion From this activity we can conclude that yeast reproduces rapidly and produces carbon dioxide during respiration. Bubbles of the gas fill the dough and increase its volume.

Viva Questions

1. What is the purpose of adding sugar to the mixture?
2. If someone wants to speed up the process, what modification can be made to the procedure ?

ACTIVITY 3 (Page 20)

Aim To carry out fermentation of sugar.

Materials Required Beaker, water, sugar, yeast powder, lid and spoon.

Procedure

1. Take a 500 mL beaker filled upto 3/4 with water.
2. Dissolve 2-3 teaspoons of sugar in it.
3. Add half a spoon of yeast powder to the sugar solution.
4. Keep it covered with a lid in a warm place for 4-5 hours.
5. Smell the solution.

Observation We will observe a pungent smell.

Conclusion From this activity we can conclude that sugar has been converted into alcohol by yeast. This process of conversion of sugar into alcohol is known as fermentation.

Viva Questions

1. Why is it important to keep the solution covered in a warm place for 4-5 hours?
2. If the amount of yeast powder is increased in the experiment, predict how it might impact the rate or intensity of fermentation?

ACTIVITY 4 (Page 22)

Aim To show that microorganisms decompose plant waste.

Materials Required Pot *A* and *B*, soil, plant waste, polythene bag, empty glass bottles and broken plastic toys.

Procedure

1. Take two pots and fill each pot half with soil and mark them *A* and *B*.
2. Put plant waste in pot *A*.
3. Put polythene bags, empty glass bottles and broken plastics toys in pot *B*.
4. Put both the pots aside. Observe them after 3-4 weeks.

Observation We will observe that contents of pot *A* would be converted into manure by the action of microbes present in the soil. However, there would be no change in the contents of pot B as microorganisms could not act on the materials present in it

Conclusion From this activity, we can conclude that microorganisms decompose plant waste and convert it into manure, but they do not act on inorganic substances like polythene bags, plastic toys, etc.

Viva Questions

1. Why it is essential to observe the pots after 3-4 weeks and not immediately after setting up the experiment?
2. If the plant waste used in the experiment was treated with pesticides how might it affect the decomposition process?

Mind Map

MICROORGANISMS: FRIEND AND FOE

Groups of Microorganisms
These are living things, too small to be seen with naked eye, viewed under a microscope.

Bacteria
Unicellular having rigid cell wall, e.g. *Lactobacillus*, *E. coli*, etc.

Fungi
- Do not contain chlorophyll.
- Can be either unicellular or multicellular, e.g. *Rhizopus*.

Algae
Plant like organism can be either unicellular or multicellular, e.g. *Chlamydomonas*

Protozoa
Single-celled, that have animal like characteristics e.g. *Amoeba*.

Viruses
- Different from other microbes.
- Reproduce only inside host organism.

Habitat of Microorganisms
Live in all types of environment, e.g. hot springs, ice cold climate, deserts, marshy land, inside the animals bodies.

Nitrogen Fixation
- *Rhizobium* fixes nitrogen in leguminous plants.
- Lives in symbiotic relationship with legume root.
- Lightining also fix nitrogen.

Nitrogen Cycle
Atmospheric nitrogen
Nitrogen fixing bacteria and blue-green algae fix atmospheric nitrogen
Lightning fixes nitrogen
Bacteria, in turn, fix nitrogen into nitrogenous compounds
Uptake by plants
Animals eat plants
Nitrogenous waste from excretion and death
Bacteria turn compounds of nitrogen into gaseous nitrogen
Compounds of nitrogen in the soil

Microorganisms and us

Making of Curd
Bacterium *Lactobacillus* turned milk into curd.

Making of Bread
- Yeast release CO_2 in bread dough.
- Increase its volume.
- Increase sponginess in bread.

Microbes in Environment
- Microbes decompose dead organic waste of plants and animals.
- It degrades harmful smelly substances.

Microorganisms in Soil Fertility
- Some bacteria and cyanobacteria (blue green algae) fix nitrogen from the atmosphere.
- Nitrogen fixes increase soil fertility.

Microorganism in Antibiotics Production
- Stop the growth of the disease causing microorganism.
- Produced by bacteria or fungi, e.g. streptomycin, tetracycline and erythromycin.

Microorganisms in Vaccine Production
- It is a preparation of dead or weakened microbes.
- Promotes the production of specific antibodies.
- Cholera, tuberculosis, smallpox and hepatitis can be prevented by vaccination.

Harmful Microorganisms
- Pathogens are disease causing microorganisms.
- Communicable diseases spread through air, water, food or physical contact.

Common human diseases caused by microorganisms

Human diseases	Causative microorganisms	Modes of transmission
Tuberculosis	Bacteria	Air
Measles	Virus	Air
Chickenpox	Virus	Air/contact
Polio	Virus	Air/water
Cholera	Bacteria	Food/water
Typhoid	Bacteria	water
Hepatitis A	Virus	Water
Malaria	Protozoan	Mosquito

Common animal diseases caused by microorganisms

Animal diseases	Microorganisms	Animal affected
Anthrax	Bacteria	Cattle and human
Foot and mouth disease	Virus	Cattle

Common plant diseases caused by microorganisms

Plant diseases	Microorganisms	Modes of transmission
Citrus canker	Bacteria	Air
Rust of wheat	Fungi	Air, seeds
Yellow vein mosaic of bhindi (Okra)	Virus	Insect

Food Preservation

Chemical Method
- Preservatives added to food to check the growth of microbes.
- Salts, edible oils, sodium benzoate and sodium meta-bisulphate are presevatives.

Preservation by Common Salt
- Salts is used to preserve meat and fish.
- Salting preserve amla, raw mangoes, tamarind, etc.

Presevation by Sugar
- Sugar reduce moisture content.
- Inhibit growth of bacteria.
- Jams, jellies and squashes are preserved by sugar.

Preservation by oil and Vinegar
Oil and vinegar preserves pickles.

Heat and Cold Treatment
- Boiling kills many microorganisms.
- Low temperature inhibits growth of microbes.

Pasteurisation
- Discovered by Louis Pasteur.
- Used for preservation of milk.
- Milk is heated at 70°C for 15 to 30 sec. and then chilled.
- Prevents the growth of microbes.

Storage and Packing
- Dry fruits and vegetables sold in sealed air tight packets.
- Air tight packet prevents growth of microbes.

NCERT FOLDER

Complete Explanations of all NCERT's Questions

Intext Questions

Q.1 Paheli saw that her mother added a little curd to warm milk to set curd for the next day. She wonders why? **Page 19**

Ans. Curd contains several microorganisms, including the bacterium *Lactobacillus* that promotes the formation of curd. It gets multiplied in the milk and converts it into curd.

Q.2 Why are children/ infants given vaccination? **Page 21**

Ans. When vaccines are introduced into the healthy body of a child (or a person), the body fights and kills the invading bacteria by producing suitable antibodies.

These antibodies remain in the body and the child is protected from the disease causing microbes.

Q.3 How do you prevent the spread of communicable diseases? **Page 23**

Ans. We can prevent the spread of communicable diseases by taking some precautions, e.g. keeping a handkerchief on the nose and mouth while sneezing and keeping a distance from infected persons.

Q.4 Why the teacher keeps telling the students not to let water collect anywhere in the neighbourhood? **Page 23**

Ans. We should not let water collect anywhere in the neighbourhood because all mosquitoes breed in the water and spread diseases like malaria.

Q.5 Paheli wonders how food can become a 'poison'? **Page 25**

Ans. Microorganisms that grow on our food sometimes produce toxic substances which make the food poisonous causing serious illness and even death.

Q.6 Why does the milk that comes in packets not spoil? What is pasteurisation? **Page 26**

Ans. The milk that comes in packets does not spoil because it is a pasteurised milk. It can be consumed without boiling as it is free from harmful microbes.

Pasteurisation is a process in which milk is heated to about 70°C for 15-30 seconds and then suddenly chilled and stored. This prevents the growth of microbes. This process was discovered by Louis Pasteur.

Exercise

Q.1 Fill in the blanks.

(a) Microorganisms can be seen with the help of a ....

(b) Blue-green algae fix .... directly from air and enhance fertility of soil.

(c) Alcohol is produced with the help of ....

(d) Cholera is caused by ....

Ans. (a) microscope (b) nitrogen
(c) yeast (d) bacteria

Q.2 Tick the correct answer.

(a) Yeast is used in the production of
(i) sugar (ii) alcohol
(iii) hydrochloric acid (iv) oxygen

(b) The following is an antibiotic
(i) sodium bicarbonate
(ii) streptomycin
(iii) alcohol
(iv) yeast

(c) Carriers of malaria-causing protozoan is
(i) female *Anopheles* mosquito
(ii) cockroach
(iii) housefly
(iv) butterfly

(d) The most common carrier of communicable diseases is
(i) ant (ii) housefly
(iii) dragonfly (iv) spider

(e) The bread or idli dough rises because of
(i) heat
(ii) grinding
(iii) growth of yeast cells
(iv) kneading

(f) The process of conversion of sugar into alcohol is called
(i) nitrogen fixation
(ii) moulding
(iii) fermentation
(iv) infection

Ans. (a) (ii) Alcohol is produced by the action of yeast.
(b) (ii) Streptomycin is an antibiotic.
(c) (i) Female *Anopheles* mosquito is the carrier of malaria. It picks up the parasite of the disease from an infected person when it bite to obtain blood.
(d) (ii) Housefly is the most common carrier of communicable disease.
(e) (iii) The bread or idli dough rises because of growth of yeast cells.
(f) (iii) Fermentation is the process of conversion of sugar into alcohol.

Q.3 Match the organisms in Column A with their action in Column B.

Column A	Column B
A Bacteria	(i) Fixing nitrogen
B *Rhizobium*	(ii) Setting of curd
C *Lactobacillus*	(iii) Baking of bread
D Yeast	(iv) Causing malaria
E A protozoan	(v) Causing cholera
F A virus	(vi) Causing AIDS
	(vii) Producing antibodies

Ans. A-(v), B-(i), C-(ii), D-(iii), E-(iv), F-(vi)

Q.4 Can microorganisms be seen with the naked eye? If not, how can they be seen?

Ans. Microorganisms or microbes are too small to be seen by naked eyes. They can be seen with the help of a magnifying glass or microscope.

Q.5 What are the major groups of microorganisms?

Ans. Microorganisms are divided into four major groups which are as follows

(i) **Bacteria** These are single-celled organisms having rigid cell was like plant cells. Diseases like typhoid and tuberculosis (TB) are caused by bacteria.
(ii) **Fungi** These are non-green organisms which obtain their food from the dead organic matter.
(iii) **Protozoa** These are unicellular animals which cause diseases like malaria and dysentery.
(iv) **Algae** These are photoautotrophic organisms, that may be unicellular or multicellular.

Q.6 Name the microorganisms which can fix atmospheric nitrogen in the soil.

Ans. Bacteria such as *Rhizobium* and certain blue-green algae (*Anabaena, Nostoc*) present in the soil can fix atmospheric nitrogen and convert it into usable nitrogenous compounds.

Q.7 Write 10 lines on the usefulness of microorganisms in our lives.

Ans. Microorganisms are useful for the humans and plants in following ways

(i) They are used in preparation of food items such as breads.
(ii) Bacteria are used in the conversion of milk into curd.
(iii) They are used for the large scale production of alcohol, wine and acetic acid.
(iv) A number of medicines such as antibiotics are being produced from bacteria and fungi.
(v) They are used to check microbial infections in animals.
(vi) Vaccines are made by dead or weakened microbes.
(vii) Some bacteria and blue-green algae increase the soil fertility by fixing atmospheric nitrogen.
(viii) They decompose the dead organic wastes of plants and animals.
(ix) They are used in cleaning up of the environment.
(x) Certain microbes are also used in the biological treatment of sewage and industrial effluents.

Q.8 Write a short paragraph on the harmful effects of microorganisms.

Ans. Microorganisms are harmful for human beings in many ways. They cause diseases in humans, plants and animals, e.g. In humans, bacteria cause diseases such as cholera, typhoid, tuberculosis, etc.
In cattle, the foot and mouth disease is caused by a virus.
Also several microbes cause diseases in plants, e.g. Citrus canker disease, late blight of potato.
Some microbes grow on food and secrete toxic substances which make the food poisonous.

Q.9 What are antibiotics? What precautions must be taken while taking antibiotics?

Ans. Refer to text on page no. 23 and 24.

REVIEW EXERCISE

Including Competency Based Questions

Part I

Multiple Choice Questions

1. The greyish white patches that develop on moist bread during rainy season are
(a) fungi (b) protozoan
(c) bacteria (d) virus

2. Diseases like dysentery and malaria are caused by
(a) protozoans (b) algae
(c) fungi (d) bacteria

3. *Spirogyra* is
(a) an algae (b) a fungi
(c) a bacteria (d) a protozoan

4. *Chlamydomonas* and *Amoeba* are the example of
(a) protozoan and virus (b) fungi and algae
(c) algae and protozoan (d) virus and bacteria

5. Which of the following reproduces only inside a host cell? **NCERT Exemplar**
(a) Bacteria (b) Virus
(c) *Amoeba* (d) Fungus

6. A disease in human beings caused by virus is **NCERT Exemplar**
(a) typhoid (b) influenza
(c) dysentery (d) cholera

7. The two microorganisms which live in symbiotic association in lichens are
(a) fungus and protozoan (b) algae and bacteria
(c) bacteria and protozoan (d) algae and fungus

8. The gas released during the preparation of bread is
(a) oxygen (b) carbon dioxide
(c) nitrogen (d) sulphur dioxide

9. Alcohol is produced with the help of **CBSE Question Bank**
(a) sodium chloride (b) yeast
(c) nitrogen (d) carbon dioxide

10. Scientist who discovered the fermentation?
(a) Alexander Fleming (b) Louis Pasteur
(c) Johann Mendel (d) Charles Darwin

11. Pathogenic microorganisms present in host cells are killed by medicines called **NCERT Exemplar**
(a) pain killer (b) antibodies
(c) antibiotics (d) vaccines

12. Which of the element is mixed with the feed of livestock and poultry to check microbial infection in animals?
(a) Vaccine (b) Antibiotic
(c) Yeast (d) Alcohol

13. Antibiotics are not effective against
(a) cold and flu (b) tuberculosis
(c) cholera (d) typhoid

14. Edward Jenner discovered the vaccine for
(a) smallpox (b) chicken pox
(c) tuberculosis (d) diphtheria

15. Polio drops given to children are actually a
(a) bacteria (b) algae
(c) vaccine (d) medicine

16. Payal dug two pits, *A* and *B* in her garden. In pit *A*, she put a polythene bag packet with some agricultural waste. In pit *B*, she dumped the same kind of waste, but without packing it in a polythene bag. She then covered both the pits with soil. What did she observe after a month? **Competency Based Que.**
(a) Waste in pit *A* degraded faster than that in pit *B*
(b) Waste in pit *B* degraded faster than that in pit *A*
(c) Waste in both pits degraded almost equally
(d) Waste in both pits did not degrade at all

17. Female *Anopheles* mosquito carries the parasite of
(a) dengue (b) malaria
(c) cholera (d) tuberculosis

18. Dengue fever is transmitted by
(a) female *Aedes* mosquito
(b) housefly
(c) female *Anopheles* mosquito
(d) sandfly

19. The disease caused by a protozoan and spread by an insect is
(a) dengue (b) malaria
(c) polio (d) measles

20. An example of bacterial disease occurring in animals is
(a) foot and mouth disease (b) bird flu
(c) anthrax (d) swine flu

Answers

1. (a)	2. (a)	3. (a)	4. (c)	5. (b)
6. (b)	7. (d)	8. (b)	9. (b)	10. (b)
11. (c)	12. (b)	13. (a)	14. (a)	15. (c)
16. (b)	17. (b)	18. (a)	19. (b)	20. (c)

Fill in the Blanks

1. All microorganisms are classified into .... major groups.
2. *Paramecium* is a slipper- shaped ....
3. Alexander Fleming discovered mould ....
4. Pathogens are .... causing organisms.
5. .... could be due to the consumption of food spoilt by some microorganisms.

Answers

1. four 2. protozoan 3. penicillin
4. disease 5. Food poisoning

True/False

1. Microorganisms can be seen with naked eyes.
2. Microorganisms can be found only in air and water.
3. Viruses can only multiply in a living cell.
4. All microbes are disease causing.
5. Microorganisms are also used in cleaning up of the environment.

Answers

1. False, microorganisms are very small and cannot be seen by naked eyes. They can be seen with the help of a microscope.
2. False, microorganisms are found everywhere in air, water, inside our body, etc.
3. True
4. False, some microbes are useful, e.g. *Lactobacillus*.
5. True

Match the Columns

1. Match the microorganisms given in the Column I to the group to which they belong in Column II. **NCERT Exemplar**

Column I	Column II
A. *Lactobacillus*	1. Algae
B. *Aspergillus*	2. Protozoa
C. *Spirogyra*	3. Fungi
D. *Paramecium*	4. Bacteria

2. Match the items given in Column I with those of Column II.

Column I	Column II
A. Polio	1. Legumes
B. Malaria	2. Antibiotics
C. *Rhizobium*	3. Yeast
D. Alexander Fleming	4. Viral disease
E. Bread making	5. Protozoan disease

3. Match the names of scientists given in Column I with the discovery made by them given in Column II. **NCERT Exemplar**

Column I	Column I
A. Louis Pasteur	1. Penicillin
B. Robert Koch	2. Anthrax bacterium
C. Edward Jenner	3. Fermentation
D. Alexander Fleming	4. Smallpox vaccine
	5. Typhoid

Answers

1. A-4, B-3, C-1, D-2
2. A-4, B-5, C-1, D-2, E-3
3. A-3, B-2, C-4, D-1

Assertion-Reason Questions

The following questions consist of two statements Assertion (A) and Reason (R). Answer these questions by selecting the appropriate option given below

(a) Both A and R are true and R is the correct explanation of A
(b) Both A and R are true, but R is not the correct explanation of A.
(c) A is true, but R is false
(d) A is false, but R is true.

1. **Assertion** (A) *Lactobacillus* converts curd into milk.
Reason (R) The conversion of milk into curd is known as fermentation.
2. **Assertion** (A) Streptomycin and tetracycline are the examples of antibiotics.
Reason (R) Antibiotics helps in the growth of disease causing microorganisms.
3. **Assertion** (A) Sodium benzoate and sodium metabisulphite are common preservatives.
Reason (R) They are used to control the growth of microbes.

4. **Assertion** (A) Pasteurised milk cannot be consumed without boiling.

   Reason (R) Pasteurised milk is free from microorganisms.

5. **Assertion** (A) *Rhizobium* is an example of nitrogen fixing bacteria.

   Reason (R) This bacteria converts nitrogen compounds into nitrogen gas.

Answers

1. (d) A is false, but R is true. A can be corrected as *Lactobacillus* converts milk into curd.
2. (c) A is true, but R is false. R can be corrected as Antibiotics are the medicines that kill or stop the growth of disease causing microorganisms.
3. (a) Both A and R are true and R is the correct explanation of A.
4. (d) A is false, but R is true. A can be corrected as Pasteurised milk can be consumed without boiling.
5. (c) A is true, but R is false. R can be corrected as *Rhizobium* bacteria coverts nitrogen gas into nitrogenous compounds which are utilised by plants.

Case Based Question

1. Manoj adds some yeast to two test tubes containing sugar solution. He ties balloons on the mouth of each of test tube. One test tube is kept in ice and the other at room temperature. The picture shows what happens after three hours. Competency Based Que.

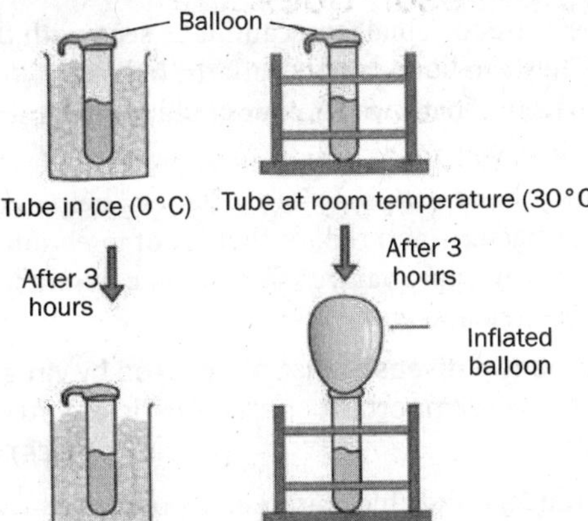

(i) What is Manoj investigating?

(a) Does yeast grow in sugar solution only?

(b) Does yeast convert sugar into alcohol?

(c) Does temperature affect the growth of yeast?

(d) Which gas is produced as yeast grows in sugar solution?

(ii) How can Manoj confirm, if the gas produced in the test tube at room temperature was due to the yeast growing in it?

(a) He should repeat the same experiment

(b) He should leave the test tube undisturbed for six hours

(c) He should repeat the experiment with test tubes containing more sugar solution

(d) He should keep an extra set of test tubes with sugar solution, but without the yeast

(iii) What should Manoj keep the same in both the test tubes for a fair experiment? Circle 'Yes' or 'No' for each row.

	Should this be kept same for both the test tubes?	Yes or No
(a)	The concentration of sugar solution	Yes/No
(b)	The colour of the balloons	Yes/No
(c)	The amount of yeast added to each test tube	Yes/No

(iv) What type of organism is yeast?

(a) Fungi (b) Algae

(c) Bacteria (d) Protozoa

Answers

1. (i) (c) Does temperature affect the growth of yeast?

   (ii) (d) He should keep an extra set of test tubes with sugar solution without the yeast.

   (iii) (a) Yes

   (b) No

   (c) Yes

   (iv) (a) Fungi

Part II

Very Short Answer Type Questions

1. Write the name of device by which we can study microorganisms successfully.

Ans. Microscope is the device that has made the study of microorganisms successful.

2. Ashish left an orange in his bag and forgot about it. After a week, when he looked in his bag, he found something growing on his orange.

(i) What was growing on Ashish's orange?

(ii) Can these organism be seen with a magnifying glass? **Competency Based Que.**

Ans. (i) Mould

(ii) Yes, Fungi can be seen with a magnifying glass.

3. Identify protozoan from the list of microorganisms given: *Rhizopus, Rhizobium, Penicillium, Amoeba.*

Ans. *Amoeba* is a protozoan in the list given.

4. Name the group of microorganisms which can photosynthesise.

Ans. Algae are the group of microorganisms which can photosynthesise.

5. Mention the kind of organisms that are classified under algae. Give examples.

Ans. Simple plant-like organisms that contain chlorophyll are classified under algae, e.g. *Spirogyra, Chlamydomonas.*

6. Mention a characteristic of viruses.

Ans. Viruses are a cellular tiny microscopic organisms that can reproduce only inside the cells of host organisms.

7. Write the name of two groups of microorganisms which live in colonies.

Ans. The groups of microorganisms which live in colonies are bacteria and fungi.

8. We add a little curd to warm milk to set curd for the next day. Why?

Ans. Curd contains several microorganisms. Of these, the bacterium *Lactobacillus* promotes the formation of curd. It multiplies in milk and converts it into curd.

9. An ingredient is added to idlis and bhatura to make them soft. What is it?

Ans. Curd is added to idlis and bhatura to make them soft.

10. A gas is responsible for increase in volume of dough. Name it.

Ans. Carbon dioxide given out by yeast is responsible for increase in volume of dough.

11. Yeast is used for commercial use. Write one commercial use of yeast. **NCERT Exemplar**

Ans. Baking bread is one of the commercial use of yeast. It is also used in alcohol manufacturing.

12. Name the process in yeast that converts sugars into alcohol. **NCERT Exemplar**

Ans. Fermentation is the process by which yeast converts sugars into alcohol.

13. Should antibiotics be used in cold and flu? Give reason for your answer.

Ans. No, antibiotics should not be used in cold and flu because these diseases are caused by viruses and antibiotics are not effective against viruses.

14. Vaccine is essential for what purpose? Mention two diseases for which vaccines are available.

Ans. Vaccine is essential to protect all children against several diseases. Polio and hepatitis are two diseases for which vaccines are available.

15. Where is the mode of transmission in yellow vein mosaic of okra?

Ans. Yellow vein mosaic of okra is a viral disease transmitted by a insect.

Short Answer Type Questions

1. Ankur's mother told him to wash his hands with soap before eating because his hands might have bacteria. Ankur did not believe her because he could not see anything on his hands. Why could not Ankur see the bacteria on his hands? Why washing hands with soap and water before eating is generally recommended? State how bacteria can be harmful to humans?

Ans. Bacteria are too small and cannot be seen with the naked eye. They can be seen only with the help of microscope.That's why Ankur could not see the bacteria on his hands.

Washing hand with soap and water can help to remove various bacteria and reduce the risk of infection. Bacteria can cause various diseases like dysentry, typhoid, cholera, etc.

2. (i) Name two diseases that are caused by virus.
(ii) Write one important characteristic of virus. **NCERT Exemplar**

Ans. (i) Influenza and chickenpox are two diseases caused by virus in humans.

(ii) Virus can reproduce only inside the cells of host of an infected person.

3. Yeast is very useful for baking industry. Elucidate the role of yeast.

Ans. Yeast plays an important role in the baking industry. It reproduces rapidly and produces CO_2 during respiration. Bubbles of CO_2 fill the dough and increase its volume, making the products such as bread, cake fluffy.

4. Justify with the help of two examples that microorganisms can be beneficial for humans. CBSE Question Bank

Ans. Two examples that justify that microorganisms can be beneficial for humans are as follows

(i) **Baking industry** The dough for making bread, cakes and pastries is prepared by adding yeast to flour. Yeast reproduces rapidly and produes carbon dioxide during respiration. These gases fill the dough and increase its volume. It adds sponginess to cake and bread.

(ii) **Production of Antibiotics** Antibiotics are produced by several groups of microbes such as bacteria and fungi. These microbes produce antibiotics as their natural defense system against other microbes.

5. How do vaccines work?

Ans. Refer to text on page no. 24.

6. Polio drops are not given to children suffering from diarrhoea. Why?

Ans. If the child is suffering from diarrhoea, the polio drops that are orally given vaccine may be excreted out because of frequent motions and thus becomes ineffective.

7. Why should we avoid standing close to a tuberculosis patient while he/she is coughing? NCERT Exemplar

Ans. Tuberculosis is an air-borne disease which easily spreads when the infected person coughs as coughing spreads germs in the air. These bacterium can be inhaled by healthy person in close proximity and causes infection. This is why, we should avoid standing close to a TB patient.

8. Classify the following into friendly and harmful microorganisms. NCERT Exemplar
Yeast, malarial parasite, *Lactobacillus*, bread mould, *Rhizobium*, *Bacillus anthracis*.

Ans.

Friendly	Harmful
Yeast	Malarial parasite
Lactobacillus	Bread mould
Rhizobium	*Bacillus anthracis*

9. While returning from the school, Boojho ate chaat from a street hawker. When he reached home, he fell ill and complained of stomach ache. What could be the reason?

Ans. The reason could be that the chaat was contaminated by pathogénic microorganisms. It can be due to unhygienic conditions near the shop or the utensil used for serving could have been contaminated. The unhygienic environment of the shop attracts flies and promotes the growth of infections. Most street hawkers sell food items in an open area which get contaminated with dust and flies carrying germs. This unhygienic condition can lead to spoilage of food which when consumed can lead to serious illness.

10. What will happen to 'pooris' and 'unused kneaded flour' if they are left in the open for a day or two? Competency Based Que.

Ans. The 'unused kneaded flour' if left in warm conditions, gets infected by microbes which cause fermentation and spoils the flour. The pooris' on the other hand would remain in relatively good condition because these were deep fried in heated oil that kills microbes.

11. Sachin opened two packets of milo drink. He left one in the refrigerator and another on the table. Three days later, he got a bad smell from the packet left on the table. The packet of milo drink in the refrigerator did not have a bad smell. Why? Explain.

Ans. The packet which was put in the refrigerator did not have a bad smell because there was a cold temperature and bacteria could and not grow there. Milo drink left outside the refrigerator smell bad because it came in contact with air and bacteria. The higher temperature outside the refrigerator proved favourable for the growth of microorganisms.

12. Explain the various method of nitrogen fixation.

Ans. Refer to text on page no. 26.

Long Answer Type Questions

1. Discuss the different ways in which communicable diseases spread from person to person.

Ans. Refer to text on page no. 24.

2. How can we prevent the following diseases?
(i) Cholera (ii) Typhoid
(iii) Hepatitis-A NCERT Exemplar

Ans. (i) **Cholera** By maintaining personal hygiene and good sanitation practices.

(ii) **Typhoid** By eating properly cooked food, drinking boiled water and by getting vaccinated against the disease.

(iii) **Hepatitis** By drinking boiled water and getting vaccinated against the disease.

3. Give causative microorganism, mode of transmission and one preventive measure of human diseases like Polio, Cholera and Hepatitis-B.

Ans.

Diseases	Causative microorganisms	Mode of transmission	Preventive measures
Polio	Virus	Air/Water	Vaccination should be given at suitable age
Cholera	Bacteria	Water/Food	Maintain personal hygiene and good sanitary habits
Hepatitis-B	Virus	Water	Drinking boiled water and proper vaccination.

4. Explain food preservatives with examples.

Ans. Refer to text on page no. 26.

5. Give reasons for the following.

(i) Fresh milk is boiled before consumption while processed milk is stored in packets and can be consumed without boiling.

(ii) Raw vegetables and fruits are kept in refrigerators, whereas jams and pickles can be kept outside.

(iii) Farmers prefer to grow beans and peas in nitrogen deficient soils.

(iv) Mosquitoes can be controlled by preventing stagnation of water though they do not live in water. Why?

Ans. (i) Fresh milk is boiled before consumption to kill the microorganisms in it. But packed milk is pasteurised and does not contain any microorganisms. Thus, it can be consumed without boiling.

(ii) Raw vegetables and fruits get easily infected by microorganisms and get spoiled. They are kept in refrigerator as low temperature inhibits growth of microbes. Jams and pickles contain sugar and salt as preservatives. They do not get infected by microbes as these preservatives do not allow the growth of microbes.

(iii) Beans and peas are leguminous plants and have *Rhizobium* in their root nodules. These bacteria can fix atmospheric nitrogen to enrich the soil with nitrogen and increase its fertility.

(iv) Though mosquitoes live on land, their larvae grow in water. If water stagnation is prevented, their larvae cannot survive, thus reducing mosquito population.

6 Explain the main steps of nitrogen cycle with the help of a diagram.

Ans. Refer to text on page no. 27.

Case Based Questions

1. A trash can contains the following materials. Plastic straw, Aluminium foil, Tissue paper, Glass bottles, Chicken bones **Competency Based Que.**

(i) Select the materials from the list that can be decomposed by microbes?

(ii) Rohit is suffering from stomach ache and is passing watery stool. What should Rohit do to prevent the spread of infection to other family members?

(a) He should eat properly cooked food

(b) He should wear a mask all the time

(c) He should maintain distance from other family members

(d) He should wash his hands with soap after using the bathroom

2. **Suman wants to see how quickly carrots lose colour. Loss of colour shows rotting of carrot. She observes carrot slices on a plate under three different conditions as shown below**

Competency Based Que.

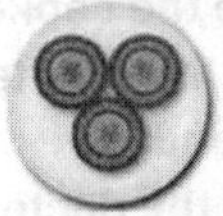
Under the Sun

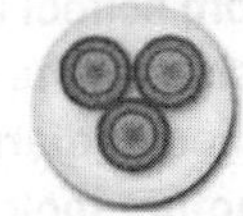
In a moist room at 25 °C

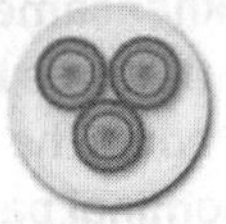
In the refrigerator

She notes how long the carrot slices on each plate take to change colour.

	Under the Sun	In a moist room at 25°C	In the refrigerator
Time carrot slices take to change colour	2 days	5 days	8 days

(i) What can Suman conclude from her activity?

(a) Carrots when kept under the Sun do not rot easily.

(b) Carrots at room temperature lose colour more quickly.

(c) Carrots can be best preserved in hot and moist conditions.

(d) Carrots take more time to lose colour under cold conditions.

(ii) Use the results of the activity to finish the graph below. The first bar is drawn for you. Put a label in the space provided for the axis on the left.

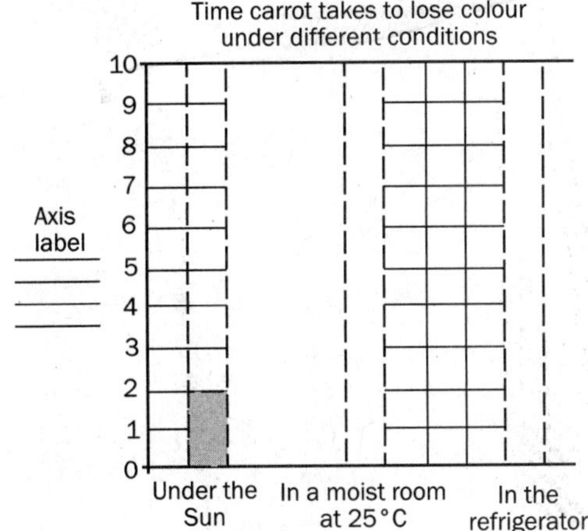

3. **The picture shows the nitrogen cycle.**

Competency Based Que.

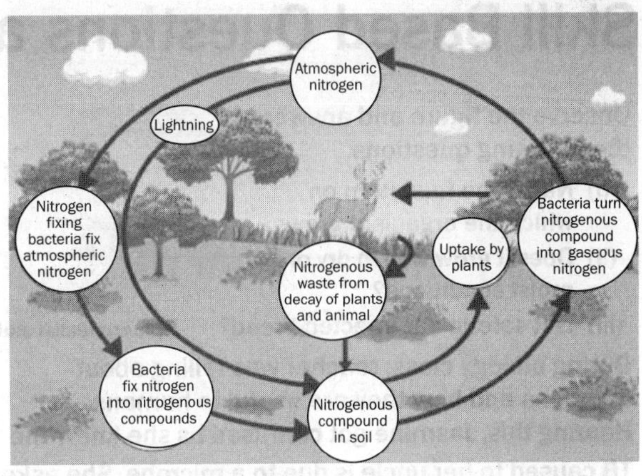

(i) How do plants take up nitrogen?

(ii) Plants and animals are continuously using nitrogen. Will there be a depletion of nitrogen in the environment due to this continuous use? Explain your answer.

Answers

1. (i) Tissue paper, Chicken bones.

   (ii) (d) He should wash his hands with soap after using the bathroom.

2. (i) (d) Carrots take more time to lose colour under cold conditions.

   (ii)

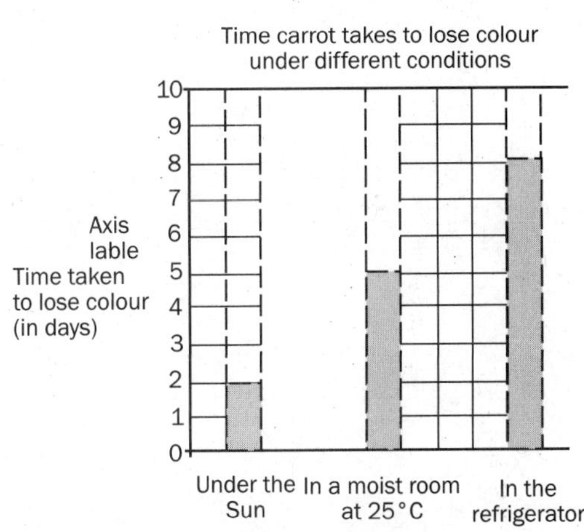

3. (i) Plants take up nitrogen from the nitrogenous compounds in the soil.

   (ii) No, nitrogen in the environment will not get depleted because it is recycled and reused in the environment.

Skill Based Questions as per NEP 2020

1. Observe the figure and answer the following questions.

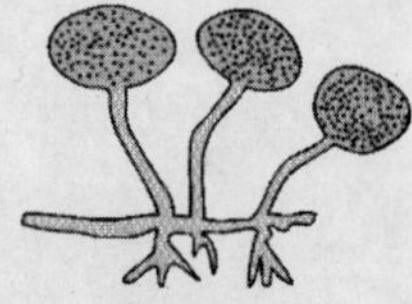

(i) Name the food item on which the organism grows.

(ii) Does it grow well in dry or in moist conditions?

(iii) Is it safe to eat infected bread? **Experimental skill**

2. During biology class, teacher was telling about microbes and how they are useful to humans. Hearing this, Jasmine got confused as she knew the TB caused to her uncle is due to a microbe. She asked her teacher about it. The teacher appreciated her for the question and explained the whole class. **Observation skill**

(i) What are microbes?

(ii) How are microbes helpful to humans?

3. Prakhar came back from school and ate the cooked rice that was kept outside on the dining table. After few hours, he complained of diarrhoea and abdominal pain. His mother took him to the doctor who explained why this happened and asked them to preserve their food properly. **Thinking skill**

(i) What must have happened to Prakhar?

(ii) Give the probable cause for his condition.

4. Arya and Unnati discuss about vaccination. Unnati came up with her fear that vaccines can be dangerous as it contains microbes itself. Arya explained and removed her fear. **Thinking skill**

(i) What is a vaccine?

(ii) Suggest what could be Arya's explanation?

ASSESSMENT EXERCISE

Part I

Multiple Choice Questions

1. Anthrax is caused by
(a) *Bacillus anthracis* (b) *Salmonella*
(c) *Clostridium* (d) *Aspergillus*

2. Polio and measles are the example of
(a) viral diseases (b) bacterial diseases
(c) protozoan diseases (d) fungal diseases

3. The spoiling of food is a .... change.
(a) physical (b) chemical
(c) natural (d) biogeochemical

4. Which of the following does not fix atmospheric nitrogen?
(a) *Nostoc* (b) *Anabaena*
(c) *Rhizobium* (d) *Amoeba*

5. Citrus canker is a common disease of
(a) human (b) plant
(c) animal (d) fungi

Fill in the Blanks

6. The process in which sugar is converted into alcohol is called..... .

7. .... is a process of heating the milk at high temperature then cooling it suddenly and storing it.

8. ...... is the vector of dengue virus.

True/False

9. Jams, jellies and squashes are preserved by adding salt.

10. The atmospheric nitrogen cannot be utilised by the living organisms.

11. Viruses can be seen by simple microscopes.

Match the Columns

12. Match the Column I with Column II.

	Column I		Column II
A.	Tuberculosis	1.	Edward Jenner
B.	Chickenpox	2.	Alexander Fleming
C.	Malaria	3.	Louis Pasteur
D.	Rust of wheat	4.	Fungi
E.	Pasteurisation	5.	Virus
F.	Antibiotic	6.	Bacteria
G.	Vaccination	7.	Protozoa

Assertion-Reason Questions

The following questions consist of two statements **Assertion** (A) and **Reason** (R). Answer these questions by selecting the appropriate option given below.
(a) Both A and R are true and R is the correct explanation of A.
(b) Both A and R are true, but R is not the correct explanation of A.
(c) A is true, but R is false.
(d) A is false, but R is true.

13. Assertion (A) Antibiotics are effective against cold and flu.
Reason (R) Cold and flu are caused by virus.

14. Assertion (A) Decomposer clean the environment.
Reason (R) They decompose the harmful dead and decaying remains of plants and animals.

Part II

Very Short Answer Type Questions

15. Is the decomposition of the bodies of dead plants and animals by microorganisms desirable?

16. Yeast is used to prepare food items name them.

Short Answer Type Questions

17. Why dry fruits and vegetables are sold in sealed air tight packets?

18. How do algae differ from fungi?

19. Write the importance of nitrogen fixing bacteria in soil.

Long Answer Type Question

20. Write the role of immunisation in eradicating diseases from a country.

Answers

1. (a) **2.** (a) **3.** (b) **4.** (d) **5.** (b)
6. Fermentation **7.** Pasteurisation **8.** *Aedes*
9. False **10.** True
11. False
12. A-6, B-5, C-7, D-4, E-3, F-2, G-1
13. (d)
14. (a)

CHAPTER 03

Coal and Petroleum

We use various resources present on Earth to fulfill our basic needs. Some of them are found naturally, e.g. air, water and soil whereas others have been made by human efforts like paper, plastics, etc. In this chapter, we will study about some natural resources like coal, petroleum and natural gas.

3.1 Natural Resources

The various resources which are obtained from the nature are called natural resources, e.g. air, water, soil, plants, petroleum, etc. These are necessary for the survival of all living beings. Based on their availability in nature, natural resources can be classified into the following two types

1. Inexhaustible Natural Resources

Those natural resources which are present in unlimited quantity in nature and are not likely to be exhausted (used up) by human activities are called inexhaustible natural resources, e.g. sunlight, air, water, etc.

2. Exhaustible Natural Resources

Those natural resources which are present in a limited quantity in nature and can be exhausted (used up) by human activities are called exhaustible natural resources, e.g. coal, petroleum, natural gas, minerals, forests, wildlife, etc.

Coal, petroleum and natural gas are collectively known as **fossil fuels**. As they were formed from remains of dead organism (fossils).

3.2 Coal

It is a hard, black combustible fuel. Coal is found in the deep coal mines under the surface of Earth. It burns in the presence of air and produces CO_2, gas and heat. Earlier, it was used in railway engines to produce steam to run the engine.

Formation of Coal

About 300 million years ago, the Earth had dense forests in low lying wetland areas. Natural processes like flooding, earthquakes, volcanoes, etc., buried these forests under the surface of the Earth.

As more soil deposited over them, they were compressed. The temperature also rose as they sank deeper and deeper. Under high pressure and temperature dead plants got slowly converted into coal.

This slow process of conversion of dead vegetation buried deep under the Earth into coal is called **carbonisation**.

Coal as a Source of Energy

Coal contains mainly carbon and when heated in air, it burns and produces mainly carbon dioxide gas and heat. The reaction can be written as

$$\underset{\text{(Coal)}}{\text{Carbon}} + \underset{\text{(From air)}}{\text{Oxygen}} \longrightarrow \text{Carbon dioxide} + \text{Heat}$$

Uses of Coal

Some of the uses of coal are given below

(i) Coal is one of the fuels used to cook food.

(ii) It is used in thermal power plants to produce electricity.

(iii) It is used as a fuel in various industries.

(iv) It is used for the manufacture of coke, coal tar and coal gas.

Products Obtained from Coal

Coal is processed in the industry to get some useful products. Which are coke, coal tar and coal gas.

1. Coke

It is a tough, porous and black substance. Coke is an almost pure form of carbon. When coal is heated in the absence of air, then coal gas and coal tar are eliminated and coke is left behind as a black residue.

Uses of Coke

Coke is mainly used

(i) in the extraction of metals such as iron, zinc, etc.

(ii) in the manufacture of steel. (iii) as a fuel.

2. Coal Tar

It is a thick, black liquid having an unpleasant smell. It is a mixture of about 200 different carbon compounds.

Uses of Coal Tar

Some of the uses of coal tar are as follows

(i) The various compounds obtained from coal tar are used as starting materials for manufacturing substances used in everyday life and in industries.

For example, perfumes, photographic materials, roofing materials, drugs, explosives, plastics and paints etc.

(ii) Naphthalene balls are obtained from coal tar and are used to repel moths and other insects.

(iii) Coal tar has been used for metalling the roads. But, these days bitumen (a petroleum product) is being used for metalling the roads.

3. Coal Gas

It is a gaseous fuel which is obtained during the processing of coal in the absence of oxygen to get coke. It is mainly a mixture of methane and hydrogen with some carbon monoxide.

Uses of Coal Gas

Some of the uses of coal gas are as follows

(i) It is used as a fuel in many industries situated near the coal processing plants.

(ii) It has also been used for lighting purposes.

SCIENCE INSIGHT Coal gas was used for street lighting for the first time in London in 1810 and in New York around 1820. This is because when it burns, it produces a good amount of light. Now a days, it is used as a source of heat rather than light.

Try These 3.1

1. **Are man made resources exhaustible or inexhaustible?**
2. **Coal, petroleum and natural gas are known as non-renewable sources. Why?**
3. **Name the product of coal which is thick black liquid having an unpleasant smell.**
4. **Name the important source from which naphthalene balls are obtained.**

3.3 Petroleum

It is a dark coloured, thick crude (raw) oil having an unpleasant odour. The name petroleum means 'rock oil' (*petra* = rock, *oleum* = oil). It is found deep below the Earth's crust trapped in rocks in certain areas.

Petrol and **diesel** are obtained from petroleum. Petrol is used as a fuel in light automobiles (e.g. motorcycles, scooters and cars), whereas diesel is used in heavy motor vehicles (e.g. trucks and tractors).

Formation of Petroleum

Petroleum was formed by the decomposition of the remains of plants and animals buried under the sea millions of years ago.

The plants and animals which lived in the sea, died and their bodies settled at the bottom of the sea. The dead remains got covered with mud, sand and clay. Due to high temperature, high pressure and the absence of air, these were slowly converted into petroleum and natural gas as shown in figure.

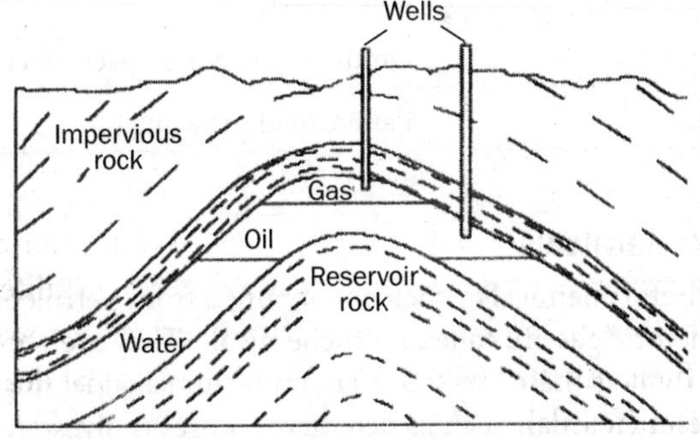

Petroleum and natural gas deposits

The layer containing petroleum oil and gas is found above than water. It is because oil and gas are lighter than water and do not mix with it.

Petroleum is extracted by drilling holes (oil wells) in the Earth's crust. In the drilling process, natural gas comes out first with a great pressure and for a time, the crude petroleum oil comes out by itself due to gas pressure.

> The world's first oil well was drilled in Pennsylvania, USA in 1859. In 1867, oil was struck at Makum in Assam. In India, oil is found in Assam, Gujarat, Mumbai (off shore area) and in the river basins of Godavari and Krishna rivers.

Refining of Petroleum

Petroleum is a mixture of petroleum gas, petrol, diesel, lubricating oil, paraffin wax, etc.

Before the use of petroleum for specific purposes, it has to be refined (or purified). The process of separating the various useful constituents (fractions) of petroleum is known as refining. It is carried out in a **petroleum refinery**.

Various Constituents of Petroleum and their Uses

The various constituents of petroleum and their uses are given below in the table.

Constituents of petroleum	Uses
Petroleum gas in liquid form (LPG)	Fuel for home and industry
Petrol	Motor fuel, aviation fuel, solvent for dry cleaning
Kerosene	Fuel for stoves, lamps and for jet aircrafts
Diesel	Fuel for heavy motor vehicles, electric generators
Lubricating oil	Lubrication
Paraffin wax	Ointments, candles, vaseline, etc.
Bitumen	Paints, road surfacing

Petrochemicals

The useful chemicals which are obtained from petroleum and natural gas are called petrochemicals. They are very important as these are used to manufacture a wide range of useful materials such as detergents, fibres (polyester, nylon, acrylic, etc), plastics (polythene, etc).

Hydrogen gas obtained from natural gas is used in the production of fertilisers such as urea. Thus, due to its great commercial importance, petroleum is also called '**black gold**'.

Try These 3.2

1. **Why does petrol burn faster than coal?**
2. **Name some products of petroleum obtained by petroleum refinery.**
3. **Write the two products of petroleum which are not used as fuels.**

3.4 Natural Gas

It mainly consists of methane (95%). Other constituents are ethane and propane. It occurs deep under the Earth's crust either alone or along with oil above the petroleum.

In India, natural gas has been found in Tripura, Rajasthan, Maharashtra and in the Krishna Godavari delta.

It is a very important fossil fuel as it is easy to transport through pipes. When it is compressed by applying pressure, it is called **Compressed Natural Gas** (CNG).

This gas is used for power generation. It is now being used as a fuel for transport vehicles as it is a clean fuel.

Natural gas is used as a starting material to manufacture of a number of chemicals (petrochemicals) and fertilisers.

3.5 Conservation of Natural Resources

Coal, petroleum and natural gas are fossil fuels and will last only a few hundred years. Fossil fuels, forests and minerals, etc. are exhaustible natural resources. If consumed at a rate faster than the rate at which these are formed in nature, they will get exhausted very soon. Once the present stock of these gets exhausted, no new supplies of these fossil fuels will be available to us in the near future. This is because it requires millions of year to get converted the dead organisms into these fuels.

Moreover, the burning of these fuels is a major cause of air pollution. Their use is also linked to global warming.

So, we should use these fuels only when absolutely necessary as

(i) It will reduce air pollution and thus lead to better environment.

(ii) It will reduce the risk of global warming.

(iii) It will ensure their availability for a longer period of time.

How to Save Petrol/Diesel while Driving?

Petrol and diesel are the main fuels used for driving vehicles. So, we should make every effort to save these precious fuels.

In India, the **Petroleum Conservation Research Association** (PCRA) advises people how to save petrol/diesel while driving the vehicles.

The various tips to avoid wastage of these fuels while driving are as follows:

(i) Drive at a constant and moderate speed as far as possible.

(ii) Switch off the engine of vehicle at traffic lights or at a place where you have to wait.

(iii) Ensure correct tyre pressure of the vehicle. Low tyre pressure consumes more fuel.

(iv) Ensure regular maintenance of the vehicle.

Try These 3.3

1. When natural gas is compressed by applying pressure, what is it called?

2. Coal, petroleum and natural gas cannot be prepared in the laboratory. Why?

3. Write the name of main fuels which are used for driving vehicles.

Science Glossary

Coal A fossil fuel obtained from deep under the Earth's crust.

Coal gas It is obtained during the processing of coal to get coke. It can be used as fuel.

Coke A tough, porous and black substance, almost pure form of carbon.

Coal tar A black thick liquid obtained by processing of coal.

Fossil fuel Fuels obtained from the decomposition of dead remains of plants and animals are known as fossil fuel, e.g. petrol, coal, etc.

Natural gas It is a fossil fuel which mainly contains methane gas and can be transported through pipes.

Petroleum It is a dark coloured crude oil having an unpleasant odour.

Petroleum refining Petroleum is seperated into different fractions by this process.

Petrochemicals They are useful chemicals which are obtained from petroleum and natural gas.

Mind Map

Natural Resources (Resources which are obtained from nature)

Types

Exhaustible Natural Resources

Which can be exhaust by human and are present in limited quantity, e.g. water coal, petroleum, etc.

Inexhaustible Natural Resources

Which cannot be exhaust by human and are present in unlimited quantity, e.g. air, sunlight, etc.

Coal

It is a hard, black combustible fuel. Coal is found in the deep coal mines under the surface of Earth. It burns in the presence of air and produces CO_2 gas and heat.

Uses of Coal

- Used to cook food.
- Used in thermal power plants to produce electricity.
- Used as a fuel in various industries.
- Used for the manufacture of coke, coal tar and coal gas.

Petroleum

It is a dark coloured, thick crude (raw) oil having an unpleasant odour.

Constituents

- **Petroleum**-Gas in liquid form (LPG)-Fuel for home and industry.
- **Petrol**–Used as motor fuel, aviation fuel, etc.
- **Kerosene**–Fuel for stoves, lamps, etc.
- **Diesel**-Fuel for heavy motor vehicles, etc.
- **Lubricating oil**-Used for lubricaiton.
- **Paraffin wax**- Ointments, candles, vaseline, etc.
- **Bitumen**-Used as paints, road surfacing.

Natural gas

- It mainly consists of methane (95%).
- It occurs deep under the Earth's crust either alone or along with oil above the petroleum.
- When it is compressed by applying pressure, it is called Compressed Natural Gas (CNG).
- This gas is used for power generation and as a fuel for transport vehicles.

Products of Coal

Coke

- Tough, porous and black substance.
- Almost pure form of carbon.
- Used in the manufacture of steel and as a fuel.

Coal Tar

- Black, thick liquid with unpleasant smell.
- Used as starting material for manufacturing of various substances.

Coal Gas

- Obtained during the heating of coal in the absence of oxygen.
- It is mainly a mixture of methane and hydrogen with some carbon monoxide.
- Used as a fuel in many industries situated near the coal processing plants.

NCERT FOLDER

Complete Explanations of all NCERT's Questions

Intext Questions

Q.1 Can we use our natural resources forever? Page 32

Ans. No, we cannot use our natural resources forever. Some resources are present in limited quantities which take millions of years to form and will exhaust one day, e.g. minerals, fossil fuel, etc.

Q.2 Where do we get coal from and how is it formed?

Ans. We get coal by the slow process of conversion of dead plants and animals buried deep under the Earth's surface.The process is known as carbonisation. Page 33

Q.3 Can coal, petroleum and natural gas be prepared in the laboratory from dead organisms? Page 37

Ans. No, their formation is a very slow process and the conditions of formation cannot be created in the laboratory.

Exercise

Q.1 What are the advantages of using CNG and LPG as fuels?

Ans. The advantages of using CNG and LPG as fuels are as follows

(i) CNG and LPG are clean fuels.
(ii) They do not produce pollution.
(iii) They are easily available.
(iv) They can be used directly for burning.

Q.2 Name the petroleum product used for surfacing of roads.

Ans. Bitumen.

Q.3 Describe how coal is formed from dead vegetation. What is this process called?

Ans. Refer to text on page no. 2.

Q.4 Fill in the blanks.

(a) Fossil fuels are ......, ... and ....
(b) Process of separation of different constituents from petroleum is called ....
(c) Least polluting fuel for vehicle is ....

Ans. (a) coal, petroleum, natural gas (b) refining
(c) Compressed Natural Gas (CNG)

Q.5 Tick True/False against the following statements.

(a) Fossil fuels can be made in the laboratory.
(b) CNG is more polluting fuel than petrol.
(c) Coke is almost pure form of carbon.
(d) Coal tar is a mixture of various substances.
(e) Kerosene is not a fossil fuel.

Ans. (a) False, Fossil fuels are made by natural process.
(b) False, CNG is a clean fuel and less polluting fuel than petrol.
(c) True (d) True
(e) False, Kerosene is a kind fossil fuel.

Q.6 Explain, why fossil fuels are exhaustible natural resources?

Ans. Refer to text on page no. 3.

Q.7 Describe characteristics and uses of coke.

Ans. Refer to text on page no. 2.

Q.8 Explain the process of formation of petroleum.

Ans. Refer to text on page no. 2.

Q.9 The following table shows the total power shortage in India from 1991-1997. Show the data in the form of a graph. Plot shortage percentage for the years on the *Y*-axis and the year on the *X*-axis.

S.No.	Year	Shortage (%)
1.	1991	7.9
2.	1992	7.8
3.	1993	8.3
4.	1994	7.4
5.	1995	7.1
6.	1996	9.2
7.	1997	11.5

Ans. Scale along X-axis, 1 unit = 1 year and along Y-axis, 1 unit = 1%

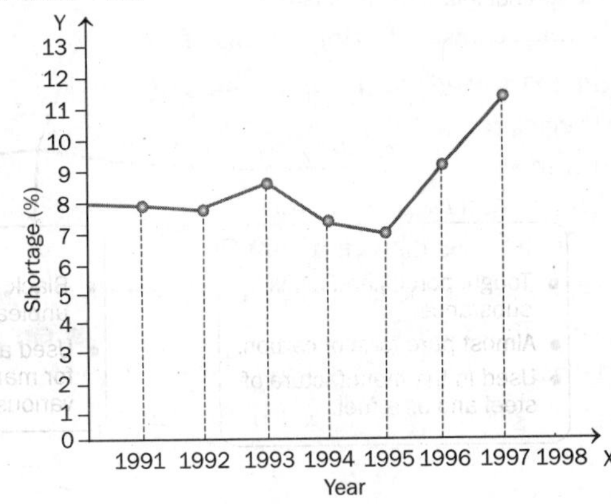

REVIEW EXERCISE

Including Competency Based Questions

Multiple Choice Questions

1. **Various materials which are obtained from nature are called natural resources. Which of the following is not a natural resource?** NCERT Exemplar

(a) Minerals (b) Water
(c) Soil (d) Plastic

2. **The source of energy for the Earth's water cycle is**

(a) seas (b) Sun
(c) Earth's rotation (d) evaporation

3. **Air is a natural resources and cannot be exhausted by human activities. It is known as inexhaustible natural resource. Which of the following is another inexhaustible natural resource?** Competency Based Que.

(a) Coal (b) Petroleum
(c) Sunlight (d) Minerals

4. **Which of the following is a pair of exhaustible natural resources?**

(a) Coal and soil (b) Air and sunlight
(c) Water and petroleum (d) Trees and minerals

5. **Exhaustible natural resources are**

(a) made by human efforts
(b) not dependent on nature
(c) limited in quantity
(d) not exhausted by human activities

6. **Which of the following is exhaustible natural resource?**

(a) Soil (b) Air
(c) Sunlight (d) Coal

7. **Fossil fuels are obtained from**

(a) remains of non-living materials
(b) dead remains of birds only
(c) dead remains of insects only
(d) dead remains of living organisms

8. **Coal is formed from the remains of**

(a) vegetation only
(b) animals only
(c) Both vegetation and animals
(d) Neither vegetation nor animals

9. **Which substance is formed by the carbonisation of dead vegetation?** NCERT Exemplar

(a) Coal (b) Coke
(c) Coal gas (d) Coal tar

10. **When coal burns in air**

(a) nitrogen is formed
(b) sulphur dioxide is formed
(c) oxygen is formed
(d) carbon dioxide is formed

11. **Coal is processed in industries to get some useful products. Which of the following is not obtained from coal?**

(a) Coke (b) Coal tar
(c) Coal gas (d) CNG

12. **Which byproduct is obtained after processing coal?** CBSE Question Bank

(a) Diesel (b) Petrol
(c) Coke (d) Paraffin wax

13. **Purest form of carbon is**

(a) coal (b) charcoal
(c) coke (d) All of these

14. **Naphthalene balls are obtained from coal tar and are used as**

(a) mosquito repellant (b) honey bee repellant
(c) moth repellant (d) snake repellant

15. **A byproduct obtained after processing coal is useful in manufacturing plastics, synthetic dyes, naphthalene balls, etc. The byproducts is ....** CBSE Question Bank

(a) coal gas (b) coal tar
(c) coke (d) paraffin Wax

16. **Petroleum was formed from organisms**

(a) living on the land (b) living on the plants
(c) living in the sea (d) living on the rocks

17. **Which of the following is not a constituent of petroleum?** NCERT Exemplar

(a) Paraffin wax (b) Lubricating oil
(c) Petrol (d) Coke

18. **Which petroleum product is used to run heavy motor vehicles?** CBSE Question Bank

(a) Petrol (b) Diesel (c) Natural gas (d) Bitumen

19. **The slow process by which the plants and trees buried deep under the Earth get converted to coal is caused**

(a) carboration
(b) carbonisation
(c) carbocation
(d) carbonation

20. **Choose the correct statement from the following.**

(a) It is difficult to transport natural gas through pipes
(b) The disadvantage of natural gas is that it cannot be used directly for burning in homes
(c) Natural gas is stored under high pressure as compressed natural gas
(d) Natural gas cannot be used for power generation

Answers

1. (d)	**2.** (b)	**3.** (c)	**4.** (c)	**5.** (c)
6. (d)	**7.** (d)	**8.** (c)	**9.** (a)	**10.** (d)
11. (d)	**12.** (c)	**13.** (c)	**14.** (c)	**15.** (d)
16. (a)	**17.** (d)	**18.** (b)	**19.** (b)	**20.** (c)

Fill in the Blanks

1. **Forests and coal are ...... natural resources.** NCERT Exemplar
2. **Coal is one of the ...... used to cook food.**
3. **Sunlight is an .... natural resource.**
4. **Petroleum, ... and ...... are fossil fuels.**
5. **The slow process of conversion of dead vegetation into coal is called ....**

Answers

1. exhaustible
2. fuels
3. inexhaustible
4. coal, natural gas
5. carbonisation

True/False

1. **Resources which are present in unlimited quantity in nature are called exhaustible natural resources.**
2. **Oxygen in air is an exhaustible natural resource.**
3. **Wildlife is an exhaustible natural resource.**
4. **CNG is less polluting fuel than petrol and diesel.** NCERT Exemplar
5. **Under high temperature and pressure, dead plants get slowly converted to coal.**

Answers

1. False, Resources which are present in unlimited quantity in nature are called on inexhaustible natural resources.
2. False, Oxygen in air is an inexhaustible natural resources because it is continuously recycled in the atmosphere.
3. True
4. True
5. True

Match the Columns

1. Match the Column I with Column II. NCERT Exemplar

Column I		Column II	
A.	Used for road surfacing	1.	Black gold
B.	Natural gas	2.	Vaseline and candles
C.	Petroleum	3.	Bitumen
D.	Paraffin wax	4.	CNG

2. Match the Column I with Column II.

Column I		Column II	
A.	Coke	1.	Fuel for home
B.	Good fuels	2.	Produce more energy
C.	LPG	3.	Fractions of petroleum
D.	Petrol and diesel	4.	Purest form of carbon

Answers

1. A–3, B–4, C–1, D–2
2. A–4, B–2, C–1, D–3

Assertion-Reason Questions

The following questions consist of two statements Assertion (A) and Reason (R). Answer these questions selecting the appropriate option given below.

(a) Both A and R are true and R is the correct explanation of A
(b) Both A and R are true, but R is not the correct explanation of A
(c) A is true, but R is false
(d) A is false, but R is true.

1. **Assertion** (A) Sunlight is an inexhaustible natural resource.
   Reason (R) Sun will continue to radiate energy.
2. **Assertion** (A) Kerosene is used in jet aircrafts.
   Reason (R) Kerosene is not a fossil fuel.
3. **Assertion** (A) Coke is a pure form of carbon.
   Reason (R) It is used in the manufacture of steel.
4. **Assertion** (A) CNG stands for compressed natural gas.
   Reason (R) CNG is stored under high pressure.
5. **Assertion** (A) Exhaustible resource are limited in nature.
   Reason (R) Fossil fuel are example of exhaustible resources.

Answers

1. (a) Both A and R are true and R is the correct explanation of A.
2. (c) A is true, but R is false. R can be corrected as Petrol, diesel and kerosene are obtained from petroleum refining, hence, kerosene is also a fossil fuel.
3. (b) Both A and R are true, but R is not the correct explanation of A.
4. (a) Both A and R are true and R is the correct explanation of A.
5. (a) Both A and R are true and R is the correct explanation of A.

Case Based Questions

1. Ravi prefers to go to school by pooling car. On other occasions he like to opt for public transport rather than private transport. For short distances, he walks or uses bicycle.

(i) Which means of transport do you think is best for short distances?

(a) Small vehicles (b) Bicycles
(c) Large vehicles (d) Motor bike

(ii) Which department advices people to save petrol/diesel while driving?

(a) UNESCO (b) Traffic department
(c) PCRA (d) NHAI

2. The picture shows how petroleum and natural gas are extracted through oil wells Competency Based Que.

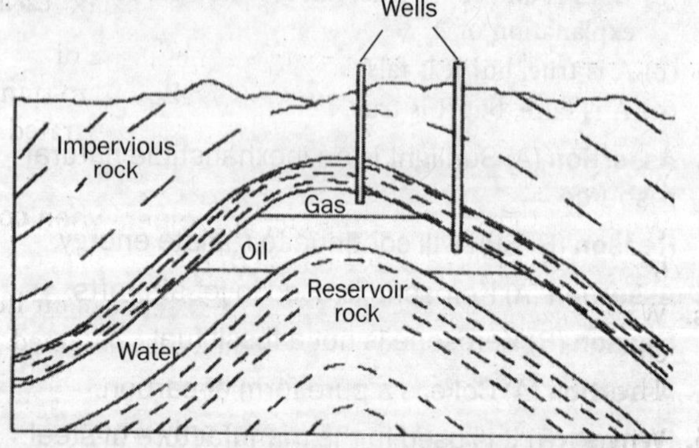

(i) Which of the following statements are supported by the picture?
Circle 'Yes' or 'No' for the correct response.

	Is this statement supported by the picture?	Yes or No
(a)	Petroleum is insoluble in water.	Yes/No
(b)	Natural gas is denser than petroleum.	Yes/No
(c)	Petroleum and natural gas deposits are found under rock layers.	Yes/No

(ii) Which of these conditions is required for the formation of natural gas?

(a) Low pressure
(b) Presence of air
(c) High temperature
(d) Presence of water

(iii) Which of these petroleum products is used for heavy motor vehicles?

(a) LPG (b) Diesel (c) Petrol (d) Kerosene

(iv) What is the advantage of using CNG instead of petrol in light motor vehicles?

(a) It can be stored easily
(b) It can be extracted easily
(c) It causes less air pollution
(d) It releases more energy on combustion

Answers

1. (i) (b) Bicycle, As it is ecofriendly and cost effective mode of transport which can be used for short distance.
   (ii) (c) PCRA (Petroleum Conservation Research Association) advices people to save petrol/diesel while driving.
2. (i) (a) Yes
   (b) No, gases are lighter than liquid (petroleum)
   (c) Yes.
   (ii) (c) High temperature
   (iii) (b) Diesel
   (iv) (c) It causes less air pollution.

Part II

Very Short Answer Type Questions

1. Give two natural resources. Why these are called natural resources?

Ans. Air and water are the natural resources because they are obtained from nature.

2. We will use all our natural resources forever. Can it be possible?

Ans. No, we cannot use all our natural resources forever. Some natural resources are going to exhaust.

3. Can air, water and soil be exhausted by human activities?

Ans. No, these will not be exhausted by human activities.

4. Coal, petroleum and natural gas are called fossil fuels. Why?

Ans. Coal, petroleum and natural gas are called fossil fuels because they are formed by the decomposition of the remains of pre-historic plants and animals (fossils) buried under the Earth long ago.

5. What do you mean by carbonisation?

Ans. The slow process of conversion of dead vegetation into coal is called carbonisation.

6. Name two fuels obtained from petroleum, which can be used as domestic fuels.

Ans. Petrol, liquefied petroleum gas (LPG) as obtained from petroleum and can be used as domestic fuels.

7. Where coal is found in India?

Ans. In India, coal is found mainly in Jharkhand, West Bengal, Odisha and Madhya Pradesh.

8. How can you define coke?

Ans. Coke is tough, porous and black substance and almost pure form of carbon.

9. Which product of coal is used in the extraction of metals ?

Ans. Coke

10. Write two important uses of coke. NCERT Exemplar

Ans. Coke is used for extraction of many metals and also for the manufacturing of steel.

11. Name the petroleum product used as fuel for stoves, lamps and jet aircrafts. NCERT Exemplar

Ans. Kerosene is used as fuel for stoves, lamps and jet aircrafts.

12. Name the process of separating the various useful constituents of petroleum.

Ans. Petroleum refining.

13. How CNG is a good fuel than petrol and diesel in vehicles?

Ans. CNG is a good alternative to petrol and diesel in vehicles because it is a clean fuel and cause less air pollution.

14. Which gas is used as a starting material for the manufacture of a number of chemicals and fertilisers and why?

Ans. Natural gas is used as a starting material for the manufacture of a number of chemicals (petrochemicals) and fertilisers as it is a source of hydrogen gas needed to manufacture the fertilisers.

Short Answer Type Questions

1. Some natural resources are given below. Classify them into the exhaustible and inexhaustible natural resources.

Air, coal, natural gas, sunlight, petroleum, minerals, forests, oxygen NCERT Exemplar

Ans. Exhaustible natural resources are coal, natural gas, petroleum, minerals, forests. Inexhaustible natural resources are air, sunlight, oxygen.

2. Sunlight and air are inexhaustible natural resources. Comment.

Ans. These resources are present in an unlimited quantity in nature and are not likely to be exhausted by human activities.

3. You are provided with a mixture of petroleum and water. Can you suggest a method to separate the two? NCERT Exemplar

Ans. Decantation can be used to separate a mixture of petroleum and water. The mixture is allowed to stand. Carefully, lighter layer can be poured and separated without disturbing the heavier one.

4. Write the name of the products obtained when coal is heated strongly in the absence of air.

Ans. When coal is heated strongly in the absence of air in closed retorts, various useful products are obtained. These are coke, coal tar and coal gas.

5. Why should we use petrol/diesel only when absolutely necessary?

Ans. We should use these fuels only when absolutely necessary because

(i) it will reduce air pollution and thus lead to better environment.

(ii) it will reduce the risk of global warming.

(iii) it will ensure their availability for a longer period of time.

6. Where do we get coal from and how is it formed?

Ans. About 300 million years ago, the Earth had dense forests in low lying wetland areas. Due to natural processes like flooding, these forests got buried under the soil and deposited as fossil. Due to high temperature and pressure, dead plants got slowly converted into coal.

7. Write the difference between coke and coal.

Ans. Differences between coke and coal are as follows:

Coke	Coal
It is almost pure form of carbon.	It contains mainly carbon.
It is an amorphous form of carbon.	It is a non-crystalline form of carbon.
It is obtained by heating coal in the absence of air.	It is obtained by the decay of vegetation which existed millions of year ago.

8. Write the characteristics and some important uses of coal.

Ans. Characteristics of coal are as follows

(i) Coal is a hard, black combustible fuel.

(ii) It is a fossil fuel.

(iii) It mainly contains carbon.

(iv) When heated in air, coal burns and produces mainly carbon dioxide gas.

(v) It is a source of energy.

For important uses of coal Refer to text on page no. 42.

9. Write the various fractions of petroleum.

Ans. The various fractions of petroleum are

(i) Petroleum gas in liquid form (LPG)

(ii) Petrol (iii) Kerosene

(iv) Diesel (v) Lubricating oil

(vi) Paraffin wax (vii) Bitumen

10. Look at the figure where petroleum and natural gas deposits are shown. Why do we find oil layer above water layer? NCERT Exemplar

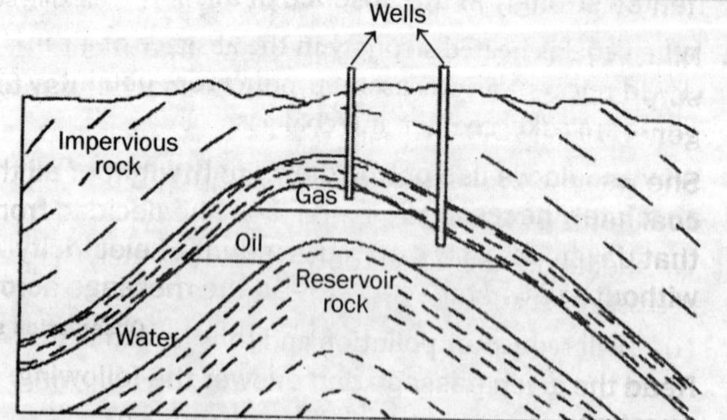

Ans. Oil and water do not mix with each other and they form two layers when mixed. OH is lighter than water therefore it floats over water and is shown above the water layer.

Long Answer Type Questions

1. Why petrol is exhaustible natural resource whereas sunlight is not? Explain. NCERT Exemplar

Ans. The natural resources which are present in a limited quantity in nature and can be exhausted (used up) by human activities are called exhaustible natural resources, e.g. coal, petroleum, natural gas, minerals, forests, wildlife, etc.

It requires millions of years for the conversion of the dead organisms into petroleum, from which petrol is separated.

So, once the present stock of it gets exhausted, no new supplies of it will be available to us in the near future, whereas sunlight is present in an unlimited quantity in nature, so it is inexhaustible natural resource. It is not likely to be exhausted by human activities.

2. Name the products obtained and their uses when coal is processed in industry.

Ans. Refer to text on page no. 43.

3. While driving what are the tips we must follow to save petrol/diesel/natural gas? NCERT Exemplar

Ans. Refer to text on page no. 45.

Case Based Questions

1. The table shows two groups of natural resources.

Group 1	Group 2
Air, Sunlight, Water	Coal, Petroleum, Natural gas

(i) How is group 1 different from group 2? Competency Based Que.

(ii) Which resource in group 2 will cause the least amount of air pollution on burning?

2. The table shows two groups of natural resources. Competency Based Que.

Swamp
300 million years ago

Before the dinosaurs, many giant plants died in swamps

Water
100 million years ago

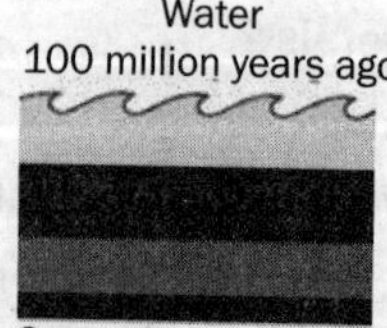

Over millions of years the plants were buried underwater and dirt

Heat and pressure turned the dead plants into coal

(i) Which of these statements is true about coal?

Circle 'Yes' or 'No' for the correct response.

	Is this true about coal?	Yes or No
(a)	Dirt makes up a large part of coal.	Yes/No
(b)	Coal is produced from plant fossils.	Yes/No
(c)	Formation of coal requires heat and pressure.	Yes/No

(ii) Where is a coal reserve most likely to be found?

(a) Inside volcanoes (b) Beneath glaciers

(c) On ocean floors (d) Under land surfaces

(iii) Which gas is mainly emitted during the combustion of coal?

(vi) Coke is a product obtained by the processing of coal.

Which of these is a byproduct of making coke?

(a) Coal tar (b) Bitumen

(c) Coal gas (d) Kerosene

3. The material *X* is a fossil fuel. It is formed from the buried large land plants (vegetation) by a very slow process *Y*. When *X* is heated in the absence of air, it gives three products *A*, *B* and *C*.

A is used in steel making *B* is used as an industrial fuel, whereas the product *C* has been traditionally used for metalling the roads. It is now replaced by a petroleum product, bitumen.

Now give the answer of the following questions.

(i) What is the material *X*?

(ii) What is the physical state and colour of *X*?

(iii) Name the processes *Y*.

(iv) What are the products *A*, *B* and *C*?

Ans. 1. (i)

Group 1	Group 2
Present in unlimited quantity	Present in limited quantity
Will not exhaust even if used continuously	Will exhaust if used continuously
Take thousands of years to form	Take millions of years to form
Contain high percentages of carbon	Contain low percentages of carbon

(ii) Natural gas will contribute to least amount of air pollution on burning among resources in group 2.

2. (i) (a) No

(b) Yes, coal is formed from plant remains buried deep under the Earth.

(c) Yes, formation of coal requires high temperature and high pressure.

(ii) (d) Under land surfaces.

(iii) Carbon dioxide

(iv) (c) Coal gas.

3. (i) Coal.

(ii) It is solid and black coloured.

(iii) *Y* is carbonisation.

(iv) *A* is coke, *B* is coal gas while *C* is coal tar.

Skill Based Questions as per NEP 2020

1. Find out the location of major thermal power plants in India. What could be the reasons for their being located at those places? **Thinking skill**

2. Mohan uses a diesel car which causes lot of pollution. But his friend Sohan has purchased an electric car which does not use fossil fuel and does not cause air pollution. Sohan told his friend that major pollution of air is caused by industries and combustion of fossil fuels by vehicles. Sulphur dioxide and nitrogen dioxide are released into air by burning coal and petroleum. Air is precious for our life, but air pollution causes many diseases like asthma, bronchitis and heart related disease.

Read the given passage and answer the following questions.

(i) What are the disadvantages of diesel car other than air pollution?

(ii) What are the effects of increase in carbon dioxide in the atmosphere?

(iii) What values are possessed by Sohan? **Thinking skill**

3. Nikita visited a thermal power plant. She was surprised to see the use of tonnes of coal per day to generate electricity.

She was highly disturbed when she thought of all the coal getting exhausted in one day. She decided from that day to use only required amount of electricity without any wastage and spread the message across. **Observation skill**

Read the given passage and answer the following questions.

(i) What role does coal play in a thermal power plant?

(ii) What values are possessed by Nikita?

ASSESSMENT EXERCISE

Part I

Multiple Choice Questions

1. Coal is a .... fuel.
(a) clean (b) flammable
(c) combustible (d) non- combustible

2. The resources which are obtained from nature are called....................... .
(a) natural resources
(b) man-made resources
(c) renewable resources
(d) inexhaustible resources

3. Dead remains of living organisms which got burried under the soil, thousands of years ago are called............... .
(a) petroleum (b) natural gas
(c) fossils (d) coke

4. When coal is heated in air, it produces ....
(a) carbon monoxide (b) carbon dioxide
(c) nitrogen gas (d) oxygen gas

5. Naphthalene balls are used to repel moths and other insects. It is made up of
(a) coal gas (b) coal tar
(c) petroleum (d) natural gas

Fill in the Blanks

6. In India .... advises people to save petrol diesel while driving the vehicles.

7. The main constituent of natural gas is ....

True/False

8. Bitumen is used for lubrication in vehicles.

9. Coal tar has been used for metalling the roads.

Match the Columns

10. Match the Column I with Column II.

Column I	Column II
A. Coal gas	1. Naphthalene balls
B. Coal tar	2. Used for lightning processes
C. Coke	3. Manufacture of steel
D. Coal	4. Fossil fuel

Assertion- Reason Questions

The following questions consist of two statements **Assertion** (A) and **Reason** (R). Answer these questions by selecting the appropriate option given below.
(a) Both A and R are true and R is the correct explanation of A.
(b) Both A and R are true but R is not the correct explanation of A.
(c) A is true, but R is false.
(d) A is false, but R is true.

11. Assertion (A) We get different constituents such as petrol, kerosene, diesel, etc. from petroleum.
Reason (R) The process of separating the various useful constituents (fractions) of petroleum is known as refining.

12. Assertion (A) Coal should not be burned in a closed room.
Reason (R) Coal releases carbon dioxide.

13. Assertion (A) Natural gas is a very important fossil fuel.
Reason (R) It produces oxygen while burns.

Part II

Very Short Answer Type Questions

14. Name the petroleum product commonly used for electric generators.

15. Write the purest form of carbon.

16. Is it possible to extract petroleum from under the sea?

17. How coke is obtained from coal?

18. How we can save petrol/diesel while driving? Explain the statement.

Short Answer Type Questions

19. Write the advantages of using LPG as fuel.

20. Why should we use fossil fuels only when absolutely necessary?

21. CNG is a non-polluting fuel commonly used now-a-days. Explain in brief.

22. Write about the extraction of coal.

Long Answer Type Question

23. What do you understand by exhaustible and inexhaustible natural resources? Explain two examples of each in detail.

Answers

1. (c) **2.** (a) **3.** (c) **4.** (b) **5.** (b)
6. PCRA (Petroleum Conservation Research Association)
7. methane **8.** False **9.** True
10. The correct match is A–2, B–1, C–3, D–4
11. (a) **12.** (a) **13.** (c)

CHAPTER 04

Combustion and Flame

We use different kinds of fuels for various purposes at home, in industry and for running automobiles. These can be cowdung, wood, coal, charcoal, petrol, diesel, Compressed Natural Gas (CNG), Liquefied Petroleum Gas (LPG), etc. Some materials burn with flame (e.g. candle) whereas some burn without flame (e.g. coal). Let us know the chemical process of burning and the types of flame produced during this process.

4.1 Combustion

A chemical process in which a substance reacts with oxygen to give off heat is called **combustion**. The substance that undergoes combustion is said to be **combustible substance**. It is also called a **fuel** which can be solid, liquid or gas. Sometimes, light is also given off during combustion either as a flame or as a glow. For example, wood burns by producing a flame, but charcoal burns by producing light in the form of glow.

Fuel For Our Body

Food is a fuel for our body. During respiration, the digested food (glucose) is broken down by reaction with oxygen producing carbon dioxide, water and heat. This heat energy is utilised by our body. Thus, respiration is a type of slow combustion of food.

Combustible and Non-Combustible Substances

All substances around us do not burn. Based on this, substances are divided into two types

(i) **Combustible Substances** The substances which burn in the presence of air or oxygen are called combustible substances, e.g. petrol, LPG, kerosene, etc.

(ii) **Non-combustible Substances** The substances which do not burn in the presence of air or oxygen are called non-combustible substances, e.g. water, glass, sand, etc.

Necessary Conditions for Combustion

There are three necessary conditions for combustion. These are as follows

1. Presence of a Combustible Substance

Presence of substance like petrol, LPG, wood, coal, etc. is necessary for combustion process.

2. Presence of a Supporter of Combustion

A substance which helps in combustion is called a supporter of combustion, e.g. oxygen (or air).

For example, when the clothes of a person catch fire, the person is covered with a blanket to extinguish the fire. The blanket cuts off the supply of air which is needed for the burning of clothes. This shows that air is necessary for combustion.

3. Ignition Temperature

The lowest temperature at which a substance catches fire and starts burning is called its **ignition temperature**. Before a substance catches fire and starts burn, it must be heated to a certain minimum temperature by supplying heat. A combustible substance cannot catch fire if its temperature is lower than its ignition temperature.

For example, a matchstick does not catch fire on its own at room temperature. When matchstick rubbed on the rough side of matchbox the heat produced increases its temperature to ignition temperature and its start burning.

History of Matchstick

More than five thousand years ago, small pieces of pinewood dipped in sulphur were used as matches in ancient Egypt. A mixture of antimony tri-sulphide, potassium chlorate and white phosphorus with some glue and starch was applied on the head of a match made of suitable wood. These days the head of the safety match contains only antimony tri-sulphide and potassium chlorate. When the match is struck against the rubbing surface, some red phosphorus gets converted into white phosphorus. This immediately reacts with potassium chlorate in the matchstick head to produce enough heat to ignite antimony trisulphide and start the combustion.

Inflammable Substances

The substances which have very low ignition temperature and can catch fire easily with a flame are called **inflammable substances**, e.g. petrol, alcohol, Liquefied Petroleum Gas (LPG), etc.

Try These 4.1

1. **Is light always given off as flame in combustion process?**
2. **Is it possible to burn a paper in a room where only CO_2 and nitrogen gases are present?**
3. **A heap of dry grass burns easily while a wet one does not. Why?**
4. **Why inflammable substance like petrol, kerosene is used to burn substance having high ignition temperature?**

4.2 How Fire can be Controlled?

We have learnt that there are three essential requirements for producing fire. These are fuel (combustible substance), supporter of combustion (i.e. air or oxygen) and heat (to raise the temperature of the fuel beyond the ignition temperature).

Fire can be controlled by any three ways given below

(i) By removing the fuel, but in most cases, fuel cannot be eliminated.

(ii) By removing the heat to bring down the temperature.

(iii) By cutting off the air supply to the burning substances.

Fire Extinguishers

Substances which are used to cut off the supply of oxygen to the fire are known as **fire extinguishers**, e.g. water and carbon dioxide, etc.

(i) The most common fire extinguisher is water, but works only when things like wood and paper are on fire. It extinguishes fire by cooling the burning substances. However, water cannot be used for extinguishing fire in electrical equipments. Water conducts electricity hence, can cause electrical shock if electrical equipment is on fire. Water is also not suitable for fires involving oil and petrol because it sinks below the oil and oil keeps burning on the top.

(ii) For fires involving electrical equipment and inflammable substances like petrol, carbon dioxide (CO_2) is the best extinguisher. CO_2 is denser than air and thus forms a layer around the burning substances, i.e. it covers the fire like a blanket due to which oxygen cannot reach the burning substances and fire is controlled. Carbon dioxide can be stored as a liquid at high pressure in cylinders (as shown in figure below). It expands enormously in volume when released from the cylinder and cools down.

Carbon dioxide fire extinguisher

(iii) Another way to obtain CO_2 is to release large amount of powdered baking soda (sodium bicarbonate) or potassium bicarbonate over the fire. Heat of the fire releases CO_2 gas from baking soda which cut off the fire.

SCIENCE INSIGHT When a LPG cylinder catchs fire, it is wrapped with a wet cloth. It lowers the temperature of fire and cuts off its contact with oxygen.

4.3 Types of Combustion

There are various types of combustion. Three important types of combustion are as follows

1. Rapid Combustion

The combustion in which a large amount of heat and light are produced in a short time, is called **rapid combustion**, e.g. immediate burning of cooking gas (LPG) in a gas stove when a burning matchstick lighter is brought near it, burning of kerosene oil in a kerosene stove, etc.

2. Spontaneous Combustion

The combustion in which a material suddenly bursts into flames without any external heat is called **spontaneous combustion.**

The heat required to start the spontaneous combustion is produced internally by the chemical reaction of substance with oxygen, e.g. white phosphorus burns in air at room temperature on its own.

Some spontaneous combustion can be very dangerous.

For example,

(i) The spontaneous combustion of coal dust has resulted in many disastrous fires in coal mines.

(ii) Sometimes, due to the heat of the Sun or due to the spark of lightning from the sky, spontaneous combustion of straw (dry grass) and forest wood takes place which leads to forest fire.

3. Explosions

A sudden combustion in which a large amount of heat, light and sound are produced is called **explosion**. A large amount of gases formed is released quickly in an explosion, e.g. when a cracker is ignited, a sudden explosion takes place with the evolution of heat, light and sound.

Explosion can also take place if pressure is applied on the cracker.

Try These 4.2

1. How can water extinguish a fire when thrown over it?
2. How can a fire from cooking oil be extinguished?
3. Sodium burns at room temperature by reacting with air. What type of combustion is this?
4. What is the process of burning of a cracker called?

4.4 Flame

A flame is a region where combustion of gaseous substance or vapour takes place.

The substances which vaporise during burning, give flames, e.g. kerosene oil and molten wax rise through the wick and are vaporised during burning and form flames. While charcoal does not vaporise and so does not produce a flame and it just glows.

Given below is the list of some materials which either form or does not form flame on burning.

Materials forming flame on burning

Material	Forms flame	Does not form flame
Candle	✓	✗
Magnesium	✓	✗
Camphor	✓	✗
Kerosene stove	✓	✗
Charcoal	✗	✓

Types of Flame

On the basis of availability of oxygen, flame can be of following types

(i) When the supply of oxygen is not sufficient, the fuels burn incompletely producing mainly a **yellow flame,** e.g. the colour of candle flame is yellow.

(ii) When the supply of oxygen is sufficient, the fuels burn completely producing mainly a **blue flame,** e.g. in LPG stoves, the LPG burns with a blue flame.

Structure of a Flame

A flame consists of three zones

(i) **Innermost Zone** It is a **dark** or **black coloured zone,** which consists of hot, unburnt vapours of combustible material. It is the least hot part of the flame.

(ii) **Middle Zone** It is the **bright** and **luminous zone.** which produces a moderate temperature. Here, partial combustion of the fuel takes place.

(iii) **Outermost Zone** It is **non-luminous zone.** Here, complete combustion of the fuel takes place because there is plenty of air around it. It has the highest temperature in the flame, i.e. is the hottest part of the flame. This is the reason why goldsmiths blow the outermost zone of a flame with a metallic blow-pipe for melting gold and silver to form the desired shapes for making jewellery.

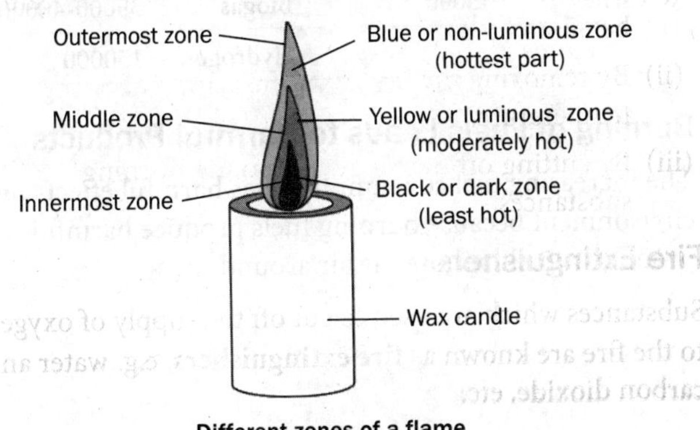

Different zones of a flame

4.5 Fuel

A substance which produces heat on burning is called a **fuel**, e.g. wood, charcoal, petrol, kerosene, LPG, natural gas, etc. These are the sources of heat energy. These fuels can be in solid, liquid or gaseous state.

A good fuel is one which has the following characteristics

(i) Readily available
(ii) Cheap
(iii) Burns easily in air at a moderate rate.
(iv) Produces a large amount of heat.
(v) Does not leave behind any undesirable substances.
(vi) Low ignition temperature.

Ideal Fuel

An ideal fuel is one, which is readily available, cheap and having high calorific value and produces less amount of pollution. There is probably no fuel that could be considered as an ideal fuel.

4.6 Fuel Efficiency

Different fuels produce different amounts of heat on burning. The amount of heat energy produced on complete combustion of 1 kg of a fuel is called its **calorific value**. The calorific value of a fuel is expressed in a unit called **kilojoule per kg** (kJ/kg).

Calorific values of some fuels are given below

Calorific values of different fuels

Fuel	Calorific value (kJ/kg)	Fuel	Calorific value (kJ/kg)
Cowdung cake	6000-8000	Diesel	45000
Wood	17000-22000	Methane	50000
Coal	25000-33000	CNG	50000
Petrol	45000	LPG	55000
Kerosene	45000	Biogas	35000-40000
		Hydrogen	150000

Burning of Fuels Leads to Harmful Products

The increasing fuel consumption has harmful effects on the environment because burning fuels produce harmful products which pollute the air around us.

These are as follows

(i) Burning of carbon fuels like wood, coal and petroleum release unburnt carbon particles in air which are dangerous pollutants causing respiratory diseases such as **asthma**.

(ii) Also using of wood as a fuel leads to deforestation which is quite harmful for living being.

(iii) Incomplete combustion of carbon fuels gives **carbon monoxide gas** which is very poisonous gas. Excessive inhaling of this gas can kill a person.

It is dangerous to burn coal in a closed room. The carbon monoxide gas produced can kill a person sleeping in that room. So, we should never sleep in a room with burning or smouldering coal fire in it.

(iv) Burning of most fuels releases carbon dioxide into air. Increased concentration of carbon dioxide in the air is believed to be the cause of rise in temperature of the atmosphere of the Earth.

This is called **global warming**. Due to this, the ice in polar regions will melt very fast, producing a lot of water. It may cause a rise in the sea level leading to floods in coastal areas.

(v) Burning of coal and diesel releases **sulphur dioxide gas.** It is an extremely suffocating and corrosive gas. It may damage our lungs. Moreover, petrol and diesel engines give off gaseous oxides of nitrogen.

These oxides dissolve in rain water and form acids. Such rain is called **acid rain.** It is very harmful for crops, buildings and soil.

Compressed Natural Gas (CNG)

The use of diesel and petrol as fuels in automobiles is being replaced by CNG (Compressed Natural Gas) because it produces the harmful products in very small amounts. CNG is a cleaner fuel.

Try These 4.3

1. Between the yellow and blue flames of a candle, which one should be used for burning a material?
2. In which zone of a flame can unburnt vapour be present?
3. Among LPG, rubber and wood, which will be a nearly ideal fuel?
4. Which oxides cause acid rain?

Science Glossary

Acid rain When oxides of sulphur and nitrogen react with water molecules in the atmosphere, it forms an acid. This acid mixes with rainwater and causes acid rain.

Calorific value It is the amount of heat energy produced on complete combustion of 1 kg of fuel.

Combustion It is a process in which a substance reacts with oxygen and gives off some heat or light.

Deforestation Cutting of trees leads to deforestation which is quite harmful to the environment.

Explosion When a cracker is ignited a sudden reaction takes place. A large amount of gases is evolved in the process along with heat, light and sound. Such a reaction is called explosion.

Flame A flame is a region where combustion of gaseous substances or vapour takes place.

Fire extinguishers These are used to block the contact of fuel with the promoter of combustion such asoxygen.

Fuel It is a combustible substance which catches fire easily and produces heat energy.

Fuel efficiency It is the amount of heat that a fuel produce for a fixed amount of mass.

Global warming It is the process of rise in the average temperature of the earth's atmosphere due to the release of carbon dioxide on combustion of fuels.

Ideal fuel An ideal fuel is cheap, readily available, readily combustible and easy to transport.

Ignition temperature It is the minimum temperature that must be reached before a substance starts burning.

Inflammable substances These substances have a lower ignition temperature and burns easily with little heating.

Let's Investigate

ACTIVITY 1 (Page 41)

Aim To show that quality of burning flame depends on the amount of air available around it.

Materials Required A candle, glass chimney, few wooden blocks and a glass plate.

Procedure

1. Fix a lighted candle on a table.
2. Put a glass chimney on the candle.
3. Rest this arrangement of chimney on the wooden blocks .
4. Make sure that air can enter the chimney as shown in the figure (a).
5. Remove the wooden blocks and let the chimney rest on the table as fig. (b).
6. Finally, put a glass plate over the chimney as fig. (c).
7. Note the observations.

Observation When the chimney is on wooden blocks, candle burns freely as the air enters into the chimney as shown in the fig. (a). When the wooden blocks are removed, the air does not enter into the chimney. Due to this the candle starts to produce smoke as shown in fig. (b). You will also observe the flame of candle flickering. Now, when we put the glass plate over the chimney, the flame finally goes off as shown in fig. (c).

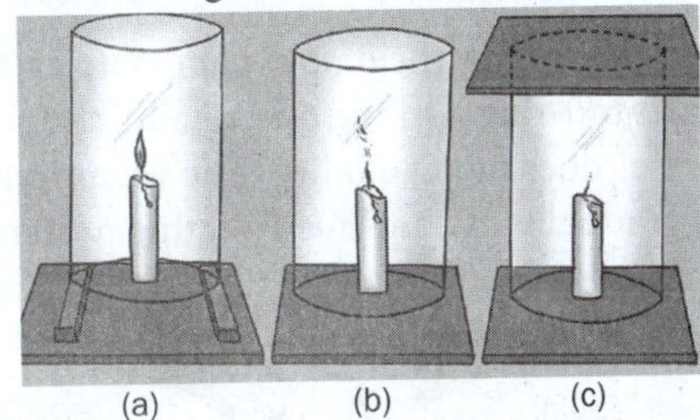

Burning of candles with different availability of air

Conclusion We can conclude that air is necessary for burning. Partial availability of air causes the smoke to produce. Complete lack of air causes the flame to goes off.

Viva Questions

1. What does flickering of candle indicate?
2. Does the candle burn unaffected when the glass plate is put over the chimney?

ACTIVITY 2 (Page 42)

Aim To show the supply of air needed for combustion.

Materials Required Piece of wood or charcoal, iron plate or tawa, a glass jar or a transparent plastic jar.

Procedure

1. Place a piece of burning wood or charcoal on the iron plate or tawa.
2. Cover it with the glass jar or the transparent plastic jar.
3. Note the observation.

Observation Wood or charcoal burns under the jar and continues burning for some time. But, after some time burning stop.

Conclusion Wood and charcoal stops burning after the wood is covered with glass jar or transparent plastic jar which shows that air is necessary for combustion.

Viva Questions

1. Does charcoal burn with a flame or a glow?
2. Will the burning stop if the jar had a hole?

ACTIVITY 3 (Page 43)

Aim To show that ignition temperature is essential for substance like paper to burn.

Materials Required Sheet of paper, water and candles.

Procedure

1 Make two paper cups by folding a sheet of paper.
2 Pour about 50 mL of water in one of the cups.
3 Heat the cups separately with the help of candle.
4 Note your observations.

Observation We see that the empty paper cup catches fire easily and starts burning. On the other hand, the paper cup containing water does not catch fire. The water in the cup becomes hot gradually. If continued heating, water will start even boiling in the paper cup.

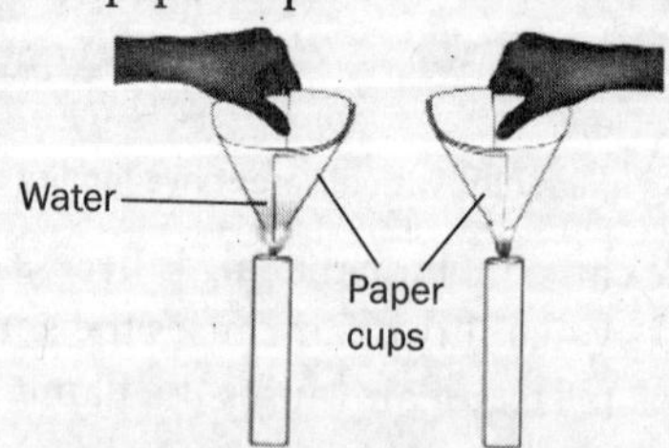

Heating water in a paper cup

Conclusion

(i) When we heat empty paper cup, it's ignition temperature is reached quickly. It catches fire and starts burning.

(ii) When we heat the paper cup having water, the heat is transferred to water by conduction. The ignition temperature of paper does not reach and hence, it does not burn.

This shows that ignition temperature is essential for a substance to burn.

Viva Questions

1. Why does paper cup filled with water not catch fire when placed over a flame?
2. What happens to the paper cup with water?

ACTIVITY 4 (Page 47)

Aim To show that the innermost zone of a candle flame consists of unburnt wax vapour.

Materials Required A candle, a glass tube, pair of tongs and a matchstick.

Procedure

1. Light the candle carefully.
2. Hold the glass tube with a pair of tongs.
3. Introduce one end of the glass tube in the dark zone of a non-flickering candle flame.

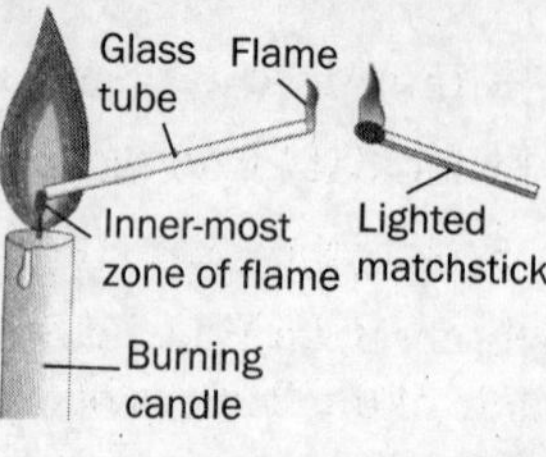

4. Bring the lighted matchstick near the other end of the glass tube as shown in figure given above.
5. Note your observations.

Observation When lighted matchstick is brought near the other end of the glass tube, we observe a flame at this end.It is because the innermost zone (dark zone) of the candle flame consists of unburnt wax vapours. Some vapours from it enter the glass tube. When the lighted matchstick is brought near it, the wax vapours starts burning and produces a flame.

Conclusion A flame burns at the other end of the glass tube when matchstick is lighted near it. Hence, we can conclude that the innermost zone (dark zone) of candle flame has unburnt wax vapours.

Viva Questions

1. Are the vapours of wax coming out of glass tube, cause of the flame produced?
2. In which zone of the flame were these wax vapours present?

ACTIVITY 5 (Page 47)

Aim To show that the middle zone of a candle flame consists of unburnt carbon particles.

Materials Required A candle, a glass plate, and a pair of tongs.

Procedure

1 Light the candle.

2 Hold the glass plate with pair of tongs as shown in figure.

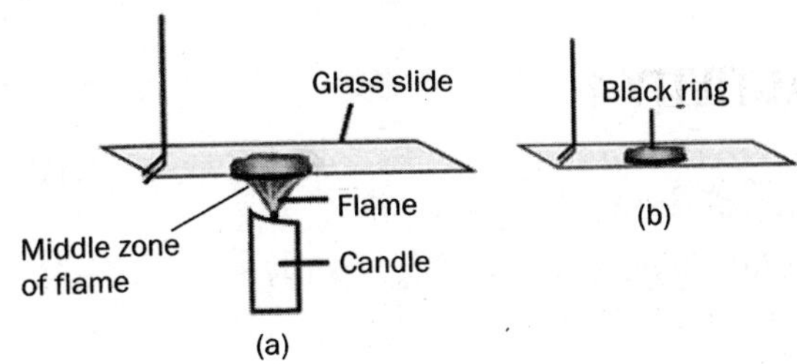

Glass plate kept in luminous zone of candle flame

3 Introduce the glass plate in the middle zone.

4 Hold it for 10 seconds and then remove.

5 Note the observation.

Observation When the glass plate is kept over the middle zone of the flame, a blackish circular ring is formed. The blackish ring is produced due to deposition of unburnt carbon particles present in the luminous zone of the flame.

Conclusion The observation concludes that the partial combustion of wax vapours in the luminous zone produced unburnt carbon particles.

Viva Questions

1. What is the luminous zone of the flame?
2. What do you observe when the glass plate is slided into the luminous zone of the flame?

ACTIVITY 6 (Page 47)

Aim To show that the outermost zone of a flame is the hottest zone.

Materials Required A copper wire, pair of tongs and a candle.

Procedure

1 Take a copper wire.

2 Hold it's one end with pair of tongs.

3 Introduce it's other end just inside the flame (outermost zone) for about 30 seconds.

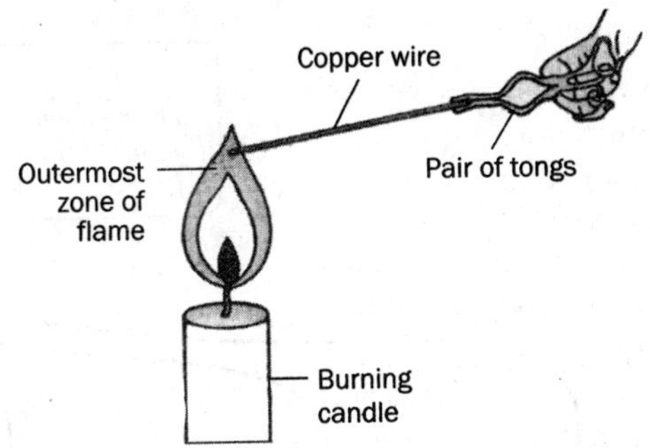

Heating of copper wire in the outemost zone of flame

4 Note the observation.

Observation We observe that the portion of the copper wire just inside the flame gets red hot.

Conclusion The observation concludes that the outermost, non-luminous zone of the flame has a high temperature. Hence, It is the hottest part of the flame.

Viva Questions

1. Which is the least hot part of the flame?
2. To ignite a cracker, should it be introduced in middle of the flame or top of the flame.

COMBUSTION AND FLAME

Combustion
It is the process in which a substance undergoes a chemical reaction in the presence of air to produce heat and light.

Condition Required for Combustion
- Presence of combustible material.
- Presence of supporter. i.e. air or oxygen.
- Ignition temperature. Lowest temperature at which a combustible substance catches fire.

Inflammable Substance
The substance which have very low ignition temperature and catches fire easily, e.g. LPG, etc.

How Fire can be Controlled?
- By removing the fuel, but in most cases, fuel cannot be eliminated.
- By removing the heat to bring down the temperature.
- By cutting off the air supply to the burning substances.

Fire Extingushers
Substances which are used to cut off the supply of oxygen to the fire are known as fire extinguishers, e.g. water and carbon dioxide, etc.

Types of Combustion

Explosion
Sudden combustion in which large amount of heat, light and sound are produced, e.g. buring of crackers.

Spontaneous Combustion
The combustion in which a material suddenly bursts into flames without any external heat, e.g. white phosphorus burns in air at room temperature on its own.

Rapid Combustion
The combustion in which a large amount of heat and light are produced in a short time, e.g. immediate burning of cooking gas (LPG) in a gas stove when a burning matchstick lighter is brought near it.

Flame
A flame is a region where combustion of gaseous substance or vapour takes place.

Zones of Flame
- Outermost zone — Blue or non-luminous zone (hottest part)
- Middle zone — Yellow or luminous zone (moderately hot)
- Innermost zone — Black or dark zone (least hot)

Fuel
A substance which produces heat on burning, e.g. wood, charcoal, petrol, kerosene, LPG, natural gas, etc.

Fuel Efficiency (calorific value)
It is the measure of amount of heat energy produced on complete combustion of 1 kg of a fuel.

Effects of Burning of Fuels
- Carbon fuels like wood, coal release unburnt carbon which are dangerous pollutants causing respiratory diseases such as asthma.
- Incomplete combustion of these fuels gives carbon monoxide gas. Excessive inhaling of this gas can kill a person.
- Burning of coal and diesel releases sulphur dioxide gas. These oxides dissolve in rainwater and form acids. It is very harmful for crops, buildings and soil.

NCERT FOLDER

Complete Explanations of all NCERT's Questions

Intext Questions

Q.1 We were told that food is a fuel for our body. Why? Page 40

Ans. The food that we eat is broken down in our body by reaction with oxygen and energy is produced, which is utilised by our body as a fuel.

Q.2 We have read that the Sun produces it's own heat and light. Is it also some kind of combustion? Page 42

Ans. No, it is not combustion. The heat and light in the Sun are produced by nuclear reaction.

Q.3 Why is it important to know the telephone number of the fire service in your area? Page 44

Ans. It is important to know the telephone number of fire service so that, in case of a fire, the fire brigade can reach on time and extinguish the fire.

Q.4 Why should we never sleep in a room with burning or smouldering coal fire? Page 49

Ans. It is because carbon monoxide gas produced can kill persons sleeping in the room with burning or smouldering coal fire.

Exercise

Q.1 List the conditions under which combustion can take place.

Ans. Necessary conditions for combustion are as follows

(i) Presence of combustible substance.

(ii) Proper supply of air to provide oxygen.

(iii) Attainment of ignition temperature.

Q.2 Fill in the blanks.

(a) Burning of wood and coal causes ...... of air.

(b) A liquid fuel used in homes is ....

(c) Fuel must be heated to its .... before it starts burning.

(d) Fire produced by oil cannot be controlled by ....

Ans. (a) pollution (b) kerosene

(c) ignition temperature (d) water

Q.3 Explain how the use of CNG in automobiles has reduced pollution in our cities.

Ans. CNG has replaced diesel and petrol as fuel in automobiles because petrol and diesel produced a lot of unburnt carbon particles and emitted carbon dioxide, nitrogen oxide and sulphur dioxide. These all gases are poisonous gases and cause various environmental hazards. The main causes of acid rain are nitrogen oxides and sulphur dioxide.

But CNG is safe because it produces these harmful substances in very small amounts. Thus, the use of CNG is reducing pollution in our cities.

Q.4 Compare LPG and wood as fuels.

Ans. Differences between LPG and wood are as follows

LPG	Wood
It is a gaseous fuel.	It is a solid fuel.
It does not produce smoke.	It produces smoke.
It is easily stored in cylinders.	It requires more space to store.
It does not cause any pollution.	It causes more pollution.
Its calorific value is high, i.e. 55000 kJ/kg.	Its calorific value is less, i.e. 17000-22000 kJ/kg.

Q.5 Give reasons.

(a) Water is not used to control fires involving electrical equipment.

(b) LPG is a better domestic fuel than wood.

(c) Paper by itself catches fire easily, whereas a piece of paper wrapped around an aluminium pipe does not.

Ans. (a) Water is not used to control fires involving electrical equipments because water conducts electricity. So, it can causes danger electric shocks.

(b) LPG is a better domestic fuel than wood because LPG has more calorific value and produces no pollution while wood has less calorific value and produces smoke and causes more pollution.

(c) It is because the ignition temperature of paper is less, so it catches fire easily. It does not catch fire, when wrapped around aluminium pipe because aluminium absorbs the heat by conduction, so paper does not attain its ignition temperature.

Q.6 Make a labelled diagram of a candle flame.

Ans.

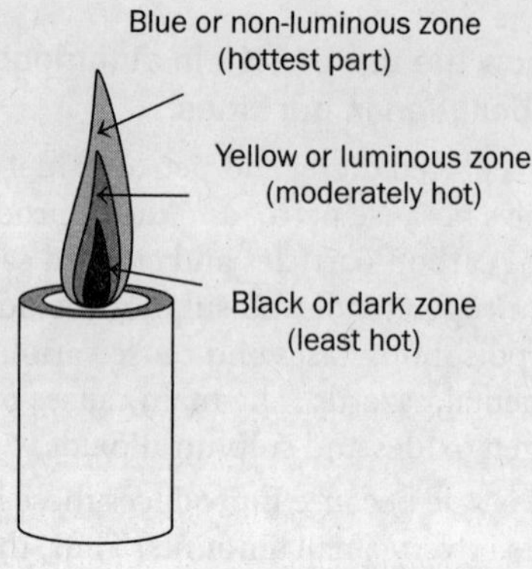

Different zones of flame

Q.7 Name the unit in which the calorific value of a fuel is expressed.

Ans. Calorific value of a fuel is expressed in kilojoule per kilogram (kJ/kg).

Q.8 Explain how CO_2 is able to control fires?

Ans. Carbon dioxide (CO_2) is the best fire extinguisher. Being heavier than oxygen, it covers the fire like a blanket. Since, the contact between the fuel and oxygen is cut-off and hence, the fire is controlled. It also brings down the temperature of the fuel.

Q.9 It is difficult to burn a heap of green leaves but dry leaves catch fire easily. Explain.

Ans. It is difficult to burn a heap of green leaves because the green leaves contain some water, due to which the ignition temperature of leaves increases and they do not catch fire easily, while dry leaves have no water, so they catch fire easily.

Q.10 Which zone of flame does a goldsmith use for melting gold and silver and why?

Ans. A goldsmith uses the outer zone or non-luminous zone of a flame for melting gold and silver because it is the hottest zone of a flame and has more temperature.

Q.11 In an experiment, 4.5 kg of a fuel was completely burnt. The heat produced was measured to be 180000 kJ. Calculate the calorific value of the fuel.

Ans. The amount of heat energy produced on complete combustion of 1 kg of a fuel is called its calorific value.

Given, total mass of fuel = 4.5 kg
Total heat produced = 180000 kJ
Now, heat produced in burning 1 kg of fuel, i.e. calorific value

$$= \frac{\text{Total heat produced}}{\text{Total mass of fuel}} = \frac{180000}{4.5}$$

$$= \frac{180000 \times 10}{45} = \frac{1800000}{45}$$

$$= \frac{360000}{9} = 40000 \text{ kJ/kg} \quad \text{(dividing by 9)}$$

Hence, calorific value of fuel = 40000 kJ/kg

Q.12 Can the process of rusting be called combustion? Discuss.

Ans. The process of rusting cannot be called combustion because in this process, no heat and light is produced. Due to this reason, iron is not considered as combustible substance.

Q.13 Abida and Ramesh were doing an experiment in which water was to be heated in a beaker. Abida kept the beaker near the wick in the yellow part of the candle flame. Ramesh kept the beaker in the outermost part of the flame. Whose water will get heated in a shorter time?

Ans. The water heated by Ramesh will get heated in a shorter time because he kept his beaker near the hottest (non-luminous) zone of the flame.

REVIEW EXERCISE

Including Competency Based Questions

Part I

Multiple Choice Questions

1. Combustion is a process that

(a) releases light and heat
(b) absorbs light and heat
(c) produces only heat
(d) produces only light

2. Combustion is generally

(a) a physical process (b) a chemical process
(c) Both (a) and (b) (d) None of these

3. The product(s) of combustion is/are

(a) only oxygen (b) oxygen and water
(c) carbon dioxide and water (d) only carbon dioxide

4. Magnesium ribbon on burning in air produces

(a) magnesium oxide, water and light
(b) magnesium oxide and heat
(c) magnesium oxide, heat and light
(d) magnesium oxide, water and heat

5. Coal burns with

(a) flame (b) only glow
(c) Both flame and glow (d) None of these

6. The substance that does not burn with flame is NCERT Exemplar

(a) LPG (b) camphor (c) dry grass (d) charcoal

7. Which of these materials is combustible?

(a) Steel (b) Wood
(c) Glass (d) Marble

8. Which of the following is not a combustible substance?

(a) Camphor (b) Glass
(c) Straw (d) Alcohol

9. A substance which reacts with oxygen giving heat is called a combustible substance. Which one of the following is a combustible substance?

(a) Iron nail (b) Glass
(c) Stone piece (d) Wood

10. If a person's clothes catch fire, the best way to extinguish the fire is to NCERT Exemplar

(a) throw water on the clothes
(b) use fire extinguisher
(c) cover the person with a woolen blanket
(d) cover the person with a polythene sheet

11. The substance expected to have the highest ignition temperature out of the following is

(a) kerosene (b) petrol (c) coal (d) alcohol

12. Water was poured over a large oil fire to extinguish it. What would happen and why?

(a) The fire will be put off since water extinguishers fires
(b) The fire will spread since oil floats on water
(c) The fire will be put off since water dissolves oil
(d) The fire will spread since water contains hydrogen that is a combustible gas

13. In a fire extinguisher, which substance is commonly used for cutting off the oxygen supply to the fire?

(a) Water (b) Sand
(c) Carbon dioxide (d) Gasoline

14. On placing an inverted tumbler over a burning candle, the flame extinguishes after some time. This is because of non-availability of NCERT Exemplar

(a) oxygen (b) water vapour
(c) carbon dioxide (d) wax

15. Which of the following case is an example of spontaneous combustion?

(a) Lighting a gas store
(b) A car engine starting
(c) A pile of dry leaves catching fire in summer
(d) A chemical reaction in laboratory

16. Bunsen burner contains a gas *X* which burns with a blue flame. What is the reason behind the blue coloured flame? Competency Based Que.

(a) Complete combustion of gas *X*
(b) Presence of impurities in the gas
(c) Low temperature of the flame
(d) Incomplete combustion of gas *X*

17. Unburnt carbon particles are present in the

(a) luminous flame (b) non-luminous flame
(c) dark flame (d) flickering flame

18. Which is the hottest zone in a candle flame?

(a) Blue zone (b) Yellow zone
(c) Dark zone (d) Grey zone

19. What is the main product of incomplete combustion of coal?

(a) Carbon dioxide (b) Oxygen
(c) Water vapour (d) Nitrogen dioxide

20. **The calorific value of a fuel is expressed in a unit called**

(a) kilojoule per litre (b) kilogram per millilitre
(c) kilojoule per gram (d) kilojoule per kilogram

21. **Which one among the following is considered as the cleanest fuel?** NCERT Exemplar

(a) Cowdung cake (b) Petrol
(c) Kerosene (d) Hydrogen gas

22. **In villages, people use wood as fuel because**

(a) it is considered to be an ideal fuel
(b) of its easy availability and low cost
(c) it is environment friendly
(d) it catches fire easily

23. **Shyam was cooking potato curry on a chulha. To his surprise, he observed that the copper vessel was getting blackened from outside. It may** NCERT Exemplar

(a) proper combustion of fuel
(b) improper cooking of potato curry
(c) improper combustion of the fuel
(d) burning of copper vessel

24. **Which one of the following has the highest calorific value?**

(a) Kerosene (b) Biogas (c) LPG (d) Petrol

25. **Our beautiful Taj Mahal is suffering from 'marble cancer'. Acid rain reacts with marble and limestone to form calcium sulphate. It causes damage to big sculptures and marble constructions.**
Identify the gases that contribute to the formation of acid rain. CBSE Question Bank

(a) Nitrogen oxides and carbon oxides
(b) Carbon dioxide and carbon monoxide
(c) Sulphur oxides and carbon oxides
(d) Nitrogen oxides and sulphur oxides

26. **When a lighted candle placed partly in a trough of water is covered by an inverted glass, water rushes up as shown and the flame extinguishes. If the above hypothesis is true, what will happen after the candle blows out in the new experimental set-up.** Diksha

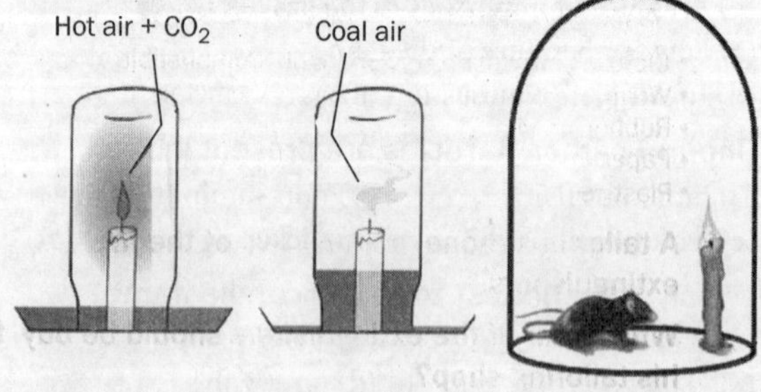

(a) The mouse will die or show signs of suffocation
(b) The mouse will become visible more active
(c) The glass will break and the mouse will escape
(d) There will be no change in mouse's behaviour

Answers

1. (a)	2. (b)	3. (c)	4. (c)	5. (b)
6. (d)	7. (b)	8. (b)	9. (d)	10. (c)
11. (c)	12. (b)	13. (c)	14. (a)	15. (c)
16. (a)	17. (a)	18. (a)	19. (a)	20. (d)
21. (d)	22. (b)	23. (c)	24. (c)	25. (d)
26. (a)				

Fill in the Blanks

1. **A...... process in which a substance reacts with ...... to give off heat is called combustion.** NCERT Exemplar

2. **When the clothes of a person catch ......, the person is covered with a ...... to extinguish fire.**

3. **The substances which gave very ...... ignition temperature and can easily catch fire with a flame are called ...... substances.** NCERT Exemplar

4. **The substances which vaporise during.................... give flame.** NCERT Exemplar

5. **Wood, paper and CNG are .... substances.**

Answers

1. chemical, oxygen 2. fire, blanket
3. low, inflammable 4. burning
5. combustible

True/False

1. **Air is necessary for combustion.** NCERT Exemplar

2. **Magnesium is a non-combustible metal.**

3. **Carbon dioxide is an excellent fire extinguisher.**

4. **Water is the best extinguisher for fires involving electrical equipment.**

5. **Middle zone is the hottest zone of a flame.**

Answers

1. True
2. False, magnesium is a combustible metal.
3. True
4. False, carbon dioxide is the best extinguisher for fires involving electrical equipment.
5. False, outer zone is the hottest zone of a flame.

Match the Columns

1. Match the Column I with Column II. **NCERT Exemplar**

Column I	Column II
A. Oxides of sulphur and nitrogen	1. Fire extinguisher
B. CNG	2. Incomplete combustion of coal
C. Oxygen	3. Very low ignition temperature
D. Inflammable substance	4. Acid rain
E. Carbon dioxide	5. Necessary for combustion
F. Carbon monoxide	6. Fuel for automobiles

2. Match the following for the flame of a candle. **NCERT Exemplar**

Column I	Column II (zone)	Column III (colour)
A. Hottest part	1. Innermost zone of unburnt wax vapours	(x) Blue
B. Moderately hot	2. Middle zone of partial combustion	(y) Black
C. Least hot	3. Outer zone of complete combustion	(z) Yellow

Answers

1. A–4, B–6, C–5, D–3, E–1, F–2
2. A–3—x, B–2—z, C–1—y

Assertion-Reason Questions

The following questions consist of two statements. Assertion (A) and Reason (R). Answer the following questions by selecting the appropriate options given below.

(a) Both A and R are true and R is the correct explanation of A.
(b) Both A and R are true, but R is not the correct explanation of A.
(c) A is true, but R is false.
(d) A is false, but R is true.

1. Assertion (A) Fireworks produce different colours.
Reason (R) Different chemicals are used in the fireworks to produce different colours.

2. Assertion (A) Spontaneous combustion can occur in materials like dry leaves.
Reason (R) Spontaneous combustion happens due to the presence of excess oxygen in materials.

3. Assertion (A) LPG gas can catch fire easily.
Reason (R) LPG have high ignition temperature.

4. Assertion (A) When a burning candle is covered with a glass jar, the flame goes out.
Reason (R) The glass jar prevents the flow of oxygen to the candle flame.

Answers

1. (a) Both A and R are true and R is the correct explanation of A.
2. (c) A is true, but R is false. R can be corrected as Spontaneous combustion occurs in materials which have low ignition temperature. Through internal chemical reaction with oxygen, they release heat and burn on their own.
3. (c) A is true but R is false. R can be corrected as LPG have low ignition temperature, so it catches fire easily.
4. (a) Both A and R are true and R is the correct explanation of A.

Case Based Questions

1. The picture shows four types of fire extinguishers. Each extinguisher is suited for specific sources of fire. **Competency Based Que.**

(i) A tailor has money for any two of the fire extinguishers. Which pair of fire extinguishers should be buy for his tailoring shop?

(a) P and Q
(b) Q and S
(c) P and R
(d) S and R

(ii) **Fire extinguisher K is suitable for kitchen fires.**

Kitchen fires

Which fire extinguisher can perform most of the work of K?

(a) P (b) Q (c) R (d) S

(iii) **How does dumping sand on fire extinguish the flame?**

2. The table shows the calorific value and pollutants released by four types of fuels. **Competency Based Que.]**

Fuel	Calorific value(kilojoule / kg)	Pollution factor
Type 1	25000- 33000	CO_2, sulphur oxides and nitrogen oxides
Type 2	55000	CO_2, water vapour
Type 3	45000	Carbon monoxide, CO_2, nitrogen oxides
Type 4	35000 - 40000	CO_2 and methane

(i) **Which fuel can boil the water in a vessel the fastest?**

(a) Type 1

(b) Type 2

(c) Type 3

(d) Type 4

(ii) **Which fuel can cause acid rain on combustion?**

(a) Type 1 only

(b) Type 4 only

(c) Both type 1 and type 3

(d) Both type 2 and type 4

(iii) **Which fuel type is likely to be biogas?**

(a) Type 1

(b) Type 2

(c) Type 3

(d) Type 4

Answers

1. (i) (c) (ii) (b)

(iii) Sand absorbs heat and cuts off the oxygen supply hence, it helps in extinguishing the flame.

2. (i) (d)

(ii) (c)

(iii) (d)

Part II

Very Short Answer Type Questions

1. Which type of substances produce flame? Does charcoal burn with flame?

Ans. The substances which vaporise during burning produce flame. No, charcoal does not burn with flame, it glows only.

2. What are the products obtained when combustion takes place?

Ans. The products of combustion are carbon dioxide, water vapour, heat and light.

3. Name the substance which gives heat and light after combustion.

Ans. The substance which provides heat and light is called fuels

4. If you burn a candle and coal, what is the difference in their burning?

Ans. Candle burns with a flame whereas coal burns by producing light in the form of glow.

5. How is heat produced in our body?

Ans. In our body, food is broken down by reaction with oxygen. During such reactions, heat is produced. This heat keeps our body warm.

6. Name two fuels which we use in our homes for cooking food.

Ans. Two fuels which we use in our homes for cooking food are LPG and kerosene oil.

7. Like fuels, the Sun also provides heat and light. What is the source of heat and light in the Sun?

Ans. In the Sun, heat and light are produced by nuclear reactions.

8. Out of kerosene oil or wood, which has higher ignition temperature?

Ans. Wood has higher ignition temperature than kerosene oil.

9. In which form, CO_2 can be stored in cylinders?

Ans. CO_2 can be stored in cylinders in liquid form.

10. Do all the substances catch fire at the same temperature?

Ans. No, different substances need different temperature to catch fire due to their different ignition temperature.

11. Two glass jars *A* and *B* are filled with carbon dioxide and oxygen gases respectively. In each jar, a lighted candle is placed simultaneously. In which jar, will the candle remain lighted for a longer time and why? **Competency Based Que.**

Ans. In jar *B*, the candle remains lighted for a longer time because oxygen is a supporter of combustion.

12. Why should we take special care in storing kerosene oil?

Ans. We need to take special care in storing kerosene oil because it has low ignition temperature and it can catch fire easily.

13. Anu wants to boil water quickly in a test tube. On observing the different zones of the flame, she is not able to decide which zone of the flame will be best for boiling water quickly. Help her in this activity. **NCERT Exemplar**

Ans. Anu should keep her test tube in the outermost zone or non-luminous zone of the flame because it is the hottest zone of a flame.

14. Why is the use of diesel and petrol as fuels in automobiles being replaced by Compressed Natural Gas (CNG) in big cities?

Ans. It is because CNG produces harmful products in very small amount and it is a clean fuel.

15. What do you understand by fuel efficiency? **NCERT Exemplar**

Ans. Fuel efficiency is determined by its calorific value which is the amount of heat energy produced on complete combustion of 1 kg of a fuel. The calorific value of a fuel is expressed in kJ/kg.

Short Answer Type Questions

1. If you hold a piece of iron wire with a pair of tongs inside a candle flame or a Bunsen burner flame, what will you observe? Will it produce a flame?

Ans. Iron wire will become red hot and glow. It will not produce a flame.

2. Define combustible and non-combustible substances? Explain with two examples of each.

Ans. Refer to text on page no. 1.

3. Boojho wants to separate the following materials as combustible and non-combustible. Can you help him? Charcoal, chalk, stone, iron rod, copper coin, straw, cardboard, glass, paper, candle, wood. **NCERT Exemplar**

Ans. (i) Combustible — charcoal, straw, cardboard, paper, candle, wood.

(ii) Non-combustible — chalk, stone, iron rod, copper coin, glass.

4. What are the factors which help in combustion?

Ans. Refer to text on page no. 1.

5. Why a person is covered with a blanket when the clothes of that person catch fire?

Ans. When the clothes of a person catch fire, the person is covered with a blanket to extinguish the fire. This is because the supply of air to the burning clothes is cut off by blanket, due to which the clothes stop burning and the fire gets extinguished.

6. How does matchstick burn?

Ans. The head of the safety match contains antimony trisulphide and potassium chlorate. The rubbing surface has powdered glass and a little red phosphorus. When the match is struck against the rubbing surface, some red phosphorus gets converted into white phosphorus. This immediately reacts with potassium chlorate in the matchstick head to produce enough heat to ignite antimony trisulphide and start combustion.

7. Why a matchstick can burn a splinter of wood directly, but cannot burn a log of wood directly? How can we burn a log of wood?

Ans. A matchstick can burn a splinter of wood directly because it has low ignition temperature, whereas a matchstick cannot burn a log of wood directly as it has high ignition temperature.

In order to burn a log of wood, a small fire is first started by burning straw (or dry grass), or paper by a matchstick, then the log of wood is placed over this fire. This fire heats the log of wood to its ignition temperature due to which it starts burning.

8. A matchstick does not catch fire on its own. But when it is rubbed, it starts burning. Why?

Ans. A matchstick does not catch fire on its own at room temperature because the ignition temperature of matchstick is much higher than the room temperature. The matchstick starts burning on rubbing it on the rough side provided on the matchbox. It is because the heat produced by friction heats the chemical at the head of the matchstick to its ignition temperature and makes it burn.

9. The calorific values of petrol and CNG are 45000 kJ/kg and 50000 kJ/kg, respectively. If you have vehicle which can run on petrol as well as CNG, which fuel will you prefer and why? **Competency Based Que.**

Ans. We will prefer CNG (Compressed Natural Gas) because the calorific value of CNG is higher than that of petrol. Therefore, CNG will be more economical. CNG will produce large amount of heat energy than petrol. At the same time, it produces the least air pollutants.

10. Cracker on ignition produces sound. Why?

Ans. When a cracker is ignited, a sudden reaction takes place with the evolution of heat, light and sound and a large amount of gas is liberated. Such a reaction is called explosion.

So, cracker on ignition produces sound because of sudden formation of large amount of gas due to chemical reaction.

Long Answer Type Questions

1. Give two examples each for a solid, liquid and gaseous fuel along with some important uses. NCERT Exemplar

Ans. **Solid fuels** Examples are wood and coal. These are used to cook food in homes. Coal is also used in industries.

Liquid fuels Examples are kerosene and petrol. Kerosene is used in stoves and in lamps to cook food and petrol is used as a fuel in automobiles.

Gaseous fuels Examples are natural gas and petroleum gas. These are used in industries, CNG is used to run automobiles.

2. How can you burn wood or coal using kerosene oil?

Ans. We have to use kerosene oil to start fire in wood or coal. It is because coal has high ignition temperature. A burning matchstick cannot produce sufficient heat to reach the ignition temperature of coal. Since, ignition temperature of kerosene oil is low, so if some kerosene is sprinkled over the wood, the kerosene starts burning by a lighted matchstick.

The heat produced by the burning of kerosene makes the wood to burn. The coal pieces are then placed over the burning wood. The large heat produced by the burning wood heats the coal to its ignition temperature. In this way, the coal starts burning.

3. What are the three essential requirements to produce fire? How fire extinguisher is useful for controlling the fire?

Ans. Three essential requirements to produce fire are as follows

(i) Fuel (ii) Air and

(iii) Heat to acquire the ignition temperature.

The job of fire extinguisher is to cut off the supply of air or to bring down the temperature of fuel or both. The most common fire extinguisher is water. But water works only when things like wood and paper are on fire. For fires involving electrical equipment and inflammable materials like petrol, carbon dioxide (CO_2) is the best extinguisher. CO_2 being heavier than oxygen, covers the fire like a blanket. Since, the contact between the fuel and oxygen is cut-off, so the fire can be controlled.

4. Although wood has a very high calorific value, we still discourage its use as a fuel. Explain.

Ans. Burning of wood has several disadvantages inspite of having high calorific value. These are as follows

(i) Burning of wood produces a lot of smoke which causes respiratory diseases like asthma.

(ii) The cutting down of trees to obtain as a wood fuel leads to deforestation which is very harmful to the environment.

(iii) Trees provide us many useful substances. To obtain fuel wood, when trees are cut down, then all useful substances which can be obtained from trees are lost.

5. Forest fire produces a lot of air pollution. Write in brief about the reasons of forest fires. NCERT Exemplar

Ans. Reasons of forest fires are as follows

(i) At high temperature, sometimes dry grass catches fire which spreads throughout the forest.

(ii) Camp fire may also be a reason of fire.

(iii) Lightning.

(iv) The use of fires by villagers to ward off wild animals.

(v) Fire lit intentionally by people living around forests for recreation.

(vi) The friction of bamboos due to high wind velocity and rolling stones.

6. Manu was heating oil to fry potato chips. The cooking oil all of a sudden caught fire, he poured water to extinguish the fire. Do you think, this action was suitable? If yes, why? If not, why not? In such a condition what should Manu have done? Competency Based Que.

Ans. Pouring water to extinguish the fire due to oil is not suitable action. It is because oil is lighter than water. So, water will settle down below the oil. In such condition, sand or soil should be used. They cut off the supply of air to the fire. Thus, fire can be controlled. But sand or soil will not be available at that place. So, Manu should have switched off the flame of the burner and put a lid on the frying pan. By doing this, the contact between fuel and oxygen is cut off and the flame could go off.

Case Based Questions

1. Sparkling rods light up when inserted in a flame. The hotter the flame, the quicker the rod lights up. The picture shows four different zones of a flame. **Competency Based Que.**

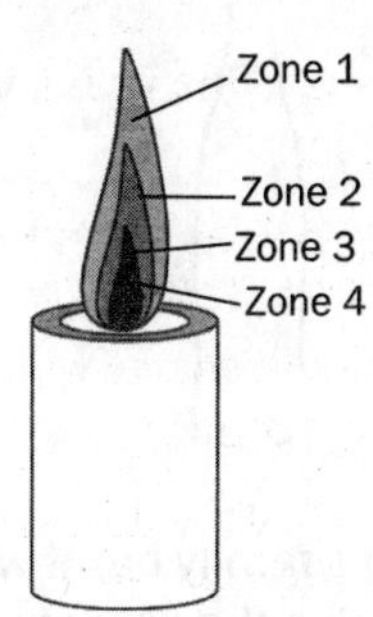

Flame of a candle

Sparking rod

(i) In which zone should a sparkling rod be inserted to light it the fastest?

(a) Zone 1

(b) Zone 2

(c) Zone 3

(d) Zone 4

(ii) Why does the flame of a candle go off when all the wax melts?

(iii) Which zone has unburnt carbon particles?

(a) Zone 1 (b) Zone 2

(c) Zone 3 (d) Zone 4

2. Observe the given picture and answer the following questions

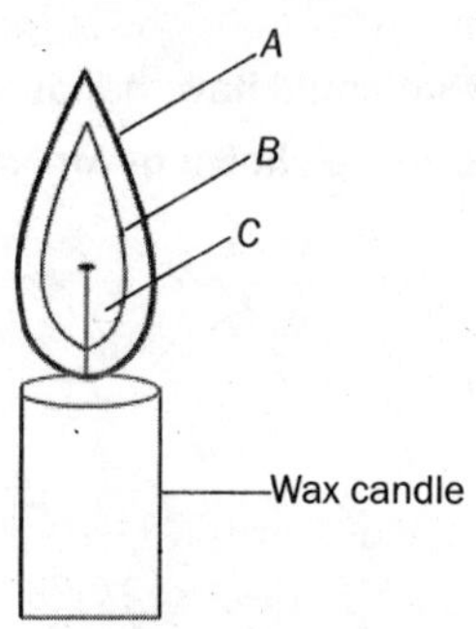

Parts of a flame

(i) Which is the hottest part of the flame in the given figure of a candle.

(ii) Why does the middle zone of the candle flame glow with yellow colour?

(iii) State any two conditions under which combustion takes place.

3.

	Compressed Natural Gas	Diesel
Carbon monoxide production	2.97 g/km	1.09 g/km
Greenhouse gas emissions	2,364 g/mj	2,680 g/mi
Energy density	47.2 Mj/kg	45.8 Mj/kg

(i) In an experiment 6.5 kg of a fuel was completely burnt. The heat produced was measured to be 1,90,000 KJ. Calculate the calorific value of the fuel in KJ per kg.

(ii) CNG is a better fuel when compared to petrol or diesel. With reference to the data in the table, evaluate this statement.

Ans. 1. (i) (a) Zone 1

(ii) The flame of the candle goes off because no more wax is available on the candle which can burn and give flame.

(iii) (c) Zone 3

2. (i) A or the outermost part of the flame.

(ii) Middle zone of the candle flame contains unburnt carbon particles which give the flame yellow colour.

(iii) Presence of a supporter of combustion and presence of a combustible substance are two required conditions for the combustion.

3. (i) Calorific value = Energy/Mass

$$= \frac{190000}{6.5} = 29230 \text{ kJ/kg}$$

(ii) CNG produces less carbon monoxide than diesel and produces, less green house gas than diesel. Also CNG has higher energy density than diesel.

Skill Based Questions as per NEP 2020

1.

Fire triangle

On the basis of fire triangle given above answer the following questions.

(i) Which part of the fire triangle is removed to control fire in the following cases?

(a) Putting a fire blanket on fire.

(b) Removing dead leaves and dead grass in forest fire.

(ii) Ramya's mother kept a container with cooking oil on the gas stove to heat. Suddenly she found that cooking oil caught fire. Analyse the given situation and suggest measures that may be taken by Ramya's mother to prevent the spread of fire.

Research skill

2. Place a candle in a bowl and ignite it as shown in the figure. Open a bottle of pepsi and quickly pour it in the bowl. What change do you observe in the flame of the candle? **Experimental skill**

3. In severe cold weather, Mohan's family burnt wood in the room during the night keeping the windows close. After some time, they felt suffocation. Mohan immediately opened the windows and get relief.

(i) What did actually happen?

(ii) What values are associated with Mohan?

Thinking skill

4. A factory was started near a village. Suddenly, villagers started feeling the presence of irritating vapours in the village. Mr. Lalit Jain was school teacher in that village. He noted that the cases of headache, chest pain, cough, dryness of throat and breathing problems are increasing among the villagers. He blamed the emission from the chimney of the factory for such problems. He gave the written complain in behalf of all the villagers.

Read the given passage and answer the following questions.

(i) Explain what could have happened in the village.

(ii) What values are shown by Mr. Lalit Jain?

Observation skill

ASSESSMENT EXERCISE

Part I

Multiple Choice Questions

1. Which type of combustion is characterised by a lack of oxygen during the burning process?

(a) Spontaneous combustion (b) Incomplete combustion
(c) Rapid combustion (d) Controlled combustion

2. What is the minimum temperature at which a substance catches fire and burns on it's own?

(a) Boiling point (b) Melting point
(c) Ignition temperature (d) Freezing point

3. Which of the following fire extinguishers is suitable for tackling electrical fires?

(a) Water fire extinguisher
(b) Foam fire extinguisher
(c) Carbon dioxide fire extinguisher
(d) Powder fire extinguisher

Fill in the Blanks

4. .... fuel is cheap, readily available and cause less pollution.

5. .... gas is a promoter of combustion.

True/False

6. LPG fire is an inflammable substance.

7. Spontaneous combustion takes place in the absence of external heat.

Match the Columns

8. Match the Column I with Column II.

	Column I		Column II
A.	LPG	1.	Non-combustible
B.	Iron nails	2.	Cheap fuel
C.	Candle	3.	Cooking gas
D.	Wood	4.	Flame

Assertion-Reason Questions

The following questions consist of two statements **Assertion** (A) and **Reason** (R). Answer these questions by selecting the appropriate option given below.

(a) Both A and R are true and R is the correct explanation of A
(b) Both A and R are true but R is not the correct explanation of A
(c) A is true, but R is false
(d) A is false, but R is true

9. Assertion (A) Electrical components can catch fire.

Reason (R) Electrical fire can be extinguished using water.

10. Assertion (A) Candle can burn a block of wood.

Reason (R) Ignition temperature of wood is high.

Part II

Very Short Answer Type Questions

11. Name two inflammable fuels.

12. Name the most common fire extinguisher.

13. How many zones are there in a flame?

Short Answer Type Questions

14. What is meant by rapid combustion? Give two examples.

15. Explain how the use of CNG in automobiles has reduced pollution in cities?

16. Give two examples each of (i) solid fuels and (ii) liquid fuels.

Long Answer Type Question

17. Explain how burning of fuels such as coal, petrol and diesel leads to acid rain? Give the harmful effects of acid rain.

Answers

1. (b) **2.** (c) **3.** (c) **4.** Ideal **5.** Oxygen
6. True **7.** True

8. A-3, B-1, C-4, D-2
9. (c) **10.** (d)

CHAPTER 05

Conservation of Plants and Animals

Conservation is a term used to describe the careful and sensible use of natural resources. The Earth's natural resources include air, water, soil, minerals, fuels, plants and animals.

In this chapter, we will study about their conservation, i.e. the practice of caring for these resources so that all living things are benefitted from them in present as well as in the future.

5.1 Deforestation and its Causes

A forest is a large area covered with trees and plants. It provides habitat for various plants and animals.
The process of clearing away forests by cutting them down or burning them is called **deforestation**. Various causes that lead to deforestation are

(i) **Procuring land for cultivation** Forest trees are cut down to obtain more agricultural land for cultivation of crops to feed the increasing population.

(ii) **Building houses and factories** The trees are cut down to build homes, factories, roads, dams, etc.

(iii) **Making various products** Paper or wood for making doors, windows, etc., are obtained from trees.

(iv) **Natural causes** Forest fires, severe droughts, etc. also leads to deforestation.

Consequences of Deforestation

Deforestation has an adverse effect on the environment and on various living organisms. Some major consequences discussed here are

1. Global Warming

Green plants uses carbon dioxide for photosynthesis (preparation of food). When fewer trees will be left due to deforestation, less carbon dioxide will be used up resulting in its increased amount in the atmosphere.

Carbon dioxide gas traps heat rays reflected by the surface of the Earth. Trapping of heat rays by carbon dioxide increases the temperature of Earth's atmosphere thus leading to **global warming**.

2. Disturbance in Water Cycle

The consequent increase in the temperature of Earth disturbs water cycle. This leads to the decrease in rainfall that lowers the groundwater level and could cause **droughts**.

3. Soil Erosion and Desertification

Roots of trees bind the particles of top soil, preventing them from being carried away by wind and water. When the forest trees are cut, there are no roots and the bare top soil becomes loose quickly and erodes rapidly. This results in soil erosion. Removal of top soil exposing the lower layer that is hard, rocky and has less humus and is less fertile. Other properties like nutrient content, texture, etc. of soil also change. Over the time, continued soil erosion can thus convert the land into a desert. This is called desertification.

4. Floods

The roots of forest trees help in absorbing the rainwater and make it to get percolated into the ground. Due to the deforestation, there is decrease in the water-holding capacity of the soil. The movement of water from the soil surface into the ground (in filtration rate) is reduced. This results in floods (excess water overflowing from the banks of the river into the adjoining areas).

5. Shortage of Wood and Other Forest Products

Deforestation will lead to shortage of wood used for various purposes. Also, there will be lack of other forest products such as honey, gum, lac, etc. if cutting down forest trees continues.

Try These 5.1

1. **State the term used for the process of clearing away forests, involving cutting down or burning trees.**
2. **What could be a potential consequences of the increased amount of carbon dioxide in the atmosphere due to fewer trees?**
3. **What will happen if the forest trees are cut and there will be no roots available in the soil?**
4. **Which plant part help to increase the water holding capacity of plants?**

5.2 Conservation of Forest and Wildlife

Now we know that deforestation leads to many harmful effects on the environment so, it is important to conserve forests and wildlife present in them.

This can be accomplished by protecting specific areas, where plantation, cultivation, grazing, felling trees, hunting and poaching are prohibited. Such areas are marked by the government as **protected areas**. The government lays down rules, methods and policies to protect and conserve these areas.

The three main types of protected areas are as follows

1. Biosphere reserves
2. Wildlife sanctuaries
3. National parks

5.3 Biosphere Reserve

It is a large protected area of land meant for the conservation of wildlife, biodiversity and the traditional lifestyle of the tribal people living in the area.

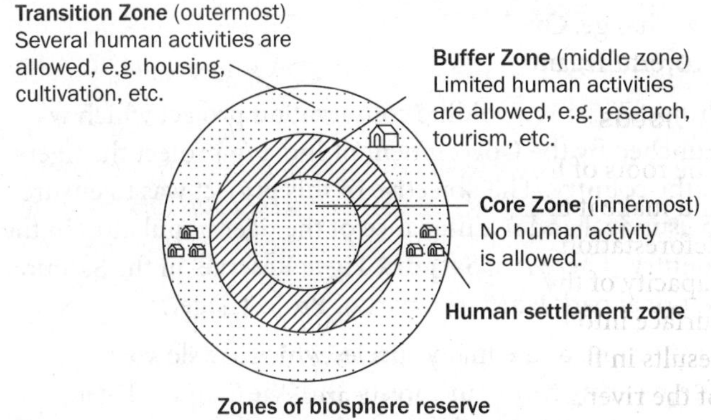

Zones of biosphere reserve

A biosphere reserve may also contain other protected areas in it, e.g. the Pachmarhi biosphere reserve consists of one National park named Satpura and two wildlife sanctuaries, i.e. Bori and Pachmarhi. The biodiversity found in Pachmarhi biosphere reserve is similar to those of the upper Himalayan peaks and to those belonging to the lower Western Ghats.

Great Nicobar Biosphere Reserve and Tiger Reserve are some examples of biosphere reserves located in India.

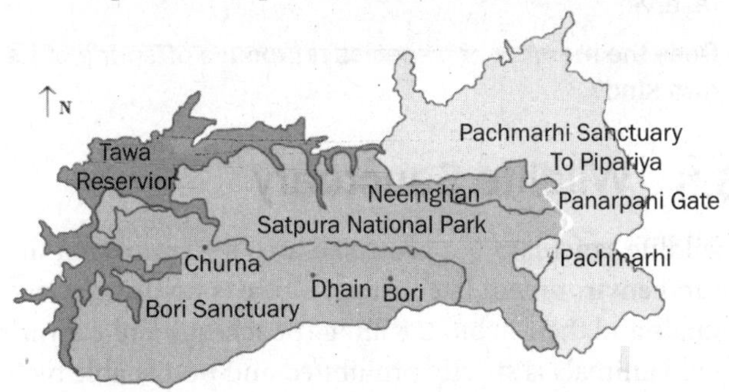

Pachmarhi biosphere reserve

5.4 Flora and Fauna

Some animals and plants typically belong to a particular area and are known as flora and fauna, respectively of that area. These are found naturally in that area, e.g. Cheetal, wolf, leopard, chinkara, blue bull, barking deer and wild dog are the examples of fauna of the Pachmarhi biosphere reserve.

While, teak, jamun, sal, mango, silver fern and arjun are the flora of Pachmarhi biosphere reserve.

Endemic Species

Endemic species are the species of plants and animals which are found exclusively in a particular area. They are not naturally found anywhere else, e.g. sal and wild mango are the examples of endemic flora of the Pachmarhi biosphere reserve. Bison, Indian giant squirrel and flying squirrel are endemic fauna of this area. The endemic species may vanish in the near future due to a number of factors, such as destruction of their habitat, increasing population, introduction of new species, etc. Such factors affects the natural habitat of endemic species and endangering their existence.

> **Species**
>
> It is a group of population which is capable of interbreeding. This means that the members of a species can reproduce fertile offspring (one which can reproduce its own kind) only with the members of their own species and not with members of other species. Members of a species have common characteristics.

Try These 5.2

1. In what ways does government play a role in safeguarding protected areas?
2. It is important to accomplish specific area where flora and fauna can be protected. Name any two such areas.
3. Name some endemic flora of Pachmarhi biosphere reserve.
4. Does the member of a species reproduce offspring of its own kind?

5.5 Wildlife Sanctuary

A wildlife sanctuary is a protected area for animals in their natural environment like forests. There is no disturbance to animals and their habitat. Killing (poaching) and capturing of wild animals is strictly prohibited and punishable by the law. It provides protection and suitable living conditions to wild animals.

Bharatpur wildlife sanctuary (Rajasthan) and Lockchao wildlife sanctuary (Manipur) are some examples of wildlife sanctuary located in India.

Some of the **threatened wild animals** like black buck, white eyed buck, elephant, golden cat, pink headed duck, gharial, marsh crocodile, python, rhinoceros, etc. are protected and preserved in wildlife sanctuaries.

Indian sanctuaries have unique landscapes, i.e. broad level forests, mountain forests and bush lands in deltas of big rivers.

Zoo

Zoos or zoological parks are the large areas where many types of wild animals and birds brought from different parts of the world are kept in cages or enclosures, so that people can see them.

Though zoos and wildlife sanctuaries both provide protection to wild animals, yet they are different from each other. Various differences between both are given below

Differences between zoo and wildlife sanctuary

Zoo	Wildlife sanctuary
In zoo, the wild animals and birds live in artificial setting such as cages and enclosures.	In wildlife sanctuary, the wild animals and birds live in their natural habitat in the forest.
A zoo contains wild animals and birds brought from the different parts of the country and from various other countries of the world.	A wildlife sanctuary contains wild animals and birds found locally.
Wild animals and birds are not comfortable living in the artificial environment of a zoo.	Wild animals and birds are very comfortable in the natural environment of a wildlife sanctuary.
A zoo is open to public for a fixed time everyday.	A wildlife sanctuary is not open to public freely like a zoo. Public can visit a wildlife sanctuary only when accompanied by the forest guards.

5.6 National Park

A national park is an area reserved for wildlife where they can freely use the habitats and natural resources.

It is relatively-large protected area and is maintained by the government to preserve flora and fauna, landscape and historic objects of the area. These areas are diverse enough to protect whole sets of ecosystems.

National park also provide human recreation and enjoyment. People are allowed to enter these areas, but exploitation of natural resources is strictly prohibited.

Satpura National Park

The **first reserve forest** of India is **Satpura National Park** in **Madhya Pradesh**. The finest **Indian teak** is found in this forest. The evidences of prehistoric human life in the jungles called **rock shelters** are also found inside the Satpura National Park which gives us an idea of the life of primitive people. Also many **rock paintings** are found in these shelters and the figures of animals and men fighting, hunting, dancing and playing musical instruments are depicted in these paintings. Many tribals still live in this area. A total of 55 rock shelters have been identified in Pachmarhi Biosphere Reserve.

Project Tiger

Project Tiger is a wildlife conservation project which was launched by the Government of India to protect the tigers in the country. The objective of this project was to ensure the survival and maintenance of the tiger population in the country. There is a **'Satpura Tiger Reserve'** in the Satpura National park which is a part of Project Tiger.

Tiger is one of the many species which are slowly disappearing from our forests. But, the Satpura Tiger Reserve is unique in the sense that a significant increase in the population of tigers has been seen here. Once upon a time, animals like barasingha, wild buffaloes, lions and elephant were also found in the Satpura National Park. All these animals have now vanished from this area due to illegal activities of people living in nearby areas.

Endangered Animals and Extinct Animals

The species which no longer exist anywhere on the Earth are called **extinct animals**. These have died out completely. A species becomes extinct when the last living member of that species dies, e.g. dinosaurs.

Animals whose numbers are diminishing to a level that they might face extinction in near by future are called **endangered animals**. These are on the verge of vanishing from the Earth and if appropriate actions to save them are not taken, they may become extinct.

The small animals are much more in danger of becoming extinct than the bigger animals. At times, we kill snakes, frogs, lizards, bats and owls ruthlessly without realising their importance in the ecosystem. They might be small in size, but their role in the ecosystem cannot be ignored.

Hence, we are indirectly harming ourselves by killing them. These small animals forms parts of food chains and food webs which are essential for maintaining balance in nature. For instance, when snake is killed for its skin. It disrupts the food chain by leading to an increase in the population of pests such as mice, which in turn can cause damage to crops.

Note An ecosystem is made up of all the plants, animals and microorganisms in an area along with non-living components such as climate, soil, river, deltas, etc.

Try These 5.3

1. **How do wildlife sanctuaries in India ensure suitable living conditions for wild animals?**
2. **Where is the first reserve forest in India located?**
3. **Name one species besides the tiger that was once present in Satpura National Park.**
4. **What term applies to species that have vanished from the Earth, signalling their complete disappearance?**

5.6 Red Data Book

A Red Data Book contains list of species whose continued existence is threatened, i.e. endangered animals and plants.

Red Data Book is maintained internationally by an organisation, known as International Union for Conservation of Nature (IUCN). India also maintain Red Data Book for plants and animals found in India.

5.7 Migration

The phenomenon of the movement of animal (or bird) to move from one place to another on the basis of season is called migration.

It is an adaptation to escape the harsh and cold conditions of their normal habitat, so as to survive and reproduce. Birds who cover long distances to reach another land are known as **migratory birds.**

Migratory birds fly to far away areas every year during a particular time because of climate changes. They fly for laying eggs as the weather in their natural habitat becomes very cold and inhospitable. For example, Siberian cranes, flamingoes, etc. that flock to India during the winter.

5.8 Recycling of Paper

Paper is made from wood pulp that is produced from the wood of forest trees. Therefore, it is one of the important products we get from the forests and thus, a major cause of deforestation. It is estimated that 17 full grown trees are needed to make **one tonn of paper.** So, we should save paper as much possible.

We can save paper by completely filling every sheet of paper, by reusing and recycling paper (as paper can be recycled 5 to 7 times for use). 'Recycling of paper' means to process the waste paper, to make new paper that can be used again.

We should save, reuse and recycle paper for the following reasons

(i) To save forest trees from being cut.
(ii) To save water used in paper making.
(iii) To save energy (electricity) used in making paper.
(iv) To reduce the amount of harmful chemicals used in paper making.

5.9 Reforestation

Reforestation is known as the phenomenon of restocking of the destroyed forests by planting new trees (generally of the same species which were cut). We should at least plant as many trees as have been cut down.

Reforestation can take place naturally also. If the deforested area is left undisturbed, it re-establishes itself. In natural reforestation, there is no role of human beings.

If we have to retain our green wealth, i.e. forests for future generations, plantation of more trees is the only option.

In India the Government has enacted the **Forest Conservation Act (1980)** to save forests. It aims at preservation and conservation of natural forests, while meeting the basic needs of the people living in or near the forests at the same time.

SCIENCE INSIGHT Chipko Andolan was a 1970 environmental movement in India where people hugged trees to prevent deforestation highlighting the need for environmental conservation.

Try These 5.4

1. **Which factors influence the timmings and purpose of migratory bird's annual journey?**
2. **Is there any connection between paper production and deforestation? Justify.**
3. **State the crucial role played by human beings in natural reforestation.**

Science Glossary

Biodiversity Diversity of plants, animals and microorganisms in a particular area.

Biosphere reserve Large protected area where plants and animals are protected along with natural resources.

Deforestation Large scale removal of trees from forests.

Desertification Conversion of fertile land to desert due to deforestation.

Ecosystem It constitutes of living and non- living components.

Endangered species Species which are threatened and can become extinct if not conserved or protected.

Endemic species Species of plants and animals which are found exclusively in a particular area.

Extinct Species which no longer exist any where on the Earth.

Flora Plants present in an area.

Fauna Animals living in an area.

Migratory birds Birds who cover long distances to reach another land.

National park Areas reserved for wildlife where they can freely use the habitats and natural resources.

Reforestation Restocking of destroyed forests by planting new trees.

Red Data Book Official record of all endangered plants and animals.

Sanctuary Protected area for animals in their natural environment.

CONSERVATION OF PLANTS AND ANIMALS

Endangered Animals

- Animals whose numbers are diminishing to a level that they might face extinction in near by future.
- These are on the verge of vanishing from the Earth.

Extinct Animals

Species which no longer exist anywhere on the Earth, e.g. dinosaurs.

Flora and Fauna

Animals and plants typically belong to a particular area.

Endemic Species

Species found exclusively in a particular area, e.g. Sal and as flora wild mango tree and bison and Indian giant squirrel as Pachmarhi Biosphere Reserve.

Red Data Book

Sources or contains list of species whose continued existence is threatened.

Recycling of Paper

- Process the waste paper to make new paper that can be used again.
- 17 full grown trees are needed to make one tonn of paper.

Deforestation

Clearing forests by cutting or burning them.

Causes

- Natural causes
- Procuring land for cultivation.
- Building houses and factories.
- Making various products.

Consequences

- Global warming.
- Disturbance in water cycle.
- Soil erosion and desertification.
- Floods.
- Shortage of wood and other forest products.

Reforestation

- Restocking of the destroyed forests by planting new tree.
- Forest conservation Act entacted in 1980 to save forest.

Migration

Movement of organism from their natural habitat to a hospitable place due to a climate change.

Conservation of Wildlife

National Parks

- An area reserved for wildlife where they can freely use the habitats and natural resources.
- Provide human recreation and enjoyment.
- People are allowed to enter these areas.
- Exploitation of natural resources is strictly prohibited.

Biosphere Reserve

- A large protected area of land meant for the conservation of wildlife, biodiversity and the traditional lifestyle.
- A biosphere reserve may also contain other protected areas in it
- The Pachmarhi biosphere reserve consists of one National park named Satpura and two wildlife sanctuaries.

Wildlife Sanctuary

- A protected area for animals in their natural environment like forests.
- No disturbance to animals and their habitat.
- Killing (poaching) and capturing of wild animals is strictly prohibited.
- Provides protection and suitable living conditions to wild animals.

Zoo

- The wild animals and birds live in artificial setting such as cages and enclosures.
- Provide protection to wild animals.
- A zoo is open to public for a fixed time everyday.

NCERT FOLDER

Complete Explanations of all NCERT's Questions

Intext Questions

Q.1 Paheli is curious to know the purpose of making National parks, Wildlife sanctuaries and Biosphere reserves. **Page 53**

Ans. National parks, Wildlife sanctuaries and Biosphere reserves are made to protect the flora and fauna whose numbers are diminishing.

Q.2 Boojho is curious to know how deforestation reduces rainfall on one hand and lead to floods on the other **Page 53**

Ans. Refer to text on page no. 75.

Q.3 Animal life is also affected by deforestation. How? **Page 54**

Ans. The natural habitats of the wild animals get destroyed due to deforestation and they tend to move to other habitats or left to die without proper shelter.

Q.4 List the factors disturbing the biodiversity of your area. Some of these factors and human activities may disturb the biodiversity unknowingly. List these human activities. How can these be checked? **Page 56**

Ans. There are various factors which can disturb the biodiversity of an area, such as volcanic eruptions earthquakes, thunderstorm, etc. Some human activities such as deforestation pollution, poaching, etc. also destroy biodiversity of an area. These human activities can be checked by educating people or applying strict laws.

Q.5 Paheli has heard that some of the endemic species may vanish. Is it true? **Page 57**

Ans. Yes, endemic species may vanish due to destruction of their habitat, increasing population and introduction of new species.

Q.6 Boojho wants to know the difference between zoo and a wildlife sanctuary? **Page 58**

Ans. Refer to text on page no. 76.

Q.7 Boojho wants to know whether tigers are still found in the forest? He is excited to see a tiger. **Page 59**

Ans. Tiger is one of the many species which are slowly disappearing from forests. But Satpura tiger reserve is unique in the sense that a significant increase in the population of tiger has been seen here.

Q.8 Paheli wants to know whether only big animals are facing the danger of extinction? **Page 59**

Ans. No, the small animals are much more in danger of becoming extinct than the bigger animals. This is because the small animals like snakes, frogs, etc. get killed ruthlessly without realising their importance in the ecosystem.

They might be small in size, but their role in the ecosystem cannot be ignored.

Q.9 Boojho wonder if there is a record of the endangered species. **Page 60**

Ans. Red Data Book is the source book which keeps a record of all endangered animals and plants.

Q.10 Paheli is curious to know what would happen if we had no wood? Is there any alternative available for wood? Boojho says that paper is one of the important products we get from forests. Boojho asks whether there are any alternatives available for paper. **Page 60**

Ans. Without wood, we would not have access to fuel and many other household necessities like paper, matchsticks, furniture, etc. The use of digital technology could replace paper.

Q.11 Boojho wants to know if there is any permanent solution for the problem of deforestation. **Page 60**

Ans. The permanent solution for the problem of deforestation is reforestation. It is restocking of the destroyed forests by planting new trees.

Exercise

Q.1 Fill in the blanks.

(a) A place where animals are protected in their natural habitat is called...... .

(b) Species found only in a particular area is known as ....

(c) Migratory birds fly to far away places because of .... changes.

Ans. (a) wildlife sanctuary

(b) endemic species

(c) climatic

Q.2 Differentiate between the following.

(a) **Wildlife sanctuary and Biosphere reserve**

(b) **Zoo and Wildlife sanctuary**

(c) **Endangered and Extinct species**

(d) **Flora and Fauna**

Ans. (a) Difference between wildlife sanctuary and biosphere reserve is as follows

Wildlife sanctuary	Biosphere reserve
It is a place where wild animals are protected in their natural environment. e.g. Wildlife sanctuary.	It is an area where biodiversities (both plants and animals) are conserved, e.g. Pachmarhi biosphere reserve.

(b) Differences between zoo and wildlife sanctuary are as follows

Zoo	Wildlife sanctuary
It is a place where animals are protected and displayed for public view.	It is a place where wild animals are protected in their natural environment.
It is an artificial habitat, e.g. Delhi National Zoological Park.	It conserves the natural habitat of animals, e.g. Pachmarhi.

(c) Difference between endangered species and extinct species is as follows

Endangered species	Extinct species
It is a population of species that is on the verge of becoming extinct, e.g. tiger.	It is a population of species that no longer exists. Hence, it is extinct, e.g. dinosaurs.

(d) Difference between flora and fauna is as follows

Flora	Fauna
It is the variety of plants in a particular area, e.g. sal, teak, mango, etc. form the flora of Pachmarhi biosphere reserve.	It is the variety of animals in a particular area, e.g. leopard, wolf, etc. form the fauna of Pachmarhi biosphere reserve.

Q.3 Discuss the effects of deforestation on the following.

(a) **Wild animals** (b) **Environment**

(c) **Villages (rural areas)** (d) **Cities (urban areas)**

(e) **Earth** (f) **The next generation**

Ans. (a) **Wild animals** Deforestation causes destruction of habitat of wild animals. This leads them to danger of extinction.

(b) **Environment** Deforestation increases the amount of CO_2 in the environment which results in increase in temperature. Due to this, the water cycle is disturbed which may lead to drought. It also reduces the water holding capacity of soil that leads to flood.

(c) **Villages** (rural areas) The lifestyle of villagers depend much on forests for wood, vegetables, fruits, meat, grass, etc. Deforestation leads their life to struggles for all of these. Also, their life becomes threatened by wild animals.

(d) **Cities** (urban areas) Deforestation causes drought, flooding and environmental pollution which affect the life of people living in cities.

(e) **Earth** The various cycles on Earth like water, oxygen, carbon dioxide are disturbed due to deforestation. It increases the temperature and pollution level on the Earth and is also the main cause of global warming.

(f) **The next generation** The major effect of deforestation on the next generation is the limitation of natural resources like wood, oxygen, water, etc.

Q.4 What will happen, if

(a) **we go on cutting trees.**

(b) **the habitat of an animal is disturbed.**

(c) **the top layer of soil is exposed.**

Ans. (a) If we go on cutting trees, then

(i) Many animals will loose their shelters.

(ii) There would be scarcity of materials like fruits, paper, which we get from forests.

(iii) Flood and drought will become more frequent.

(iv) Earth will loose its most fertile layer and transform into desert.

(b) The habitat of an animal provides it with necessities such as shelter, food and protection. If the habitat of an animal is disturbed, then it will be forced to go to other places in search of food and shelter. As a result, the animal could get killed.

(c) Removal of the top layer of the soil exposes the lower, hard and rocky layers. This soil has less humus and is less fertile. Gradually, the fertile land gets converted into deserts. It is called desertification.

Q.5 Answer in brief.

(a) Why should we conserve biodiversity?

(b) Protected forests are also not completely safe for wild animals. Why?

(c) Some tribals depend on the jungle. How?

(d) What are the causes and consequences of deforestation?

(e) What is Red Data Book?

(f) What do you understand by the term migration?

Ans. (a) We should conserve biodiversity because each and every organism in nature plays an important role in balancing of natural system.

(b) Protected forests are not completely safe for wildlife because some local people kill animals on large scale for their valuable skin, teeth, etc.

(c) Some tribals depend on the jungle because they get most of their resource to live from the jungle like shelter, wood, food, etc.

(d) The main causes of deforestation are the cutting of trees for wood and use of lands for industries and houses. Its consequences are flooding, drought, extinction of species and many more harmful activities.

(e) Red Data Book is a source book that maintains an international list of all endangered animals and plant species.

(f) Migration refers to the movement of an organism or a group of organisms from its natural habitat to another place at a particular time because of climatic change. Birds who cover long distances to reach another land are known as migratory birds.

Q.6 In order to meet the ever-increasing demand in factories and for shelter, trees are being continually cut. Is it justified to cut trees for such projects? Discuss and prepare a brief report.

Ans. The continuous cutting of trees is not justified for any project because it leads to deforestation, desertification, flooding, danger to the lives of wild animals. It also disturbs the balance of nature.

Q.7 How can you contribute to the maintenance of green wealth of your locality? Make a list of actions to be taken by you.

Ans. We can contribute to the maintenance of green wealth of our locality by taking these actions.

(i) Taking care of the plants and trees growing in or around the locality.

(ii) Encourage people to plant more trees by informing them about the importance of growing trees.

Q.8 Explain how deforestation leads to reduced rainfall?

Ans. Refer to text on page no. 74.

Q.9 Find out about National parks in your state. Identify and show their location on the outline map of India.

Ans. One of the National parks located near Delhi is the Jim Corbett National Park in Uttarakhand.

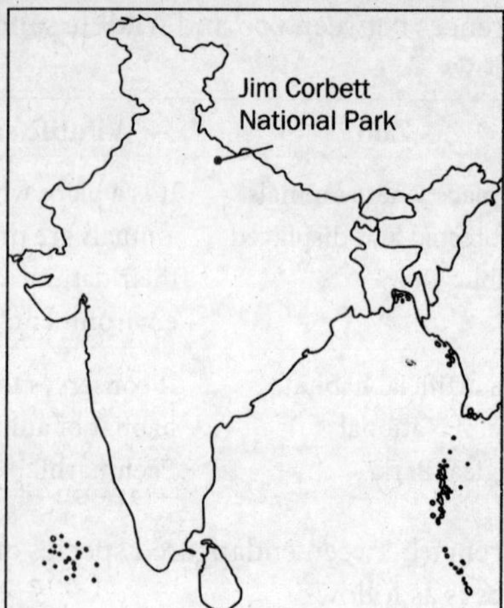

Q.10 Why should paper be saved? Prepare a list of ways by which you can save paper.

Ans. Paper should be saved because it takes our important natural resource, i.e. trees to make it (around 17 full grown trees to make one tonne of paper). Trees as we know, are important to maintain a balance in nature.

Therefore, in order to save trees and prevent the impact of their loss in the living world, we need to save paper. We can save paper by following ways

(i) Paper should be recycled.

(ii) Use both side of a paper for writing purpose.

(iii) Spread awareness regarding the value of saving paper.

REVIEW EXERCISE

Including Competency Based Questions

Part I

Multiple Choice Questions

1. There is a list of some events.

1. Tilting of soil for sowing seeds on a deserted land.
2. Cutting of trees for making table and chairs.
3. Establishing forest on a land that had trees before.
4. Clearing forest for building houses.

Deforestation will be caused by which of the following events?

(a) 1 and 2 (b) 3 and 1 (c) 2 and 4 (d) 2 and 3

2. How is a decline in trees connected to a water shortage?

(a) Deforestation increase Earth's temperature resulting in less rainfall
(b) Deforestation decrease Earth's temperature which reduces the moisture content of air
(c) Deforestation disturbs the soil composition leading to high water retention by the soil
(d) Deforestation prevents the absorption of water by the plants reducing groundwater level

3. Deforestation increases the level of one of the following in the atmosphere.

(a) Ozone (b) Carbon dioxide
(c) Oxygen (d) Water vapour

4. In our country, large patches of forests are being cleared for cultivation of crops. The environmental impact of such a practice will lead to NCERT Exemplar

(a) soil erosion (b) soil pollution
(c) soil conservation (d) soil fertility

5. The amount of soil erosion is lower in areas with more trees. How do trees stop the Earth from eroding?

(a) The roots of the trees hold the top layer of the soil firmly
(b) The trees absorb more Sun rays which increases soil density
(c) The trees store extra food in the soil which increases the soil content
(d) The trees add dead leaves into the soil which increases the soil quantity

6. Which one of the following changes may occur due to desertification? NCERT Exemplar

(a) Decrease in atmospheric temperature
(b) Increase in water holding capacity of soil
(c) Increased chances of floods
(d) Conversion of fertile land into a desert

7. Cutting down trees and clearing forests are common construction method for industries. What is its potential impact on nature?

(a) Decrease in the number of wildlife
(b) Sudden boost in the plant growth
(c) Availability of more food for wildlife
(d) Increase in the percentage of land occupied with trees

8. Which one of the following statements is true about a biosphere reserve? NCERT Exemplar

(a) It is a protected area where only endemic species live
(b) It is meant only for the conservation of plants and animals
(c) It is meant to conserve both, the biodiversity and the culture of that area
(d) There are no other protected areas within its limits

9. Radha went for a trip to a Pachmarhi Biosphere Reserve in Madhya Pradesh and Jim Corbett National Park in Uttarakhand. Which common activity is likely to be observed in both the protective areas? Competency Based Que.

(a) Both provide protective environment to fauna only
(b) Both provide shelter to humans as well as wildlife
(c) Both allow human activities for interaction with wild animals
(d) Both do not interferes with the natural environment of the wildlife

10. The place of living of an organism in environment is called

(a) home (b) resort
(c) habitat (d) reservoir

11. What do black buck, elephant, python and golden cat together represent in a forest?

(a) Fauna (b) Ecosystem
(c) Flora (d) Species

12. **There is a list of some organisms.**

1. Star fish	2. Cheetah
3. Fern	4. Shrub
5. Cactus	6. Wolf

Which choice properly categorises the flora and fauna?

(a)	**Flora**	Star fish, cheetah, fern
	Fauna	Shrub, cactus, wolf
(b)	**Flora**	Shrub, cactus, fern
	Fauna	Star fish, cheetah, wolf
(c)	**Flora**	Star fish, wolf, fern
	Fauna	Shrub, cactus, cheetah
(d)	**Flora**	Star fish, cheetah, wolf
	Fauna	Shrub, cactus, fern

13. **Which one of the following statements is true about endemic species?** **NCERT Exemplar**

(a) They are found exclusively in a specific habitat
(b) Endemic species can never become endangered
(c) They are found only in zoos and botanical gardens
(d) They are not affected by the destruction of their habitat

14. **Satpura National Park and Bori sanctuary are present in the Pachmarhi Biosphere Reserve. How does these regions contribute to the protection of wildlife and plants?**

(a) These large areas provide artifical habitat to wildlife
(b) These large areas conserve organisms and their habitats
(c) These large areas control the number of wildlife by preventing natural breeding
(d) These large areas prevent the interaction of organisms with wildlife to keep them safe

15. **A tiger reserve is a forest area where the tiger population is protected. Why did Indian government declare parts of many forests as tiger reserves?**

(a) Tiger is a mammal
(b) Tiger is our national animal
(c) Tiger is an endangered species
(d) Tiger is the top predator of forest ecosystem

16. **Which statement is incorrect about endangered species?** **NCERT Exemplar**

(a) Their number has decreased drastically
(b) They might become extinct in the near future
(c) They pose danger to other animals
(d) Their natural habitat needs to be protected

17. **Wild buffalo is an endangered species because**

(a) its population is diminishing
(b) it has become extinct
(c) it is found exclusively in a particular area
(d) its poaching is strictly prohibited

18. **Snakes are killed in large numbers because**

(a) they are very poisonous (b) they kill rats
(c) their skin is expensive (d) they damage the crops

19. **The Red Data Book keeps a record of all the**

(i) endemic species
(ii) extinct species
(iii) endangered plants
(iv) endangered animals **NCERT Exemplar**

(a) (i) and (ii) (b) (ii) and (iii)
(c) (iii) and (iv) (d) (i) and (iv)

20. **The migratory birds come to India every year in winter for a few months.**

(a) To escape the severe summer
(b) To escape the severe winter
(c) To escape the heavy rains
(d) To escape from predators

21. **Why should we recycle paper?** **Competency Based Que.**

(a) Paper is biodegradable
(b) Recycled paper is stronger
(c) Production of paper requires lot of wood pulp
(d) Recycling of paper produces useful by products

22. **What kind of approach should one take to lessen deforestation?**

(a) Limiting the use of paper
(b) Using only fine quality paper for work
(c) Throwing old newspapers in dustbins
(d) Bury used and waste paper instead of burning it

23. **Planting new trees is called**

(a) species (b) deforestation
(c) desertification (d) reforestation

24. **What is expected to be accomplished by planting trees in the forest?**

(a) Conservation of forest and animals
(b) Increase in the number of extinct species
(c) Decrease in the number of predator species
(d) Availability of more information for Red Data Book

Answers

1. (c)	2. (a)	3. (b)	4. (a)	5. (a)
6. (d)	7. (a)	8. (c)	9. (d)	10. (c)
11. (a)	12. (b)	13. (a)	14. (b)	15. (c)
16. (c)	17. (a)	18. (c)	19. (c)	20. (b)
21. (c)	22. (a)	23. (d)	24. (a)	

Fill in the Blanks

1. ...... traps the heat of Sun rays.
2. Conversion of fertile land into desert is called ......
3. Pachmarhi is an example of ....
4. Plants found in a particular area are termed as ....
5. Group of populations which are capable of interbreeding are called. ....

Answers

1. Carbon dioxide 2. desertification
3. biosphere reserve 4. flora 5. species

True/False

1. Deforestation leads to an increase in the water holding capacity of the soil.
2. There can be a wildlife sanctuary within a biosphere reserve.
3. Pachmarhi biosphere reserve consists of one National park and two wildlife sanctuaries.
4. Plants of a particular area are collectively termed as fauna. **NCERT Exemplar**
5. Bison is an endemic fauna of Pachmarhi biosphere reserve. **NCERT Exemplar**

Answers

1. False, because deforestation leads to decrease in water holding capacity of soil which causes floods.
2. True 3.True
4. False, because fauna is a collective term used for the animals of a particular area.
5. True

Match the Columns

1. Match Column I with Column II.

	Column I		Column II
A.	Satpura	1.	Protect animals
B.	Deforestation	2.	Killing of animals
C.	Global warming	3.	Cutting of trees
D.	Poaching	4.	National park
E.	Zoo	5.	Increasing carbon dioxide

Answer

A–4, B–3, C–5, D–2, E–1

Assertion-Reason Questions

The following question consist of two statements Assertion (A) and Reason (R). Answer these questions by selecting the appropriate options given below.

(a) Both A and R are true and R is the correct explanation of A
(b) Both A and R are true, but R is not the correct explanation of A
(c) A is true, but R is false
(d) A is false, but R is true

1. **Assertion (A)** Deforestation leads to drought.
   Reason (R) The consequent increase in temperature on the Earth disturbs the water cycle. This leads to decrease in rainfall.
2. **Assertion (A)** Conserving biodiversity is a necessity.
   Reason (R) Biodiversity is a part of the web of life and its loss can have effect on other species and ecosystem.
3. **Assertion (A)** Bison is an example of endemic fauna.
   Reason (R) Endemic species are those species which no longer exists any where on the Earth.
4. **Assertion (A)** Members of a species have common characteristics.
   Reason (R) Species is a group of population, which are not capable of interbreeding.
5. **Assertion (A)** Project tiger was launched by the government of United States.
   Reason (R) It was launched to ensure the survival and maintenance of the tiger population in the country.

Answers

1. (a) Both A and R are true and R is the correct explanation of A.
2. (a) Both A and R are true and R is the correct explanation of A.
3. (c) A is true, but R is false. R can be corrected as
   The endemic species are those species of plants and animals, which are found exclusively in a particular area. For example, bison is an endemic fauna of Pachmarhi biosphere reserve.
4. (c) A is true, but R is false. R can be corrected as
   Species is a group of population which are capable of interbreeding.
5. (d) A is false, but R is true. R can be corrected as
   'Project Tiger' was launched by the government of India.

Case Based Questions

1. Which of these are the effects of deforestation? Circle 'Yes' or 'No' for the correct response.

Is this an effect of deforestation?	Yes or No
Decrease in the fertility of soil	Yes/No
Decrease in the occurrence of floods	Yes/No
Increase in the occurrence of droughts	Yes/No

Competency Based Que.

2. The Gangetic Dolphin is a freshwater aquatic mammal.
Which of these measures will protect the Gangetic Dolphin species?
Circle 'Yes' or 'No' for the correct response.

Will this measure protect the Gangetic Dolphin?	Yes or No
Setting up industries near the riverbanks	Yes/No
Transporting the dolphins to seas and oceans	Yes/No
Making protected areas in certain stretches of the river	Yes/No

Competency Based Que.

Answers

1. Yes, No, Yes
2. No, No, Yes

Part II

1. Arrange the following in order to show how deforestation leads to water pollution?

I. The roots of the trees no longer have a firm grip on the soil.
II. Rainfalls onto the ground.
III. The trees of a forest are cut down.
IV. The loose soil gets washed away into a nearby body of water.

Ans. III $\rightarrow$ I $\rightarrow$ II $\rightarrow$ IV

2. A gas is utilised by the trees and plants in photosynthesis. The same gas also traps the heat rays reflected by the Earth and is also given out by humans during respiration. Name the gas and the phenomenon of increase in temperature for which it is responsible. Competency Based Que.

Ans. The gas is carbon dioxide and the phenomenon is global warming.

3. Why is it important to conserve forests?

Ans. Forest conservation maintains the balance in nature. It acts as carbon sinks absorbing CO_2 and keeps global warming at bay.

4. Mention any one action that you have undertaken to conserve trees. NCERT Exemplar

Ans. I have planted some trees and look after them carefully so that they are well protected. This is the action, I have taken to conserve trees.

5. 'Variety of all forms of life found in a region' is known by a specific name, what is it?

Ans. Biodiversity.

6. Name the protected area, built to support the biodiversity.

Ans. Biosphere reserve supports the biodiversity.

7. Out of the three–a biosphere reserve, a National park or a wildlife sanctuary, which is the largest?

Ans. Biosphere reserve is the largest of the three and it may contain a National park or a wildlife sanctuary.

8. Endemic fauna is restricted to a particular area. Name few in India.

Ans. Bison and flying squirrel are endemic fauna of Pachmarhi Biosphere Reserve in India.

9. What is the unique feature of the biodiversity found in Pachmarhi Biosphere Reserve?

Ans. The biodiversity found in Pachmarhi Biosphere Reserve is similar to those of the upper Himalayan peaks and to those belonging to the lower Western Ghats.

10. How are even small animals important in an ecosystem? NCERT Exemplar

Ans. Small animals might be small in size, but their role in the ecosystem cannot be ignored. They are important in an ecosystem as they form part of food chains and food webs.

11. A group of cats are found in a forest that interbreed freely. What is the term used for them?

Ans. A species is a group of same kind of organisms which can interbreed to produce fertile offspring.

12. Name the plant found in Satpura forests.

Ans. The finest Indian teak is found in the Satpura forests.

13. Name the first reserve forest of India. NCERT Exemplar

Ans. Satpura National park is the first reserve forest of India.

14. Mention the aim of Forest (Conservation) Act.

Ans. The aim of Forest (Conservation) Act is preservation and conservation of natural forests and meeting the basic needs of the people living in or near the forests.

15. Can a forest regenerate naturally in a short period of time? NCERT Exemplar

Ans. Reforestation can take place naturally by leaving the deforested area undisturbed for a long period of time. During this period, the area re-establishes itself without the interference of human beings.

Short Answer Type Questions

1. We have often read in the newspaper about careful use of natural resources. What is the term used for it? Mention some of the Earth's natural resources that need to be used carefully.

Ans. 'Conservation' is a term used to described the prudent (careful and sensible) use of natural resources.

The Earth's natural resources that needs to be conserved are air, water, soil, minerals, fuels, plants and animals.

2. Soil erosion and desertification are the consequences of deforestation. Justify.

Ans. Deforestation causes soil erosion, i.e. removal of top layer of soil. It also changes the physical properties of soil. Thus, exposing the lower, hard and rocky layers of soil that has less humus and is less fertile. Gradually, the fertile land gets converted into deserts. This is called desertification.

3. A new species *X* is introduced in a forest. How is it likely to affect the local species of that area? Competency Based Que.

Ans. The new species is likely to affect the local species as it poses threats in following manner

(i) Preying on native species.

(ii) Out competing for food or other resources.

(iii) Causing or carrying disease.

(iv) Preventing native species from reproducing.

(v) Changing food webs.

4. Sometimes, animals enter human habitation, killing people and causing damage to materials. Why do the animals behave like this?

Ans. Animals behaviour can be understood from the explanation given below

As human populations expand into wild animal habitats, their territory is displaced. Reduction in the availability of food sources, forces the animal to seek alternate sources. Thus, drawing them towards human habitation.

5. Roshni attended a seminar on forest and Wildlife conservation. She on returning home, discussed it with her brother. Give some measures, she would have mentioned to conserve forests and wildlife.

Ans. Forests and wildlife can be conserved by following

(i) **Protection by law** It is very necessary to have strict laws and their enforcement for the protection and preservation of wildlife, e.g. hunting regulation.

(ii) **Reforestation** It is the act of planting more trees to replace the ones that are cut.

(iii) **Habitat preservation** In this method, protected areas such as Wildlife sanctuaries, National parks, Biosphere reserve, etc. are established. These areas are large enough to protect the diverse and whole set of ecosystems.

6. Why are endemic organisms in greater danger of becoming extinct? NCERT Exemplar

Ans. Endemic organisms are confined to a limited geographical area. They cannot adapt to or live outside their natural habitat; any disturbance to their habitat will adversely affect them. Thus, they are in greater danger of becoming extinct.

7. Why are wildlife sanctuaries important for conservation of plants and animals? NCERT Exemplar

Ans. In a wildlife sanctuary, killing and capturing wild animals are strictly prohibited. It does not allow any human activity which disturbs the wild animals or their habitat. So, in these areas, animals live in a natural environment, protected from people. This is why sanctuaries are important.

8. Describe briefly about national parks.

Ans. Refer to text on page no. 76.

9. Recycling and saving of papers are related to deforestation. Justify.

Ans. Trees are used in making papers. About 17 fully grown trees are used to make one tonne of paper. So, wastage of paper is also a cause of deforestation.

Therefore, we should recycle and save the papers. If we save papers, we can save many trees in a year. In this way, recycling and saving of papers are directly related to deforestation.

Long Answer Type Questions

1. Deforestation has adverse effects on plants, animals as will as humans. List some causes of deforestation.

Ans. Refer to text on page no. 74.

2. Is deforestation associated with global warming? Explain. NCERT Exemplar

Ans. Trees (and other plants) use carbon dioxide gas from the atmosphere for the process of food making called 'photosynthesis'. When a lot of trees are cut down during deforestation, then lesser number of trees will be left. The lesser number of trees will use up less carbon dioxide due to which the amount of carbon dioxide in the atmosphere will increase. In this way, deforestation increases the level of carbon dioxide in the atmosphere. Carbon dioxide gas traps the sun's heat rays reflected by the Earth (causing greenhouse effect). Trapping of heat rays by carbon dioxide increases the temperature of Earth's atmosphere.

This will lead to global warming. The gradual increase in the overall temperature of Earth's atmosphere due to greenhouse effect caused by the increased level of carbon dioxide in the atmosphere is called global warming.

3. How does deforestation leads to frequent floods and droughts? **NCERT Exemplar**

Ans. When the forest trees are cut down, then the number of trees decrease which results in less transpiration. Reduced transpiration causes decrease in the amount of water vapour in the atmosphere resulting in less rainfall.

When there is less rainfall in an area, then less water percolates into the ground. Due to this, the groundwater level also gets lowered. The shortage of surface water (in ponds, lakes, etc.) and groundwater due to persistent low rainfall in an area can lead to droughts.

Deforestation also leads to decrease in the water holding capacity of the soil. The movement of water from the soil surface into the ground is reduced.So, there are floods.

Case Based Questions

1. The table shows an example of the different types of threat for the Gangetic Dolphin.

Type of threat	Example of the threat
Habitat degradation	Construction of dams in rivers
Human-Dolphin conflict	Getting caught in fishing nets
Water pollution	Dumping of chemical wastes

Competency Based Que.

Surface runoffs containing pesticides also threaten the survival of the Gangetic Dolphin. Which type of threat in the table does this belong to? Explain your answer.

2. The table shows two groups of natural resources.

Wildlife sanctuary	National park
Protects certain specific species of animals	Protects all plants, animals, landscape and historical objects
Restricts killing and capturing of animals	Restricts all kinds of disturbances for animals, plants and historical objects
Visitors are allowed without permission	Visitors are allowed only after authorised permission
Found in all types of terrain	Found in all types of terrain

Competency Based Que.

(i) Radha visited a protected forest area where she can enter at her own will and can collect samples of herbs.

Which type of protected forest area did Radha visit? Explain your answer.

(ii) Which of these statements is supported by the table?

(a) Mining is allowed in National parks

(b) Zoo is an example of a wildlife sanctuary

(c) National parks are larger than wildlife sanctuaries

(d) Wildlife sanctuaries are always found in river basins

Answers

1. Surface runoffs containing pesticides is an example of water pollution. Pesticides are harmful chemicals that pollute water bodies and threaten the survival of the Gangetic Dolphin.

2. (i) Radha visited wildlife sanctuary as in wildlife sanctuary visitors are allowed without permission and can collect the plant samples.

   (ii) (c) National parks are larger than wildlife sanctuaries.

Skill Based Questions as per NEP 2020

1. Analyse a set of data on the population trends of species over a bison few years. What patterns can be identified from the graph below about the growth of bison? Also mention where the threatened species are protected. **Thinking skill**

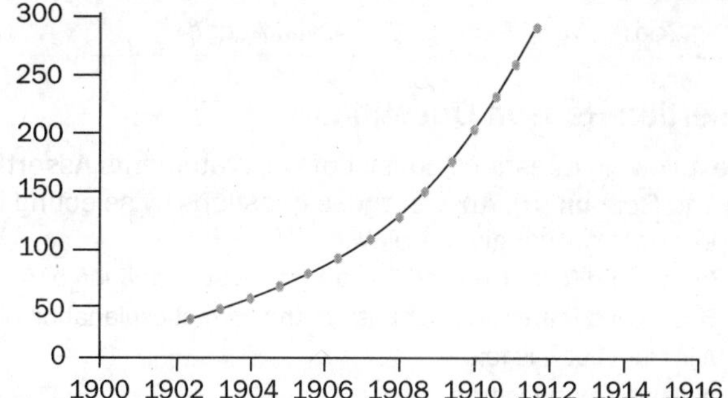

2. The biodiversity of Earth including plant and animal species are mandatory to maintain the balance and functioning of all ecosystems on Earth. Still people are destroying their habitats to fetch benefits out of it. What fundamental principles one should follow for the preservation of biodiversity. **Observation skill**

3. During an educational trip to a renowned forest, Amit saw a highway being constructed which passes through the middle of the forest. He was unhappy seeing that and contacted the wildlife department to stop the work.
   (i) If the highway is constructed, what would be the effect?
   (ii) Forests are useful to mankind. Comment.
   Research skill

4. Seeing a crowd of students in one corner of the school, the principal rushed to see the matter and found some children beating and chasing a small lizard. On seeing the principal, all children fled to their classes except Alok who requested the principal to arrange for some medical assistance for the injured animal. The principal rewarded him for his attitude.
   (i) Species of few animals are very less in number. What are these species known as?
   (ii) It is wrong to harm the animals. Give reason.
   (iii) Give example of some endemic species of India.
   Observation skill

5. Complete the word puzzle.

Down
1. Species on the verge of extinction.
2. A book carrying information about endangered species.
5. Consequence of deforestation.

Across
1. Species which have vanished.
3. Species found only in a particular habitat.
4. Variety of plants, animals and microorganisms found in an area

Thinking skill

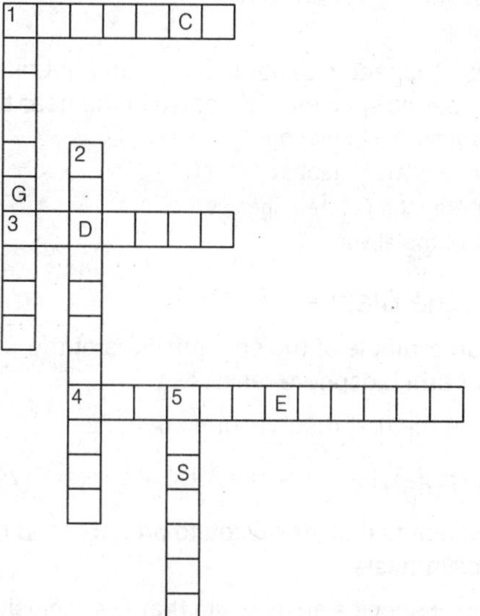

ASSESSMENT EXERCISE

Part I

Multiple Choice Questions

1. Which term is used for the species that are found only in a particular area?
(a) Extinct (b) Endemic
(c) Endangered (d) Threatened

2. Which of these books keeps a record of all the endangered animals and plants?
(a) Red Data Book
(b) Blue Data Book
(c) Black Data Book
(d) Green Data Book

3. Which of the following is not true regarding deforestation?
(a) Causes soil erosion
(b) Causes decrease in temperature
(c) Causes global warming
(d) Causes drought

4. Animals whose numbers are diminishing to level that they might face extinction is known as
(a) endemic
(b) endangered
(c) extinct
(d) fauna

5. Choose the factor/s that proves that if not taken care the endemic species may vanish in the near future.
(a) Increasing population
(b) Distruction of habitat
(c) Introduction of new species
(d) All of the abvoe

Fill in the Blanks

6. ... is an example of the endemic flora of the Pachmarhi Biosphere reserve.

7. .... is the first reserve forest of India.

True/False

8. Green plants utilises oxygen to prepare food through photosynthesis.

9. Endemic species are the one that are exclusively found in a particular area.

Match the Columns

10. Match Column I with Column II.

	Column I		Column II
A.	National park	1.	Tiger reserve
B.	Biosphere reserve	2.	An artificial environment
C.	Wildlife sanctuary	3.	Jim Corbett
D.	Zoo	4.	Lockchao

Assertion-Reason Questions

The following questions consist of two statements **Assertion** (A) and **Reason** (R). Answer these questions by selecting the appropriate option given below.
(a) Both A and R are true and R is the correct explanation of A.
(b) Both A and R are true, but R is not the correct explanation of A.
(c) A is true, but R is false.
(d) A is false, but R is true.

11. **Assertion** (A) Wildlife sanctuary, National park and Biosphere reserve are protected areas.

Reason (R) In these areas, plantation cultivation, grazing felling trees, hunting and poaching is prohibited.

12. **Assertion** (A) Rock shelters are found inside the Satpura National park.

Reason (R) A total 55 rock shelters have been identified in Pachmarhi Biosphere reserve.

Part II

Very Short Answer Type Questions

13. Mention a function of Wildlife sanctuary.

14. Write a statement to differentiate flora and fauna.

Short Answer Type Questions

15. Distinguish between deforestation and reforestation

16. Conservation of forests is necessary. Why?

Long Answer Type Question

17. Animals are protected in a zoo also. Is there any difference between a zoo and Wildlife sanctuary? Where do you think animals will be happier?

Answers

1. (b) **2.** (a) **3.** (b) **4.** (b) **5.** (d)
6. Sal
7. Satpura National Park
8. False
9. True
10. A–3, B–1, C–4, D–2
11. (a) **12.** (b)

CHAPTER 06

Reproduction in Animals

The process through which living beings produce new young ones of their own kind is called **reproduction**. It is essential for

(i) the continuation of similar kinds of individuals.

(ii) replacement of dead organisms.

(iii) transfer of variations from one generation to another.

6.1 Modes of Reproduction

Depending upon the number of parents involved in the process, the phenomenon of reproduction is divided into following two main types

(i) Sexual reproduction (ii) Asexual reproduction

6.2 Sexual Reproduction

In this type of reproduction, new individual is produced by the fusion of male and female gamete. During sexual reproduction, gametes from both parents fuse together to form a **zygote**, that develops into a new individual. It mainly occurs in multicellular organisms, For example, in humans, hen, dogs, fish, etc.

6.3 Sexual Reproduction in Humans

In human beings, reproduction involves mainly two sexes, i.e. male and female. Each sex has a different reproductive system with distinct organs performing different functions.

Male Reproductive Organs

In males, the reproductive organs include a pair of testes (singular : testis), two sperm ducts and a penis.

(i) **Testes** These are paired, oval-shaped structures located outside the abdominal cavity. These produce the male gametes called **sperms**.

Sperm (male gamete) It is tiny, motile single-celled structure with a head, a middle piece and a tail. The long tail helps it to move through the female tract. Millions of sperms are produced by the testes in single ejaculation.

(ii) **Sperm ducts** (vas deferens) These connect testes to the urethra.

(iii) **Penis** It is an external male genital organ that transfers sperms into the body of a female.

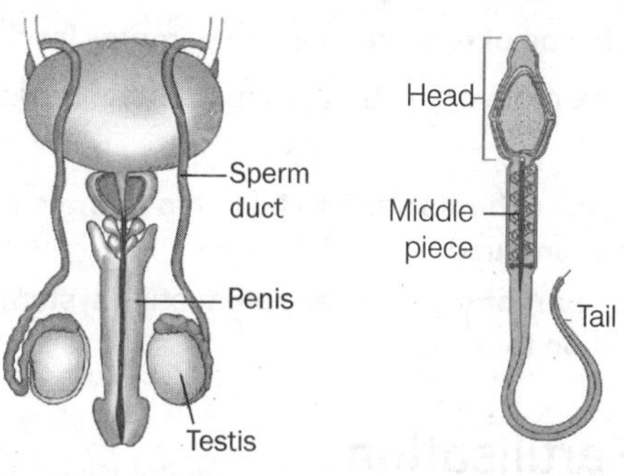

Male reproductive organs Human sperm

Female Reproductive Organs

In females, the reproductive organs include a pair of ovaries, oviducts and uterus.

(i) **Ovaries** These are paired, oval-shaped organs located in the lower part of abdominal cavity. It produces female gametes called **ova** (egg).

Ova/Egg (female gamete) It is a microscopic, round, single cell with nucleus, cytoplasm and a cell membrane.

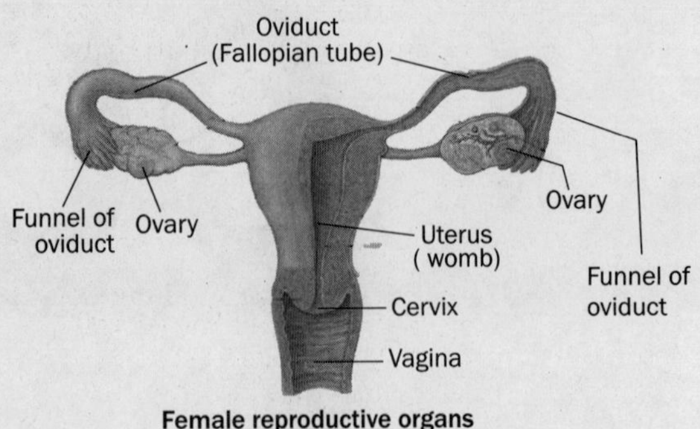

Female reproductive organs

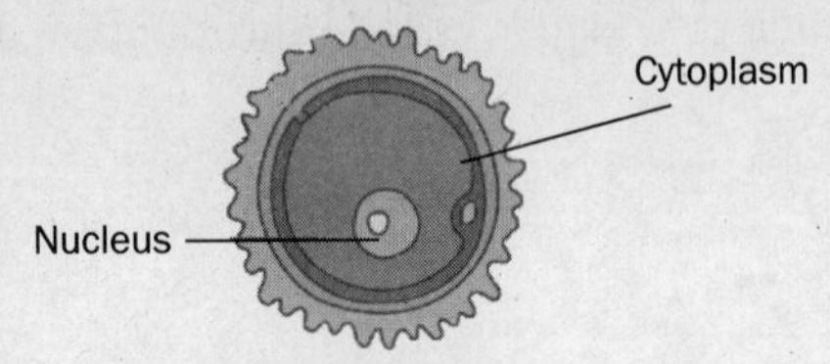

Female ovum

(ii) **Oviduct** (or Fallopian tube) It is a tube like structure with a funnel-shaped opening near the ovary. In human beings a single matured egg is released into the oviduct by one of the ovaries every month. It is also known as the site of fertilisation in human females.

(iii) **Uterus** (womb) It is a hollow, bag-like structure, where growth and development of foetus takes place.

Try These 6.1

1. **What process is essential for the continuation of similar kinds of individuals?**
2. **In which type of reproduction are gametes involved?**
3. **Name the male organ that produces male reproductive cell.**
4. **Which part of human sperm help it to swim to move into female reproductive tract?**
5. **In which part of the female reproductive system does fertilisation take place?**

6.4 Fertilisation

The process of fusion of the egg and the sperm is called **fertilisation**. It is the first step of sexual reproduction.

During fertilisation, when nuclei of the sperm comes in contact with an egg, it fuses to form a single nucleus. This results in the formation of a **fertilised egg** or **zygote**. The zygote marks the beginning of a new individual.

The process involves the meeting of an egg cell from the mother and a sperm cell from the father. So, the new individual inherits some characteristics from the mother and some from the father. You must have noticed that some of your siblings characters are similar to those of your mother and some to those of your father.

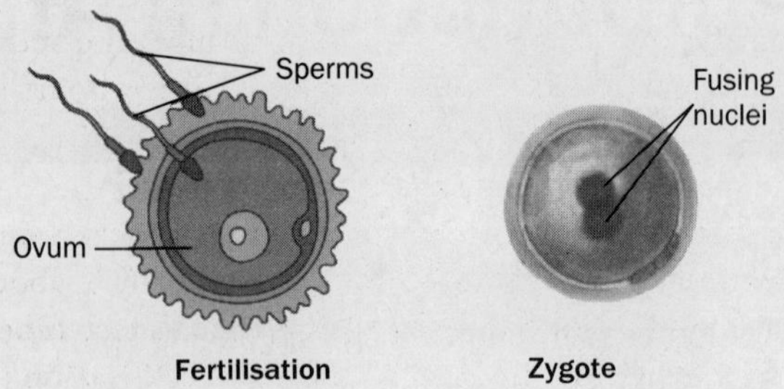

Fertilisation Zygote

There are various methods by which fertilisation takes place in different organisms. These are

1. External Fertilisation

Fertilisation that takes place outside the body of a female is called external fertilisation. For example, in aquatic animals such as fishes, starfish and frogs fertilisation takes place mainly in water.
They lay their eggs and sperms together on the surface of the water. The sperms fuse with the eggs in water to form zygote. The zygote develop into new individuals in the water itself. Animals living in or near ponds and lakes also undergo external fertilisation.

During spring (or rainy) season, frogs and toads move to the water in ponds and slow-flowing streams. When the male and female come together in water, the female lays hundreds of eggs. The eggs are delicate and do not have a shell, unlike the hen's eggs. A layer of jelly-like substance holds the eggs together and provides protection to them.

As the eggs are laid, the male ejects millions of sperms directly on them. Each sperm swims randomly in water with the help of its long tail. The sperms come in contact with the eggs floating in water. This results in fertilisation.

As the gametes are released in water, many of them may be carried away by the movement of water, wind, etc. or may be eaten by other aquatic animals, so a large number is released to compensate for the loss.

2. Internal Fertilisation

Fertilisation that takes place inside the female body is called internal fertilisation. For example, in higher animals such as reptiles, birds and mammals, e.g. humans, cows, dogs and hens.

> ***In Vitro* Fertilisaiton**
>
> Some women are unable to have babies because their oviducts are blocked and sperms cannot reach the egg for fertilisation. This prevents the ova from being fertilised. This problem can be overcome through **test-tube baby technology** or ***In vitro* fertilisation.**
>
> In this technique, freshly matured ova are collected from a woman's ovaries (by using a special syringe) and sperm from the man. They are kept together for few hours in an incubator (*in vitro*).
>
> The sperms fertilise the ova to form a zygote. After a week, the embryo thus formed is then inserted into the woman's womb where the embryo develops into a baby in about nine months. The baby thus born is called a **test-tube baby**. This technique is called ***In Vitro* Fertilisation (IVF)** (Fertilisation outside the body). The success rate is only about 30-40%.
>
> This term is misleading because babies cannot grow in test tubes.

Development of Embryo in Humans

Development of embryo in human beings takes place through following steps

(i) In human beings, soon after fertilisation, the zygote travels down the oviduct and divides repeatedly to form a ball of cells by cell division.

(ii) The cells then begin to form groups that finally develop into different tissues and organs of the body. This developing structure is called the **embryo**. It gets embedded in the wall of the **uterus** for further development.

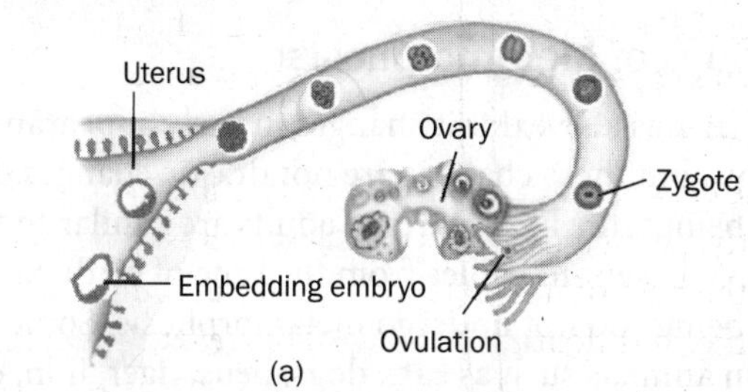

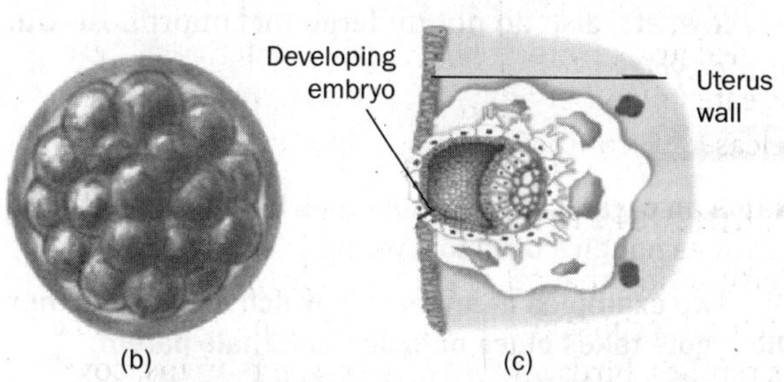

(a) Zygote formation and development of an embryo from the zygote (b) Ball of cells (enlarged) (c) Embedding of the embryo in the uterus (enlarged)

(iii) The embryo continues to develop in the uterus and gradually develops different body parts such as head, hands, legs, eyes, ears, etc.

(iv) The stage of the embryo in which all body parts can be recognised is called a **foetus**. When the development of the foetus is complete, the mother gives birth to the baby.

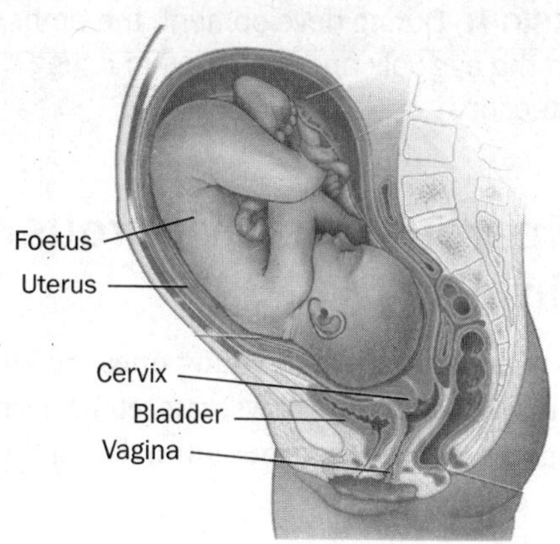

Foetus in uterus

Try These 6.2

1. **Name few animals in which fertilisation takes place inside the female body.**
2. **Can fertilisation occur in females with blocked Fallopian tubes?**
3. **How are the eggs of a female frog protected in water?**
4. **Where does the foetus grow?**

Development of Embryo in Hen

Hen is a bird that also undergoes internal fertilisation as humans. But it does not give birth to a young one. You will be wondering how chicks are born. Let's discuss in the section given below

(i) Soon after fertilisation (inside the female hen), the zygote divides repeatedly and travels down the oviduct.

(ii) Many protective layers are formed around it as it makes its way down. The hard shell that we see in a hen's egg is one such protective layer (outermost).

(iii) After the hard shell is formed around the developing embryo, the hen finally lays the egg.

(iv) The hen then sits on the eggs to provide sufficient warmth for the development of eggs. The embryo takes about 3 weeks to develop into a complete chick. The development of the chick takes place inside the egg shell during this period.

(v) After the chick is completely developed, it bursts, open the egg shell and comes out of it.

Development of Embryo in other Animals

In animals (such as frogs, fish, etc.) which undergo external fertilisation, development of the embryo takes place outside the female body. The embryos continue to grow within their egg coverings. After the embryos develop, the eggs hatch and the young ones come out.

SCIENCE INSIGHT During development, the embryo gets its food from the egg yolk and the albumin in egg helps in protection.

6.5 Viviparous and Oviparous Animals

The animals which give birth to young ones are known as viviparous animals, e.g. dogs, cows, cats, etc. The animals which lay eggs are called oviparous animals, e.g. birds, fishes, etc.

Differences between viviparous and oviparous animals

Viviparous animals	Oviparous animals
Animals that give birth to their young ones directly.	Animals that reproduce by laying eggs.
Development of zygote takes place inside the body of female parent.	Development of zygote takes place outside the female parent.
e.g. mammals, including humans.	e.g. birds, fishes, crocodiles, snakes and lizards.

6.6 Young Ones to Adults

The new individuals which are born or hatched from the eggs continue to grow till they become adults.

In some animals such as amphibians (e.g. frog) and certain insects (e.g. silkworm), the young one may look very different from the adults.

This process of change by which a larva is transformed into an adult is called **metamorphosis.**

Life Cycle of Frog

A frog lays eggs in large numbers (spawning). The baby that hatches out of the frog's eggs is called **tadpole**. The tadpole undergoes several changes before it becomes an adult frog.

egg → tadpole → adult

A tadpole undergoes metamorphosis to become an adult frog. These adult frogs are capable of jumping and swimming.

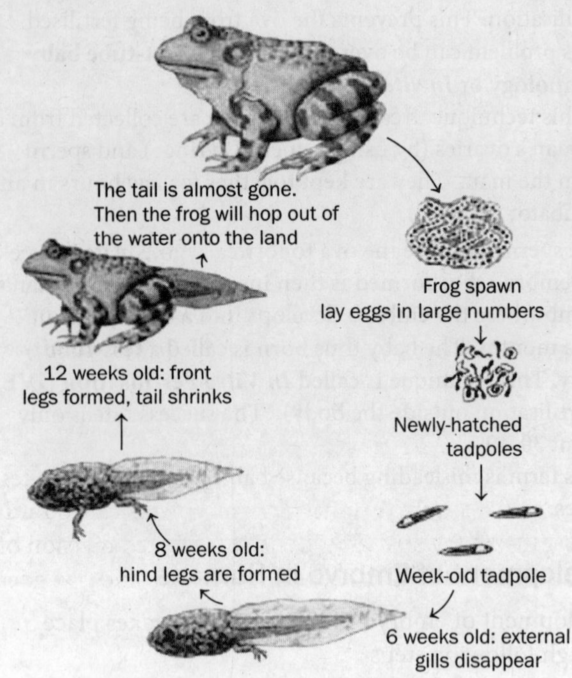

Life cycle of a frog

Differences between tadpole and frog

Tadpole	Frog
It has a long tail and fins to swim in water.	It has webbed feet to swim in water and hop on land.
It breathes through gills.	It has lungs for breathing.

Exceptions of Metamorphosis

Human beings also exhibit changes in body appearance as they grow, but these changes are not drastic changes. In human beings, the body parts in adults are similar to those which are present in babies from the time of birth. So, human beings do not undergo metamorphosis. Some common animals such as cats, dogs, hens, tiger, lion, deer, horse, cow, etc. also do not undergo metamorphosis during their life cycle.

Try These 6.3

1. **Name an organism that undergoes internal fertilisation but does not give birth to a young one.**
2. **Give two examples of animals in which the development of the zygote takes place outside the female parent.**
3. **Do all organisms given birth to young ones?**
4. **In some animals the young ones may look very different from the adults. Give examples of two such animals.**

6.7 Asexual Reproduction

In this method, a new organism is produced from a single parent without the fusion of gametes. The offsprings produced are identical to the parents. There are various modes of asexual reproduction. Some of them are discussed below

1. Budding

It is a type of asexual reproduction in which a bud(or a bulge) develops from the parent body. This bud enlarges and gets detached from the parent. It later develops into a similar/identical organism that can live independently, e.g. *Hydra*, yeast, etc.

Budding in *Hydra*

It is a multicellular animal that reproduces by budding. In this, one or more small, bulb-like outgrowths called **buds** are formed on the side of its body by repeated division of cell. The nucleus of the parent body divides and one goes into the bud.

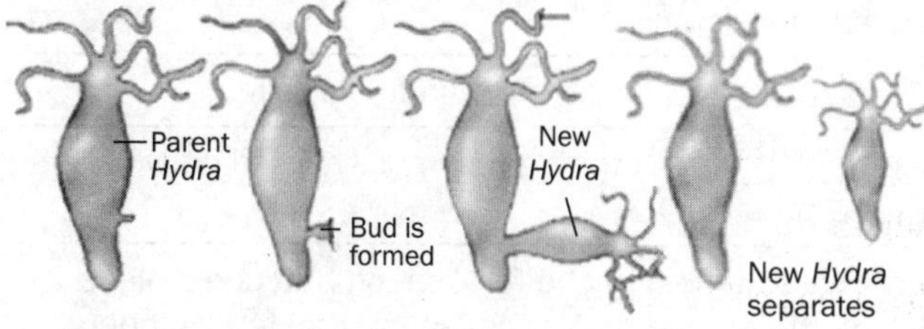

Budding in *Hydra*

The bud grows and finally gets detached from the parent body of *Hydra*. It begins to live as an independent individual.

2. Binary Fission

The process of reproduction in which a parent organism divides (both nucleus and cytoplasm divide), into two daughter cells each of which grow and mature into two separate new individuals is called binary fission, e.g. *Amoeba, Paramecium.*

Fission in *Amoeba*

It is a single-celled organism. It reproduces by this method under favourable conditions. Firstly, the nucleus divides into two, it is then followed by the division of the cytoplasm. A constriction develops in the body which gradually deepens to form two daughter amoebae.

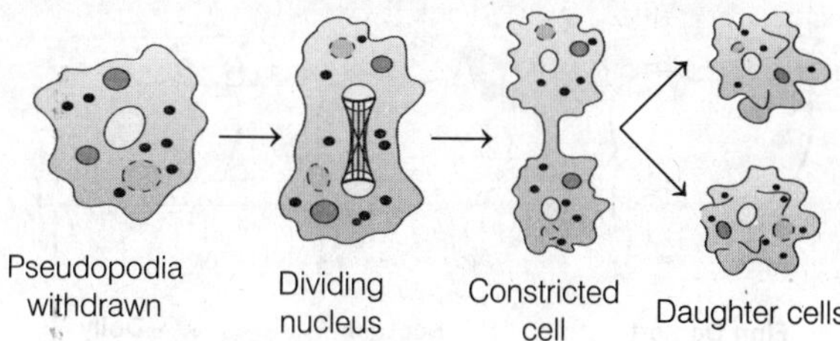

Fission in *Amoeba*

Besides these two processes, there are other methods of asexual reproduction (such as fragmentation, spore formation, vegetative propagation). These methods will be studied by you in higher classes.

Differences between sexual and asexual reproduction

Sexual reproduction	Asexual reproduction
It is characterised by the union of male and female gametes coming from two parents.	It does not involve fusion of gametes. It results from multiplication of body cells from a single parent.
Offsprings differ from the parents.	Daughter cells are identical to the parent.
Fertilisation takes place.	No fertilisation occur.
It leads to variations and thus, contributes to evolution of species.	Since there is no variation, so it does not contribute to evolution of species.

6.8 Cloning

Cloning is defined as the production of an exact copy of a cell or any other living part or a complete organism.

Story of Dolly, the Clone

Cloning of an animal was successfully performed for the first time by **Ian Wilmut** and his colleagues at the **Roslin**

Institute in Edinburgh, Scotland. They successfully cloned a sheep named **Dolly**. Dolly was born on 5th July, 1996 and was the first mammal to be cloned.

Finn Dorsett sheep | Scottish blackface ewe | Dolly

Steps Followed in Cloning.

- During the process of cloning Dolly, a cell was collected from the mammary gland of a female **Finn Dorsett sheep**.
- Simultaneously, an egg was obtained from a Scottish **blackface ewe**.
- The nucleus was removed from the egg. Then, the nucleus of the mammary gland cell from the Finn Dorsett sheep was inserted into the egg of the Scottish blackface ewe whose nucleus had been removed.
- The egg thus produced was implanted into the Scottish blackface ewe.
- Development of this egg followed normally and finally Dolly was born.

Though Dolly was given birth by the Scottish blackface ewe, it was found to be absolutely identical to the Finn Dorsett sheep from which the nucleus was taken. Since, the nucleus from the egg of the Scottish blackface ewe was removed, Dolly did not show any character of the Scottish blackface ewe.

Dolly was a healthy clone of the Finn Dorsett sheep and produced several offspring of her own through normal sexual means. Unfortunately, Dolly died on 14th February, 2003 due to a certain lung disease.

Since Dolly, several attempts have been made to produce cloned mammals. However, many die before birth or die soon after birth. The cloned animals are many-a-time found to be born with severe abnormalities.

Try These 6.4

1. **Name the method of reproduction in which the offspring produced are identical to the parents.**
2. **Name the process of asexual reproduction in which small bulb-like outgrowth is formed on the side of the parents body by repeated cell division.**
3. **Name a single-celled organism that reproduces by binary fission.**

Science Glossary

Asexual reproduction The type of reproduction in which only a single parent is involved.

Budding In this, new individual develops from bud.

Eggs Female reproductive cells produced by ovary.

External fertilisation The fertilisation that takes place outside the female body is called external fertilisation.

Embryo The zygote divides repeatedly to give rise to an embryo. It gets embedded in the wall of the uterus for further development.

Fertilisation The fusion of ovum and sperm.

Foetus The stage of the embryo in which all body parts are identifiable.

Internal fertilisation The fertilisation that takes place inside the female body is called internal fertilisation.

Metamorphosis The transformation of larva into an adult through drastic change.

Oviparous animals Animals which lay eggs.

Sexual reproduction Reproduction resulting from the fusion of male and female gametes.

Sperms Male reproductive cells produced by testes.

Viviparous animals Animals which give birth to young ones.

Zygote Fertilisation results in the formation of a fertilised egg or zygote.

Let's Investigate

ACTIVITY 1 (Page 69)

Aim To observe frog's eggs.

Procedure

1. Visit some ponds or slow-flowing streams during spring or rainy season.
2. Try to find out clusters of frog's eggs floating in water.
3. Note the colour and size of the eggs.

Observation We will observe that the colour of the eggs is transparent when unfertilised. If fertilised, a tiny black tadpole appears in the middle.

Eggs measure about 2-3mm in size.

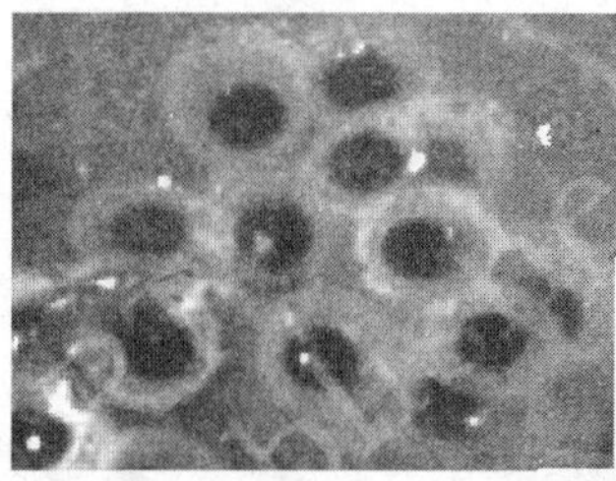

Viva Questions

1. Do frog's eggs have a shell?
2. Why they sometimes appear black in the middle?

ACTIVITY 2 (Page 71)

Aim To collect the eggs of different oviparous animals.

Procedure

1. Collect the eggs of as many oviparous animals as possible (e.g. frog, lizard, butterfly, bird, etc).
2. Make drawings of the eggs that you have collected.

Observation We will observe that the eggs of different oviparous animals are of different colour and sizes.

Bird's egg
(usually white, oval)

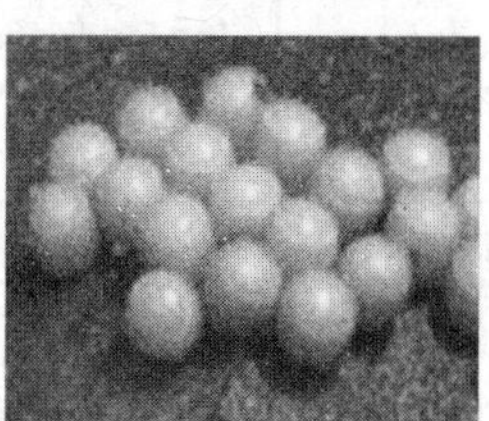

Butterfly eggs
(spherical or ovate)

Lizard's eggs
(white, shelled)

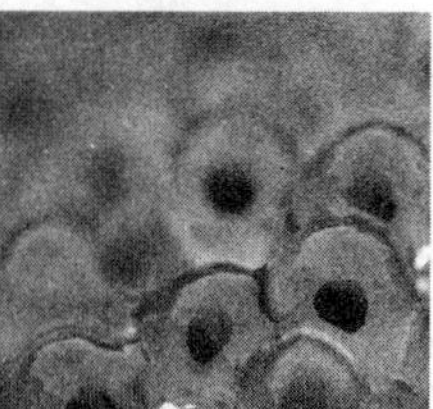

Frog's egg
(transparent, small)

Conclusion From this activity, it is concluded that it is easy to collect the egg of oviparous animals because they lay them outside their bodies.

Viva Questions

1. What are oviparous animals?
2. Give few example of viviparous animals.

ACTIVITY 3 (Page 73)

Aim To study budding in *Hydra* with the help of permanent slides.

Materials Required Permanent slide of *Hydra*, microscope.

Procedure

1. Get permanent slides of *Hydra* and observe them using a microscope.
2. Look out carefully for any bulges from the parent body.
3. Count the number of bulges that you see in different slides.
4. Draw the diagram of *Hydra* as you see it.

Observation We will observe a small single outgrowth or protuberance on the parent body. This bud develops into a tiny individual which when fully mature detaches from the parent body.

Conclusion From this activity we can conclude that *Hydra* reproduces through budding.

Viva Questions

1. Does *Hydra* reproduce through binary fission or budding?
2. Define budding.

REPRODUCTION IN ANIMALS

Cloning
First mammal cloned was Dolly sheep in 1996 on 5th July

Metamorphosis
The process of change by which a larva is transformed into an adult, e.g. insects, butterfly, frog, etc.
Commonly seen in frogs
egg → tadpole → adult

***In Vitro* Fertilisation**
(Test tube baby technique)

- Allows fertilisation outside the body and inside the laboratory.
- Women who are unable to have babies because their oviducts are blocked and sperms cannot reach the egg for fertilisation.
- The problem can be overcome through test-tube baby technology.
- Success rate is 30-40%.
- Mainly treats infertile couples.

Asexual Reproduction

- **Budding:** *Hydra*, yeast.
- **Fission:** *Amoeba, Paramecium.*

Sexual Reproduction

- Occurs mainly in multicellular organisms including human beings.
- Involves two parents (i.e. male and female).

Male Reproductive System (Humans)

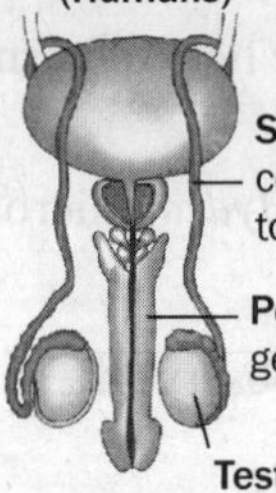

Sperm duct connects testes to urethra.
Penis external genital organs.
Testis produces male gamete.

Fertilisation

- The process of fusion of male and female gamete, i.e. sperm and ovum respectively.
- It is the first step of sexual reproduction.
- Nuclei of the sperm comes in contact with an egg, it fuse to form a single nucleus.

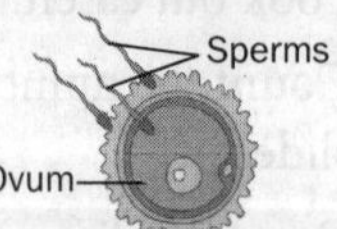

Female Reproductive System (Humans)

Oviduct (Fallopian tube) Acts as a site of fertilisation

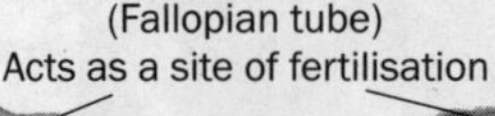

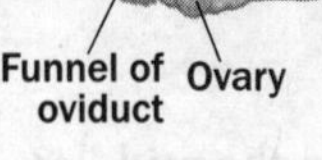

Funnel of oviduct
Ovary produces ova egg or female gamete.
Funnel of oviduct
Ovary
Uterus (womb) growth and development of foetus takes place here.
Cervix
Vagina

Formation of a

Zygote
It marks the begining of a new individual.

Leads to

Development of an embryo

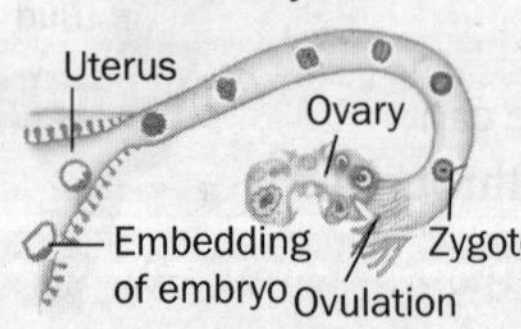

External Fertilisation
The fertilisation takes place outside the body of a female especially in water, e.g. fish, frogs, etc.

Results in

Oviparous Animals

- Animals that reproduce by laying eggs.
- Development of zygote takes place outside the female parent.

Internal Fertilisation
The fertilisation takes palce inside the body of a female, e.g. cow, dog, cat, human beings, etc.

Results in

Viviparous Animals

- Animals that give birth to their young ones directly.
- Development of zygote takes place inside the body of female parent.

NCERT FOLDER

Complete Explanations of all NCERT's Questions

Intext Questions

Q.1 How are the chicks born? Page 66

Ans. Refer to text on page no. 93.

Q.2 Does sperm appear to be a single cell? Page 67

Ans. Yes, each sperm is a single cell with all the usual cell components.

Q.3 What purpose does the tail in a sperm serve? Page 67

Ans. The tail in sperm provides mobility to it and helps it to reach female gamete, i.e. ovum for fusion.

Q.4 Why do fish and frogs lay eggs in hundreds whereas a hen lays only one egg at a time? Page 69

Ans. Fish and frog lay egg in hundred in number whereas, a hen lays only one egg at a time because fish and frog undergo external fertilisation, and a hen undergoes internal fertilisation. In case of fish and frog, the gametes are released in water, many of them may be carried away by the movement of water, wind, etc. or may be eaten by other aquatic animals. So, to enhance the chances of fertilisation a large number of eggs are released by them.

Q.5 How could a single cell become such a big individual ? Page 70

Ans Refer to text on page no. 92

Exercise

Q.1. Explain the importance of reproduction in organisms.

Ans. Reproduction helps in the production of new individuals of same kind and transmission of certain characters from parents to offspring.

Q.2 Describe the process of fertilisation in human beings.

Ans. In human beings, fertilisation takes place inside the female body.

It is the fusion of male and female gamete, i.e. sperm and an ovum. It is the first stage in the process of reproduction. During fertilisation, the nuclei of egg and sperm fuse together to form a single nucleus. This results in the formation of fertilised egg or zygote.

Q.3 Choose the most appropriate answer.

(a) Internal fertilisation occurs

(i) in female body
(ii) outside female body
(iii) in male body
(iv) outside male body

(b) A tadpole develops into an adult frog by the process of

(i) fertilisation **(ii) metamorphosis**
(iii) embedding **(iv) budding**

(c) The number of nuclei present in a zygote is

(i) none **(ii) one**
(iii) two **(iv) four**

Ans. (a) (i) Internal fertilisation occurs in female body.

(b) (ii) The process of development of tadpole into an adult frog is known as metamorphosis.

(c) (ii) In zygote, only one nuclei is present which is formed by the fusion of two nuclei, one from each parent.

Q.4 Indicate whether the following statements are True or False.

(a) Oviparous animals give birth to young ones.
(b) Each sperm is a single cell.
(c) External fertilisation takes place in frog.
(d) A new human individual develops from a cell called gamete.
(e) Egg laid after fertilisation is made up of single cell.
(f) *Amoeba* reproduces by budding.
(g) Fertilisation is necessary even in asexual reproduction.
(h) Binary fission is a method of asexual reproduction.
(i) A zygote is formed as a result of fertilisation.
(j) An embryo is made up of a single cell.

Ans. (a) False, oviparous animals (female) lay eggs.

(b) True

(c) True

(d) False, a new human individual develops from a cell called zygote.

(e) True

(f) False, *Amoeba* reproduces by binary fission.

(g) False, fertilisation does not take place in asexual reproduction as no gametes are formed and only a single parent is involved.

(h) True (i) True

(j) False, because an embryo is a developing structure formed from a group of dividing cells of zygote.

Q.5 Give two differences between a zygote and a foetus.

Ans. Difference between a zygote and a foetus are as follows

Zygote	Foetus
It is formed by the fusion of male and female gamete.	It is formed by the developing embryo.
It is made up of single cell.	It is made up of many cells, in which all the body parts can be identified.

Q.6 Define asexual reproduction. Describe two methods of asexual reproduction in animals.

Ans. Refer to text on page no. 95.

Q.7 In which female reproductive organ does the embryo get embedded?

Ans. Embryo gets embedded in the uterus of female for further development.

Q.8 What is metamorphosis? Give examples.

Ans. Refer to text on page no. 94.

Q.9 Differentiate between internal fertilisation and external fertilisation.

Ans. Difference between internal fertilisation and external fertilisation are as follows

Internal fertilisation	External fertilisation
It is the fertilisation that takes place inside the female body.	It is the fertilisation that takes place outside the female body, generally in water.
Sperms are released in female body.	Sperms and ova are released in water, outside the female body.
It is common in terrestrial animals, e.g. humans, cats, dogs, etc.	It is very common in aquatic animals, e.g. frogs, fishes, etc.

REVIEW EXERCISE

Including Competency Based Questions

Part I

Multiple Choice Questions

1. Which of the following is not a part of the human male reproductive system?

(a) Testes (b) Oviducts
(c) Seminal vesicles (c) Epididymis

2. Sets of reproductive terms are given below. Choose the set that has an incorrect combination. NCERT Exemplar

(a) Sperm, testis, sperm duct, penis
(b) Menstruation, egg, oviduct, uterus
(c) Sperm, oviduct, egg, uterus
(d) Ovulation, egg, oviduct, uterus

3. Which of the following statements about reproduction in humans is correct?

(a) Fertilisation takes place externally
(b) Fertilisation takes place in the testes
(c) During fertilisation, egg moves towards the sperm
(d) Fertilisation takes place in the human female

4. A stage of sexual reproduction is represented below. Select the correct statement describing the process shown in the image.

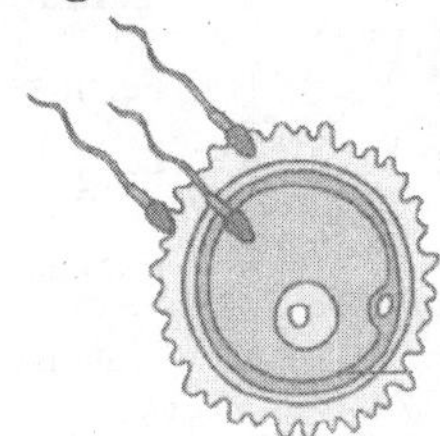

(a) Several ova penetrate the egg cell and fertilise it to form a zygote
(b) Several sperms penetrate the egg cell and fertilise it form a zygote
(c) A single ova penetrates the egg cell and fertilise it to form a zygote
(d) A single sperm penetrates the egg cell and fertilise it to form a zygote

5. After fertilisation, the resulting cell which gives rise to a new individual is the NCERT Exemplar

(a) embryo (b) ovum (c) foetus (d) zygote

6. Which of these animals reproduce by external fertilisation? Competency Based Que.

(a) Snake (b) Frog
(c) Horse (d) Elephant

7. Internal fertilisation occurs

(a) inside the male body (b) outside the male body
(c) inside the female body (d) outside the female body

8. Where does the fertilisation of eggs occur in the process of *In Vitro* Fertilisation (IVF)? Competency Based Que.

(a) Ovary (b) Water (c) Uterus (d) Petri dish

9. In human beings, the correct sequence of events during reproduction is NCERT Exemplar

(a) gamete formation, fertilisation, zygote formation embryo
(b) embryo, zygote formation, fertilisation, gamete formation
(c) fertilisation, gamete formation, embryo, zygote formation
(d) gamete formation, fertilisation, embryo, zygote formation

10. Animals exhibiting external fertilisation produce a large number of gametes. Pick the appropriate reason from the following NCERT Exemplar

(a) The animals are small in size and want to produce more offspring
(b) Food is available in plenty in water
(c) To ensure better chance of fertilisation
(d) Water promotes production of large number of gametes

11. In human beings, after fertilisation, the structure which gets embedded in the wall of uterus is

(a) ovum (b) embryo (c) foetus (d) zygote

12. In humans, the development of fertilised egg takes place in the

(a) ovary (b) testis (c) oviduct (d) uterus

13. Baby before being born is termed as

(a) embryo (b) foetus
(c) zygote (d) egg

14. Aquatic animals in which fertilisation occurs in water are said to be NCERT Exemplar

(a) viviparous without fertilisation
(b) oviparous with external fertilisation
(c) viviparous with internal fertilisation
(d) oviparous with internal fertilisation

15. Which is not oviparous animal?

(a) Hen (b) Frog (c) Butterfly (d) Dog

16. In the list of animals given below, hen is the odd one out. **NCERT Exemplar**
Human being, cow, dog, hen.
The reason for this is
(a) it undergoes internal fertilisation
(b) it is oviparous
(c) it is viviparous
(d) it undergoes external fertilisation

17. Which of the following is not a viviparous animal?
(a) Rat (b) Lizard
(c) Rabbit (d) Cat

18. Which table given below correctly represents the classification of the animals into viviparous and oviparous animals?

(a)

Viviparous Animals	Oviparous Animals
Frog, dog, lizard	Cow, cat, hen

(b)

Viviparous Animals	Oviparous Animals
Frog, cat, lizard	Dog, hen, cow

(c)

Viviparous Animals	Oviparous Animals
Dog, cow, cat	Frog, hen, lizard

(d)

Viviparous Animals	Oviparous Animals
Frog, hen, cow	Lizard, dog, cat

19. Tadpole is the larva of
(a) fish (b) frog
(c) mosquito (d) butterfly

20. Reproduction by budding takes place in **NCERT Exemplar**
(a) *Hydra* (b) *Amoeba*
(c) *Paramecium* (d) Bacteria

21. Reproduction by binary fission occurs in
(a) *Hydra* (b) *Amoeba*
(c) *Paramecium* (d) yeast

22. The production of an exact copy of an animal by asexual reproduction is known as
(a) budding (b) mating
(c) cloning (d) hatching

Answers

1. (b) 2. (c) 3. (d) 4. (d) 5. (d)
6. (b) 7. (c) 8. (d) 9. (a) 10. (c)
11. (b) 12. (d) 13. (b) 14. (b) 15. (d)
16. (b) 17. (b) 18. (c) 19. (b) 20. (a)
21. (b) 22. (c)

Fill in the Blanks

1. Sperms are produced in ....
2. ...... reproduces by budding.
3. *Amoeba* is a ...... celled organism. It reproduces by ...... reproduction. The process of reproduction begins by the division of its ...... into two. This is followed by the division of its ...... into two. This type of reproduction is called ...... fission. **NCERT Exemplar**

Answers

1. testes 2. *Hydra*
3. single, asexual, nucleus, cytoplasm, binary

True/False

1. All living animals reproduce to produce new young ones.
2. Human egg has a head, middle piece and tail.
3. Sperms are produced by ovaries.
4. The male gametes are called ova.
5. In adult human females, a single mature egg is released into an oviduct every month.

Answers

1. True
2. False, human sperms has a head, middle piece and tail.
3. False, sperms are produced by testes.
4. False, male gametes are called sperms.
5. True

Match the Columns

1. Match the Column I with Column II.

Column I	Column II
A. Budding	1. Fertilised egg
B. Sperm	2. Frog
C. Ovary	3. Asexual reproduction
D. Zygote	4. Male gamete
E. Oviparous	5. Female organ

Answers

A–3, B–4, C–5, D–1, E–2

Assertion-Reason Questions

The following questions consist of two statements Assertion (A) and Reason (R). Answer these questions by selecting the appropriate option given below.
(a) Both A and R are true and R is the correct explanation of A
(b) Both A and R are true, but R is not the correct explanation of A
(c) A is true, but R is false
(d) A is false, but R is true

1. **Assertion** (A) The animals which undergo external fertilisation lay hundreds of eggs.

   Reason (R) To enhance the chances of fertilisation.

2. **Assertion** (A) Internal fertilisation occurs in many animals including humans, cows, dogs and hens.

   Reason (R) Fertilisation which takes place inside the female body in called internal fertilisation.

3. **Assertion** (A) It is easy to collect the eggs of viviparous animals.

   Reason (R) They lay egg outside their body.

4. **Assertion** (A) Human beings do not undergo metamorphosis.

   Reason (R) The body parts in adults are not similar to those of babies.

5. **Assertion** (A) Binary fission and budding are two methods of asexual reproduction.

   Reason (R) Only a single parent is involved.

Answers

1. (a) Both A and R are true and R is the correct explanation of A.
2. (b) Both A and R are true and R is not the correct explanation of A.
3. (d) A is false, but R is true. A can be corrected as It is easy to collect the eggs of oviparous animals.
4. (c) A is true, but R is false. R can be corrected as The body parts in adults are similar to those of babies.
5. (a) Both A and R are true R is the correct explanation of A.

Case Based Questions

1. **Consider the below diagram and answer the following question.** **Competency Based Que.**

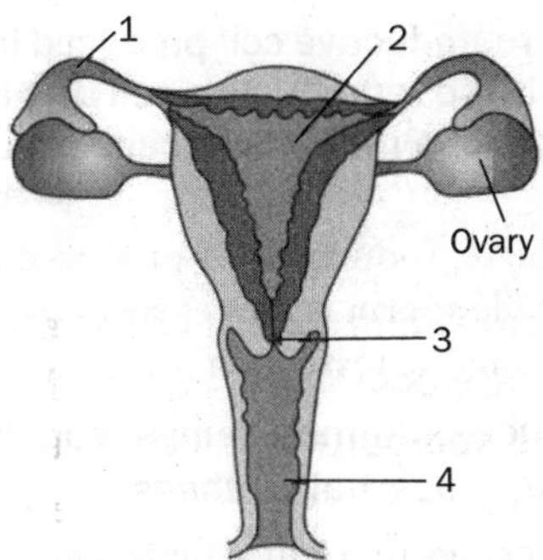

Female reproductive system

(i) **A mature egg and a sperm unite to form a zygote. In which part of the female reproductive system does a zygote form?**

(a) 1 (b) 2 (c) 3 (d) 4

(ii) **How many eggs are usually released each month by the ovary of a woman?**

(a) One (b) Two
(c) Fourteen (d) Twenty-four

(iii) **In which part of the female reproductive system does an embryo implant?**

(a) 1 (b) 2 (c) 3 (d) 4

2. **Which of these statements is true about a foetus? Circle 'Yes' or No for the correct response.**

Is this statement true about a foetus?	Yes or No
(i) All body parts can be identified properly.	Yes/No
(ii) It is covered by a hard shell of protective layers.	Yes/No
(iii) It resembles a large ball made up of millions of cells	Yes/No

3. **The table shows the processes of external fertilisation and internal fertilisation.** **Competency Based Que.**

External fertilisation	Internal fertilisation
The female releases the eggs (ova) outside its body. The male releases the sperms on the eggs. Fertilisation takes place outside the female body.	The male releases the sperms inside the body of the female. Fertilisation takes place inside the female body.

Which of these is true about external fertilisation and internal fertilisation?

	External fertilisation	Internal fertilisation
A.	Both parents are necessary	Both parents are necessary
B.	Embryo is not formed	Embryo is formed
C.	Involves development of egg shell	Involves development of egg shell
D.	Takes place among invertebrates	Takes place among vertebrates

4. **The picture shows the life cycle of a moth.** **Competency Based Que.**

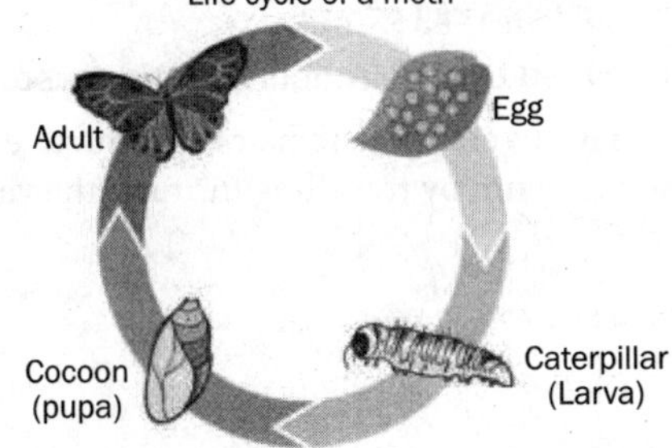

What can be concluded from the picture?
Circle 'Yes' or 'No' for the correct response.

Can this be concluded from the picture?	Yes or No
(a) Moth is an oviparous animal.	Yes/No
(b) A moth looks different in each stage of its life cycle.	Yes/No
(c) There are two different stages in the life cycle of a moth.	Yes/No

5. The pictures show three types of reproduction in animals. **Competency Based Que.**

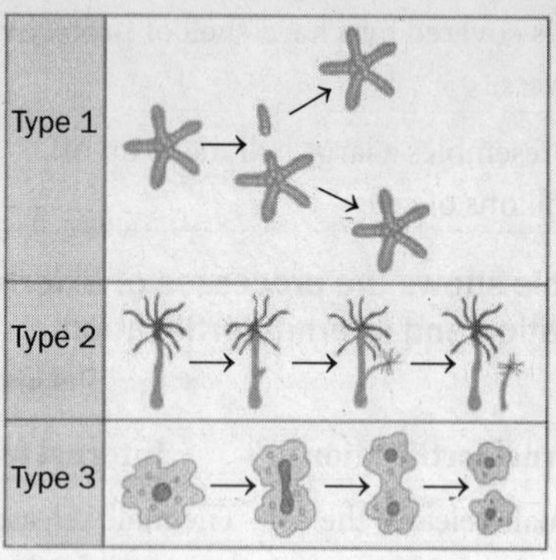

Which of these statements is true?

(a) Type 1 reproduction is called binary fission

(b) Type 2 reproduction produces two non-identical offspring.

(c) Type 3 reproduction involves unequal distribution of genetic materials.

(d) Types 1, 2 and 3 methods of reproduction involve single parent only.

Answers

1. (i) (a) 1
   (ii) (a) One
   (iii) (b) 2
2. (a) Yes
   (b) No
   (c) No
3. Both parents are necessary.
4. (a) Yes
   (b) Yes
   (c) No
5. (d) Type 1, 2 and 3 methods of reproduction involves single parent only.

Part II

Very Short Answer Type Questions

1. What is the name of the process by which young ones are formed?

Ans. Reproduction is the biological process of formation of young ones of their own kind by living organisms.

2. Name two main types of reproduction prevalent in animals.

Ans. Two main types of reproduction prevalent in animals are asexual and sexual reproduction.

3. A type of reproduction involves gametes. Name it.

Ans. Sexual reproduction is the type of reproduction that involves gametes.

4. The male and female gamete in human beings are known by which names?

Ans. In human beings, male gamete is known as sperm and female gamete as egg or ova.

5. 'Sperms need to have mobility'. Give reason.

Ans. Sperms have to enter the female reproductive passage and fertilise the ovum by travelling through the vagina and uterus to reach the Fallopian tube. This is the reason why sperms need to have mobility.

6. Only male gametes have a tail, can you think of a reason for this?

Ans. Male gametes or sperms have tail to facilitate movement of sperms which help them to reach the egg (female gamete) for fertilisation.

7. In humans, which organ produces the sperm?

Ans. Testes produce sperms in humans.

8. *X* is the reproductive cell produced in a woman's *Y* while *Z* is the reproductive cell that is produced in the testes of a man. What can *X*, *Y* and *Z* be? **Competency Based Que.**

Ans. **Egg** is the reproductive cell produced in a woman's **ovary** while **sperm** is the reproductive cell that is produced in the **testes** of a man.

9. State whether human beings reproduce by sexual methods or asexual methods.

Ans. Human beings reproduce by sexual method.

10. Give the other name of oviducts.

Ans. Fallopian tube is the other name of oviducts.

11. Arrange the following stages of development of human body in correct sequence.
Foetus, Zygote and Embryo.

Ans. Zygote, embryo and foetus.

12. A fertilisation takes place outside the body. What is it called as?

Ans. The process of fertilisation that takes place outside the body of the female is called external fertilisation.

13. Stages in the life cycle of silkworm are given below. Write them in sequential order.
Pupa, Egg, Silkmoth, Caterpillar **NCERT Exemplar**

Ans. The stages in the life cycle of silkworm occurs in following sequence
Egg $\rightarrow$ Caterpillar $\rightarrow$ Pupa $\rightarrow$ Silkmoth
The drastic change in the structure from caterpillar to silkmoth is called metamorphosis.

14. The eggs of frogs do not have shells for protection, yet they are safe in water, how? **NCERT Exemplar**

Ans. Frog's eggs are without any external covering or shell, but a layer of jelly-like coat hold the eggs together, thus providing them protection.

15. Give the name of the organism and the mode of reproduction represented in the given diagram.

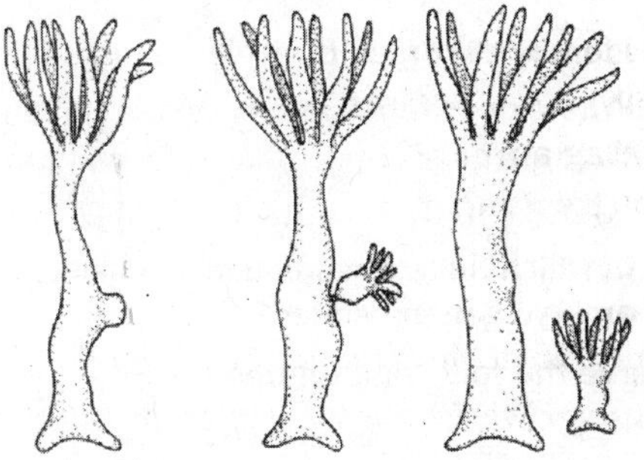

Ans. The name of the organism is *Hydra* and the mode of reproduction is asexual (budding).

Short Answer Type Questions

1. Describe the two modes of reproduction.

Ans. Two modes of reproduction are

(i) **Asexual reproduction** It does not involve the fusion of gametes, it results from multiplication of body cells from a single parent. Daughter cells are identical to the parent. No fertilisation takes place.

(ii) **Sexual reproduction** It is characterised by the union of male and female gametes coming from two parents. offspring differ from the parents genetically. Fertilisation takes place.

2. It is necessary to produce large number of eggs and sperms by the animals which reproduce by external fertilisation. Why?

Ans. It is necessary to produce large number of eggs and sperms by the animals which reproduce by external fertilisation to enhance the chances of fertilisation. As the gametes are released in water, many of them may be carried away by movement of water, wind, etc. or may be eaten by other aquatic animals, so a large number is released to compensate for the loss.

3. Mother gives birth to a baby, but the baby has characters of both parents. How is this possible? **NCERT Exemplar**

Ans. Although mother gives birth to a baby, but the baby is formed from the fertilisation of male and female gametes involving two parents. The nuclei of both the parent gametes fuse together to form zygote thus passing their characters to the offspring. This zygote develops inside the female body (uterus) and finally takes birth as baby.

4. Although two cells called gametes fuse, the product formed is a single cell called zygote, Justify. **NCERT Exemplar**

Ans. During fertilisation, only the nucleus of the sperm enters the egg cell to form a single-celled structure which is called zygote.

5. Can a woman with a blocked Fallopian tube give birth to a baby? How?

Ans. A woman with a blocked Fallopian tube cannot produce babies in normal way because the eggs released by their ovary cannot meet the sperms and get fertilised in the oviducts. But such women can have babies by using '*in vitro* fertilisation' technique.

6. The test-tube babies are called so as they grow inside a test tube. Give your opinion.

Ans. The babies born through IVF technique are called test-tube babies because the fertilisation takes place in a glass test tube. This is however, a misleading name as a very brief period is spent in a test tube. After which, the entire growth and development of the baby takes place inside the uterus of the woman as in normal pregnancy.

7. Observe the figure given and answer the questions that follow.

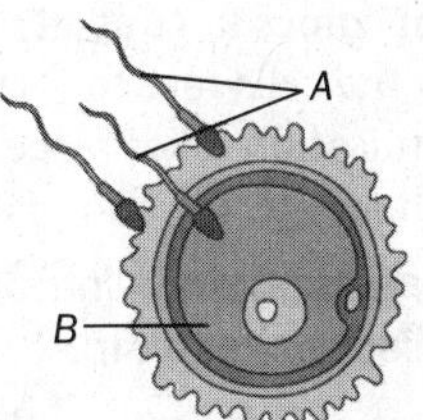

(i) Label *A* and *B*. **(ii) Identify the process.**

(iii) What happens during the process and what is formed?

Ans. (i) *A*–sperm, *B*–ovum (egg).
(ii) The process is fertilisation.
(iii) During this process, the sperm nucleus fuses with the egg nucleus to form a zygote.

8. The term metamorphosis is not used while describing human development. Why? **NCERT Exemplar**

Ans. The term 'metamorphosis' is not used while describing human development because in human beings, body parts of an adult are present from the time of birth itself, i.e., while beginning of life as a baby and until you are an adult, the basic plan of body does not change. On the contrary, in metamorphosis, the parts of the adult are different from those at the time of birth.

9. What does the figure represent?

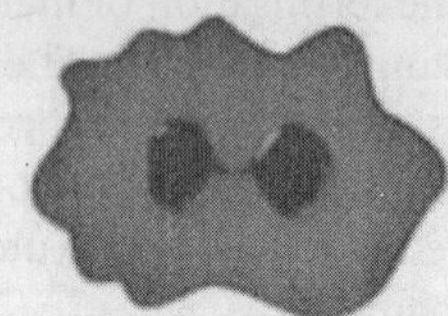

Ans. The figure represents the process of binary fission in *Amoeba*. During fission, a single *Amoeba* divides (both nucleus and cytoplasm) to form two daughter cells that develop into two independent *Amoeba*.

10. How is reproduction in *Hydra* different from that in *Amoeba*?

Ans. Both *Hydra* and *Amoeba* reproduces asexually, involving only, single parent, but the modes are different. As *Hydra* reproduces from bulges or buds arising from the parent body that grows and matures into another organism, *Amoeba* reproduces by forming two daughter cells by division of both nucleus and cytoplasm through binary fission.

Long Answer Type Questions

1. Describe sexual reproduction

Ans. Refer to text on page no. 91 and 92.

2. How can we say that fish exhibits external fertilisation? **NCERT Exemplar**

Ans. Female fish lays eggs in water while male fish releases sperms in water. Sperms swim and reach the eggs of fish randomly due to water currents.

When a sperm comes in contact with the viable egg, nuclei of both the cells fuse to form a zygote. This process of fertilisation takes place in water outside the female body, hence fertilisation is external in fishes.

3. Hens and frogs are both oviparous exhibiting different types of fertilisation, explain.

Ans. Hens lay eggs after fertilisation, therefore their eggs are covered with hard shell to protect the young ones. This shows that fertilisation in hen is internal. The frogs on the other hand lay both sperms and eggs in water prior to fertilisation. Thus, the fertilisation in frog takes place in water, hence it is external.

Case Based Questions

1. The picture shows the basic parts of a salmon fish sperm.

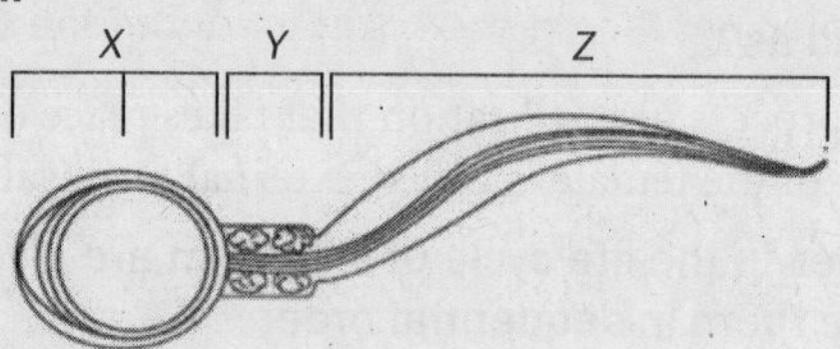

Which part of the sperm helps it to swim in water and reach the egg?

2. Observe the diagram and answer the following questions **Competency Based Que.**

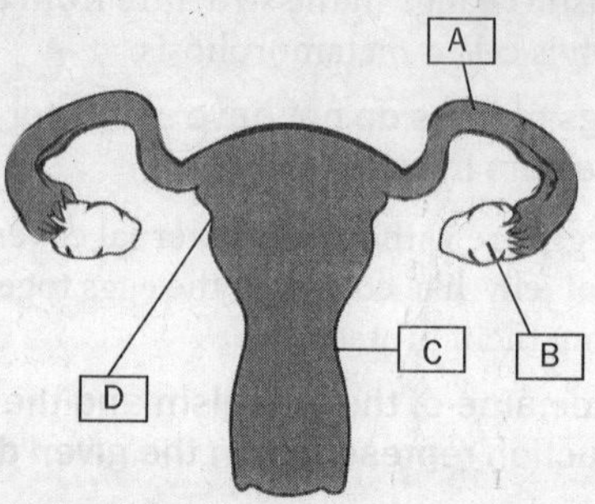

(i) Identify the organ *B*.

(ii) Where does fertilisation occur in the above diagram?

(a) *A* (b) *B* (c) *C* (d) *D*

(iii) In which female reproductive organ does the embryo get embedded?

3. Observe the following figures.

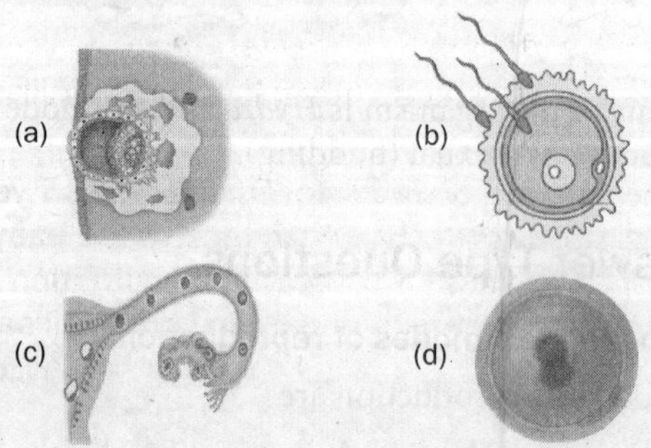

(i) Identify the stages (a) to (d) in figure during development of human baby.

(ii) Arrange the stages in correct sequence of development.

(iii) Explain the development that takes place in any one stage. **NCERT Exemplar**

4. After observing figure below answer the following.

(i) Read the following statements and label them in the figure.

(a) The part which produces female gametes.

(b) The part where development of the baby takes place.

(c) The part through which the developing embryo passes to reach the uterus.

(ii) Explain the future development of the embryo that would take place after it gets embedded in the uterus. **NCERT Exemplar**

Ans. 1. Part '*Z*' which represents the tail of the sperm helps it to swim in water and reach the egg.

2. (i) Organ *B* is identified as ovary.

(ii) (a) (A) Fallopian tube or oviduct.

(iii) (D) The embryo gets embedded in the uterus.

3. (i) The figures showing stages during development of embryo are identified as

(a) Embedding of the embryo in the uterus (implantation).

(b) Fertilisation (fusion of egg and sperm).

(c) Zygote formation and development of an embryo from the zygote.

(d) Zygote (showing fusion of gametes) single-celled.

(ii) The sequence of the above stages is as follows

(b) Fertilisation → (d) Zygote formation → (c) Development of embryo → (a) Implantation of embryo in uterus.

(iii) **Embryo development**

The embryo after being implanted in uterus, continues to develop and differentiate into body parts. This stage of embryo is termed as foetus. After the foetus is completely developed, the mother gives birth to the baby.

4.. (i) The parts in the figure are labelled below.

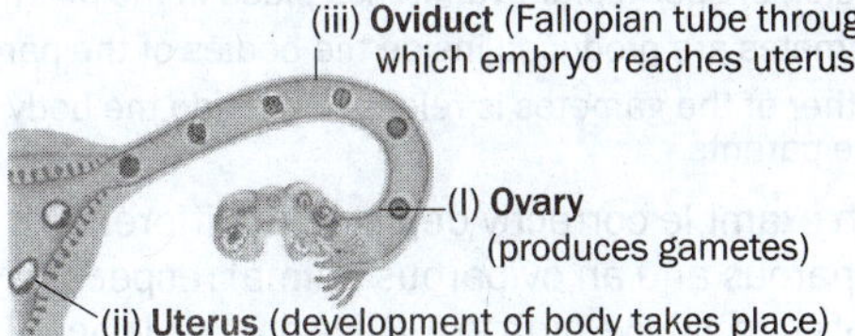

(ii) The embryo continues to develop after it gets embedded into the uterus. It divides and differentiates into three germ layers which give rise to different body parts such as hands, legs, head, eyes, ears, etc. This stage where all the body parts are distinct and easily identified in developing embryo is called foetus. After completion of development of foetus, mother gives birth to the baby.

Skill Based Questions as per NEP 2020

1. Visit a poultry farm with your parents.Talk to the incharge of the farm and try to find out the answers of the following questions. **Observation skill**

(i) Do hens lay unfertilised eggs?

(ii) Are the eggs that we get in the stores fertilised or unfertilised?

2. A couple visited a doctor as even after their 7 year of marriage they were unable to conceive the baby on their own. The doctor after seeing the situation recommended them to undergo *in vitro* fertilisation. **Observation skill**

(i) What is the basis behind *in vitro* fertilisation?

(ii) Why some women are unable to conceive?

3. Gametes are the haploid cells formed within the body of both male and female in the reproductive gonads. These gametes fuse together to form a zygote that later develop into an embryo and delivered out from the body of a female.

Inspite of being delivered by a mother the baby bears characters of both parents. What according to you could be the basis behind this act? Discuss. **Thinking skill**

ASSESSMENT EXERCISE

Part I

Multiple Choice Questions

1. Sexual reproduction begins with
(a) implantation (b) fertilisation
(c) zygote formation (d) development of embryo

2. The process of internal fertilisation differs from external fertilisation as
(a) fusion of sperm and ovum takes place inside the female body
(b) fusion of sperm and ovum takes place in the ovaries
(c) gametes are produced inside the bodies of the parents
(d) either of the gametes is released outside the body of the the parents

3. Which example correctly depicts the difference between a viviparous and an oviparous animal respectively?
(a) Cats directly give birth to a young one, while hens lay eggs
(b) Frogs lay soft shelled eggs, while birds lay hard-shelled eggs
(c) Frogs lay unfertilized eggs in the water, while hens lay fertilised eggs
(d) Dogs give birth to many puppies, while elephants give birth to just one calf

4. Select the animal which undergoes metamorphosis during its life cycle.
(a) Dog (b) Cat (c) Hen (d) Tadpole

5. The multicellular organism which reproduces by budding is
(a) *Amoeba* (b) yeast
(c) *Paramecium* (d) *Hydra*

Fill in the Blanks

6. Reproduction by binary fission occurs in ....

7. .... reproduces by fragmentation.

True/False

8. Cow and dogs are viviparous animals.

9. Budding is a method of asexual reproduction.

Match the Columns

10. Match Column I with Column II.

	Column I		Column II
A.	Scrotum	1.	Produces sperm
B.	Testes	2.	Receives sperms
C.	Penis	3.	Holds testes
D.	Oviduct	4.	Transfer sperm into female body

Assertion-Reason Questions

The following questions consist of two statements **Assertion** (A) and **Reason** (R). Answer these questions by selecting the appropriate option given below.
(a) Both A and R are true and R is the correct explanation of A
(b) Both A and R are true but R is not the correct explanation of A
(c) A is true, but R is false
(d) A is false, but R is true

11. Assertion (A) During metamorphosis tadpole is transformed into caterpiliar.

Reason (R) Metamorphosis is a process in which a larva is transformed into an adult.

12. Assertion (A) Cloning of an animal was successfully performed for the first time by Ian Wilmut and his colleagues.

Reason (R) Cloning is the production of different copy of a cell or any living part or a complete organism.

Part II

Very Short Answer Type Questions

13. Name the organs of the female reproductive system in humans.

14. In sexual reproduction, does fertilisation take place or not?

15. What do you understand by foetus?

Short Answer type Questions

16. Testes produce male germ cells. What are these cells called? Name its parts.

17. Human male gamete has a tail, but female gamete does not. Why?

18. Explain what happens after a hen lays a fertilised egg?

Long Answer Type Question

19. Eluciate the life cycle of frog.

Answers

1. (b) **2.** (a) **3.** (a) **4.** (d) **5.** (d)
6. *Amoeba* **7.** *Spirogyra*
8. True **9.** True
10. A–3, B–1, C–4, D–2
11. (a) **12.** (c)

Reaching the Age of Adolescence

CHAPTER 07

In the previous chapter, we have learnt how human beings reproduce by giving birth to babies, but the human beings can do so only after growing up to a 'certain age'. This is because the reproductive system starts working only after a certain age. In this chapter, we will learn about the changes that take place in a human body, making them capable of reproduction.

7.1 Adolescence and Puberty

Growth is a process that begins from the day, a baby is born. It is a slow and a natural process. The period of life, when the body undergoes changes, leading to reproductive maturity is called **adolescence**.

It begins around the age of 11 to 18 or 19 years of age. Since, adolescence period include the teenage period (i.e.13-19 years of age), adolescents are also called **teenagers.**

The period of adolescence varies from person to person. In girls, it may begin a year or two earlier than in boys.

Puberty

It is a period, during which the human body undergoes certain changes by which adolescents become capable of reproduction. The puberty ends when an adolescent reaches the reproductive maturity.

7.2 Changes at Puberty

Growth of the body is an important character during puberty. The rapid growth is due to two main types of hormones, i.e. **sex hormones** and **growth hormones.**

Some of the conspicious changes which takes place during puberty are given below

Increase in Height

A sudden increase in height is the most prominent change during puberty. The long bones (i.e. the bones of the arms and the legs) elongate at this time, making a person tall. The rate of growth in height varies from person to person. Girls grows faster than boys initially, but by about 18 years of age, both reach their maximum height. Sometimes the arms and the legs or the hands and the feet of adolescent boys and girls look oversized and out of proportion with the body. But soon the other parts catch up with them in growth resulting in a more proportionate body.

The average rate of growth in height of boys and girls with age is given in the table

Average growth in height with age

Age in years	% of full height	
	Boys	Girls
8	72%	77%
9	75%	81%
10	78%	84%
11	81%	88%
12	84%	91%
13	88%	95%
14	92%	98%
15	95%	99%
16	98%	99.5%
17	99%	100%
18	100%	100%

This table gives the approximate percentage of maximum or full height a person has achieved at a particular age.

The maximum height of a person (i.e. both girl and boy) can be calculated by the following formula

$$\textbf{Maximum height} \text{ (cm)} = \frac{\text{Present height (cm)}}{\text{\% of full height at this age}} \times 100$$

(as given in the table)

e.g., A boy is 9 years old and 120 cm tall. At the end of the growth period, he is likely to be

$$\frac{120}{75} \times 100 \text{ cm} = 160 \text{ cm tall}$$

It is to be noted that the height of an individual also depends upon the genes inherited from their parents. However, it is important that one should take nutritive diet for the proper growth of bones, muscles and other parts of the body during the growing period.

Change in Body Shape

During adolescence, changes in body shape takes place. These changes are different in boys and girls as follows

(i) In boys, the shoulders become broader and the chests become wider. The muscles of the body grow more prominently.

(ii) In girls, the pelvic region (region below the waist) widens, hips broaden, breasts develop and increase in size.

Change in Voice

The **voice box** or **larynx** produces sound when we are talking. At puberty, it begins to grow. It is bigger in boys and can be seen as a protruding part of the throat called **Adam's apple**.

In girls, the larynx is smaller and hardly visible from outside. This is the reason why boys develop a deep voice, whereas girls have a high pitched voice.

In adolescent boys, sometimes, the muscles of the growing voice box go out of control and the voice becomes hoarse. This state may remain for a few days or weeks after which the voice becomes normal.

Increased Activity of Sweat and Sebaceous Glands

There is an increase in the activity of sweat and sebaceous (oil) glands. This leads to increased sweating, often resulting in body odour.

Many young people get acne and pimples on the face at this time because of the increased activity of these glands in the skin.

Development of Sex Organs

The reproductive system starts functioning at puberty due to the complete growth and development of sex organs in boys and girls.

(i) In boys, the male sex organs like testes and penis develop completely. The testes start producing sperms.

(ii) In girls, the ovaries enlarge and eggs begin to mature. Also ovaries start releasing mature eggs (only one egg is released per month by either ovary).

Reaching Mental, Intellectual and Emotional Maturity

Adolescence is also a period which brings about development in a person's way of thinking. The person becomes more independent and self-conscious.

Intellectual development also occurs and they tend to spend considerable time on thinking, planning, analysing, exchanging views and ideas with others. It is the time in one's life when the brain has the highest capacity for learning.

There are a lot of **emotional** and **physical changes** during puberty. These changes in body and mind can lead to confusion and insecurity in the adolescents.

There is however, no reason to fell insecure, as puberty is a natural process of growing up that everyone passes through.

Try These 7.1

1. **What is the term used for the period of life marked by changes leading to reproductive maturity typically spanning around 11 to 18 or 19 years of age?**
2. **Can the disproportionate appearance of arms, legs, hands or feet in adolescence be a temporary phenomenon?**
3. **How does the increased activity of sweat and oil glands contribute to skin-related issues in young people?**
4. **Is it correct to worry about the bodily changes that occur during adolescence?**

7.3 Primary and Secondary Sexual Characters

Sexual characteristics are the physical traits of an organism that indicate its biological sex. These mainly include the following characters

(i) **Primary sexual characters** are present since birth and determine a child's gender, e.g. testes in males and ovaries in females.

(ii) **Secondary sexual characters** appear later at the time of puberty and are not directly involved in the process of reproduction.

Some of the secondary sexual characters that develop in boys and girls are as follows

In Boys

(i) Development of facial hairs, such as beard and moustaches.

(ii) Muscles develop and shoulders become broad.

(iii) Increase in weight.

(iv) The voice becomes deeper.

(v) Hair develop under the armpit, on the chest and in the pubic regions.

In Girls

(i) Development and enlargement of breast.

(ii) Hips region becomes broader and pelvic region widens.

(iii) Initiation of the menstrual cycle.

(iv) The voice becomes high-pitched.

(v) Hair develop under the armpit and in the pubic regions.

7.4 Hormones

These are chemical substances. They are secreted by the **endocrine glands** or **endocrine system** and are released into the bloodstream to reach the **target site** (i.e. a particular body part), which then responds to the hormone.

The changes which occur at adolescence are controlled by two hormones, i.e. **testosterone in males** and **oestrogen/estrogen in females**.

Role of Hormones in Initiating Reproductive Function

Puberty begins with a sudden increase in the production of hormones. Apart from being reproductive organs, the testes (in males) and ovaries (in female) are also endocrine glands, which secrete sex hormones that bring about changes at puberty and make their reproductive systems functional.

The **testes** releases male sex hormone, called **testosterone,** while the **ovaries** produce female sex hormone called **oestrogen**. The production of these sex hormones is under the control of another hormone secreted from an endocrine gland called **pituitary gland**.

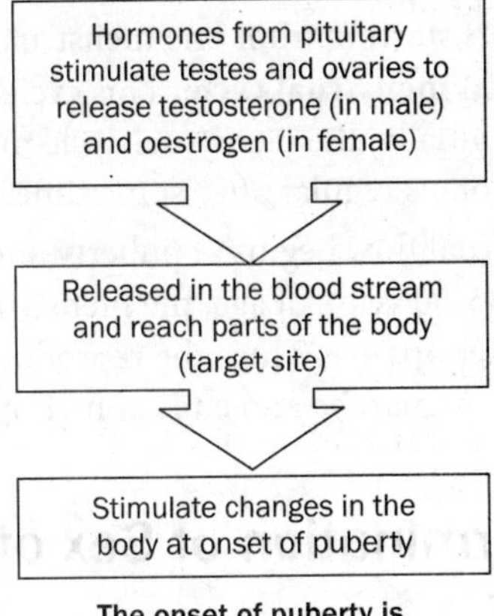

The onset of puberty is controlled by hormones

The pituitary gland secretes many hormones. One of these hormones stimulates the formation of sperms in testes and maturation of egg cells (or ova) in ovaries. Another hormone, develops the mammary glands (milk producing glands) inside the breasts in females.

7.5 Reproductive Phase of Life in Humans

Adolescents become capable of reproduction at puberty when their testes and ovaries begin to produce gametes. In males, the capacity to produce gametes (sperms) usually lasts longer than in females.

In females, the reproductive phase of life begins at puberty (10-12 years of age) and generally continues till they reach the age of approximately 45-50 years.

During reproductive phase, following changes occurs in the ovary and the uterus of female

(i) With the onset of puberty, the ova begins to mature in the ovaries of a woman. One mature ovum is released by one of the ovaries once in about 28-30 days.

(ii) During this period, the wall of the uterus becomes thick so as to receive the fertilised egg. The fertilised egg gets implanted in the thick wall of uterus for further development resulting in **pregnancy**.

(iii) If fertilisation does not occur, then the released egg, and the thickened lining of the uterus along with its blood vessels are shed off.

This causes bleeding in women which is termed as **menstruation**. Menstruation occurs once in about 28 to 30 days.

The cyclic events starting from one menstruation till the next one is called **menstrual cycle**. This cycle is controlled by hormones. Initially, the menstrual cycle may be irregular, it becomes regular after some time.

The first menstrual flow begins at puberty and is termed as **menarche**. At 45-50 years of age, the menstrual cycle stops. This is called **menopause**. Thus, the reproductive life of a woman starts at menarche and ends at menopause.

7.6 Determination of Sex of the Baby

The sex of the baby is determined by the nature of the sex chromosomes present in the fertilised egg. You have already studied that thread-like structures called **chromosomes** are present inside the nucleus of the cell.

The nucleus of each human cell contains 23 pairs of chromosomes. One pair, out of these are the **sex chromosomes** which are of two types named as X and Y.

A female has two **X-chromosomes**, while a male has one X and one **Y-chromosome**. The gametes (egg and sperm) have only one set of chromosomes.

The unfertilised egg always has one X-chromosome, but sperms are of two kinds, i.e. X-chromosome and Y-chromosome.

The sex of a child depends on what happens at fertilisation.

(i) If a sperm carrying X-chromosome, fertilises an egg cell (or ovum) then the zygote formed will have XX combination of sex chromosomes, due to which the child born will be a girl (or female).

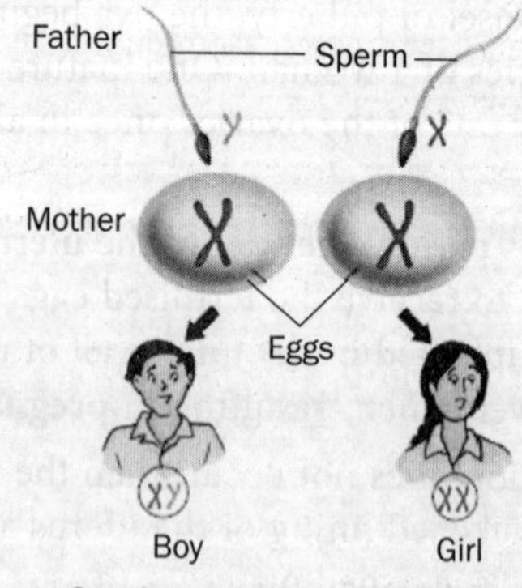

Sex-determination in humans

(ii) If a sperm carrying Y-chromosome, fertilises an egg cell (or ovum) then the zygote formed will have XY combination of sex chromosomes, due to which the child born will be a boy (or male).

From the above discussion, we can see that sex chromosome of the male parent determines the sex of an unborn baby. Traditionally, it is believed that a mother is responsible for the sex of the baby. This belief is completely wrong and unjustified.

Try These 7.2

1. **Which chemical messengers, released into circulatory system act like couriers delivering directions to specific body parts during adolescence?**
2. **Which gland, situated in the endocrine system, control production of sex hormones by the testes and ovaries during puberty?**
3. **How often does the release of one mature ovum from ovary occur?**
4. **What is the end of menstruation in females called?**
5. **The resultant sex of a child is determined by which parent, mother or father?**

7.7 Hormones Other than Sex Hormones

Certain hormones secreted by endocrine glands are required in extremely small quantities. They control growth, development, behaviour and in human beings.

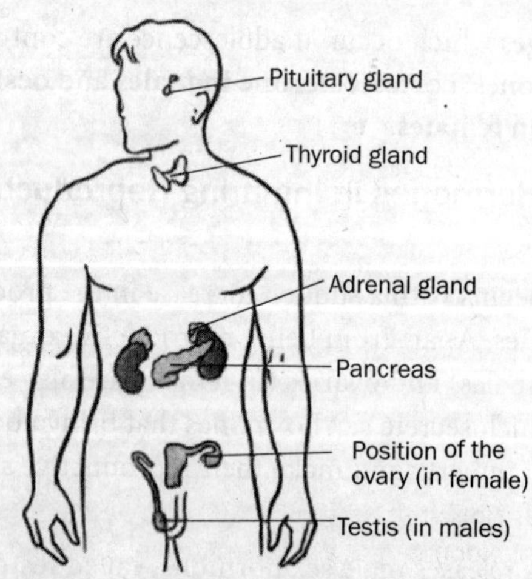

Position of endocrine glands in the human body

Some endocrine glands and their functions are given below in the table

Endocrine glands and their functions

Glands	Location	Hormones secreted	Functions
Pituitary (master gland)	Attached to the brain	Growth hormone and several other hormones	Regulates growth and the functioning of the other endocrine glands.
Thyroid	Near the larynx	Thyroxine	Controls many activities of the body including the rate at which energy is produced.
Adrenals (2 glands)	Attached to each kidney	Adrenaline	Regulate heartbeat, respiration rate and blood pressure.
Pancreas	Below the stomach	Insulin	Controls glucose level in blood.
Testes	Outside abdominal cavity	Testosterone	Promote development of secondary sexual characters.
Ovaries	Lower part of abdominal cavity	Oestrogen	Control secondary sexual characters and changes related to pregnancy.

Hormones are required in a proper amount. A less (hypo) secretion or more (hyper) secretion of a particular hormone may lead to disorders in body. Some of these are given below in the table.

Disorders of endocrine glands

Glands	Hormones	Disorders
Thyroid	Thyroxine	Hyposecretion–goitre (neck appears to be swollen) due to the deficiency of iodine in the diet.
Pancreas	Insulin	Hyposecretion–diabetes (large quantities of sugar in blood and urine).

SCIENCE INSIGHT The pancreas plays crucial role in regulating blood sugar levels by secreting insulin and glucagon. While, insulin lower blood sugar, glucagon raises it by prompting the release of glucose.

Role of Hormones in Completing the Life History of Insects and Frogs

We have studied the life cycle of frog. The tadpole passes through certain stages to become a frog. This change from larva to adult is called **metamorphosis**. The process of metamorphosis in insects is controlled by **insect hormones.**

In a frog, the process is regulated by **thyroxine hormone** produced by thyroid gland. Thyronine production requires the presence of iodine in water. A tadpole cannot become an adult if there is deficiency of iodine in the water where it is growing.

Try These 7.3

1. **What is the role of the gland located near the larynx?**
2. **Which hormone is released during the moments of stress, fear, anger and excitement, causing an elevation in heart rate and blood pressure?**
3. **Which term is used to describe the series of changes a tadpole undergoes to become an adult?**

7.8 Reproductive Health

Health is regarded as the physical and mental well-being. Reproductive health addresses the reproductive processes, functions and systems at all stages of life. During adolescence, there is rapid mental and physical growth. Therefore, growing children need special attention towards proper health.

Nutritional Needs of the Adolescents

Each individual should take balanced diet to stay healthy, but it is more important for adolescent to plan their diet carefully.

A typical **balanced diet** includes carbohydrates, fats, proteins, vitamins, minerals, roughage and water in adequate proportions.

The various types of food items which should be included in the diet of adolescent to meet their nutritional needs are as follows

(i) Cereals (like wheat and rice) which provide carbohydrates **for energy**, e.g. chapati, dosa, cooked rice, etc.

(ii) Milk, meat, nuts and pulses which provide protein **for growth**, e.g. dal, paneer, fish, etc.

(iii) Fats and sugars which **give energy**, e.g. butter, ghee, groundnuts, etc.

(iv) Fruits and vegetables which are **protective food** and provide many vitamins and minerals, e.g. citrus fruits like oranges (vitamin-C rich), carrot (vitamin-A rich).

(v) The iron-rich foods such as leafy vegetables, Indian gooseberry (amla), meat and jaggery (gud) are good for adolescents. Iron contributes to the **formation of blood**.

(vi) Milk contains a lot of calcium mineral which is necessary for making **healthy bones** of the growing adolescents.

Our Indian meal of roti (or rice), pulses (dal) and vegetables is a balanced meal. Milk is a balanced food in itself. For infants (small babies), mother's milk provides all the necessary nourishment which they need.

Avoid consuming junk foods such as burgers, noodles, etc. Chips and packed (or tinned) snacks, though very tasty should never be taken in place of regular meals because they do not have adequate nutritional value.

Personal Hygiene

Good personal hygiene is one of the most effective ways to protect ourselves and others from illness. The adolescents are advised to adopt the practices given below to maintain personal hygiene

(i) Keep all the parts of the body clean by taking bath daily. It is more necessary for teenagers because the increased activity of sweat glands sometimes makes the body smelly. Bathing removes the sweat, oil and dirt, etc. and cleans the body.

(ii) Always wash hands before and after meals.

(iii) Do not defecate in open field.

(iv) Girls should take special care of cleanliness during the time of menstrual flow. They should keep track of their menstrual cycle and be prepared for the onset of menstruation.

If personal hygiene (or cleanliness of body) is not maintained by adolescent boys and girls, there are chances of catching bacterial infections. These infections can make a person ill.

Physical Exercise

Do physical exercise regularly to keep your body fit and fine. All young boys and girls should include brisk walking, running, jogging, cycling, swimming, skipping and dancing in their routine to keep themselves fit and healthy.

Say 'No' to Drugs

Adolescence is a period of transition between childhood and adulthood. It is a period of hyperactivity in the body and mind, which is a normal process of growing up. Some adolescents feel confused or insecure about these changes. We should not worry about these changes as there is nothing abnormal about them.

If somebody suggests that you will get relief from confusion, tension, boredom, worries, etc., and feel better by taking some drugs, just say 'No' (unless the drugs have been prescribed by a doctor).
Drugs are very powerful chemical substances and should be used only under a doctor's supervision. Adolescent boys and girls should avoid drugs to live a happy life.

Some of the harmful effects of taking drugs are as follows

(i) Drugs are addictive. If you take drugs once, you feel like taking them again and again. Soon the person feels he (or she) cannot live without drugs and becomes a drug addict.

(ii) Drug addicts become irritable and loose interest in their studies or jobs.

(iii) Drugs do physical harm to the body in the long run.

(iv) The sharing of syringes for injecting drugs spreads disease like AIDS among the drug addicts.

> **AIDS (Acquired Immuno Deficiency Syndrome)**
>
> AIDS is a disease which is caused by HIV (Human Immunodeficiency Virus).
>
> This virus can easily pass from an infected person to a healthy person through the ways given below
>
> (i) Sharing the syringes for injecting drugs.
>
> (ii) Unprotected sex with an infected person.
>
> (iii) Transfusion of blood into a healthy person from an infected person.
>
> (iv) Through milk from an infected mother to an infant.

Myths, Taboos, Do's and Dont's

After learning the scientific facts about human reproduction and adolescence, you should be able to discard many wrong notions that are prevalent in the society.

Some of these myths with the facts in front of them are given below

Myths	Facts
The mother is responsible for the sex of her child.	It is the sperm that comes from the father which is responsible for the sex of the child.
A girl should not be allowed to work in the kitchen during menstruation.	This should not be done. Having your period does not make you dirty/ unclean and you are at no risk of spoiling the food items by touching them.
If you do not get your menstruation period, you are definitely pregnant.	There are various factors that can delay menstruation period such as stress, illness, drastic weight change, etc.

Adolescent Pregnancy

You might be knowing that in our country, the legal age for marriage is 18 years for girls and 21 years for boys. This is because teenage mothers are not prepared mentally or physically for motherhood.

Early marriage and motherhood cause health problems in the mother and the child. It also curtails employment opportunities for the young woman and may cause mental agony as she is not ready for responsibilities of motherhood. To avoid such pregnancies, it is very important to create understanding among the youngsters about sex-related issues.

Try These 7.4

1. **Why is it recommended for young boys and girls to participate in outdoor activities such as walking and exercise?**
2. **What is the connection between drug use and the transmission of the HIV virus?**
3. **What is most likely to happen if personal hygiene is not maintained?**

Science Glossary

Adolescence Period of life, when the body undergoes changes, leading to reproductive maturity.

Adrenaline Hormone released by adrenal gland.

Adam's apple Larynx in boys, visible as protruding part of throat.

Balanced diet A diet that contains all important constituents required by the body to grow.

Endocrine glands Ductless glands, that release their secretions called hormones directly into the blood.

Hormone Chemical substances, secreted by endocrine gland.

Insulin Hormone released from pancreas.

Oestrogen Female hormone produced from ovaries.

Puberty Time in life when an individual becomes sexually mature.

Pituitary gland Master gland of the body.

Reproductive health Condition of male and female reproductive systems during all life stages.

Secondary sexual characters The characters that are governed by the hormones released at the time of puberty.

Sex chromosome Type of chromosome, involved in sex determination.

Target site Particular body part or organ that responds to a hormone.

Testosterone Male hormone produced from testes.

Thyroxine Hormone released by thyroid gland.

Voice box Produces sound when we are talking.

ACTIVITY 1 (Page 81)

Aim To determine the maximum height that would be reached at the end of growth period.

Materials Required Graph paper, pencil, table, etc.

Procedure

1. Use the data given in the table in the previous activity to draw a graph.
2. Take age an X – axis and per cent growth in height on the Y – axis.
3. Mark the point representing your age on the graph (Let age of a girl be 11 years, height be 120 cm).
4. Find out the percentage of height already reached and calculate the height she might eventually reach.

Observation

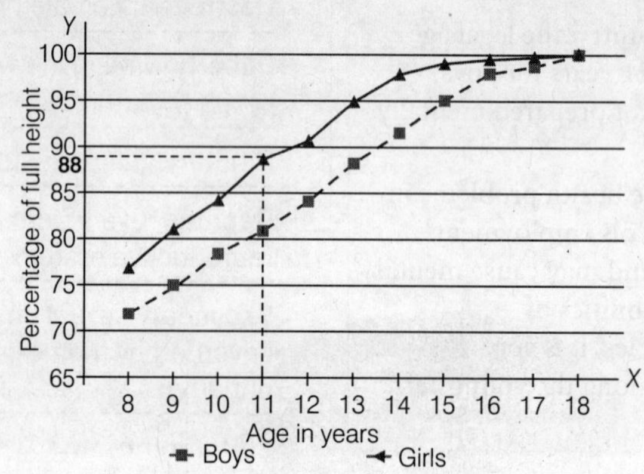

Graph depicting percentage of height

With the age of 11 years (girl), the point of age touches the 88% mark on height axis. So, the maximum height that will eventually be reached

$$= \frac{\text{Present height}}{\text{\% of full height at this age}} \times 100 = \frac{120}{88} \times 100 = 136.36 \text{ cm}$$

Conclusion From this activity we conclude that we can determine the maximum height that would be reached at the end of growth period using the formula.

Viva Questions

1. A 12 year old boy is 135 cm tall. If the present height of the boy is 84% of his full height, calculate the full height which the boy will eventually reach at the end of growth period?
2. What is the most conspicuous change during puberty?

Mind Map

REACHING THE AGE OF ADOLESCENCE

Adolescence
- Period of life when the body undergoes changes leading to reproductive maturity.
- Rapid physical, mental growth occurs during this phase.

Puberty
- Period when body undergoes certain changes leading to reproductive maturity.
- It includes changes such as change in body shape, change in voice, increased activity of sweat and sebaceous glands, development of sex organs, mental intellectual and emotional maturity occurs.

Sexual Characters

Primary Sexual Characters
Present since birth and determines sex or gender of a child.

Secondary Sexual Characters
Appears later at the time of puberty.

Secondary Sexual Characters in Boys
- Development of facial hair.
- Muscle development.
- Increase in weight.
- Pubic hair, hair on chest, armpit.

Secondary Sexual Characters in Girls
- Development of breasts.
- Widening of pelvic region.
- Menstruation.
- Voice high pitched.

Hormones
Chemical substances secreted by various endocrine glands.

Pituitary gland Secretes growth hormone and several other hormones. Regulates growth and the functioning of the other endocrine glands.

Thyroid gland Secretes thyroxine that controls many activities of the body including the rate at which energy is produced.

Adrenal gland Secretes adrenaline that regulate heartbeat, respiration rate and blood pressure.

Pancreas Secretes insulin that controls glucose level in blood.

Ovary Secretes oestrogen that control secondary sexual characters and changes related to pregnancy.

Testis Secretes testosterone that promote development of secondary sexual characters.

Reproductive Health
- It addresses reproductive processes, functions and systems at all ages of life.
- It includes the following
- Balanced diet.
- Personal hygiene.
- Physical excercise.

Reproductive Phase

Menarche
- Onset of menstruation.
- It begins at puberty.

Menstrual Cycle
- The cyclic events starting from one menstruation to the next.
- It is controlled by hormones.
- It occurs once in about 28-30 days.

Pregnancy
Fertilised egg gets implanted in the thick wall of the uterus.

Menopause
- Stoppage of menstruation.
- It occurs at 45-50 years of age.

Determination of Sex of a Baby
- It is determined by the nature of the sex chromosomes present in fertilised egg.
- Female has XX chromosomes, males have XY chromosomes.

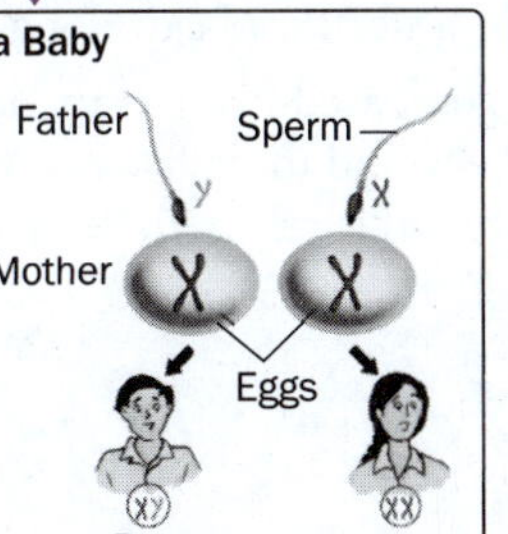

NCERT FOLDER

Complete Explanations of all NCERT's Questions

Intex Questions

Q.1 Boojho begin wondering how long this period marked by changes in the body would last. **Page 79**

Ans. The period marked by change, i.e. adolescence begins around the age of 11 and last upto 18 or 19 years of age.

Q.2 Paheli, on the other hand is worried about this period of life when you are neither a child nor an adult. She wondered whether this period between childhood and adulthood had a special name. **Page 80**

Ans. The period of life between childhood and adulthood is termed as adolescence.

Q.3 Paheli and Boojho realised that sudden increase in height and hairy line above the lips in boys were signs of adolescence. They wanted to know about other changes at puberty. **Page 81**

Ans. The other changes in the body are as follows

(a) Change in body shape.

(b) Increase in height.

(c) Increased activity of sweat and sebaceous glands.

Q.4 Both Boojho and Paheli wish to know, what initiates changes at puberty? **Page 83**

Ans. The changes which occur at adolescence are controlled by hormones.

Q.5 Paheli and Boojho have now understood that puberty marks the beginning of the reproductive period when one becomes capable of reproduction. But they want to know if reproductive life once begin, it continues or it ends some time. **Page 84**

Ans. The capacity for maturation and production of gametes lasts for much longer time in males than in females. In females, the reproductive phase of life begins at puberty (10 to 12 year of age) and generally last till age of approximately 45 to 50 years.

Q.6 Paheli says that the reproductive life of a woman lasts from menarche to menopause. Is she right? **Page 84**

Ans. Refer to text on page no. 112.

Q.7 Paheli heard her mother and her aunt talking about her cousin who is going to have a baby. They were discussing whether she would given birth to a boy or a girl. She wonders what makes the fertilised egg develop either into a boy or a girl.

Ans. Inside the fertilised egg or zygote is the instruction for determining the sex of the baby. This instruction is present in the thread-like structures called chromosome.

Q.8 Are there hormones in other animals also? Have they any role to play in reproduction ? **Page 86**

Ans. Yes, animals also have hormonal secretions.
Yes, hormones have their role to play in reproduction.

Q.9 If people do not have enough iodine in their diet, will they get goitre caused by lack of thyroxine? **Page 86**

Ans. Yes, if people do not have enough iodine in their diet, they will get goitre caused by lack of thyroxine.

Exercise

Q.1 What is the term used for secretions of endocrine glands responsible for changes taking place in the body?

Ans. Hormone is the term used for secretions of endocrine glands responsible for changes taking place in the body.

Q.2 Define adolescence.

Ans. Adolescence is the period of life, in which organisms become reproductively active.

In other words, it is the period of attaining reproductive maturity in boys and girls, which starts from 11-13 years and lasts upto 18-19 years in humans.

Q.3 What is menstruation? Explain.

Ans. Menstruation is the monthly reproductive cycle that occurs in women once in about 28-30 days. It is the release of unfertilised egg along with blood.

If the egg released from ovary does not get fertilised, the released egg and the thickened lining of uterus along with its blood is released out from body.

Q.4 List changes in the body that take place at puberty.

Ans. At puberty, the body undergoes the following changes

(i) Boys and girls become capable of reproduction.

(ii) Sudden increase in height.

(iii) Broad shoulders and wide chests in boys and region below the waist becomes wider in girls.

(iv) Growth of hairs on different parts of the body.

(v) Voice of girls becomes high pitched and that of boys becomes deep.

(vi) Secretions of sweat and sebaceous glands increase.

(vii) Sex organs become active. In boys, testes start to form sperms and in girls, ovaries enlarge and eggs begin to mature.

(viii) Changes at mental, intellectual and emotional level.

Q.5 Prepare a table having two columns depicting names of endocrine glands and hormones secreted by them.

Ans. The table is shown as below

Endocrine glands	Hormones
Pituitary gland	Growth hormones
Thyroid	Thyroxine
Pancreas	Insulin
Adrenal glands	Adrenaline
Ovaries	Oestrogen
Testes	Testosterone

Q.6 What are sex hormones? Why are they named so? State their functions.

Ans. The hormones which are responsible for the male and female secondary sexual characters are called sex hormones.

They are called sex hormones as they control the sexual activities and help us to distinguish boys from girls.

In boys, sex hormones control formation of sperms by testes and growth of facial hair, etc. and in girls, they help to develop breasts, control menstrual cycle, etc.

Q.7 Choose the correct option.

(a) Adolescents should be careful about what they eat, because

(i) proper diet develops their brains

(ii) proper diet is needed for the rapid growth taking place in their body

(iii) adolescents feel hungry all the time

(iv) taste buds are well developed in teenagers

(b) Reproductive age in women starts when their

(i) menstruation starts

(ii) breasts start developing

(iii) body weight increases

(iv) height increases

(c) The right meal for adolescents consists of

(i) chips, noodles, cake

(ii) chapati, dal, vegetables

(iii) rice, noodles and burger

(iv) vegetable cutlets, chips and lemon drink

Ans. (a) (ii) Adolescents should be careful about what they eat because proper diet is needed for the rapid growth taking place in their body.

(b) (i) Reproductive age in women starts when their menstruation starts.

(c) (ii) The right meal for adolescents consists of chapati, dal and vegetables.

Q.8 Write notes on

(a) Adam's apple.

(b) Secondary sexual characters.

(c) Sex-determination of the unborn baby.

Ans. (a) **Adam's apple** The protruding part of the growing voice box is called Adam's apple in males. In boys, the voice box (larynx) develops larger than in girls and this protruding part is seen as bulge in the neck area.

(b) **Secondary sexual characters** The physical features that help to distinguish males from females are called secondary sexual characters. These characters develop at the time of puberty. The secondary sexual characteristics in humans are given below

In males,

(i) Growth of pubic hair, beard and moustaches.

(ii) Hair on chest and underarms.

In females,

(i) Enlargement of breasts.

(ii) Appearance of pubic hair, hair underarms.

(c) **Sex-determination of the unborn baby** Sex of the unborn baby is determined by the sex chromosomes, i.e. X and Y.

In females, the gamete, (i.e. egg) have only one X-chromosome, but in males, the gamete, (i.e. sperm) may have an X-chromosome or Y-chromosome.

If the egg fertilises with sperm containing X-chromosome, the zygote will develop into a female (XX) and if the egg fertilises with sperm containing Y-chromosome, the zygote will develop into a male (XY).

Q.9 The table given below shows the data on likely heights of boys and girls as they grow in age. Draw graphs showing height and age for both boys and girls on the same graph paper. What conclusions can be drawn from this graph?

Age (Years)	Height (cm)	
	Boys	**Girls**
0	53	53
4	96	92
8	114	110
12	129	133
16	150	150
20	173	165

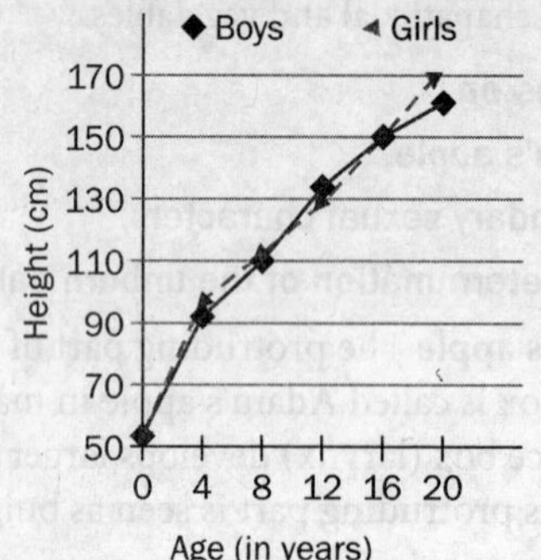

Ans. We conclude that initially, girls grow faster than boys, but by about 18 years of age, both reach their maximum height. The rate of growth in height varies in different individuals.

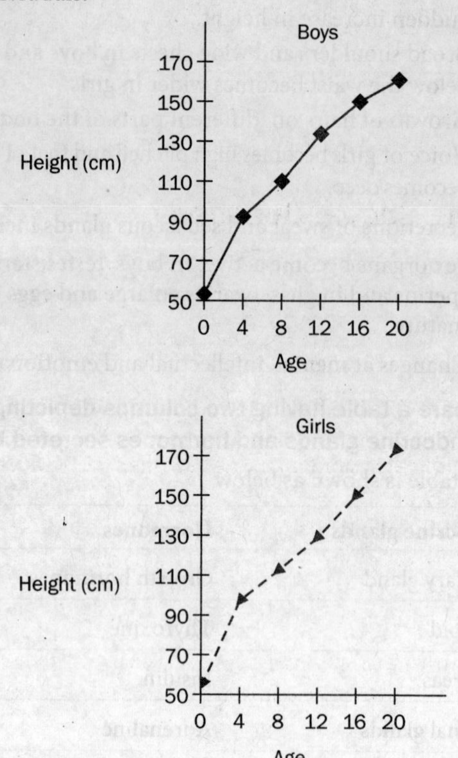

REVIEW EXERCISE

Including Competency Based Questions

Part I

Multiple Choice Questions

1. The most conspicuous visible change that occurs in boys during puberty is NCERT Exemplar

(a) development in voice box
(b) increase in height
(c) production of sperms
(d) increased sweating

2. Pimples and acne are formed due to the increased activity of

(i) adrenal glands (ii) sebaceous glands
(iii) thyroid gland (iv) sweat glands

(a) (i) and (ii) (b) (ii) and (iii)
(c) (i) and (iii) (d) (ii) and (iv)

3. The dramatic changes in body features associated with puberty are mainly because of the secretions of

(i) Thyroxine (ii) Oestrogen
(iii) Adrenaline (iv) Testosterone

(a) (i) and (ii) (b) (ii) and (iii)
(c) (i) and (iii) (d) (ii) and (iv)

4. The male hormone is

(a) oestrogen (b) progesterone
(c) testosterone (d) All of these

5. How do the endocrine gland's hormones secreted during puberty induces changes in the body?

(a) It decreases the muscle mass
(b) It reduces the metabolism increasing the food intake
(c) It stimulates changes in different parts of the body
(d) It doubles the capability of body parts to function

6. The beginning of menstruation at puberty is called

(a) ovulation (b) menstruation
(c) menarche (d) menopause

7. Given below are events that lead to pregnancy and development of embryo.

(i) Fertilisation of egg
(ii) Maturation of egg
(iii) Release of egg
(iv) Embedding of embryo in uterus

Which of the following options gives the correct order of sequence in which they occur? Competency Based Que.

(a) (i), (ii), (iii), (iv) (b) (ii), (i), (iii), (iv)
(c) (i), (iv), (ii), (iii) (d) (ii), (iii), (i), (iv)

8. Structures present in a cell which is responsible for determination of the sex of a baby is NCERT Exemplar

(a) cytoplasm (b) cell membrane
(c) nucleus (d) chromosome

9. The number of chromosomes present in human cell

(a) 22 pairs (b) 23 pairs
(c) 24 pairs (d) 26 pairs

10. The belief that the mother is completely responsible for the sex of the child is wrong because the child NCERT Exemplar

(a) gets sex chromosome only from the mother
(b) develops in the body of the mother
(c) gets one sex chromosome from the mother and the other from the father
(d) gets sex chromosome only from the father

11. Which endocrine gland is attached to the brain?

(a) Adrenal (b) Pancreas
(c) Pituitary (d) Thyroid

12. Which choice appropriately distinguishes the roles of oestrogen and insulin?

(a) Oestrogen plays a role in development of mammary glands, while insulin helps to control blood sugar level
(b) Oestrogen plays a role in promoting growth of facial hair, while insulin helps to control blood sugar level
(c) Oestrogen helps to control blood sugar level, while insulin plays a role in promoting growth of facial hair
(d) Oestrogen helps to control blood sugar level, while insulin plays a role in development of mammary glands

13. The faulty functioning of an endocrine gland can make a person very short or very tall. This gland is

(a) thyroid (b) pituitary
(c) adrenal (d) pancreas

14. What can be the consequences of drug addiction?

(a) They can harm our body
(b) They can protect our body from infections
(c) They can enhance body's immunity
(d) They can make our body resistant to harmful organisms

15. AIDS can spread from an infected person to another person through NCERT Exemplar

(a) sharing food (b) blood transfusion
(c) sharing comb (d) a mosquito bite

Answers

1. (b)	2. (d)	3. (d)	4. (c)	5. (c)
6. (c)	7. (d)	8. (d)	9. (b)	10. (c)
11. (c)	12. (a)	13. (b)	14. (a)	15. (b)

Fill in the Blanks

1. After attaining puberty, boys develop a .... voice. **NCERT Exemplar**

2. The sex hormones, ... and oestrogen are responsible for the development of sexual characters.

3. Release of sex hormones is under the control of a hormone secreted from the...... .

4. Endocrine glands release hormones directly into......for transportation to the...... .

5. In females, the uterine wall thickens to receive the...... . **NCERT Exemplar**

Answers

1. deep
2. testosterone
3. pituitary gland
4. bloodstream, target site
5. fertilised egg

True/False

1. Puberty starts later in girls than in boys.

2. Girls have high pitched voice, whereas boys have deep voice.

3. Mood swings takes place during adolescence.

4. Oestrogen is a male hormone.

5. Males have both X and Y chromosomes.

Answers

1. False, It starts early in girls than in boys.
2. True
3. True
4. False, oestrogen is a female hormone.
5. True

Match the Columns

1. Match the hormones given in Column I with their deficiency diseases given in Column II.

	Column I		Column II
A.	Thyroxine	1.	Salt imbalance
B.	Growth hormone	2.	Diabetes
C.	Insulin	3.	Goitre
D.	Adrenal hormone	4.	Dwarfism

Answer.

A–3, B–4, C–2, D–1

Assertion- Reason Questions

The following questions consist of two statements; Assertion (A) and Reason (R). Answer the following questions by selecting the appropriate option given below

(a) Both A and R are true and R is the correct explanation of A.

(b) Both A and R are true, but R is not the correct explanation of A.

(c) A is true, but R is false.

(d) A is false, but R is true.

1. Assertion (A) Height of an individual is roughly comparable to that of a family member.

Reason (R) Height depends on the genes inherited from parents.

2. Assertion (A) Young people get acne and pimples on the face at the time of puberty.

Reason (R) It is caused due to increased activity of adrenal gland.

3. Assertion (A) Exocrine glands are also called as ductless glands.

Reason (R) They release hormones into blood stream to reach a target site.

4. Assertion (A) Diet for an adolescent has to be carefully planned.

Reason (R) Chips and packed or tinned snacks should be included in a regular meal.

5. Assertion (A) Teenagers should take care of their personal hygiene.

Reason (R) The increased activity of sweat glands makes their body smelly.

Answers

1. (a) Both A and R are true and R is the correct explanation of A.
2. (c) A is true, but R is false. R can be corrected as Young people get acne and pimples on the face due to increased activity of sweat and sebaceous glands.
3. (d) A is false, but R is true. A can be corrected as Endocrine glands are called as ductless glands. They release hormones directly into blood streams to reach a target site.
4. (c) A is true, but R is false. R can be corrected as The diet for an adolescent has to be carefully planned because it is a stage of rapid growth and development. Meals should include proteins, carbohydrates, fats and vitamins in requisite proportions.
5. (a) Both A and R are true and R is the correct explanation of A.

Case Based Questions

1. Heights of students of four different sections of grade 8 are measured. The table shows the percentage of maximum height up to which the students in each section have grown **Competency Based Que.**

Section	Girls	Boys
A	80%	75%
B	100%	100%
C	92%	85%
D	100%	98%

(i) In which class have both the boys and the girls reached the end of puberty?

(a) Section A (b) Section B
(c) Section C (d) Section D

(ii) What can be concluded from the table?

(a) Girls are taller than boys in all four classes
(b) Girls attain their maximum height earlier than boys
(c) Girls grow faster than boys throughout their childhood
(d) Girls and boys attain their maximum height at the same age

2. An ovum contains one X-chromosome. A sperm contains an X or a Y-chromosome. A sperm can fertilise an ovum to produce two different zygotes.

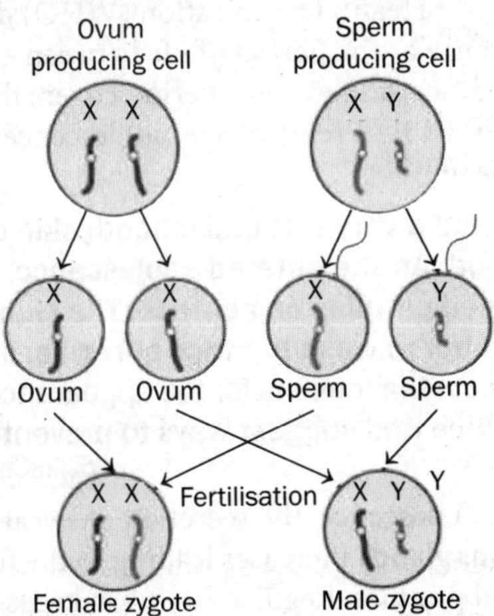

Competency Based Que.

(i) Which chromosome does the female zygote receive from the mother and the father?

	Mother	Father
(a)	X-chromosome	Y-chromosome
(b)	Y-chromosome	X-chromosome
(c)	X-chromosome	X-chromosome
(d)	Y-chromosome	Y-chromosome

(ii) Which of these statements is supported by the picture?

Circle 'Yes' or 'No' for the correct response.

Is this statement supported by the picture?	Yes or No
A. The father's sperm decides the gender of the zygote.	Yes/No
B. The Y-chromosome is shorter than the X-chromosome.	Yes/No
C. An ovum unites with two sperms at a time.	Yes/No

3. Diabetes is a condition in which the blood sugar level of a person rises above the normal level. The table below shows the average range of blood sugar levels at fasting.

	Low blood sugar level	Normal blood sugar level	High blood sugar level (diabetes)
Blood sugar level at fasting	Below 70 mg/dL	70-120 mg/dL	Above 120 mg/dL

Doctors prescribe insulin injection for patients with high blood sugar levels. However, glucagon is injected in an emergency if the blood sugar level of a person drops too low. **Competency Based Que.**

(i) Which of these is true about the gland secreting insulin in the human body?

(a) It has no ducts
(b) It is located on the skin
(c) It controls the function of all other glands
(d) It releases hormones that help in growth

(ii) Under what conditions of blood sugar level is glucagon likely to be injected?

(a) Below 60 mg/dL
(b) 80–100 mg/dL
(c) 100–120 mg/dL
(d) Above 120 mg/dL

Answers

1. (i) (b) Section B.
   (ii) (b) Girls attain their maximum height earlier than boys.
2. (i) (c) Mother X-chromosome, father X-chromosome
   (ii) A. Yes B. Yes C. No
3. (i) (a) It has no ducts (ii) (a) Below 60 mg/dL

Part II

Very Short Answer Type Questions

1. Adolescence is the period from 13-19 years of age. Is there any other term for this period?

Ans. Yes, the other term for adolescence is teenage.

2. Do all the parts of the body grow at the same rate? State yes or no.

Ans. No, all the parts of the body do not grow at the same rate.

3. What is the common name of the bulge (or projection) at the front of throat in grown up boys?

Ans. Adam's apple.

4. Some characters distinguish a boy from a girl. What are they called as?

Ans. Secondary sexual characters distinguish a boy from a girl.

5. Name the hormone that is released by testes at the onset of puberty. **NCERT Exemplar**

Ans. Testosterone is the male hormone which is released from the testes at the onset of puberty.

6. Name the female hormone produced by ovaries that helps in development of mammary glands. **NCERT Exemplar**

Ans. Oestrogen is the female hormone produced by ovaries that helps in development of breasts/mammary glands.

7. State the function of male sex hormone testosterone.

Ans. Testosterone is involved in the development of the reproductive organs and controls secondary sexual characteristics.

8. Give a suitable word for each of the following statements. **NCERT Exemplar**

(a) The site which responds to a hormone.
(b) Name of a gland which transports secretions through ducts.
(c) Chemicals which control changes at adolescence stage.
(d) It marks the beginning of reproductive period.

Ans. (a) Target site
(b) Sweat glands
(c) Hormones
(d) Puberty

9. Out of two sexes of humans, which one has a longer reproductive phase of life?

Ans. Men have a longer reproductive phase of life than women.

10. What is the name of the process in which the thickened uterus lining along with its blood vessels is removed from the body of a woman through vaginal bleeding.

Ans. Menstruation cycle.

11. Which comes earlier in the life of a woman menarche or menopause?

Ans. The reproductive life of a woman starts at menarche and ends at menopause. Thus, menarche comes earlier.

12. XX or XY, state the combination of sex chromosomes that produces a male child?

Ans. XY combination of sex chromosomes produces a male child.

13. The nucleus of a cell contains chromosomes for inheritance. How many chromosomes are there in the nuclei of a human cell?

Ans. The nucleus of each human cell contains 23 pairs of chromosomes.

14. Name the endocrine gland attached to the base of brain.

Ans. Pituitary gland.

15. Name some endocrine glands other than pituitary gland.

Ans. Some endocrine glands other than pituitary are thyroid, pancreas and adrenals.

Short Answer Type Questions

1. Give the definition of adolescence as stated by the WHO. Why is adolescence also called teenage?

Ans. The World Health Organisation (WHO) defines adolescence as the period of life between 11 and 19 years of age. Since, adolescence period covers the teens period, i.e. 13-19 years of age, adolescence is also called as 'teenage'.

2. Salma had a very soft and smooth skin during her childhood. As she entered adolescence, she developed pimples on her face. The skin specialist advised her to wash her face at regular intervals. Can you explain the reasons for the appearance of pimples on her face and suggest ways to prevent them? **Competency Based Que.**

Ans. During adolescence, the secretion of sweat glands and sebaceous glands increases leading to the formation of acne and pimples. Regular face wash keeps the face clean and dry and helps to reduce the pimples.

3. Mention any two features each that are seen in boys and girls each to distinguish them from each other at puberty. **NCERT Exemplar**

Ans. Two features seen in boys at puberty are
(i) Growth of facial hairs.
(ii) Voice becomes hoarse.

Two features seen in girls at puberty are
(i) Development of breasts.
(ii) Region below the waist becomes wider.

4. In human females, each time during maturation and release of egg, the inner wall of uterus thickens. Is this thickening permanent? Give reasons. NCERT Exemplar

Ans. No, this thickening of the uterine wall is not permanent. If the egg gets fertilised, it starts developing and gets embedded in the uterine wall resulting in pregnancy. During pregnancy, no more eggs are released and the thickened lining is discharged only when the baby is born. However, if fertilisation does not occur, the released egg and the thickened lining are shed off resulting in menstruation.

5. Fill the blank circles in figure and identify the sex of child *A* and *B*.

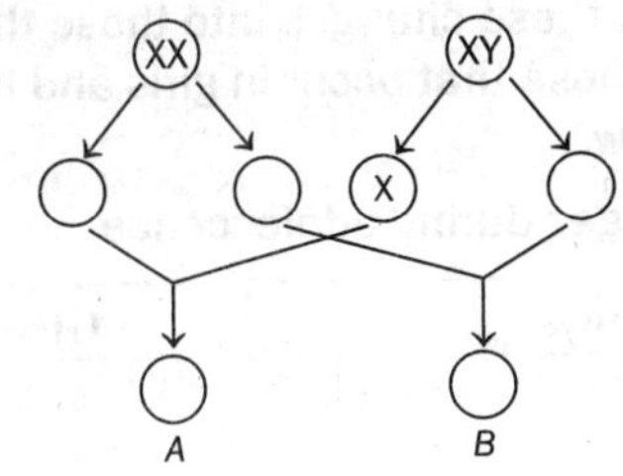

Ans.

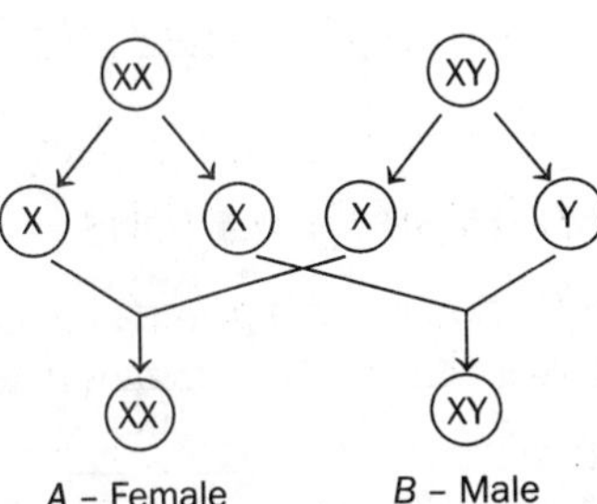

A – Female *B* – Male

6. Name the hormone which would be released during the following situations. NCERT Exemplar

(i) A frightened person

(ii) Growth of a child to adult

(iii) Development of caterpillar to moth

(iv) Development of tadpole to frog

Ans. (i) **Adrenaline** is secreted from adrenal gland during the stress conditions like fright or fear, anger, worry or embarrassment.

(ii) **Growth hormone** is secreted from pituitary gland to regulate the normal growth of a person, i.e. growth of a child to adult.

(iii) **Insect hormones** controls the development of caterpillar to moth.

(iv) **Thyroxine** is produced by thyroid gland to control the development of tadpole to frog.

7. A tadpole is kept in iodine deficient water. How will it affect its growth? Explain.

Ans. Tadpoles growing in iodine deficient water have retarded growth. This is because the growth and development is regulated by thyroxine hormone which is produced by thyroid gland.

As iodine is required for thyroxine production, retarded growth is seen in tadpoles when kept in iodine deficient water.

8. Lila always eats only dal and rice in every meal. She often falls ill and has become prone to diseases. Can you suggest changes in her diet which can make her healthy and free from disease? Competency Based Que.

Ans. Lila's diet is not a balanced diet because her meal does not contain the adequate nutritional requirement. She takes only proteins and carbohydrates in every meal. She requires vitamins and minerals in her meal to protect her from various diseases.

Thus, I would suggest her to include fruits and vegetables in her meal as a source of vitamins and minerals.

9. We should avoid taking medicines/drugs unless prescribed by a doctor. Give reasons. NCERT Exemplar

Ans. We should avoid taking medicines/drugs unless prescribed by a doctor because

(i) several medicines have adverse side effects and have specific dosage levels which if not followed may harm the body.

(ii) drugs can be addictive too and can ruin our health and happiness.

10. Given below are certain food items required for proper nourishment of adolescents. Name the nutrients present in the food items and write their functions. NCERT Exemplar

Food items	Major nutrients	Functions
Pulses and nuts		
Oranges and amla		
Sugar and roti		
Oils		
Vegetables		

Ans.

Food items	Major nutrients	Functions
Pulses and nuts	Proteins	Growth, repair of body cells.
Orange and amla	Vitamin-C and iron	Improved immunity, formation of blood.
Sugar and roti	Carbohydrates	Provide energy.
Oils	Fats	Provide energy.
Vegetables	Vitamins and minerals	Keeps the body healthy and disease free.

Long Answer Type Questions

1. Observe the chart and graph given in figure carefully and answer the following questions.

Competency Based Que.

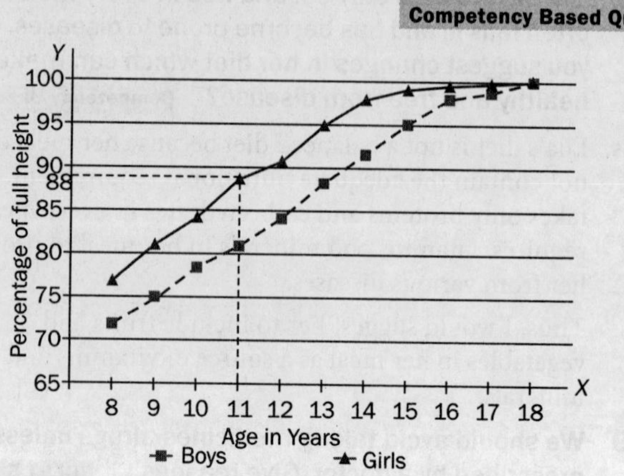

Age in years	% of full height Boy	Girl
8	72%	77%
9	75%	81%
10	78%	84%
11	81%	88%
12	84%	91%
13	88%	95%
14	92%	98%
15	95%	99%
16	98%	99.5%
17	99%	100%
18	100%	100%

(i) Which of the line represents the height of boys?

(ii) Which line represents the height of girls?

(iii) What is the difference between the pattern of increase in the height of boys and girls?

(iv) Is this pattern true for each individual?

Ans. (i) The dotted line represents the height of boys.

(ii) The solid line represents the height of girls.

(iii) At the onset of puberty, girls grow faster in height than the boys and by the age of 18 years, approximately both reach their maximum height.

(iv) No, the rate of growth in height varies among individuals. Some may grow in height suddenly at puberty and then slow down, while others may grow gradually.

2. During adolescence, the body of boys and girls undergoes certain changes. Given below are few of those changes

(a) Broad shoulders

(b) Wider chests

(c) Wider region below waist

(d) Development of muscles

(e) Development of mammary glands

(f) Growth of facial hair

(g) Acne and pimples on face

(h) Development of sex organs

(i) High-pitched voice

(j) Growth of pubic hair

Categorise these changes into those that occur in boys and those that occur in girls and fill in the table given below.

NCERT Exemplar

Body changes during adolescence

Boys	Girls

Ans. Body changes during adolescence are given below

Boys	Girls
Broad shoulders	Wider region below waist
Wider chests	Development of mammary glands
Development of muscles	Acne and pimples on face
Growth of facial hair	Development of sex organs
Acne and pimples on face	High-pitched voice
Development of sex organs	Growth of pubic hair
Growth of pubic hair	

3. Hormones play an important role during adolescence. Explain role of hormones in initiating reproductive function in humans, with a flow chart.

Ans. Refer to text on page no. 111.

4. **In figure, mark the position of the endocrine glands which release the hormones that** **NCERT Exemplar**

(i) **control the release of sex hormones.**

(ii) **are responsible for the secondary sexual characters in boys.**

(iii) **prevent diabetes.**

(iv) **maintain the correct salt balance in the blood.**

Ans. (i) **Pituitary gland** It releases hormones that control the release of sex hormones, i.e. testosterone in males and oestrogen in females.

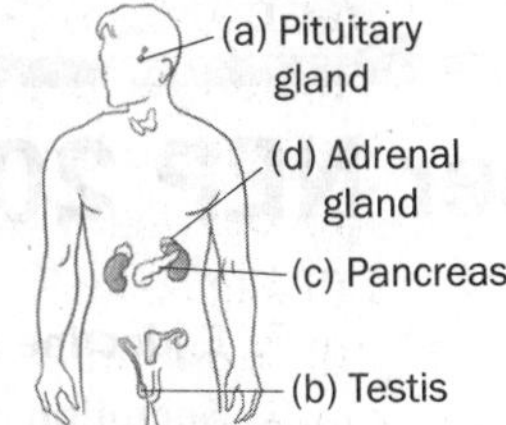

(ii) **Testis** It releases testosterone which is responsible for the secondary sexual character in boys.

(iii) **Pancreas** It releases insulin which prevents diabetes.

(iv) **Adrenal gland** It releases aldosterone that maintains the correct salt balance in the blood.

5. **It is often read in the newspapers as well as advised by our elders that we should say 'No' to drugs. What are actually these drugs? Mention some of their harmful effects.**

Ans. Refer to text on page no. 114.

6. **Our government has legalised the age for marriage for boys and girls. Give reasons as to why one should get married after a certain age?** **NCERT Exampler**

Ans. In our country, the legal age for marriage is 18 years for girls and 21 years for boys. This is because teenage mothers are not prepared mentally or physically for motherhood. Early marriage and motherhood causes health problems for both the mother and the child. It also curtails employment opportunities for the young woman and may cause mental agony as she is not ready to shoulder the responsibilities of motherhood. Also, boys before that age may not be mentally mature and financially secure enough to take on the responsibilities of a family. Thus, one should get married only after a certain age.

Case Based Questions

1. **Rohan and Seema were childhood friends. When Seema became eleven years old her breasts started developing. Rohan's voice became deeper his shoulder and chest became wider.**

(i) **Give a word for the characteristics that are developed in Rohan and Seema?**

(ii) **Name the hormone which is responsible for these sexual characteristics in Seema.**

(iii) **After a few years Rohan observed a bulge in his neck. What could be the possible reason for this bulge in his neck?**

2. **Sanjay and Seema were childhood friends. When Seema became 12 years old, she developed a little swelling in her neck. She visited a doctor who prescribed some medicines and asked her to take an iodine rich diet. After some time she felt better. Later, her friend Sanjay also developed a little protrusion on his throat. He got worried. But when he went to the doctor, he assured him that it was absolutely normal. It was just the development of secondary sexual characteristics in him.**

(i) **Describe in brief the meaning of 'secondary sexual characteristics'.**

(ii) **Explain the change that Sanjay was experiencing.**

(iii) **Recommend any two measures to Sanjay and Seema to maintain their reproductive health during adolescence.**

3. **When Sudha reached a certain age the vaginal bleeding started occurring after regular interval of time. Her mother told her to take special care of her personal hygiene during this period.**

(i) **Name the process occurring after regular intervals.**

(ii) **What does the onset of this process in females signify?**

(iii) **Give reason why her mother told her to take special care of her personal hygiene during this period.**

4. **Shobha gave birth to a healthy baby girl. Her husband was unhappy with the news and held her responsible for the baby to be a girl.**

(i) **Was her husband justified in blaming her for the birth of a baby girl?**

(ii) **Draw a diagram to show how the sex of a foetus is determined.**

Ans. 1. (i) Both Rohan and Seema have developed secondary sexual characters.

(ii) Oestrogen is the hormone responsible for these sexual characteristics in Seema.

(iii) The bulge in Rohan's neck is called Adam's apple. It is formed because male's larynx grow bigger during puberty.

2. (i) The external characters that distinguish a male from a female are called secondary sexual characters. For example, development of breast in girls and growth of moustaches in boys.

(ii) Sanjay was experiencing the enlargement of voice box. The growing voice box in boys can be seen as protruding part of the throat.

(iii) The two measures that can be taken to maintain their reproductive health are as follows

- Maintain personal hygiene
- Take balanced and nutritious diet

3. (i) This process is known as menstruation.
(ii) The onset of menstruation signifies that the reproductive system of female has started working.
(iii) Her mother told her to take special care of her personal hygiene during this period because if it is not maintained there might be chances of occurrence of bacterial infections.

4. (i) No, husband was not justified in blaming his wife for the birth of baby. As the unfertilised egg of female always has one X-chromosome. But sperm has two chromosomes, i.e. an X chromosome and the Y chromosome.
(ii) Mother- XX Father - XY

Skill Based Questions as per NEP 2020

1. In Radha's community, someone was diagnosed with AIDS. Lack of awareness led society members to cease communication and ostracise the individual. What misconceptions about AIDS contribute to this behaviour? **Observation skill**

2. According to 2011 census report of India, there are 940 adolescent females for every 1000 males. How does the patriarchal mindset impact the perception of gender and contribute to the sex ratio disparity? **Thinking skill**

3. Amit was very good in study. But as he attained the age of 13 years, he became dull and lethargic.
Asked by his teacher, Amit told that he is very worried about the changes that are taking place in his body such as hoarse voice, height, etc. The teacher smiled and explained that it is a normal process of growing up. **Observation skill**
(i) Mention some of the changes that Amit must be going through.
(ii) What is this special period of life known as?
(iii) Can you explain the reason of his hoarse voice?

4. Pooja was happy when she gave birth to her second child. Her in-laws were dissatisfied with her not giving birth to a male child and blamed her. Pooja tried to convince her in-laws that she had no role in the child's gender. They were yet not satisfied. Pooja's husband took up the matter and explained them the biological reason. They understood and apologised. **Thinking skill**
(i) What are sex chromosomes?
(ii) Is it right to blame mother for the child's gender? Give reason for your answer.

5. Word game : Use the clues to work out the words.

Across
3. Protruding voice box in boys
4. Glands without ducts
7. Endocrine gland attached to brain
8. Secretion of endocrine glands
9. Pancreatic hormone
10. Female hormone

Down
1. Male hormone
2. Secretes thyroxine
3. Another term for teenage
5. Hormone reaches here through blood stream
6. Voice box
7. Term for changes at adolescence

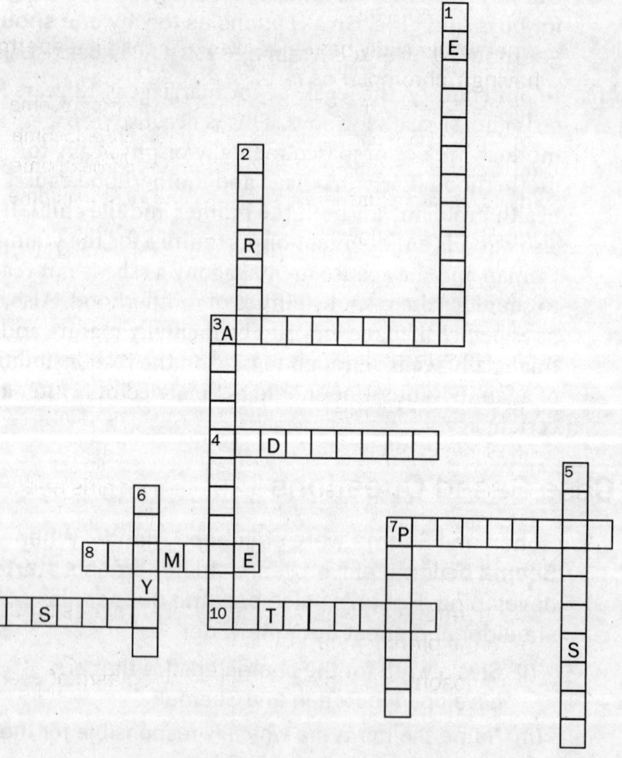

ASSESSMENT EXERCISE

Part I

Multiple Choice Questions

1. What physiological changes take place in females during puberty?
(a) Development of large voice box
(b) Development of hair on face and chest
(c) Region below the waist becomes wider
(d) Shoulder broaden

2. During puberty, hormones are produced. What secondary sexual characteristics typically emerges when testosterone is released in males?
(a) High pitched voice
(b) Development of Adam's apple
(c) Development of mammary glands
(d) Growth of hair on head

3. Which of the following option correctly describes women's menstrual cycle?
(a) The release of the fertilised egg from the uterus that occurs once in a month
(b) The release of the unfertilised egg from the uterus that occurs once in 28-30 days
(c) The release of the unfertilised egg from the ovary that occurs once in 28-30 days
(d) The release of the fertilised egg from the ovary that occurs twice in a month

4. What would likely be the gender of a child if a sperm having Y chromosome fertilise an egg?
(a) A boy, as the unfertilised egg has one X chromosome
(b) A girl, as the unfertilised egg has one Y chromosome
(c) A girl, as the unfertilised egg has one X chromosome
(d) A boy, as the unfertilised egg has one Y chromosome

5. Which of the following is not a hormone?
(a) Thyroxine
(b) Insulin
(c) Adrenal
(d) Insect hormone

Fill in the blanks

6. AIDS is caused by ...

7. The legal age for marriage is ... years for girls and ... years for boys.

True/False

8. Sex hormones are under control of hormones produced from the pituitary gland.

9. Chromosomes are present inside cytoplasm of every cell

Match the Columns

10. Match the Column I with Column II.

	Column I		Column II
A.	XX chromosomes	1.	Female hormone
B.	Thyroid gland	2.	Adrenaline
C.	Adrenal gland	3.	Thyroxine
D.	Oestrogen	4.	Girl

Assertion-Reason Questions

The following questions consist of two statements **Assertion** (A) and **Reason** (R). Answer these questions by selecting the appropriate option given below.
(a) Both A and R are true and R is the correct explanation of A
(b) Both A and R are true, but R is not the correct explanation of A
(c) A is true, but R is false
(d) A is false, but R is true

11. Assertion (A) Menstrual cycle is controlled by hormones.

Reason (R) The first menstrual flow began at puberty and is termed as menarche.

12. Assertion (A) Testosterone is a female hormone.

Reason (R) It is involved in the development of the reproductive organs and controls secondary sexual characteristics.

Part II

Very Short Answer Type Questions

13. By which term, stoppage of menstruation is described?

14. Which hormone maintains the correct salt balance in the blood?

Short Answer Type Questions

15. Give the location of the following glands in human body
(i) Pituitary (ii) Thyroid
(iii) Adrenal

16. Why iron is needed by our body? Give reason and name some of the iron-rich foods?

Long Answer Type Question

17. What is the function of thyroxine and adrenaline?

Answers

1. (c) **2.** (b) **3.** (c) **4.** (d) **5.** (c)
6. Virus **7.** 18, 21
8. True **9.** False
10. A–4, B–3, C–2, D–1
11. (b) **12.** (d)

Force and Pressure

CHAPTER 08

In our daily life, we can observe that a batsman hits the ball by applying a force and changes the speed and direction of a ball. Similarly, a hockey player changes the direction of moving ball with a flick of the stick. Here, the force is deciding factor which helps an object to change its position and direction of motion.

In this chapter, we will study how different types of forces can produce different effects. The effect of force depends upon the magnitude of force as well as the area on which it is applied. Force acting on per unit area is referred to as **pressure**. We will also study about pressure in this chapter.

8.1 Force : A Push or a Pull

In order to move an object, it has either to be pushed or pulled. A push or a pull acting on an object is known as **force**. Thus, any object is in motion due to the application of force.

The direction in which body is pushed or pulled is called **direction of force**.

Actions like kicking, opening, shutting, lifting, hitting, etc., are examples of push or pull. These actions usually results in some kind of change in the state of motion of an object.

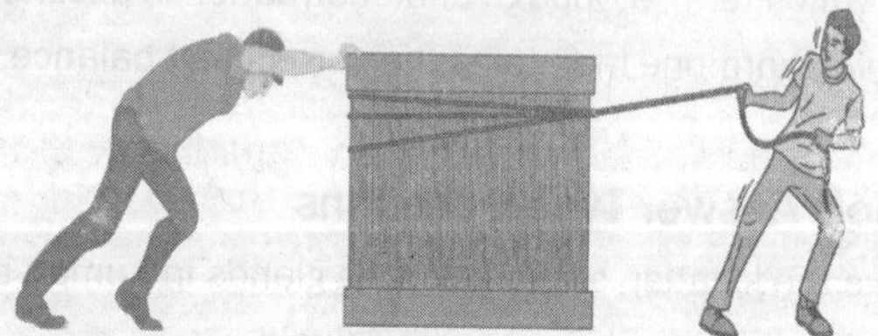

Two friends, one is pushing and other is pulling the box with rope (A push-pull force)

8.2 Force is Due to an Interaction

Force between the objects is caused by an interaction of one object with another object. If there is no interaction between two objects, then no force can show its effect. Assume that, a man is standing behind a stationary car where there is no interaction between the man and the car, so no force is acting on the car, therefore the car does not move.

A man standing behind stationary car (no interaction)

Now, consider the second diagram in which the man pushes the car and it starts moving. This is possible because the man interacts with the car.

A man pushes the car (interaction occurs)

From this example, **we can conclude that at least two objects must interact for a force to come into play.**

8.3 Exploring Forces

The strength of the force is expressed by its **magnitude** and **direction**. So, the change in the magnitude or direction of applied force always result into the change in effect produced by applied force.

- **If forces are applied on an object in the same direction, then they add to one another.** e.g. In the fig. (a), two men apply pushing force together in the same direction on the heavy box, the two forces add upto provide a much bigger force.
- **If the two forces act in the opposite directions on an object, the net force acting on it is the difference between the two forces,** e.g. In the Fig. (b), the box will move in that direction where stronger push is applied.

(a)

(b)

Two men apply pushing force on a heavy box

(a) in the same direction and (b) in the opposite direction

Another example is the game 'tug of war' in which two teams pull at a rope in opposite directions. When the two teams pull the rope equally hard by applying equal forces, then the net force acting on the rope is zero and hence, the rope does not move.

In general, **if more than one force is acting on an object, then the effect on the object will be due to net force.**

Try These 8.1

1. **If a person pushed a heavy box in north direction, then what will be the direction of force?**
2. **In which direction, an object moves when two equal forces act on an object in opposite direction?**
3. **Can force be in effect, if there is no interaction between two objects?**

8.4 Effects of Force

If we apply force on an object, it can have the following effects, depending on the type of object.

- It can change the state of motion of an object.
- It can change the size or shape of an object.

Force can Change the State of Motion

The state of motion is described by its **speed** and the **direction of motion**. The state of rest is considered to be the state of zero speed.

A force may bring a change in the state of motion of an object.

Force can increase the speed, if the force applied on the object is in the direction of its motion and decrease the speed, if the force is applied in the opposite to the direction of motion. Even, it can stop the moving object or change the direction of motion of an object.

e.g.

(i) A goalkeeper dives or jumps up to save the goal. Actually, he applies force on the moving ball. This force can stop or deflect the ball.

(ii) In the following figure, the child applies force in the direction of motion of tyre to increase its speed.

To move a tyre faster, it has to be pushed repeatedly

Sometimes the application of force does not change the state of motion. e.g. Heavy box may not move all even if you apply the maximum force that you can exert. Similarly, you cannot displace a wall by pushing that.

Force can Change the Shape of an Object

The application of force on an object may change it's shape, e.g.

(i) The shape of an inflated balloon changes by pressing it.

(ii) The shape of ball of dough changes when it is rolled to make a chapati.

We can summarise that applying force

- may make an object **move from rest.**
- may **change the speed** of an object if it is moving.
- may **change the direction** of motion of an object.
- may bring about a **change in the shape** of an object.
- may cause some or all of these effects.

8.5 Types of Force

There are different types of force which are categorised into two groups

1. Contact force

These forces come in action only when two objects are in actual contact with each other. These are also of two types

(i) **Muscular force** This force is caused by the action of muscles in our body. It enables us to perform all activities involving movement or bending of our body.

e.g. In the process of digestion, the food gets pushed through the alimentary canal, expansion and contraction of lungs while breathing, physical activities done by animals, etc.

(ii) **Frictional force** This force always acts opposite to the motion of any moving object. e.g. Ball rolling on the ground slows down, boat comes to rest if we stop rowing it, etc.

2. Non-Contact Forces

These forces came into action without any contact with one another. e.g. Magnetic force, electrostatic force and gravitational force.

(i) **Magnetic force** The force exerted by magnet is called the magnetic force. Like poles of two magnets repel each other and unlike poles attract each other.

A magnet can attract iron nails without touching them or a magnet exerts a force even without touching an object. So, it is considered as a non-contact force.

(ii) **Electrostatic force** The force exerted by a charged body on another charged body is known as electrostatic force. e.g. When a plastic comb is rubbed in dry hair, the comb gets electric charges by friction and if this electrically charged comb is brought near the small pieces of paper, then it exerts an electrostatic force of attraction on them (pieces of paper) even if they are not in touch with each other.

(iii) **Gravitational force** The force due to which every body of the universe attracts another body, whether the object is small or large is known as gravitational force.

Objects or things fall towards the earth because it pulls them. This force is called the **force of gravity or gravity** and this is an **attractive force**.

e.g. The earth attracts leaves of trees, water begins to flow towards the ground as soon as we open a tap etc.

SCIENCE INSIGHT Gravitational force of the moon is (1/6)th of the gravitational force of the earth. Due to this fact, the moon does not have its atmosphere.

Try These 8.2

1. **Is it true that force acting on an object can also change its shape?**
2. **Is it compulsory that non-contact forces are having both the properties, i.e. attraction and repulsion?**
3. **Write the force with which the earth attracts the objects towards it.**

8.6 Pressure

The force acting on a unit area of surface is defined as pressure. It can be represented as,

$$\text{Pressure} = \frac{\text{Force}}{\text{Area}}$$

For example, if we push our thumb into a wooden plank, it does not go in. But, if we push a nail by its pointed end, it goes in easily. This is because in a nail, **the force acting on per unit area of wood is very large.**

Thumb produces a smaller pressure because it acts on a large area of wood but the same force produces a much larger pressure when it is applied on a small area in a nail.

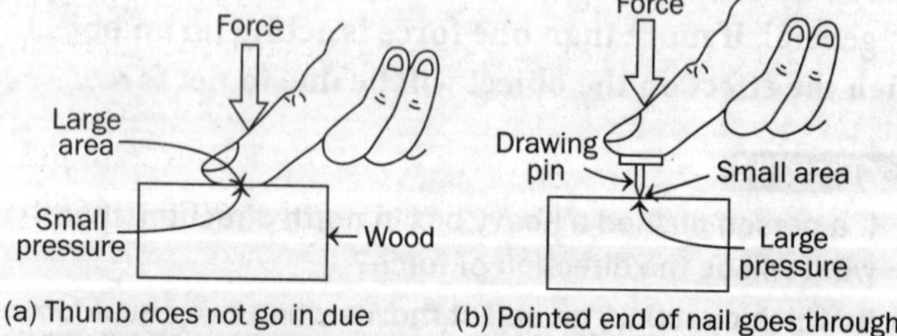

(a) Thumb does not go in due to pressure on a large area (b) Pointed end of nail goes through due to pressure on a small area

Pressure depends on the area on which it is exerted

Applications of pressure in our daily life

- **A porter reduces pressure by placing a cloth on his head, while carrying heavy load.** This increases the area of contact of load with their head due to which the pressure on the head decreases and it becomes easier for porter to carry the load.

So, the larger is the area, smaller the pressure on a surface for the same force.

- **School bags have broad straps**, so that the weight of the bag falls over a large area producing less pressure over the shoulder.
- **Tip of the needle is sharp** as it produces more pressure on a small area of the cloth. A sharp needle is able to pierce through the cloth while sewing.

Pressure Exerted by Liquids and Gases

Like solid, fluid also exerts pressure and fluid can be liquids or gases.

Pressure Exerted by Liquids

- Liquids exert pressure due to the weight that liquids possess.
- Liquids always possess pressure in the downwards direction.
- The pressure exerted by liquids at the bottom depends on the height of liquid column.
- The pressure exerted by liquids increases with depth.
- Liquids exert pressure in all the directions on the walls of the container.
- Liquids exert equal pressure at the same height.

Pressure Exerted by Gases

- Gases too exert pressure in all the directions on the walls of containers like liquids.
- Gases exert pressure due to constant collisions of it in molecules.

8.7 Atmospheric Pressure

The envelop of air around us is known as the **atmosphere.** It extends up to many kilometres above the surface of the earth.

The pressure exerted by the atmosphere is known as atmospheric pressure. It is the force that **air exerts on per unit area.** In other words, it is the weight of air present in a very tall column of unit area.

SCIENCE INSIGHT The maximum atmospheric pressure on the earth is at sea level because column of air is the largest above the sea. The pressure decreases as we go above the earth's surface because length of air column decreases. That's why, the atmospheric pressure above the mountain is less as compared to that on the earth's surface.

Some facts about atmospheric pressure are

- The weight of air above our head is about 225 kg. But, we are not crushed under the weight of this air because **the pressure inside our body is equal to the atmospheric pressure outside**.
- A suction cup sticks to a flat surface. When we press the suction cup against a flat surface, it flattens and escape out most of the air from under it.

  This creates partial vacuum inside the suction cup. **The atmospheric pressure outside is much greater and this holds the cup firmly to the surface.**

Magdeburg Hemispheres

In the 17th century, a German scientist whose name was Otto Von Guericke invented a pump to extract all the air from a vessel. This pump is called **vacuum pump.** So, he demonstrated an experiment in the town of Magdeburg to show the large atmospheric pressure.

Try These 8.3

1. **Sourav wants to measure the atmospheric pressure for an experiment. Which device should he use for it?**
2. **In which case, the pressure will be more : a force on small area or the same force on large area?**
3. **Does the atmospheric pressure decrease, as we go at higher altitude?**

Science Glossary

Force It refers to a pull push on an object.

Push It is moving an object away from the source of force.

Pull It is moving an object towards from the source of force.

Contact Force Force that is exerted by one object on another object when they are in contact with each other.

Muscular Force The force exerted by the muscles of a body.

Frictional Force The force exerted by one object to oppose its motion over another object.

Non-contact Force The force exerted by one object on another without being in contact.

Magnetic Force The force exerted by a magnet.

Electrostatic Force The force exerted by an electrically charged object.

Gravitational Force The force of attraction (pull) exerted by the earth.

Pressure It refers to the force that is exerted over a unit area of a surface.

Atmospheric Pressure It refers to the pressure exerted by the atmosphere.

Let's Investigate

ACTIVITY 1 (Page 94)

Aim To identify push or pull by observing motion of objects.

Material Required Pen and paper.

Procedure

1. Take some familiar situation of moving objects.
2. Draw a table as shown below.
3. Now, identify action involved in each case and categorise into push or pull.

Description of the situation	Action : (pushing/pulling/picking/ hitting/ lifting/ lowering /flying/ kicking/ throwing/ shutting/ flicking)	Action can be grouped	
		Push	**Pull**
Moving a book placed on a table	Pushing Pulling	Yes	Yes
Opening or shutting a door	Pushing Pulling	Yes	Yes
Drawing a bucket of water from a well	Lifting	No	Yes
A football player taking a penalty kick	Hitting kicking	Yes	No
A cricket ball hit by a batsman	Hitting	Yes	No
Moving a loaded cart	Pushing Pulling	Yes	Yes
Opening a drawer	Pulling	No	Yes

Conclusion All types of motion can be classified into pulling or pushing.

Viva Questions

1 What is the action involved in opening an almirah?

2 Repulsion between two magnets is pulling or pushing.

ACTIVITY 2 (Page 96)

Aim To learn more about forces by exploring them.

Material Required A heavy object like table or box.

Procedure

1. Push the box by yourself.
2. Now, ask your friend to help you in pushing it in the same direction. You will find that it is easier to move than before.
3. Now, ask your friend to push it from the opposite side. You will find that the box move in that direction where stronger push is applied.
4. Note the direction of motion in each case.

Two friends pushing a heavy load
(a) in the same direction and (b) in the opposite direction

Conclusion When force is applied in the same direction, then the movement of the box increases and when forces are applied from opposite direction, then box moves slowly.

Viva Questions

1. What will be the net force on a box when two equal forces of 5N are applied in the same direction?
2. Why doesn't the table move when equal forces are applied from opposite direction?

ACTIVITY 3 (Page 97)

Aim To show that when a force is applied on an object at rest, it begins to move.

Material Required A rubber ball and a table.

Procedure

1. Place the rubber ball on the level surface of the table.
2. Push the ball very slowly along the level surface.
3. The ball will start moving, push the moving ball in the direction of its motion. You will observe the speed of moving ball increases.
4. Now, place your palm in front of the moving ball.
5. Remove your palm as soon as the ball touches it.
6. You will observe that the speed of moving ball decreases.

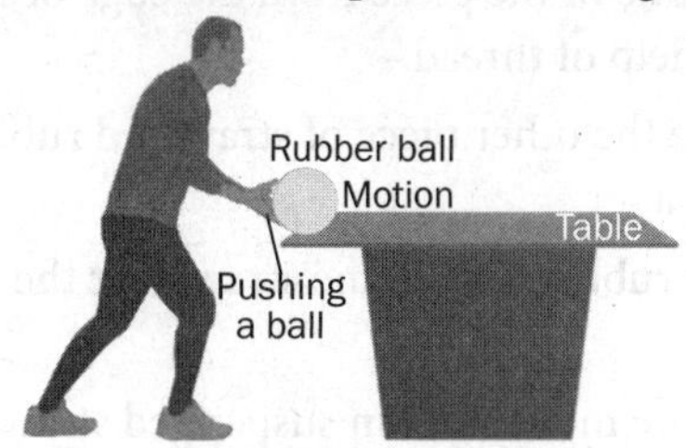

Motion of ball changes with force

Conclusion Force can increase or decrease the speed of the object.

Viva Questions

1 What will happen, if you do not remove your palm in step 5 ?

2 Does your palm apply a force on the ball ?

ACTIVITY 4 (Page 98)

Aim To determine whether force can change the direction.

Material Required A ruler and a ball.

Procedure

1. Place the ball on the level surface and push it.
2. Now, place a ruler in its path as shown in the figure.

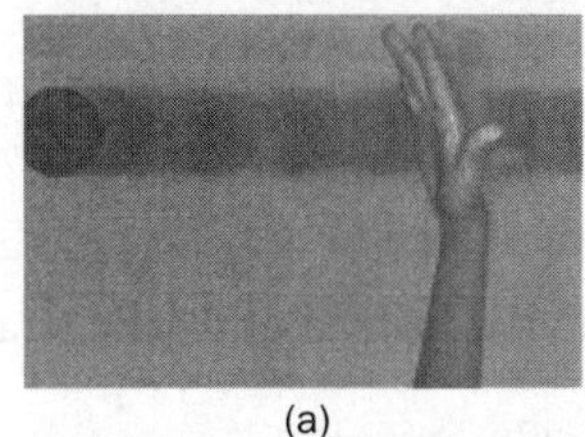
(a)

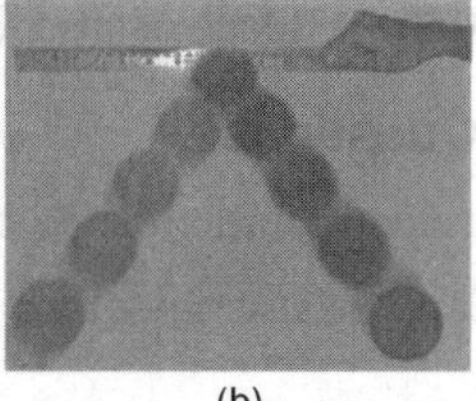
(b)

(a) A ball set in motion by pushing it along the level surface and (b) the direction of motion of the ball after it strikes the ruler placed in its path

3. Note the motion of the ball when it strikes the ruler.
4. Repeat the activity by placing ruler at different angles.

Conclusion Force can change the direction of motion.

Viva Questions

1 What will happen, if the ruler is placed at 90° to the direction of motion of object?

2 What is the direction of force on the ball when it strikes with the ruler ?

ACTIVITY 5 (Page 99)

Aim To study the effect of force on objects.

Material Required Pen and paper.

Procedure

1. List some phenomenon as mentioned in the table.
2. Now, categorise them by observing the action of force.

Effect of force on objects

Description of situation	How to apply force	Action of force			
		Change in state of motion		Change in shape	
		Yes	No	Yes	No
A lump of dough on a plate	Pressing it down with your hands		✓	✓	
Spring fixed to the seat of bicycle	By sitting on the seat		✓	✓	
A rubber band suspended from a hook/nail fixed on a wall	By hanging a weight or by pulling its free end	✓		✓	
A plastic or metal scale placed between two bricks	By putting a weight at the centre of the scale	✓		✓	

Conclusion Force does not only change the velocity, but it can change the shape also.

Viva Questions

1. Does change of shape depends upon the strength of force applied on an object?
2. Give one example in which both velocity and shape of the object are changing?

Think Like a Scientist
To prove that muscular force is contact force.

ACTIVITY 6 (Page 101)

Aim To study the type of force applied by the magnet.

Material Required A pair of bar magnets and 3 round shape pencil.

Procedure

1. Place the longer side of a magnet on the 3 rounded shape pencil as shown in figure.
2. Now, bring one end of the other magnet near the end of magnet placed on the pencil.
3. Do not touch ends of magnet, then observe the motion of the magnet.
4. Now, bring the other end of the magnet near the same end of the magnet placed on the pencil.
5. Again, observe the motion of the magnet.

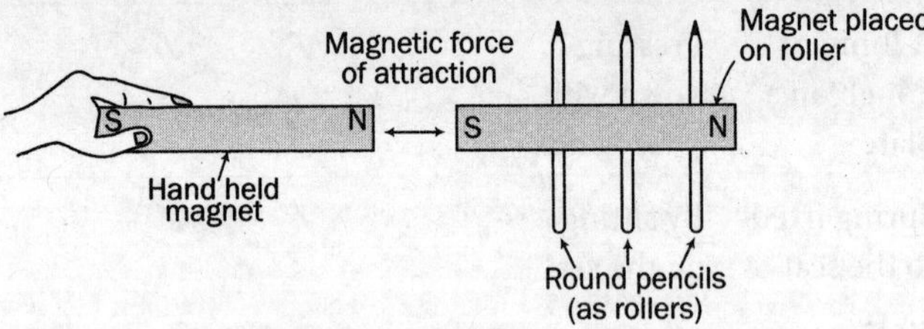

Observing the magnetic force of attraction between unlike poles (*N*-pole and *S*-pole) of two bar magnets

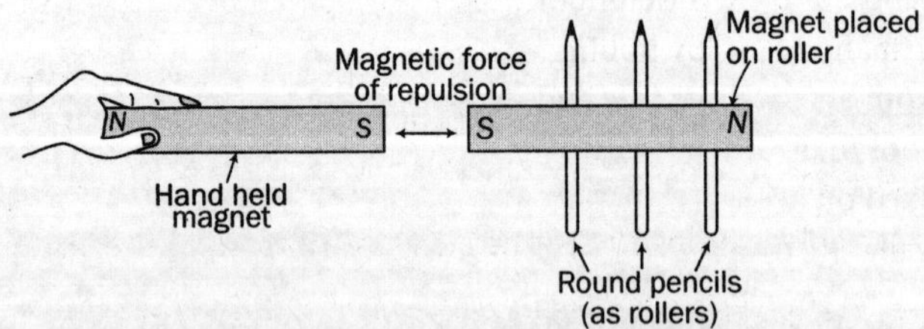

Observing the magnetic force of repulsion between like poles (*S*-pole and *S*-pole) of two bar magnets

Conclusion Magnet applies force without touching.

Viva Questions

1. Is the force exerted by a magnet on a piece of iron contact force or non-contact force ?
2. Is a magnetic force attractive or repulsive?

ACTIVITY 7 (Page 102)

Aim To identify the type of force (contact or non-contact) applied by electrically charged objects.

Material Required A table, long thread, a straw and scissor.

Procedure

1. Cut the plastic straw into nearly two equal pieces.
2. Suspend one of the piece from the edge of the table with the help of thread.
3. Now, take the other piece of straw and rub it with a sheet or paper.
4. Bring the rubbed end of the straw near the suspended straw.
5. Observe the movement in suspended straw. You will find that it will attract towards it.
6. Now, rub the free end of the suspended straw with the paper.
7. Again, bring the straw which was earlier rubbed with the paper.
8. Again, observe the motion of the suspended straw. You will find that it will repel each other.

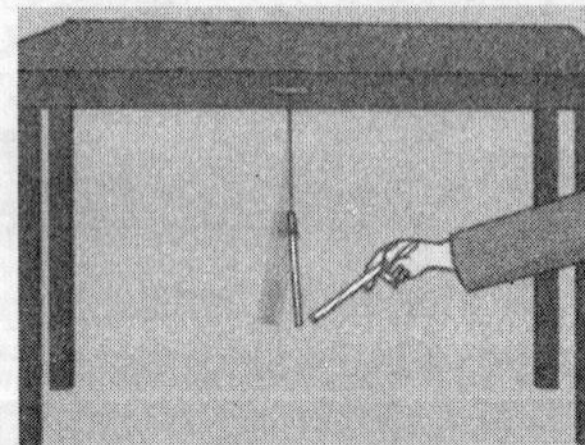
A straw rubbed with paper attracts another straw but repels it, if it has also been rubbed with a sheet of paper

Conclusion Electrostatic force is non-contact force.

Viva Questions

1. Is electrostatic force a contact force ?
2. Can you use any other material instead of plastic straw?

ACTIVITY 8 (Page 104)

Aim To demonstrate that liquid exerts pressure at the bottom of its container.

Material required A transparent plastic pipe of length 25 cm and diameter about 5-7.5 cm, a balloon and water.

Procedure

1. Fix the rubber balloon at one end of the pipe.
2. Now, hold the pipe in vertical position and ask your friend to pour some water in the pipe.
3. Note the height of water column and change in shape of the balloon.
4. Now, pour some more water and note the increase in the balloon.
5. Repeat the same process 2-3 times and try to find the relation between bulge and height of the water column.

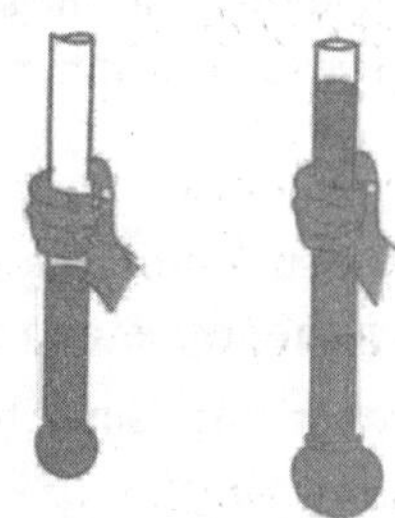

Pressure exerted by water at the bottom of the container depends on the height of its water column

Conclusion

(i) A liquid exerts pressure at the bottom of its container.

(ii) The pressure exerted by a liquid depends on the height of liquid column.

Viva Questions

1. Can we use another liquid instead of water to perform this activity?
2. Does liquid pressure depend on area of container?

ACTIVITY 9 (Page 104, 105)

Aim To demonstrate that the liquid exerts pressure on the walls of its container.

Material Required A plastic bottle, a cylindrical glass tube of few cm long, a balloon and water.

Procedure

1. Make a hole near the bottom of the bottle.
2. Fix the tube into the hole and a balloon (fixed tightly) on the other end of the tube. See the figure.
3. Now, fill the bottle upto half with water and note the bulge of the balloon.
4. Add some more water and again observe the change in the bulge.

A liquid exerts pressure on the walls of the container

Conclusion From this activity also, we can conclude that

(i) A liquid exerts pressure on the walls of its container.

(ii) The pressure exerted by the liquid on the walls of its container depends on the height of liquid level from bottom.

Viva Questions

1. Is pressure same in all liquids at given depth?
2. Why bulge of the balloon increases on increasing the water level?

ACTIVITY 10 (Page 105)

Aim To demonstrate that liquid exerts equal pressure at same depth.

Material required Empty plastic bottle and water.

Procedure

1. Drill four holes all around near the bottom of the bottle.
2. Make sure, the holes are at the same height from the bottom.
3. Pour the water in the bottle and measure the distance where the water jet falls from the bottle. You will find

that, the different streams of water coming out of the holes fall at the same distance from the bottle.

Liquids exert equal pressure at the same depth

Conclusion Liquids exert equal pressure, if they are at same depth.

Viva Questions

1. Do liquids exert equal pressure at the same height?
2. What will happen, if you drill holes at different heights?

ACTIVITY 11 (Page 106)

Aim To show the effect of pressure due to air.

Material Required A rubber sucker.

Procedure

1. Hold a good quality of rubber sucker.
2. Try to press it on a flat smooth surface, so most of the air between its cup and surface escape out.
3. We will notice that the sucker sticks to the surface.
4. Now, try to pull the sucker off the surface, you will find little hard to pull it off.

   In order to pull the sucker off the surface, the applied force should be large enough to overcome the atmospheric pressure.

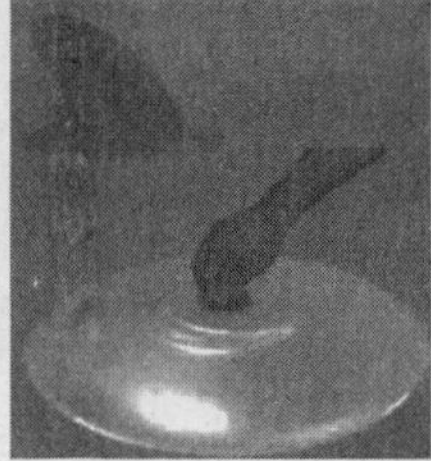

A rubber sucker pressed on a surface. Atmospheric pressure holds it with surface.

Conclusion We have concluded that the sucker sticks to the surface because the pressure of atmosphere acts on it.

Viva Questions

1. Is it possible to pull the sucker off the surface, when there is no air at all between the sucker and surface ?
2. How does the atmospheric pressure change with the height ?

Effects of Force

- **Force can change the shape of an object**
  - The shape of an inflated balloon changes by pressing it.
  - The shape of ball of dough changes when it is rolled to make chapati.
- **Force can change the state of motion**
  - Force can change the speed.
  - It can stop the object.

Exploring Forces

- The strength of force is expressed by its magnitude and direction.
- If forces are applied on an object in the same direction, then they will get added.
- If two forces act in the opposite direction on an object, the net force acting on it is the difference between them.
- If more than one force is acting on an object, then the effect on the object will be due to net force.

Force due to Interaction

- Force between the objects is caused by an interaction of one object with another object.
- If there is no interaction between two objects, there will no effect of force.

Types of Forces

- **Contact force**
  Come into action when objects are in direct contact no . e.g. Muscular force, friction force.
- **Non-contact forces**
  Come into action without any contact. e.g. Gravitational force, magnetic force.

FORCE AND PRESSURE

Force

- A push or pull acting on an object.
- Object is in motion due to application of force.
- The direction in which body is pushed or pulled is called direction of force.

Pressure

Force acting per unit area,
$p = F/A$

Application of Pressure

- Porter reduces pressure by placing a cloth to increase area.
- School bags have wides straps.
- Nails have a painted end.

Atmospheric pressure

- The pressure exerted by atmosphere is known as atmospheric pressure.
- The pressure inside our body is equal to the atmospheric pressure outside, that's why we do not crushed under the weight of air.

Pressure Exerted by Liquids and Gases

Pressure Exerted by Liquid

- Liquid exert pressure due to the weight that liquid possess.
- It always possess pressure in the downward direction.
- Liquids exert equal pressure at the same height.

Pressure Exerted by Gases

- Gases exert pressure in all the directions on the walls of containers like liquids.
- Gases exert pressure due to constant collisions of its molecules.

NCERT FOLDER

Complete Explanations of all NCERT's Questions

Intext Questions

Q.1 Have you ever wondered what makes an object slow down or go faster or change its direction of motion ? **Page 93**

Ans. Force makes an object slow down or go faster or change its direction of motion.

Q.2 Paheli remembers that a magnet attracts a piece of iron towards it. Is attraction also a pull ? What about repulsion between similar poles of two magnets ? Is it a pull or a push ? **Page 94**

Ans. Attraction or repulsion between the poles of magnet can be seen as another form of pull or push.

Q.3 Does it mean that the net force on an object is zero, if the two forces acting on it in opposite direction are equal? **Page 96**

Ans. Yes, when two forces of equal magnitude act in opposite direction, the net force is zero on that body.

Q.4 Boojho has seen children competing with one another in moving a rubber tyre or a ring by pushing it. Why does the speed of tyre or ring increase whenever it is pushed ? **Page 97**

Ans. With every push, they are applying a little more force on the moving tyre in the direction of motion. Hence, the speed of the tyre increases continuously.

Q.5 Does the application of a force would always result in a change in the state of motion of the object ? **Page 98**

Ans. No, sometimes a heavy material may not move at all even if you apply the maximum force that you can exert. e.g. When you try to push a wall, no effect of force is observed.

Q.6 Can you lift or push a book lying on a table without touching it? **Page 100**

Ans. No, we cannot lift or push a book lying on a table without touching it because it is a type of contact force.

Q.7 What happens when you apply a force on an inflated balloon by pressing it between your palms ? **Page 100**

Ans. The shape of balloon will change, if we apply a force on an inflated balloon by pressing it between our palms.

Q.8 Where does the force come from when we push an object like a school bag or lift a bucket of water? **Page 100**

Ans. This force is caused by the action of muscles in our body.

Q.9 List few examples of the force exerted by the muscles in our body. **Page 100**

Ans. Chewing of food, lifting of luggage, squeezing a sponge ball.

Q.10 Leaves and fruits fall to the ground when they get detached from the plant. Have you ever wondered why it is so ? **Page 100**

Ans. Leaves and fruits fall towards the ground because earth pull them towards it and this attractive force is known as the force of gravity or gravitational force.

Q.11 Is there any relation between pressure and force ? **Page 100**

Ans. Yes, pressure is force per unit area. Thus, we can say that pressure is directly proportional to force.

Q.12 Paheli wants to understand why porters place a round piece of cloth on their heads when they carry heavy loads ? **Page 100**

Ans. When a porter places a round piece of cloth on his head, it reduces the pressure on the head as the area of contact increases and they find it easier to carry the load.

Q.13 Can you explain why shoulder bags are provided with broad straps and not thin strap ? **Page 100**

Ans. School bags are provided with broad straps because it increases the surface area of contact with the shoulders which results in reducing the pressure on the shoulder.

Q.14 Boojho has seen fountains of water coming out of the leaking joints or holes in pipes supplying water. Is it due the pressure exerted by water on the walls of the pipes ? **Page 100**

Ans. Yes, water coming out of the leaking joints or holes in pipes supplying water is due to pressure exerted by water on the surface of the pipes.

Q.15 Why is it easy to cut the fruit with sharp knife as compared to blunt knife? Page 103

Ans. The surface area of sharp knife is lesser than that of blunt knife, so pressure applied by sharp knife is higher than blunt knife.

Q.16 If the area of my head were 15 cm × 15 cm, how much force will air exert on my head? Page 107

Ans. We know that, 1 atmospheric pressure $=10^5$ N/m^2 $= 10$ N/cm^2

$$\text{Pressure} = \frac{\text{Force}}{\text{Area}}$$

$$\text{Force} = \text{Pressure} \times \text{Area} = 10 \times (15 \times 15) = 2250 \text{ N}$$

Exercise

Q.1 Give two examples each of situations in which you push or pull to change the state of motion of objects.

Ans. The two examples are as follows

(i) We push the door to open it.

(ii) We pull a drawer to open it.

Q.2 Give two examples of situations in which applied force causes a change in the shape of an object.

Ans. The two examples are as follows:

(i) **Spring** When we compress or stretch the spring, it changes its shape.

(ii) **Foam** When we compress the foam or sponge, it changes its shape.

Q.3 Fill in the blanks in the following statements

(a) To draw water from a well, we have to .... the rope.

(b) A charged body .... an uncharged body towards it.

(c) To move a loaded trolley, we have to......... it.

(d) The north pole of a magnet .... the north pole of another magnet.

Ans. (a) pull (b) attracts

(c) push (d) repels

Q.4 An archer stretches her bow while taking aim at the target. She then releases the arrow, which begins to move towards the target. Based on this information, fill up the gaps in the following statements using the following terms: muscular, contact, non-contact, gravity, friction, shape, attraction

(a) To stretch the bow, the archer applies a force that causes a change in its ....

(b) The force applied by the archer to stretch the bow is an example of .... force.

(c) The type of force responsible for a change in the state of motion of the arrow is an example of a .... force.

(d) While the arrow moves towards its target, the forces acting on it are due to .... and that due to .... of air.

Ans. (a) shape (b) muscular

(c) contact (d) gravity, friction

Q.5 In the following situation, identify the agent exerting the force and the object on which it acts. State the effect of the force in each case.

(a) Squeezing a piece of lemon between the fingers to extract its juice.

(b) Taking out paste from a toothpaste tube.

(c) A load suspended from a spring while its other end is on a hook fixed to a wall.

(d) An athlete making a high jump to clear the bar at a certain height.

Ans.

	Agent exerting the force	Object on which it acts	Effect of the force
(a)	Fingers (squeezing the lemon)	Lemon	Extraction of juice
(b)	Hand (or fingers)	Toothpaste tube	Coming out of paste from toothpaste tube
(c)	Suspended load	Spring	Elongation of spring due to load on the one end of it
(d)	Muscles of legs	ground	Making a high jump to clear the bar at a certain height

Q.6 A blacksmith hammers a hot piece of iron while making a tool. How does the force due to hammering affect the piece of iron?

Ans. When blacksmith hammers a hot piece of iron, the force due to hammering can change the shape of the piece of iron.

In other words, we can say that force applied through the hammer by the blacksmith can mould the hot piece of iron into any kind of tool.

Q.7 An inflated balloon was pressed against a wall after it has been rubbed with a piece of synthetic cloth. It was found that the balloon sticks to the wall. What force might be responsible for the attraction between the balloon and the wall?

Ans. As the balloon has been rubbed with a piece of synthetic cloth, it has acquired some electrostatic charge and became a charged body. Now, when this charged body (which is balloon) was pressed against the wall, it will get attracted. Thus, the electrostatic force is responsible for the attraction between the balloon and the wall.

Q.8 Name the forces acting on a plastic bucket containing water held above ground level in your hand. Discuss, why the forces acting on the bucket do not bring a change in its state of motion.

Ans. The forces acting on a plastic bucket are gravitational force and muscular force. These forces do not bring a change in its state of motion because being equal and opposite in magnitude, the effect of net force on bucket becomes zero.

Q.9 A rocket has been fired upwards to launch a satellite in its orbit. Name the two forces acting on the rocket immediately after leaving the launching pad.

Ans. Two forces are as follows:

(i) Gravitational force

(ii) Friction due to air or force of friction

Q.10 When we press the bulb of a dropper with its nozzle kept in water, air in the dropper is seen to escape in the form of bubbles. Once we release the pressure on the bulb, water gets filled in the dropper. The rise of water in the dropper is due to

(a) pressure of water

(b) gravity of the earth

(c) shape of rubber bulb

(d) atmospheric pressure

Ans. (d) atmospheric pressure.

REVIEW EXERCISE

Including Competency Based Questions

Part I

Multiple Choice Questions

1. In figure, two boys *A* and *B* are shown applying force on a block. If the block moves towards the right, which one of the following statements is correct?

NCERT Exemplar

(a) Magnitude of force applied by *A* is greater than that of *B*.
(b) Magnitude of force applied by *A* is smaller than that of *B*.
(c) Net force on the block is towards *A*.
(d) Magnitude of force applied by *A* is equal to that of *B*.

2. In the circuit shown in figure, when the circuit is completed, the hammer strikes the gong. Which of the following force is responsible for the movement of hammer? Competency Based Que.

(a) Gravitational force alone
(b) Electrostatic force alone
(c) Magnetic force alone
(d) Frictional force alone

3. Force due to the charged particles is known as
(a) muscular force (b) magnetic force
(c) electrostatic force (d) gravitational force

4. During dry weather while combing hair, sometimes we experience hair flying apart. The force responsible for this is NCERT Exemplar
(a) force of gravity (b) electrostatic force
(c) force of friction (d) magnetic force

5. Which one of the following forces is a contact force?
(a) Force of gravity (b) Force of friction
(c) Magnetic force (d) Electrostatic force

6. Two objects repel each other, this repulsion could be due to
(a) frictional force
(b) electrostatic force
(c) magnetic force
(d) either a magnetic or an electrostatic force

7. Type of force where only attraction is found
(a) electrostatic force (b) magnetic force
(c) gravitational force (d) Both (a) and (b)

8. The wear and tear in the machine part is due to
(a) electrostatic force (b) muscular force
(c) frictional force (d) gravitational force

9. Like poles exert a force of
(a) attraction (b) repulsion
(c) Both (a) and (b) (d) None of these

10. A block of mass 2 kg tied with a rope is going down under the force of gravity of 20 N.

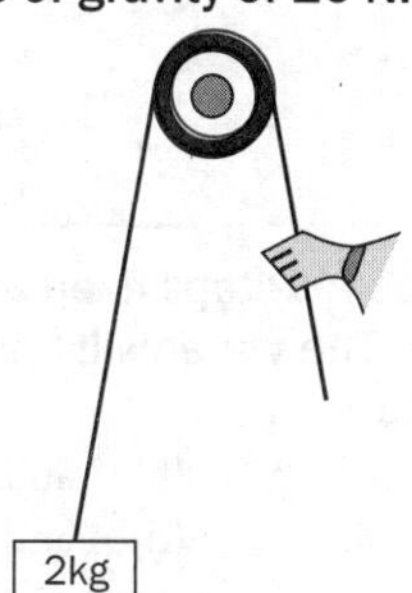

How much force is required by the hand to stop the motion of the block?
(a) 10 N (b) 20 N (c) 30 N (d) 40 N

11.

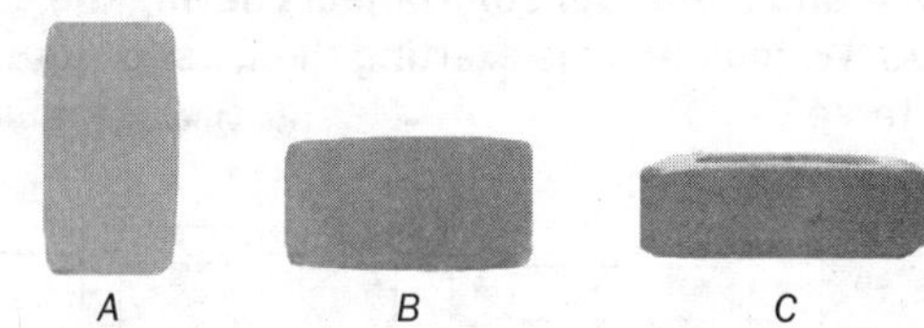

A brick is kept in three different ways on a table as shown in figure. The pressure exerted by the brick on the table will be NCERT Exemplar
(a) maximum in position *A*
(b) maximum in position *C*
(c) maximum in position *B*
(d) equal in all cases

12. **The pressure exerted by liquid due to increase in depth**

(a) reduces (b) increases
(c) remains same
(d) depends on the nature of liquid

13. **Some mustard oil is kept in the beaker. It will exert pressure**

(a) upward
(b) downward
(c) sideways
(d) in all the directions

14. **Figure shows a container filled with water. Which of the following statements is correct about pressure of water ?**

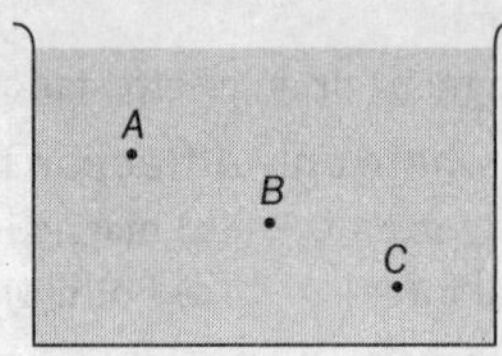

(a) Pressure at $A>$ Pressure at $B>$ Pressure at C
(b) Pressure at $A =$ Pressure at $B =$ Pressure at C
(c) Pressure at $A <$ Pressure at $B >$ Pressure at C
(d) Pressure at $A <$ Pressure at $B <$ Pressure at C

15.

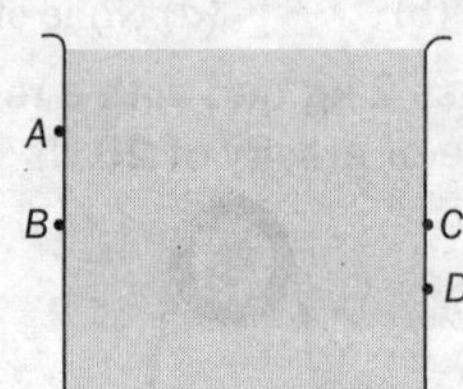

A water tank has four taps fixed at points *A, B, C, D* as shown in figure. The water will flow out at the same pressure from taps at

(a) *B* and *C* (b) *C* and *D*
(c) *A* and *B* (d) *A* and *C*

16. **The standard value of atmospheric pressure is**

(a) 78 cm of Hg (b) 76 mm of Hg
(c) 45 cm of Hg (d) 0.76 cm of Hg

17. ***P, Q, R* and *S* are four solid objects having the same mass. Which object is exerting the least pressure on the table?** **Competency Based Que.**

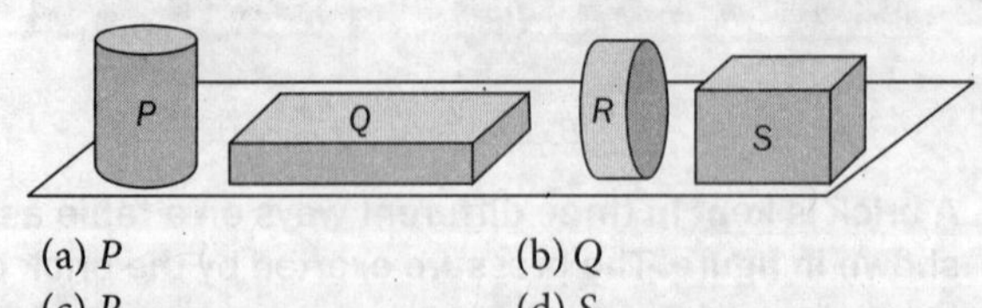

(a) *P* (b) *Q*
(c) *R* (d) *S*

18. **How much pressure would be exerted by a block exerting 20 N of force on 0.5 m^2 area?**

(a) 10 N/m^2 (b) 20 N/m^2
(c) 30 N/m^2 (d) 40 N/m^2

Answers

1. (a)	**2.** (c)	**3.** (c)	**4.** (b)
5. (b)	**6.** (d)	**7.** (c)	**8.** (c)
9. (d)	**10.** (b)	**11.** (a)	**12.** (b)
13. (d)	**14.** (d)	**15.** (a)	**16.** (b)
17. (b)	**18.** (d)		

Fill in the Blanks

1. The .... the area, larger the pressure on a surface.
2. A cyclist exerts a force of ...... on the pedal of cycle.
3. When two forces act in the same direction, then the net force acting is ...... of the two forces.
4. The force which acts when two objects are in actual contact is called ...... force.
5. Halting of moving ball on its own is an example of ...... force.
6. As we go high on the mountain, the ...... decreases.
7. If the force is applied on smaller area of contact, then pressure exerted by it ....
8. Droper and rubber sucker work on the principle of ...... pressure.

Answers

1. smaller	**2.** push
3. sum	**4.** contact
5. frictional	**6.** pressure
7. increases	**8.** atmospheric

True/False

1. If two forces act in opposite directions, then net force is the difference between the two forces.
2. In 'tug of war' when both the teams apply equal pulling force, then net force is maximum.
3. Force between two electric charges is called magnetic force.
4. Muscular force and frictional force are the examples of non-contact forces.
5. The force per unit area is the pressure on that area.
6. The nails get penetrated into the planks easily because a large force acts on a small area.
7. Water comes out more slowly from an upstair tap than from a similar downstair tap.
8. The blood pressure in our body balances the atmospheric pressure acting on our body.

Answers

1. True	**2.** False	**3.** False	**4.** False
5. True	**6.** True	**7.** True	**8.** True

Match the Columns

1. Match the Column I with Column II.

	Column I		Column II
(a)	Electrostatic force	(i)	Attract each other
(b)	Atmospheric pressure	(ii)	Exert same pressure at equal depth
(c)	Unlike poles	(iii)	76 mm of Hg
(d)	Liquids	(iv)	Force between charges
(e)	Force of gravity	(v)	Strength of force
(f)	Magnitude	(vi)	Non-contact force

Answer

1. (a) – (iv), (b) – (iii), (c) – (i), (d) – (ii), (e) – (vi), (f) – (v)

Assertion-Reason Questions

The following questions consist of two statements- Assertion (A) and Reason (R). Answer these questions by selecting the appropriate option given below

(a) Both A and R are true and R is the correct explanation of A.
(b) Both A and R are true but R is not the correct explanation of A.
(c) A is true but R is false.
(d) A is false but R is true.

1. Assertion (A) Push or pull on an object is called force.
Reason (R) Forces add together, if they are applied in opposite direction.

2. Assertion (A) In the game of tug of war, sometimes the rope does not seem to move to any side even if strong forces are applied from both sides.
Reason (R) Equal forces applied from opposite side on object make the net applied force zero.

3. Assertion (A) Electrostatic force is a contact force.
Reason (R) The force exerted by a charged body on another charged body is known as electrostatic force.

4. Assertion (A) The larger the area, smaller is the pressure.
Reason (R) The force acting on a unit area of a surface is called pressure.

Answers

1. (c) A is true but R is false because forces applied in same direction add together.
2. (a) Both statements are correct. If net force on a body is zero, then it does not move. Hence, the correct option is (a).
3. (d) A is false because electrostatic force is a non-contact force. Hence, option (d) is correct.
4. (a) According to the definition of pressure,

$$\text{Pressure} = \frac{\text{Force}}{\text{Area}} \Rightarrow \text{Pressure} \propto \frac{1}{\text{Area}}$$

Both statements are correct. Hence, option (a) is correct.

Case Based Question

1. Two groups of students are playing tug-of-war.

Competency Based Que.

(i) Choose the correct direction of force applied by Group 1 and Group 2.

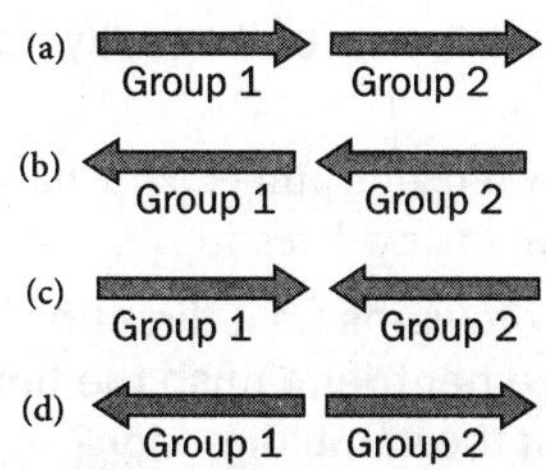

(ii) Group 1 is pulling with 250 N force and Group 2 is pulling with 300 N force. What would be the likely position of the two groups after a minute of pulling?

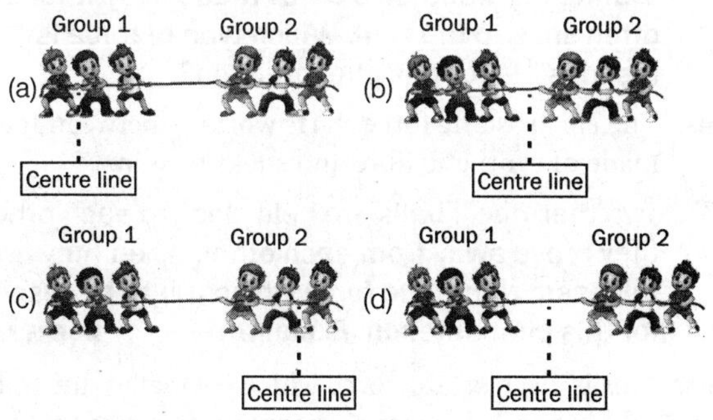

Answer

1. (i) (d), (ii) (a)

Part II

Very Short Answer Type Questions

1. Where do we apply a force while walking? **NCERT Exemplar**

Ans. We apply a force on ground while walking and ground applies reaction force on our foot due to which we are able to move forward.

2. Does the palm apply any force on the ball, when we place our palm in front of a moving ball?

Ans. Yes, when we place our palm in front of a moving ball, then the palm applies a force on the moving ball and stop it.

3. Name an activity which does not involve any pushing force.

Ans. When a person swims freestyle, he is pulling himself forward in the water.

4. A ball of dough is rolled into a flat chapati. Name the force exerted to change the shape of the dough. **NCERT Exemplar**

Ans. The shape of dough is changed due to muscular force applied by the hand.

5. In 'tug of war' when two teams pull equally hard, then what happens?

Ans. In 'tug of war', when two teams pull equally hard, then the rope does not move in any direction.

6. A girl is pushing a box towards East direction. In which direction should her friend push the box, so that it moves faster in the same direction? **Competency Based Que.**

Ans. Her friend should push the box towards East direction, so that it will start moving more fast towards East because the magnitude of force increases.

7. During dry weather, clothes made of synthetic fibre often stick to the skin. Which type of force is responsible for this phenomenon?

Ans. The electrostatic force starts working between the cloth made of synthetic fibre and sticks to skin.

8. Two thermocol balls are held close to each other but they move away from each other, when they are released. Name the force which might be responsible for this phenomenon. Explain. **NCERT Exemplar**

Ans. This is electrostatic force which is created due to the rubbing and since same charges are induced on two balls, so they move away from each other.

9. While sieving grains, small pieces fall down. Which force pulls them down?

Ans. It is the force of gravity which is responsible for the grains to fall down.

10. Does the force of gravity act on dust particles?

Ans. Yes, force of gravity acts on the dust particles.

11. A gas filled balloon moves up. Is the upward force acting on it larger or smaller than the force of gravity? **NCERT Exemplar**

Ans. The upward force will be greater than the force of gravity only, then the balloon will be able to lift up against this gravitational force.

12. Fruits detached from a tree fall down due to the force of gravity. We know that a force arises due to interaction between two objects. Name the objects interacting in this case. **Competency Based Que.**

Ans. The interacting objects in this case are: earth and fruit. Earth applies force of gravity on fruit towards its centre, so fruit falls down.

13. Rahul is pushing a magnet along his table when some paper clips on his table suddenly move. In which direction, does the force act on the paper clips?

Ans. As, the magnet will attract the paper clips, so the force acting on them will be towards the magnet.

14. Under which circumstance, a person will not experience any gravitational force?

Ans. A person who is in a space that is too far away from earth gravitational force will not suffer any gravitational force.

15. An astronaut travels from the earth to the moon, how does his weight and mass change?

Ans. Mass of an object remains constant at all the places, so mass of astronaut will not change. Weight of an object depends upon the gravity, at the moon gravity is lesser than earth, so weight of astronaut will decrease.

Short Answer Type Questions

1. Two persons are applying forces on two opposite sides of a moving cart. The cart still moves with the same speed in the same direction. What do you infer about the magnitudes and direction of the forces applied? **NCERT Exemplar**

Ans. The magnitude of forces will be equal and it acts in opposite direction, so that they are cancelling each other. We can understand this by using the following figure.

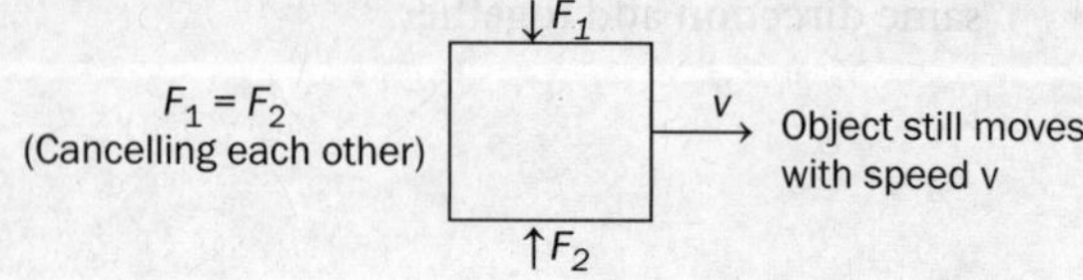

2. A man is pushing a cart down a slope. Suddenly the cart starts moving faster and he wants to slow it down. What should he do?

Ans. The man can do following things

(i) He can start pulling the cart instead of pushing it in order to balance the downward force due to gravity.

(ii) He can go the other side by moving himself very fast in the direction of motion and try to slow down the speed of cart by giving an opposite force to the moving cart.

3. A soccer ball flew towards a goalkeeper standing at the goalpost. He tried to grab it but it slipped from his hands. Describe the action of force at the point when goalkeeper grabbed the ball. **Competency Based Que.**

Ans. When the goalkeeper tried to grab the ball coming towards him, the force he applied caused it to change direction. At the same time, the force caused the ball to decrease in its speed. The force applied did not stop the ball from moving or increasing its speed.

4. Figure shows a man with a parachute. Name the force which is responsible for his downward motion. Will he come down with the same speed without the parachute? **NCERT Exemplar**

Ans. The name of force responsible for the downward motion of the parachute is called force of gravity.
No, because the air friction will become less.

5. In the circuit shown in figure, when the key is closed, the compass needle placed in the match box deflects. Name the force which causes this deflection. **NCERT Exemplar**

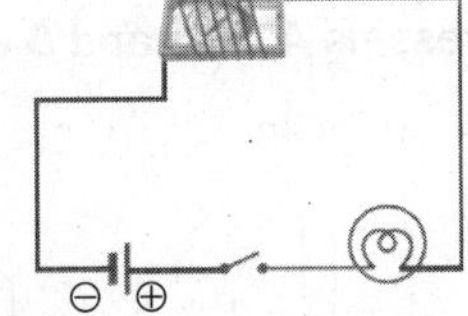

Ans. On closing the switch, the current starts flowing in the wire and due to this current, a magnetic field is established around the wire which exerts magnetic force on the needle and it gets deflected.

6. Does the force of gravitation exist between two astronauts in space?

Ans. Yes, there will be gravitational force between the astronauts because every object in universe, whether small or large, exerts a force on every other object, it is the universal law of gravitation.

7. Figure shows a car sticking to an electromagnet. Name the forces acting on the car. Which one of them is larger?

Ans. The forces working on the object (car) are
(i) Force of gravity (downwards)
(ii) Magnetic force (upwards)

Since, the car is moving upwards, so magnetic force due to electromagnet is greater.

8. The figure shows a magnet at the top of a ramp and paper clips at the base of the ramp. He observed that the paper clip move up the ramp and attached to the magnet. What forces were acting on the paper clip as it moved up the ramp?

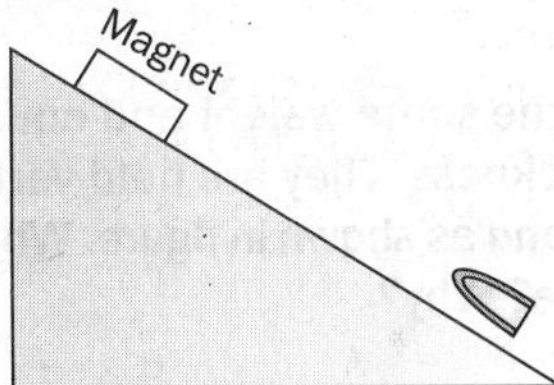

Ans. The paper clip moved up the ramp because it was attracted to the magnet, therefore there was a magnetic force acting on it.

Gravitational and frictional forces also continue to act on the paper clip as it moved up the ramp.

9. A chapati maker is a machine which converts balls of dough into chapatis. What effect of force comes into play in this process? **NCERT Exemplar**

Ans. The force per unit area is called pressure, works on the chapatis. This is the pressure which works on the dough balls and makes them chapatis with the help of machine.

10. Wooden or concrete sleepers are kept below the railway line. Explain why?

Ans. Since the area on which weight of train acts increases which results in the decrease in the pressure on the ground due to which the train moves easily on the railway line without any risk of happenings the accident. So, this is the reason for keeping the wooden or concrete below the railway line.

11. Determine the pressure when a force of 200 N acts on area

(i) $20\ m^2$ and (ii) $8\ m^2$.

Ans. Pressure $= \dfrac{\text{Force}}{\text{Area}}$

Given, $F = 200$ N

(i) For area, $A = 20\ m^2$

$$p = \frac{200}{20} = 10\ N/m^2 \text{ or } 10\ Pa$$

(ii) For area, $A = 8\ m^2$

$$p = \frac{200}{8} = 25\ N/m^2 \text{ or } 25\ Pa$$

12. Raman was very curious to know that how the porters carry heavy load on his head easily. Suddenly, he asked to his teacher and teacher told him that by reducing the pressure on the head, the porters carry heavy load.

(a) Explain how the porters carry heavy loads easily?

(b) Mention your views about Raman.

Competency Based Que.

Ans. (a) The porters usually cover their heads by thick round cloths before carrying the load. This increases the area of contact, therefore reducing pressure on the head. So, the porters carry heavy load easily.

(b) According to me, Raman is very curious to know about science.

13. Two rods of the same weight and equal length have different thickness. They are held vertically on the surface of sand as shown in figure. Which one of them will sink more? Why? **NCERT Exemplar**

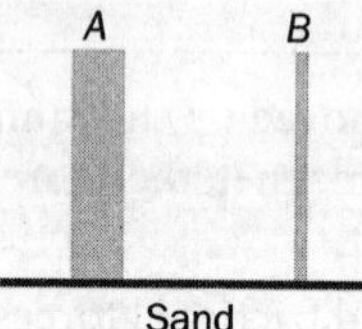

Ans. As we know that, pressure exerted by the body is inversely proportional to the area where force is applied. So, the thinner rod, i.e. rod *B* will sink more because it has less area of cross-section in contact with the surface, hence it will exert more pressure on the sand with respect to the rod *A*.

14. What type of force is involved in each of the given conditions? Put a tick mark (✓) for the response in terms of push or pull.

Condition	Push	Pull
Hitting a ball with a bat		
Sucking milk shake with a plastic straw		
Lifting a school bag from a desk		

Ans.

Condition	Push	Pull
Hitting a ball with a bat	✓	
Sucking milk shake with a plastic straw.		✓
Lifting a school bag from a desk		✓

Long Answer Type Questions

1. In walking, the pressure on the ground is more as compared to that in standing on the ground. Explain this statement.

Ans. When a person is walking on the ground, then at one time, his one foot is only on the ground. Therefore, the force of entire weight of man falls on smaller area of the ground which results into large pressure on the ground. While in another case, if the man is standing on the ground, then both his feets are on the ground. It causes the force of weight of man to fall on larger area of ground and results in less pressure on the ground.

2. Two women are of the same weight. One wears sandals with pointed heels while the other wears sandals with flat soles. Which one would feel more comfortable while walking on a sandy beach? Give reasons for your answer. **Competency Based Que.**

Ans. While walking on a sandy surface, one needs the footwears of larger area so that the pressure exerted on the ground is minimum. So, in this case, the woman having the sandals with pointed heels will be less comfortable in walking while the other woman wears sandals with flat soles feels more comfortable while walking on sandy beach.

3. It is difficult to cut cloth using a pair of scissors with blunt blades. Explain. **NCERT Exemplar**

Ans. It is difficult to cut cloth using a pair of scissors with blunt blades because blunt blades have more area and due to which applied force produces very less pressure. As we know that pressure is inversely proportional to area of cross-section, so it is difficult to cut cloth from blunt blades. $\left(\because p = \dfrac{F}{A}\right)$

4. Observe the vessels *A*, *B*, *C* and *D* as shown in figure carefully.

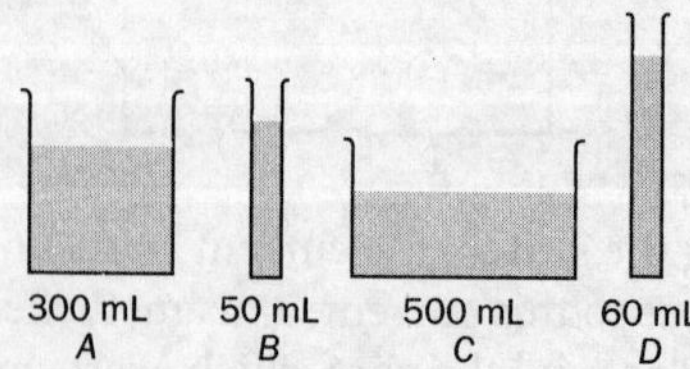

Volume of water taken in each vessel is as shown. Arrange them in the order of decreasing pressure at the base of each vessel. Explain.

Ans. Pressure at depth due to liquid column depends upon

(i) gravitational acceleration

(ii) density of liquid

(iii) height of liquid.

and in this case, gravitational acceleration and density are same, so only thing that can change pressure, is height.

So, the order of pressure exerted by the fluid A, B, C and D at the base is given by

$$p_D > p_B > p_A > p_C$$

5. An archer shoots an arrow in the air horizontally. However, after moving some distance, the arrow falls to the ground. Name the initial force that sets the arrow in motion. Explain why the arrow ultimately falls down? **NCERT Exemplar**

Ans. The archer shoots an arrow by applying muscular force by stretching the string of the bow. When the string is released, it regains its original position that provides the initial force to set the arrow in motion horizontally. The force of gravity acts on the arrow in the downward direction and hence the arrow ultimately falls to the ground.

6. It is much easier to burst an inflated balloon with a needle than by a finger. Explain.

Ans. Because needle tip has very less area of cross-section in comparison to that of our finger and we know that pressure exerted by a force is inversely proportional to the area where it has been applied, so pressure exerted will be more by the needle tip than the finger.

Case Based Questions

1. Rishi drops a metal block from same height onto different wooden blocks of same mass but different contact area. The teacher was also watching this activity. He asked some questions to Rishi which are listed below.

(i) Explain the relationship between the contact area of the wooden block and how deep the wooden block would sink into the soft ground?

(ii) A force of 100 N is applied on an area of 4 m^2. Calculate the pressure applied on the area.

(iii) Contact area of one of the wooden block is 9 cm^2. Calculate the force acting on it if pressure is 900 Pa.

2. Four students wanted to find out who could kick a football the strongest. Each student kicked the football. The table shows the distance the football travelled in air before hitting the ground.

	Student 1	Student 2	Student 3	Student 4
Distance the ball travelled in air before hitting the ground	10 m	12 m	8 m	14 m

Competency Based Que.

(i) Which student kicked the ball with the greatest force?

(a) Student 1 (b) Student 2

(c) Student 3 (d) Student 4

(ii) Which of these factors must remain the same when each student kicks the football? Choose 'Yes' or 'No' for the correct response.

	Factor that must remain the same	Yes /No
(a)	Type of ground surface	Yes/No
(b)	Direction and speed of the wind	Yes/No
(c)	Size of the shoe worn by the student	Yes/No

(iii) Shade the columns in the graph to correctly show the data in the table.

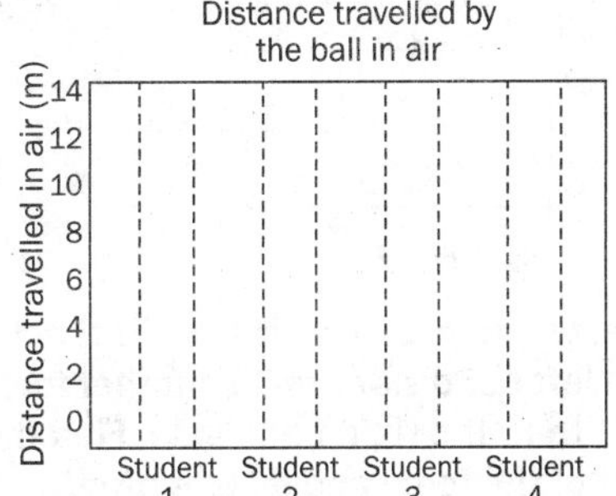

Answers

1. (i) As pressure is equal to force divided by area, hence as the contact area of the wooden block increases, the depth to which block would sink into the soft ground decreases.

$$\text{Pressure} = \frac{\text{Force}}{\text{Area}}$$

(ii) Force = 100 N, Area = 4 m^2

$\therefore$ Pressure = Force/Area = $\frac{100}{4}$ = 25 Pa

(iii) The relation between pressure and force is

$$\text{Pressure} = \frac{\text{Force}}{\text{Area}}$$

Force = Pressure × Area

= (900) (0.0009) ($\because$ 9 cm^2 = 0.0009 m^2)

= 0.81 N

2. (i) (d), (ii) (a) Yes, (b) Yes, (c) Yes

(iii)

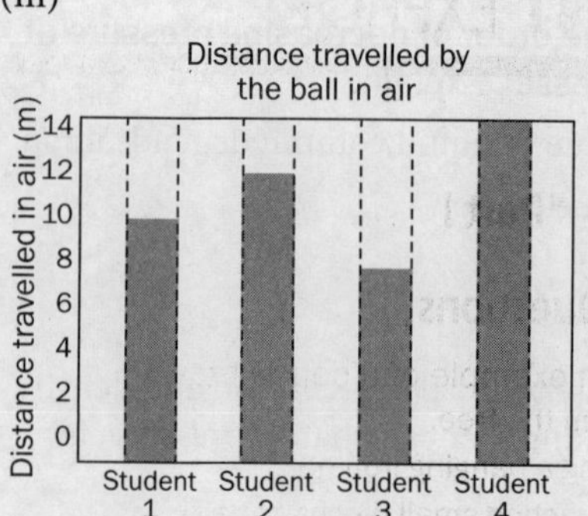

Skill Based Questions as per NEP 2020

1. Resultant forces considered in following situations

(i) If the two forces act in the same direction on a body, the net force acting on it is the sum of two forces. **Thinking Skill**

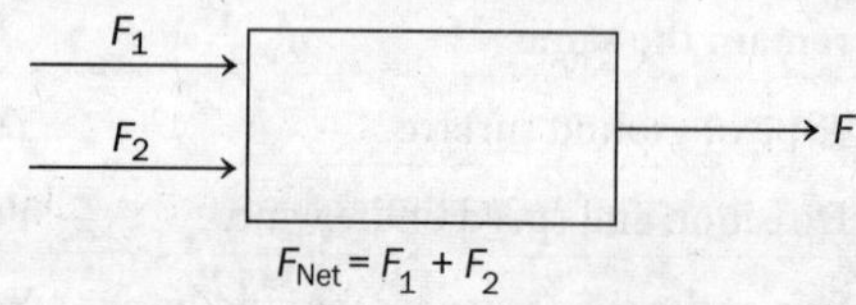

$F_{Net} = F_1 + F_2$

(ii) If the two forces act in the opposite directions on a body, the net force acting on it is the difference between two forces.

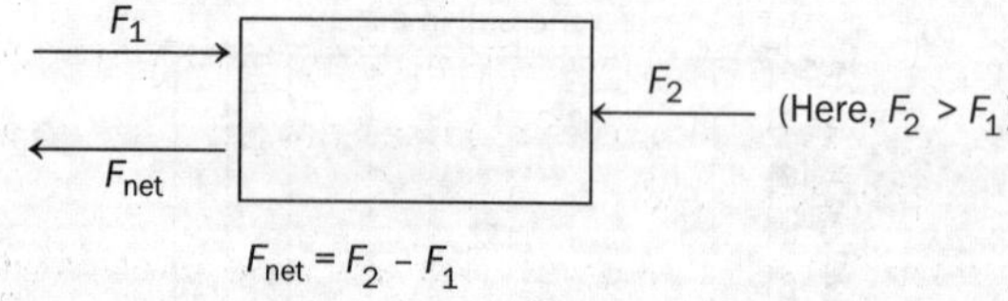

$F_{net} = F_2 - F_1$

Suppose, two forces of 15 N and 30 N act on a body from the left hand side, while another force of 35 N acts on it from the right hand side. Find the resultant of the force and its direction.

2. Watson fills a bottle completely with water. The bottle has three same sized plugged holes on its wall. Watson pulls out the plugs and checks the position of the stream of water coming out. **Thinking Skill**

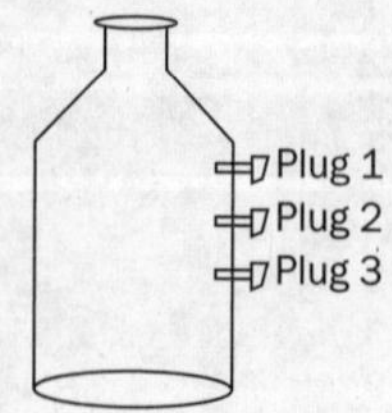

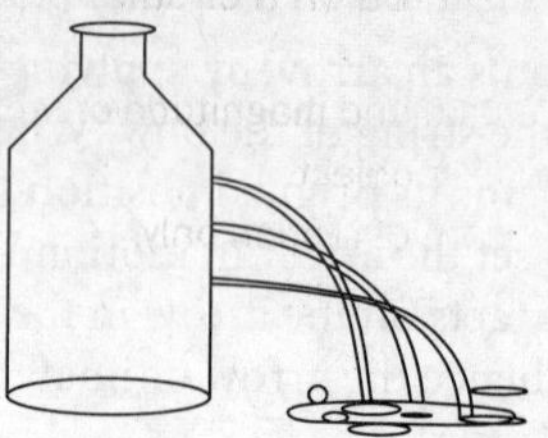

(i) What does Watson's activity show?

(a) Liquids exert pressure.

(b) Liquids contract on cooling.

(c) Liquids cannot be compressed.

(d) Liquids have no definite shape.

(ii) Liquids exert pressure on the walls of container

1. at same depth

2. at different depth

3. with same strength

Which of the following is correct?

(a) Only 1 (b) Only 3

(c) Only 2 (d) Only 1 and 3

(iii) Pressure exerted by liquids at the bottom depends on

(a) width of the liquid column

(b) shape of the column

(c) shape of the container

(d) height of the liquid column

(iv) Which of the following does not affect the pressure beneath the surface of a liquid?

(a) Strength of the gravitational field

(b) Area of the liquid

(c) Density of the liquid

(d) Depth of the liquid

ASSESSMENT EXERCISE

Part I

Multiple Choice Questions

1. Which of these is an example of a contact force?
(a) A guava falling from the tree.
(b) A magnet attracting a hanging iron nail.
(c) A plastic comb attracting small pieces of hair.
(d) A boat moving on water by the action of wind on its sail.

2. Which of these is not true for force?
(a) A force can change the state of motion of an object
(b) A force can change the shape of an object
(c) A force can act between two solid objects only
(d) Forces applied on an object in the same direction add to one another

3. When a stone is rotated on a circular path uniformly, the effect of force will be
(a) change in direction and magnitude of motion.
(b) change in shape of object.
(c) change in direction of motion only.
(d) change in magnitude only.

Fill in the Blanks

4. .... is an example for contact force.

5. When you kick a ball with your leg, you exert .... force.

6. .... is the device used to measure the atmospheric pressure.

True/False

7. The SI unit of pressure is newton.

8. Pressure is defined as the force per unit length.

9. A liquid exerts pressure in all directions.

Assertion-Reason Questions

The following questions consist of two statements- Assertion (A) and Reason (R). Answer these questions by selecting the appropriate option given below.

(a) Both A and R are true and R is the correct explanation of A.
(b) Both A and R are true but R is not the correct explanation of A
(c) A is true but R is false.
(d) A is false but R is true.

10. **Assertion (A)** Fruit falls on the ground when they get detached from the tree.

Reason (R) The force responsible for this action is electrostatic force.

11. **Assertion (A)** A football rolling along the ground, gradually slows down and finally comes to rest.

Reason (R) This happens due to force of friction between the ball and the ground.

Part II

Very Short Answer Type Questions

12. If you are pushing an object, then what actually does it mean?

13. Explain the concept of muscular force.

14. How many types of non-contact forces are available? Give the names.

15. Briefly state where will the atmospheric pressure be greater at ground level or at the top of high mountain.

Short Answer Type Questions

16. Mention the type of pressure involved in rubber sucker.

17. Explain in brief why does our head not get crushed with atmospheric pressure?

18. The rear wheels of a tractor are very wide. Explain with reason.

Long Answer Type Questions

19. Describe an activity to show that a liquid exerts equal pressure in all the direction at a given depth.

20. Gravitational force is related to weight. List some points to justify this statement.

Answer

1. (d)	**2.** (c)	**3.** (c)	**6.** Barometer	**7.** False	**8.** False
4. Frictional force		**5.** muscular	**9.** True	**10.** (c)	**11.** (a)

CHAPTER 09

Friction

In our daily life, we observe that a cricket ball moving on the ground slows down gradually and stops after sometime. Similarly, if we push a book on the table, it moves to a certain distance and stops on its own.

So, these kinds of examples show that **an opposing force comes into play between the surface of contact of two bodies, when one body moves over the surface of another body. This force is simply called force of friction**.

In this chapter, we will study the factors that affect friction, different types of friction and how the friction can be increased or decreased to our advantage.

9.1 Force of Friction

Friction force is defined as the force that opposes the relative motion between two surfaces of objects, when they come in contact.

The direction of friction force is always opposite to the direction of motion of moving body.

Spring Balance

It is the device which is used for measuring the force acting on an object. It consists of a coiled spring which gets stretched when a force is applied to it. Stretching of the spring is measured by a pointer moving on a graduated scale. The reading on the scale gives the magnitude of the force.

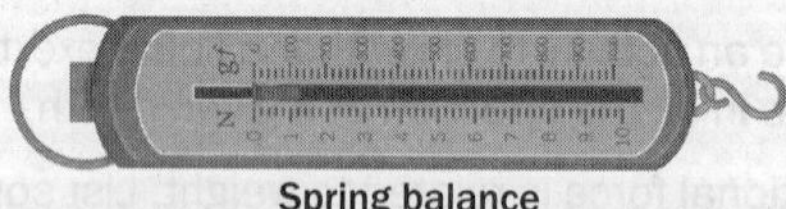

Spring balance

Factors Affecting Friction

The friction force between two surfaces depends on the two factors

(i) The nature of two surfaces.

(ii) The force with which the two surfaces are pressed together.

Friction Depends on the Nature of Two Surfaces

The force of friction is not same for all the surfaces. It depends on the roughness or smoothness of surfaces which are in contact.

When the contact surfaces are smooth, then the friction is very less. As the roughness increases, the friction also increases.

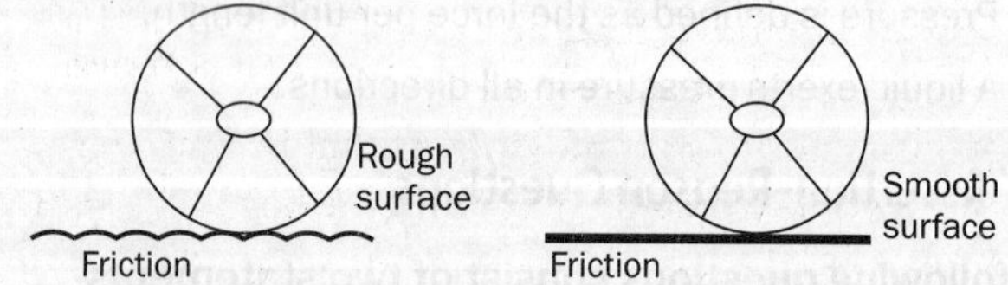

Friction Depends on the Force with which the Two Surfaces are Pressed Together

Friction is caused by interlocking of irregularities on the two surfaces of contact. So, even those surfaces which appear very smooth, have a large number of minute irregularities on them.

When two surfaces of objects are pressed together with greater force, it will increase the interlocking of irregularities. Thus, the friction force increases. This will become more clear from the following figure.

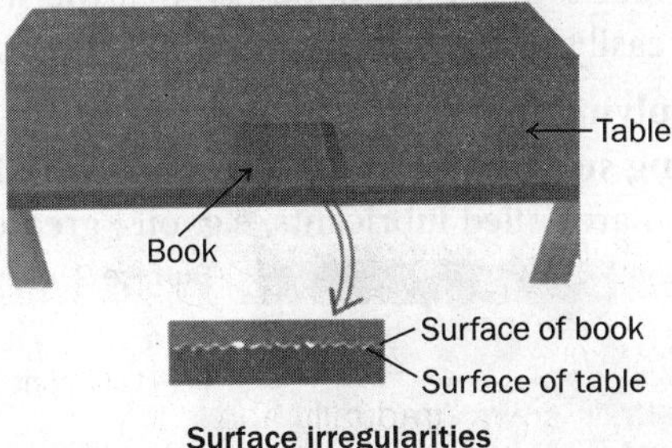

Surface irregularities

Try These 9.1

1. **Which force always acts in opposite direction to moving body ?**
2. **Aman has a toy car. If he push it with same force on smooth surface and rough surface, on which surface will it cover more distance?**
3. **Does chalk powder increases the friction?**

9.2 Types of Friction

There are generally three types of frictions which are stated below

1. Static Friction

It is the friction that acts between two surfaces when the object starts moving from its state of rest. It is more powerful than other frictions.

Static Friction

e.g. A boy pushes a heavy box but the box does not move, then he apply more force on the box and the box just tends to start moving. At that instant, the frictional force between the floor and the box is the static friction.

2. Sliding Friction

It is the friction that acts between two surfaces when the object is already in motion or sliding over another surface. e.g. Skating on snow.

Skating on Snow

During sliding, an object does not get enough time to lock into the contact points on the floor.

3. Rolling Friction

It is the friction which comes into play when a body rolls over the surface of another body.

e.g. Wheels of a skate board rolls over a road.

The direction of rolling friction is opposite to the direction of turning of wheels.

Note Sliding friction is smaller than static friction but greater than rolling friction.

9.3 Friction : A Necessary Evil

The force of friction plays an important role in our day-to-day activities. Sometimes, friction is useful while in some cases, friction is harmful.

Let us learn some advantages and disadvantages of friction.

Advantages of Friction

(i) **Friction enables us to walk easily on the ground** When we push the ground backwards while walking, the friction force pushes the foot forward. It prevents us from slipping back.

(ii) **Friction enables us to fix the nail into the wall** When we hammer a nail into the wall, the force of friction between nail and wall holds the nail tightly in the wall. Thus, we are able to fix nails in the wall.

(iii) **The brakes slow down or stop moving bicycle due to friction** If we press the brake lever to apply brakes, the brake pads rub the rims of bicycle wheels. The friction between them slows down the motion of bicycle.

Disadvantages of Friction

In some cases, friction is harmful to us and can be considered as an evil because of the following disadvantages

(i) **Wearing away of soles of our shoes takes place due to friction** There is a friction between soles of shoes and road during walking. Due to which the soles rub against the road and the tiny pieces of soles keep on breaking off slowly.

(ii) **Heat gets produced due to friction** When we rub our hands together quickly for a few seconds, they become warm because friction between the hands produces heat. Similarly, when we operate a mixer and a grinder for few minutes, its jar becomes hot due to friction.

(iii) **The efficiency of machines gets reduced due to friction** In order to run a machine, some energy is supplied to it. Due to friction between the parts of machine, some of the energy is wasted in the form of heat. This reduces the efficiency of machines.

Try These 9.2

1 **Which is greater, static friction or sliding friction ?**

2 **Arrange the types of friction in descending order on the basis of their strength.**

3 **Which force is responsible for the production of heat when we rub our hand?**

9.4 Methods of Increasing Friction

(i) **The grooves are made on the soles of shoes to increase friction.** These grooves increase the friction with the ground and the shoes get a better grip even on a slippery ground.

Soles of shoes

(ii) **The tyres of vehicles are made up of treads to increase friction.** A series of patterns made on the surface of tyre is called **tread**. The tyres are designed with treads which provide a better grip with the ground even on slippery road.

Tyres are treaded to increase friction

(iii) Kabaddi players usually rub their hands with dry soil to increase friction and to get a better grip on their opponents. Gymnasts apply some coarse substance on their hands to increase friction for better grip.

Coarse substance is applied by gymnastic player for better grip

9.5 Methods of Reducing Friction

(i) **With the help of polishing the surface** We sprinkle fine powder on the carrom board and then we polish its surface to make it smooth, so that the striker slides easily on the surface.

(ii) **By applying lubricants (like grease or oil) to the rubbing surfaces** The substances which reduce friction are called lubricants, e.g. oil , grease, etc.

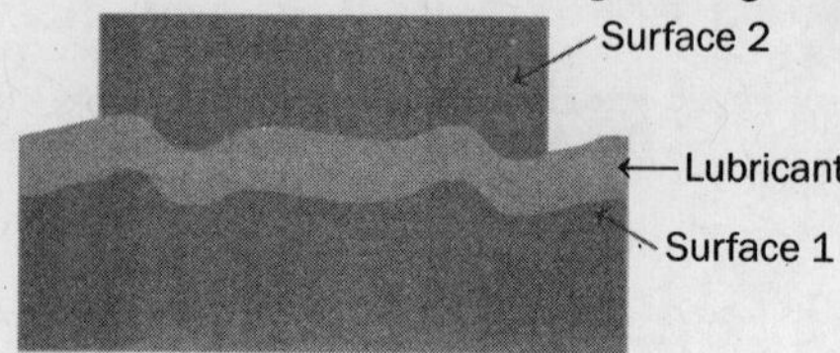

Action of Lubricants

When the oil, grease or graphite is applied between the moving part of a machine , a thin layer is formed there and moving surfaces do not directly rub against each other.

So, interlocking of irregularities is avoided to a greater extent, thus it reduces friction and the movement becomes easier.

Wheels Reduce Friction

It requires a lot of force or energy to move a heavy bag on the ground as the sliding friction is very large.

However, if we attach wheels or rollers to this heavy bag, then it experiences rolling friction.

In our daily routine, we often observe objects; like trolley bags and attaches fitted with rollers.

It easier to pull the heavy bag with the attached wheels because rolling friction is smaller than sliding friction.

Ball Bearing

These are designed to make moving parts of machines to roll over each other. It consists of metal balls fitted in between metal rings.

In bicycle , motorbike , etc., the ball bearing is inserted between the hub of wheel and the axle.

Ball bearing

When the wheel revolves, the balls of ball bearing roll and this reduce the friction. Hence, the wheel rolls smoothly over the axle.

9.6 Fluid Friction

Those substances which can flow easily are called **fluids**; like liquids and gases. There is a friction whenever an object moves through a fluid, is called fluid friction.

Air and water both exert friction force when objects move through them.

Note The frictional force exerted by fluids is also known as **drag**.

The frictional force exerted by fluid on an object moving through it depends on

(i) Speed of object with respect to fluid

(ii) Shape of object

(iii) Nature of fluid (viscosity)

Disadvantages of Fluid Friction

(i) A fluid friction opposes the motion of the object, which reduces its speed.

(ii) A fluid friction reduces the efficiency of an object. Some energy get lost in overcoming the fluid friction.

Methods of Reducing Fluid Friction

The fluid friction can be decreased by giving special (streamlined) shape to the objects.

Scientists got the idea for streamline shape from the nature. The body shape of birds and fishes help them to reduce frictional force of fluids and make them to move easily.

Note The body shape that offers a small resistance to the flow of fluid around it, is called **streamlined shape**.

In the figure, we can see that the bird and aeroplane both have a streamlined shape in the middle with two wings and a tail. Fishes are also streamlined by nature due to which they move easily in the water.

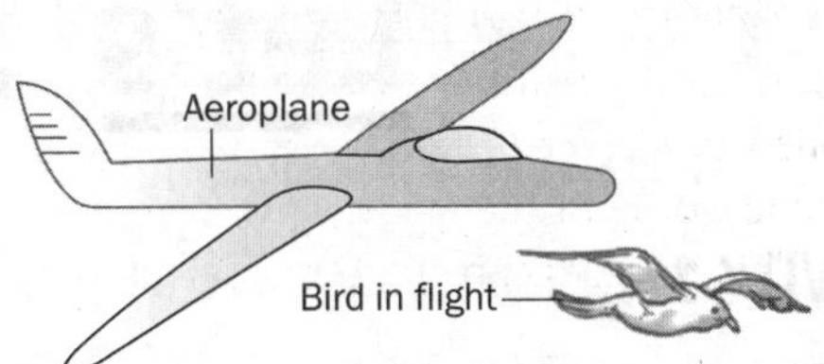

Similarity in shapes of an aeroplane and a bird

Try These 9.3

1 **What should we use to fix the cranky noise, while pedalling the bicycle?**

2 **Which shape is most suitable to reduce fluid friction?**

3 **What is the another name of fluid friction?**

Science Glossary

Force of friction The force that opposes the relative motion between two surfaces of object, when they came in contact.

Static friction The friction that acts between two surfaces, when the object starts moving from its rest state.

Sliding friction The friction that acts between two surfaces, when the object is already in motion.

Rolling friction The friction that acts between two surfaces, when a body rolls over the surface of another body.

Drag The frictional force exerted by fluids is called drag.

Let's Investigate

ACTIVITY 1 (Page 112)

Aim To observe opposing or friction force.

Material Required A table, a book

Procedure

1. Firstly, take a book and place it on table.
2. Now, push the book gently towards right. You will find that the book stops after covering some distance.
3. Now, push the book towards left, you will find that the book stops after covering some distance.

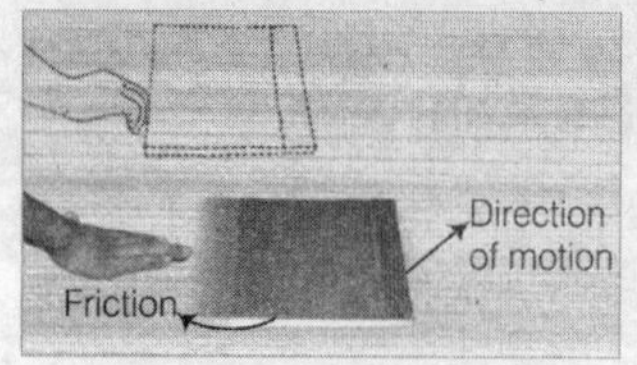

(a) Book moves towards right and friction acts towards left

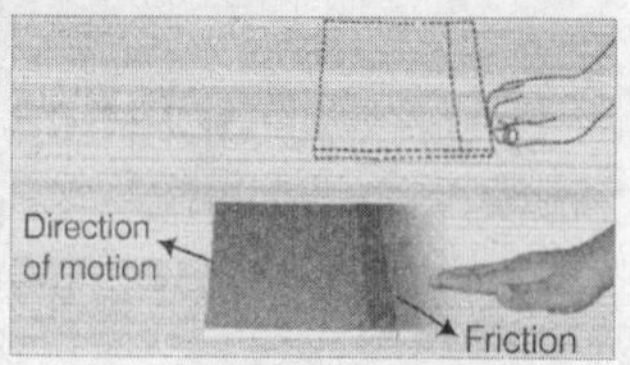

(b) Book moves towards left and friction acts towards right

Conclusion We can see that when the force is acting towards left, the friction is towards right and when the force is acting towards right , the friction is towards left. Hence, we come to the conclusion that the force of friction always acts in a direction opposite to the direction of motion of object.

Viva Questions

1. What is the direction of friction force with respect to motion of object?
2. If the friction force acts in the north direction, then what will be the direction of moving body ?

ACTIVITY 2 (Page 113)

Aim To show that the magnitude of friction is less over smooth surfaces with the help of spring balance.

Material Required A brick, a spring balance.

Procedure

1. Firstly, tie a string around a brick and connect it to the hook of the spring balance.
2. Pull the other end of the spring balance by hand till the brick just begins to move.
3. Note the reading on the spring balance. It will give you the magnitude of the force of friction between the surface of the brick and the floor.
4. Now, wrap a piece of polythene around the brick and repeat the above steps to measure the magnitude of friction force.

A brick is being pulled by spring balance

Conclusion We have concluded that the magnitude of friction is less, when we wrap the brick with a polythene. It means that smooth surfaces produce less friction.

Viva Questions

1. What is the use of spring balance?
2. Suggest some household things by which we can reduce the friction.

ACTIVITY 3 (Page 113, 114)

Aim To observe dependence of friction on the nature of surfaces.

Material Required Wooden board, a pencil cell, a piece of cloth, some books, a table.

Procedure

1. Firstly, set up an inclined plane on a smooth table by placing a wooden board supported by some books as shown in the figure.
2. Put a mark *A* on the inclined plane and let a pencil cell move down from this mark. Note the distance covered by the pencil cell on the table.
3. Now, put a piece of cloth over the table. Repeat the above steps again on the cloth spread over table. You will find that distance covered by the pencil cell is less than the distance covered in first case.

4. Again, repeat this activity by spreading a thin layer of sand over the table. You will find that the distance covered by the pencil cell is very less.

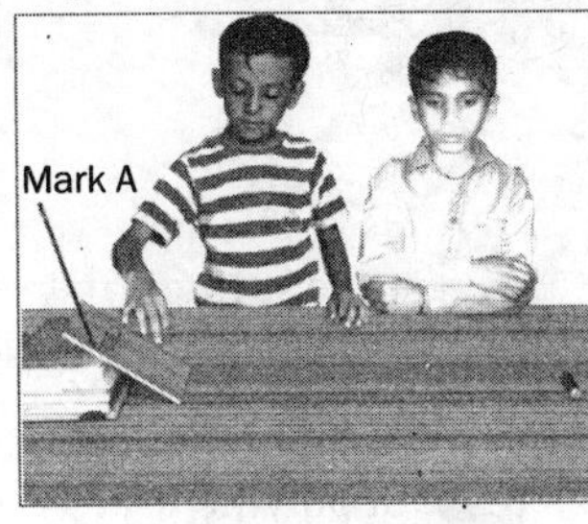

(a)

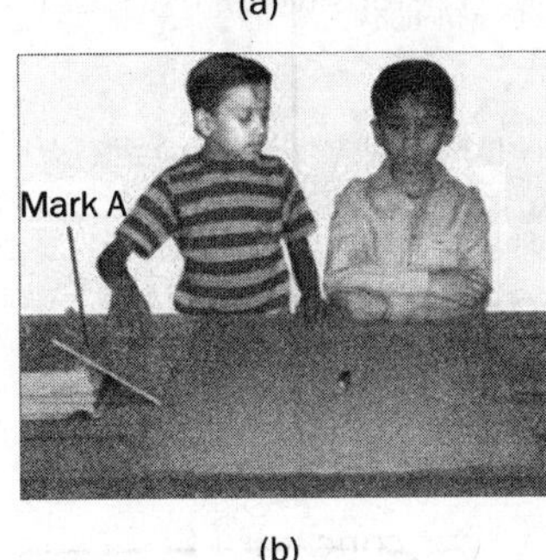

(b)

Pencil cell covers different distances on different surfaces

Conclusion We have concluded that the distance covered by pencil cell is different on different surface. Thus, the friction depends on the nature of the two surfaces in contact.

Viva Questions

1. What can be the result, if we sprinkle oil drops on the table?
2. What can be the result, if we spread small-small stones over the table?

ACTIVITY 4 (Page 118)

Aim To show that rolling friction is less than the sliding friction.

Material Required A book, few pencils.

Procedure

1. Firstly, take few pencils of cylindrical shape and place them parallel to each other on a table.
2. Place a thick book over it.
3. Now, push the book gently. You will find that the pencils rolling as the book moves.

   Here, we find easier to move the book in this way than to slide it.

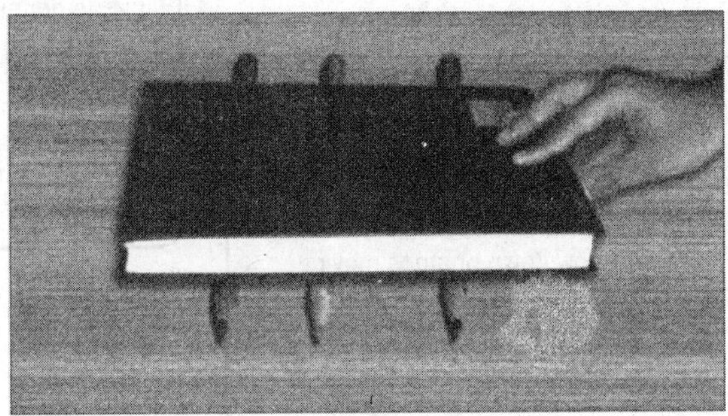

Motion of the book on the roller

Conclusion We have concluded that the friction can be reduced by attaching wheels, to move an object. It is always easier to move an object by rolling as compare to sliding it.

Viva Questions

1. Is rolling friction greater than sliding friction?
2. Give two examples of rolling friction.

Mind Map

FRICTION

Types of Friction

- **Rolling friction**
  Friction which comes into play when a body rolls over other surface.
- **Sliding friction**
  Acts between two surfaces when the object is already in motion or sliding over other surface.
- **Static friction**
  Friction that acts between two surfaces when there is no motion between the two surfaces. It acts in response trying to cause a stationary object to start moving.

Rolling friction

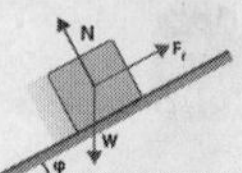
Sliding friction

Static friction

Friction : A Necessary Evil

- **Advantages of friction**
  - Friction enables us to walk easily on ground.
  - Enables us to fix the nail into the wall.
  - Brakes slow down or stops moving bicycle due to friction.
- **Disadvantages of friction**
  - Wearing away of soles of shoes due to friction.
  - Heat gets produced due to friction.
  - Efficiency of machines gets reduced due to friction.

Force of Friction

Force that opposes the relative motion between two surfaces of objects.

Factors Affecting Friction

- **Force with which surfaces are pressed together**
  - Friction is caused by interlocking of irregularities.
  - Smooth surfaces have less irregularities on them.
- **Nature of two surfaces**
  - If contact surfaces are smooth, then friction is very less.
  - If roughness increases, then friction increases.

Methods of Increasing Friction

- Grooves are made on soles of shoes.
- Tyres of vehicles are made up of treads
- Kabaddi players usually rub their hands with dry soil.

Methods of Reducing Friction

- Polishing the surface, i.e. sprinkle fine powder on carromboard and polish its surface.
- By applying lubricants to rubbing surfaces
- Wheels reduce friction.

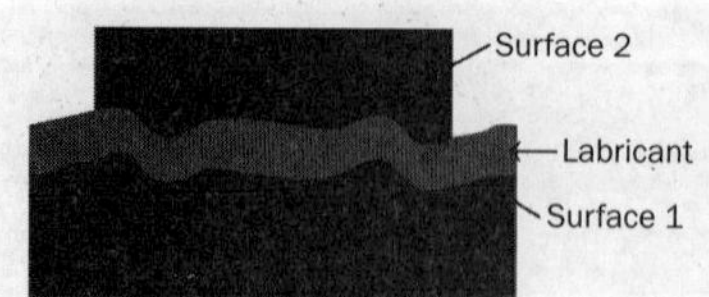

Fluid Friction

When an object moves through fluid friction acts on it, then

- **Methods of reducing fluid friction**
  - Decreased by giving special (Streamlined) shape to objects.
  - Birds and aeroplane have streamlined shape.
- **Disadvantages of fluid friction**
  - Opposes the motion of object, which reduces its speed.
  - Reduces the efficiency of an object.
- **Dependence**
  - Speed of object with respect to fluid.
  - Shape of object.
  - Nature of liquid (viscosity).

Device For Measuring Weight

Spring balance is the device which is used to measure the force acting on an object.

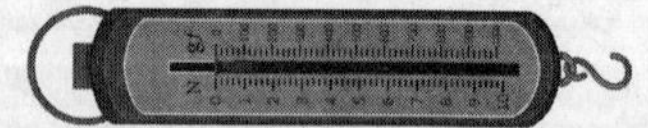

NCERT FOLDER

Complete Explanations of all NCERT's Questions

Intext Questions

Q.1 Why it is difficult to move on a wet marble floor? **Page 112**

Ans. On a wet marble floor, frictional force between the foot and floor decreases to make it slippery, thus we feel difficult to move on a wet marble floor.

Q.2 State the reason, why do we slip when we step on a banana peel? **Page 112**

Ans. As we step on a banana peel, there is no grip between our foot and the banana peel due to very less friction. So, we slip accidentally.

Q.3 Is the friction same for all the surfaces? **Page 113**

Ans. No, because friction depends on the nature of surface in contact.

Q.4 It is easier to move the box from rest or to move it when it is already in motion. Explain why? **Page 115**

Ans. When the object is at rest, we have to apply more force to overcome interlocking between irregularities. On the other hand, when the object starts moving the contact points on its surface do not get enough time to lock into the contact points on the ground. So, it is easier to move the block when it is already in motion.

Q.5 Can you imagine being able to walk at all, if there were no friction? **Page 115**

Ans. No, we can't walk at all, if there is no friction.

Q.6 Could you write, if there were no friction between the chalk and the board ? **Page 116**

Ans. No, we couldn't able to write on blackboard, if there were no friction between the chalk and the board.

Q.7 How do you feel, if you vigorously rub your palms together for few minutes? **Page 116**

Ans. We will feel that our hands feel warm. This warmth is caused by a force called friction.

Q.8 Have you ever thought why the sole of your shoe is grooved ? **Page 117**

Ans. It is done to provide the shoes better grip. The groove on shoes increases the friction between the shoes and floor.

Q.9 Why do you sprinkle fine powder on the carrom board ? **Page 117**

Ans. Powder is sprinkled on the carrom board to reduce friction.

Q.10 The pieces of luggage fitted with the rollers. Explain why? **Page 118**

Ans. In order to reduce friction, pieces of luggage are fitted with rollers so that even a child can pull the luggage easily.

Q.11 Can we reduce friction to zero by polishing surfaces or using large amount of lubricants? **Page 118**

Ans. No, friction can never be entirely eliminated. Some irregularities are always there.

Q.12 Where do you think scientists got hints for the streamlined shapes ? **Page 119**

Ans. Scientists got hints for the streamlined shapes from the body shapes of birds and fishes who have to move about in fluids all the time.

Q.13 Do you find any similarity in the shape of aeroplane and that of a bird ? **Page 119**

Ans. Yes, both have streamlined bodies, which help them to move easily in fluid.

Exercise

Q.1 Fill in the blanks.

(a) Friction opposes the .... between the surfaces in contact with each other.

(b) Friction depends on the .... of surfaces.

(c) Friction produces ....

(d) Sprinkling of powder on the carrom board .... friction.

(e) Sliding friction is ...... than the static friction.

Ans. (a) relative motion

(b) nature

(c) heat

(d) reduces

(e) less

Q.2 Four children were asked to arrange forces due to rolling, static and sliding frictions in a decreasing order. Their arrangements are given below. Choose the correct arrangement.

(a) Rolling, static, sliding
(b) Rolling, sliding, static
(c) Static, sliding, rolling
(d) Sliding, static, rolling

Ans. (c) We know that the static friction is more powerful than all other frictions. Hence, it will take first place in decreasing order. Similarly, sliding friction is smaller than static friction but greater than rolling friction. Thus, the decreasing order of the forces due to these frictions is as follows

Static > Sliding > Rolling

Q.3. Alida runs her toy car on dry marble floor, wet marble floor, newspaper and towel spread on the floor. The force of friction acting on the car on different surfaces in increasing order will be

(a) wet marble floor, dry marble floor, newspaper, towel
(b) newspaper, towel, dry marble floor, wet marble floor
(c) towel, newspaper, dry marble floor, wet marble floor
(d) Wet marble floor, dry marble floor, towel, newspaper

Ans. (a) The correct arrangement is as follows:

Wet marble floor, dry marble floor, newspaper, towel.

Q.4. Suppose your writing desk is tilted a little. A book kept on it starts sliding down. Show the direction of frictional force acting on it.

Ans. A book kept on a tilted writing desk starts sliding down. The direction of frictional force is in the opposite direction, thus frictional force will act in upward direction.

Q.5. You spill a bucket of soapy water on a marble floor accidentally. Would it make easier or more difficult for you to walk on the floor? Why?

Ans. After spilling a bucket of soapy water on a marble floor, it would be more difficult for us to walk on the floor. Because the layer of soapy water reduces the friction and the foot cannot make a proper grip on the floor.

Q.6. Explain why sportsmen use shoes with spikes?

Ans. Sportsmen use shoes with spikes in order to avoid getting slipped in the field. The spikes in the shoes increase the friction, so they can run on the ground easily.

Q.7. Iqbal has to push a lighter box and Seema has to push a similar heavier box on the same floor. Who will have to apply a larger force and why?

Ans. The heavy object will be pressed hard against the opposite surface and produces more friction. So, Seema will have to apply a larger force due to more friction.

Q.8. Explain why sliding friction is less than the static friction?

Ans. We know that friction is caused by the interlocking of irregularities in the two surfaces.

In case of static friction, interlocking between two objects is very strong but in case of sliding friction, there is a less time of getting interlocked with each other. Thus, the sliding friction is less than the static friction.

Q.9. Give examples to show that friction is both a friend and a foe.

Ans. Friction as a friend

(i) It allows us to walk comfortably.
(ii) It allows us to minimise the speed or to stop the moving objects.
(iii) It allows us to write on a board with chalk.

Friction as a foe

(i) It causes wear and tear in objects.
(ii) It causes damage to the parts of machines.
(iii) It does not allow the free movement of objects.

Q.10 Explain why objects moving in fluids must have special shapes?

Ans. The frictional force exerted by fluids is also called drag. When objects move through fluids, they have to overcome friction acting on them. In this process, they lose their energy. Efforts are made to minimise friction. So, objects are given special shapes and this type of shape is known as streamlined shape.

REVIEW EXERCISE

Including Competency Based Questions

Part I

Multiple Choice Questions

1. In figure, a boy is shown pushing the box from right to left. NCERT Exemplar

The force of friction will act on the box

(a) from right to left (←)
(b) from left to right (→)
(c) vertically downwards (↓)
(d) vertically upwards (↑)

2. To sharpen the blade of a knife by rubbing it against a surface, which of the following will be most suitable? NCERT Exemplar

(a) Stone (b) Plastic block
(c) Wooden block (d) Glass block

3. A toy car released with the same initial speed will travel farthest on

(a) muddy surface
(b) polished marble surface
(c) cemented surface
(d) brick surface

4. A boy rolls a rubber ball on a wooden surface. The ball travels a short distance before coming to rest. To make the same, ball travel longer distance before coming to rest, he may NCERT Exemplar

(a) spread a carpet on the wooden surface
(b) cover the ball with a piece of cloth
(c) sprinkle talcum powder on the wooden surface
(d) sprinkle sand on the wooden surface

5. It is difficult to walk on a well polished floor because friction between our feet and floor is

(a) increased (b) reduced
(c) same (d) None of these

6. A student wants to move a heavy block from one place to another. What method the student should apply to reduce the effort?

(a) Pull the block using a rope
(b) Place wheels under the block
(c) Slide the block along the surface
(d) Apply oil to the bottom of the block

7. The picture shows four types of shoe soles.

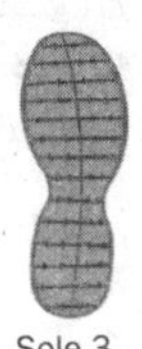

Sole 1 Sole 2 Sole 3 Sole 4

Competency Based Que.

Which shoe sole provides the best grip and friction while walking?

(a) Sole 1 (b) Sole 2
(c) Sole 3 (d) Sole 4

8. We can increase the friction by

(a) polishing
(b) making grooves and treads
(c) streamlining
(d) using ball bearing

9. If we apply oil on door hinges, the friction will NCERT Exemplar

(a) increase (b) decrease
(c) disappear altogether (d) will remain unchanged

10. Fine powder is poured on the carromboard to

(a) increase friction (b) decrease friction
(c) Both (a) and (b) (d) None of these

11. Treads are made in the tyres to

(a) increase friction (b) decrease friction
(c) speed up the vehicle (d) speed down the vehicle

12. In a large commercial complex, there are four ways to reach the main road. One of the path has loose soil, the second is laid with polished marble and the third is laid with bricks and the fourth has gravel surface. It is raining heavily and Paheli wishes to reach the main road. The path on which she is least likely to slip is Competency Based Que.

(a) loose soil (b) bricks
(c) polished marble (d) gravel

13. Which of the following statements is incorrect? NCERT Exemplar

(a) Friction acts on a ball rolling along the ground.
(b) Friction acts on a boat moving on water.
(c) Friction acts on a bicycle moving on a smooth road.
(d) Friction does not act on a ball moving through air.

14. Whenever the surfaces in contact tend to move or move with respect to each other, the force of friction comes into play Competency Based Que.

(a) only if the objects are solid
(b) only if one of the two objects is liquid
(c) only if one of the two objects is gaseous
(d) irrespective of whether the objects are solids, liquids or gases

15. The fishes swim easily in the water because they have

(a) more energy (b) streamlined shape
(c) Both (a) and (b) (d) None of these

Answers

1. (b)	2. (a)	3. (b)	4. (c)
5. (b)	6. (b)	7. (d)	8. (b)
9. (b)	10. (b)	11. (a)	12. (d)
13. (d)	14. (d)	15. (b)	

Fill in the Blanks

1. Spring balance is a device used for measuring the .... acting on the object.
2. On smooth surfaces, there are .... number of irregularities. While on rough surfaces, there are .... number of irregularities.
3. Friction can never be entirely ....
4. The soles of our shoes get worn out after a period of time. It is due to ....
5. .... is produced by friction.
6. Ball bearings reduce friction because they rolls rather than ....
7. We pour a drop of oil on the hinge of door to .... friction.
8. Cars and speedboats are .... to reduce drag.

Answers

1. force	2. less, large	3. eliminated
4. friction	5. Heat	6. slide
7. reduce	8. streamlined	

True/False

1. Friction always works in the same direction of motion of body.
2. Soapy floor is slippery due to less friction.
3. Friction increases with increase in smoothness of surface.
4. It is easy to roll the body over one another than to slide it.
5. Friction enables vehicles to move on the ground.
6. Fluid friction depends on the shape of an object placed in the fluid and nature of fluid.

Answers

1. False	2. True	3. False	4. True
5. True	6. True		

Match the Columns

1. Match the Column I with those in Column II.

Column I	Column II
(a) Friction produces	(i) Ceiling fan
(b) Lubricants	(ii) Heat
(c) Soapy floor	(iii) Oil and grease
(d) Ball bearing	(iv) Rolling friction
(e) Wheels	(v) Less friction

Answer

1. (a)–(ii), (b)–(iii), (c)–(v), (d)–(i), (e)–(iv)

Assertion-Reason Questions

The following questions consists of two statements - Assertion (A) and Reason (R). Answer these questions by selecting the appropriate option given below.

(a) Both A and R are true and R is the correct explanation of A.
(b) Both A and R are true but R is not the correct explanation of A.
(c) A is true but R is false.
(d) A is false but R is true.

1. **Assertion** (A) Force of friction is smaller in smooth surfaces than rough surface.
Reason (R) Static friction is greater than the sliding friction.

2. **Assertion** (A) Lubricants increases the friction force.

   Reason (R) Friction is a necessary evil.

3. **Assertion** (A) Birds can fly easily in sky.

   Reason (R) Streamlined body help them in minimising the friction.

4. **Assertion** (A) It is difficult to push or pull heavier object than lighter object.

   Reason (R) Interlocking of irregularities are more in between heavy object surface than light object.

Answers

1. (b) Force of friction is smaller on smooth surfaces than rough surfaces because on smooth surfaces, the irregularities present are very less as compare to rough surface.
2. (d) Lubricants are the materials which minimise the friction force. Friction has advantages as well as disadvantages. That's why, it is called as a necessary evil.
3. (a) A body shape that offers a small resistance to the flow of fluid around it, is called streamlined shape. Birds have streamlined shape by nature. That's why, they fly easily in the air.
4. (a) The interlocking of irregularities are more in between heavy object surface than light object. That's why, it is difficult to push or pull heavier objects.

Case Based Question

Friction is a force that acts between two surfaces that are sliding across each other. It always act in the opposite direction in which object is moving.
Friction is a necessary evil. It has both advantages as well as disadvantages. It prevents our shoes slipping on footpath when we walk but sometimes it may also harm us. It reduces the efficiency of a machine. There is a lot of energy loss due to friction. Friction can be reduced by some methods. For example, we use lubricants like oil, grease to reduce the friction between moving parts of a machine. In many machines, friction is reduced by using ball bearings.

(i) Which of the following can be used as a lubricant?

(a) Mustard oil (b) Soil
(c) Paper (d) Iron powder

(ii) Friction always acts in which direction with respect to moving body is

(a) perpendicular
(b) same direction
(c) opposite direction
(d) always downward

(iii) Friction can be increases by using

(a) lubricant (b) chalk powder
(c) oil (d) talcum powder

Answer

1. (i) (a) (ii) (c) (iii) (b)

Part II

Very Short Answer Type Questions

1. **Will force of friction come into play, when a rain drop rolls down a glass window pane?** **NCERT Exemplar**

Ans. Yes, friction comes into play when two surfaces are in contact but in very small amount.

2. **If a body is moving on rough horizontal surface towards east, then in which direction the frictional force will act?**

Ans. Frictional force always acts in the direction opposite to the direction of motion, so it will act towards west.

3. **Figure shows two boys applying force on a box. If the magnitude of the force applied by each is equal, will the box experience any force of friction?** **NCERT Exemplar**

Ans. No, the force applied by both boys is equal. So, net force will be zero and hence friction force will not come into play.

4. **It is easier to drag a carpet from the floor, but it is difficult to drag the carpet when someone is sitting on it. Explain the reason behind it.** **Competency Based Que.**

Ans. If the two surfaces are pressed harder, then the force of friction will increase. So, it is easy to drag a carpet when nobody is sitting on it but when a person is sitting on it, then it produces more friction.

5. **Why does a matchstick catch fire when it is rubbed on rough surface?**

Ans. On rubbing the matchstick on a rough surface, the temperature increases due to friction, making the matchstick catch fire.

6. **A jar of a mixer becomes hot when it is run for few minutes. Comment.**

Ans. Due to friction, the jar of a mixer becomes hot when it is run for few minutes.

7. Give a reason for calling friction as a necessary evil.

Ans. Friction is a necessary evil because it causes a lot of wear and tear.

8. Why do kabaddi players rub their hands with soil?

Ans. Kabaddi players rub their hands with soil to increase the friction, so that they can grip the opposite team players firmly.

9. Why do weightlifters apply chalk powder on their palms while lifting weights? **Competency Based Que.**

Ans. It increases the roughness in their hand. This provide better grip while lifting weights.

10. Why are oil, creams and grease called lubricants?

Ans. Oil, creams and grease when applied on a surface make it smooth, thus reduce friction, so these are called lubricants.

11. Can we eliminate friction completely?

Ans. No, we cannot eliminate friction completely because it is the characteristic property (molecular property) of material.

12. Which is the special shape of the objects moving in fluids?

Ans. Streamlined shape is the special shape given to objects moving in fluids.

13. Explain fluid friction in brief.

Ans. When an object moves in a fluid, then the resistance to the movement of object exerted by fluid is called fluid friction.

14. Why an arrow with a pointed tip can move faster in air than that with a flat tip?

Ans. The arrow with a pointed tip suffers small air resistance due to its pointed shape, so it moves faster.

Short Answer Type Questions

1. Imagine that an object is falling through a long straight glass tube held vertical, air has been removed completely from the tube. The object does not touch the walls of the tube. Will the object experience any force of friction? **NCERT Exemplar**

Ans. No, the object will not experience any frictional force because to experience the force of friction, two surfaces must be there and there is only one surface in this case.

2. While travelling on a rickshaw, you might have experienced that if the seat cover is very smooth, you tend to slip when brakes are applied suddenly. Explain. **NCERT Exemplar**

Ans. If the seat cover of rickshaw is very smooth, then the friction between our body and the seat is very small. Therefore, when the brakes are applied, we tend to slip.

3. Two boys are riding their bicycles on the same concrete road. One has new tyres on his bicycle while the other has tyres that are old and used. Which of them is more likely to slip while moving through a patch of the road which has lubricating oil spilled over it?

Ans. The boy having the tyres which are old and used is most likely to slip because these tyres will experience less frictional force which is insufficient to move on the oily road.

4. Explain why

(i) a pencil will write on paper but not on glass.

(ii) climbing a greasy pole is very difficult.

Ans. (i) Since, due to friction, a pencil writes on paper but there is smoothness on the surface of glass, a pencil cannot write on glass.

(ii) If a pole is polished with grease, then the surface of pole becomes smoother thus reducing friction. So, climbing a greasy pole becomes tough.

5. The handle of a cricket bat or a badminton racquet is usually rough. Explain the reason. **NCERT Exemplar**

Ans. The handle of a cricket bat or badminton racquet is rough, so that while playing, the bat or badminton racquet does not slip away from the hands of the player. Roughness is responsible for the frictional force without which gripping is not possible.

6. Is there a force of friction between the wheels of a moving train and iron rails? If yes, name the type of friction. If an air cushion can be introduced between the wheel and the rail, what effect will it have on the friction? **Competency Based Que.**

Ans. Yes, there is always a force of friction between the wheels of a moving train and iron rails. The name of this friction is rolling friction, since the wheels are rolling on the track.

On introducing air cushion, the frictional force becomes less, since there is no contact between rails and wheels.

7. A father and son pushed their car to the side of road as it had stalled in the middle of the road. They experienced that although they had to push with all their might initially to move the car, the push required to keep the car rolling was smaller, once the car started rolling. Explain. **NCERT Exemplar**

Ans. When the car is at rest, we have to apply greater force because the value of static friction is more.

As the car starts moving, the friction changes into the rolling friction which is always less than the previous one. So, we have to exert the lesser force to keep it in motion.

8. **When the cutting edge of a knife is put against a fast rotating stone to sharpen it, sparks are seen to fly? Explain the reason.** NCERT Exemplar

Ans. Due to the friction between knife and stone, the temperature of the knife and hence the stone increases and it increases to such a level that sparks are produced which can be seen while sharpening it.

9. **Cartilage is present in the joints of our body, which helps in their smooth movement. With advancing age, this cartilage wears off. How would this affect the movement of joints?** Competency Based Que.

Ans. Cartilage present in the joints of our body, reduces friction during movement of joints. But on wearing off this cartilage, the force of friction increases due to which the smoothness of movement decreases and one feels the joint pain.

10. **Explain why the surface of mortar and pestle (silbatta) used for grinding is etched again after prolonged use?**

Ans. After prolonged use, the mortar and pestle loose the roughness, due to which frictional force reduces and it does not work properly. So, we have to etch it to make it rough again.

11. **You might have noticed that when used for a long time, slippers with rubber soles become slippery. Explain the reason.** NCERT Exemplar

Ans. It is due to continuous rubbing of soles with the ground, the spikes on the sole get damaged slowly and the soles become slippery.

12. **Explain which principle is involved in machine belts.**

Ans. In many machines (like flour mills), belts are used to drive wheels for running the machines.
Greater friction is required between the belts and machine wheels, so that the belts can drive the machine wheels properly without slipping off wheels. So, in order to increase friction, machine belts are made up of special materials having rough surfaces.

13. **A marble is allowed to roll down an inclined plane from a fixed height. At the foot of the inclined plane, it moves on a horizontal surface (a) covered with silk cloth, (b) covered with a layer of sand and (c) covered with a glass sheet. On which surface, will the marble move the shortest distance. Give reason for your answer.** NCERT Exemplar

Ans. Marble will move the shortest distance on the layer of sand because it will exert a greater force of friction on the marble and other two surfaces like silk cloth and glass sheet will exert a lesser friction force comparatively.

14. **While playing tug of war, Preeti felt that the rope was slipping through her hands. Suggest a way out for her to prevent this.** NCERT Exemplar

Ans. To prevent slipping of the rope from hands, Preeti has to make her hands somewhat non-smooth, so she can rub her hands by introducing sand between them.

15. **Two friends are trying to push a heavy load as shown in figure below. Suggest a way which will make this task easier for them.**

Ans. Both the friends can put rollers below the heavy load. Since, the rolling friction is smaller than the sliding friction. Therefore, putting rollers below the heavy load will make this task easier for them.

Long Answer Type Questions

1. **Few days back, Shradha ,a student of class VIIIth was driving the car. She went to a crop field. The level of road were just above the level of ploughed field. As she wanted to stop the slow moving car, the brakes failed to work at that time. Suddenly, she turned the car towards the ploughed field. After sometime, the car came to rest.**

(a) Shradha turned the car towards the ploughed field. Explain why?

(b) Explain how the car came to rest after covering some distance in the ploughed field?

(c) Mention the values that Shradha exhibits here.

Ans. (a) She turned her car towards the ploughed field to protect herself from an accident.

(b) The car moved from road to the ploughed field due to which the force of friction between the tyre and the ground surface increases suddenly. Because the large amount of irregularities reduces the movement of tyre. Thus, the car came to a rest.

(c) The values displayed by Shradha are intelligence and awareness.

2. **In Physics classroom, a teacher told to his students that when a cricket player want to catch a ball then first he rub the hands. Thus, there is less chance of slipping the ball from hands.**

(a) Explain the reason of not slipping of ball from hand.

(b) If the player makes his hands oily instead of rubbing them, would he be able to catch the ball?

(c) Mention the type of teaching skills of teacher is being represented here. **Competency Based Que.**

Ans. (a) The player rub his hand due to which the palms become warm which absorb the moisture from the surface and make the surface rough. So, due to roughness of hands, the ball may get a better grip between the hands and will not slip.

(b) The player makes the palm surface oily. The number of irregularities decreases and the surface becomes smooth. So, the ball slips off easily from the hand.

(c) As, teacher wants to teach the students through easy example. So, this act of teaching shows the experience and ideality of teacher.

3. **Explain with the help of an example that heat is produced by friction.**

Ans. As friction opposes the relative motion between the two surfaces, it produces heat. So, when we rub our hands together vigorously for few minutes, we feel hotness. Similarly when we strike a matchstick against the rough surface, it catches fire.

In machineries also, heat is produced due to friction as the machine parts rub against each other.

4. **We have two identical metal sheets. One of them is rubbed with sand paper and the other with ordinary paper. The one rubbed with sand paper shines more than the other. Give reason.** **NCERT Exemplar**

Ans. While rubbing with sand paper, more frictional force is produced between the layers of metal sheet and sand paper which causes more force on dust particles and they are removed easily, so it will shine more. But in case of ordinary paper, the force of friction is not sufficient to remove all the dust, so it will shine less in this case.

Case Based Questions

1. **Raju wanted to find out which one of four surfaces produces the greatest friction.**
He pushed the same toy car on the four surfaces, separately.

Raju noted the distance travelled by car on each surface before stopping.

	Surface 1	Surface 2	Surface 3	Surface 4
Distance travelled by the toy car before stopping	120 cm	150 cm	100 cm	180 cm

Competency Based Que.

(i) On which surface did the car experience the greatest friction?

(a) Surface 1 (b) Surface 2
(c) Surface 3 (d) Surface 4

(ii) What must be kept the same in the activity to compare the distances travelled by the car?

(iii) What will happen to the car, if it continues to move on the surface for 1 h?

(a) The wheels will get hard.
(b) The wheels will become hot.
(c) The wheels will shrink in size.
(d) The wheels will change shape

2. **The picture shows four different rubber tubes.**

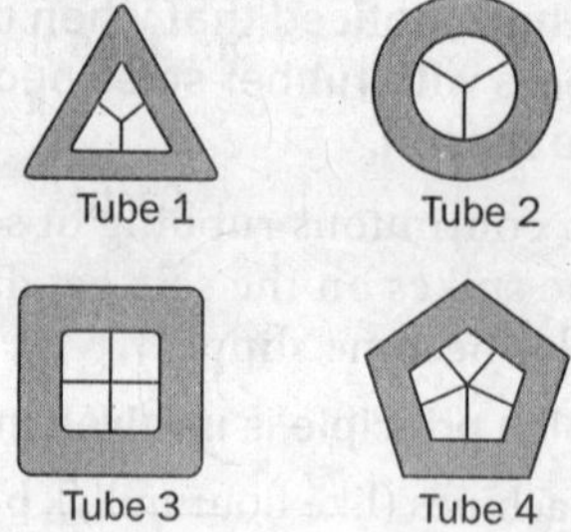

Competency Based Que.

(i) Which tube will experience the least friction while rolling on a surface? Explain your answer.

(ii) Which of these would affect the amount of friction generated on a moving object?
Circle 'Yes' or 'No' for the correct response.

Does this Affect the Amount of Friction Generated?	Yes or No
(a) Mass of the object	Yes/No
(b) Surface area of the object	Yes/No
(c) Roughness of the object	Yes/No

3. **Anshu lets a marble roll freely on four rough wooden planks.**
The table shows the time taken by the marble to reach the bottom of each plank.

	Plank 1	Plank 2	Plank 3	Plank 4
Time taken by the marble to reach bottom	2 s	3 s	X s	4 s

Competency Based Que.

(i) What could be the value of X in the table?

(a) 2 s (b) 3 s (c) 4 s (d) 5 s

(ii) Anshu polished all four planks to smoothen the surfaces. She repeated her activity on the polished planks.
Will there be any change in the results? Explain your answer.

Answers

1. (i) (c)
   (ii) Toy car and pushing forces must be kept the same in the activity to compare the distances travelled by the car.
   (iii) (b)
2. (i) Tube 2 experiences the least friction while rolling on a surface because area of contact between two surfaces is less in case of tube 2.
   (ii) (a) Yes (b) Yes (c) Yes
3. (i) (d)
   (ii) Yes, results will change. Polishing the surface make it smooth, then the friction between marble and plank decreases which results in decreasing the time taken by the marble to reach bottom.

Skill Based Questions as per NEP 2020

1. The wheel of a moving car is driven by the engine. The car is moving in the direction shown in the above diagram. In which direction, does the frictional force act on the wheel ? **Knowledge Based Que.**

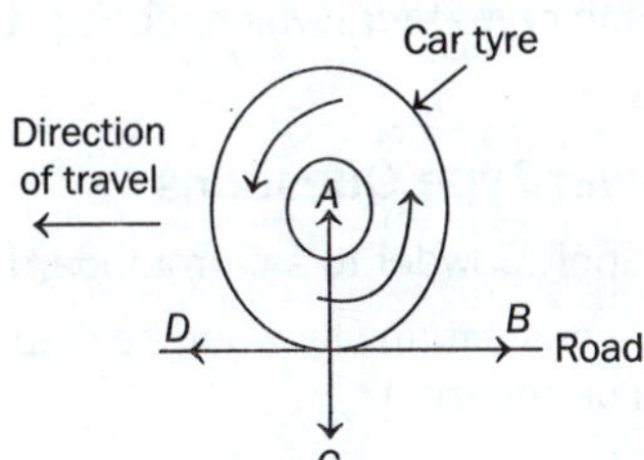

(a) A (b) B
(c) C (d) D

2. Sonakshi investigated how a pencil cell travels on a ramp when the table is covered with different surfaces (wood, cotton cloth and silk cloth). She noted the time taken by the pencil cell to travel on each surface three times. Her results are mentioned below. **Activity Based Que.**

Surface	Time (s)	Time (s)	Time (s)
Wooden	5.01	4.99	5.21
Cotton cloth	7.02	7.25	7.20
Silk cloth	4.20	4.20	4.25

(i) Name the two factors on which the magnitude of a frictional force depends.

(ii) From the chart given above, state which travelled fastest and find the average time it took.

(iii) Explain with one example how friction can be both a positive and a negative part in our everyday life?

3. The frictional force between two moving surfaces which are in contact with each other is called kinetic friction or sliding friction.

Example If a boy apply some pushing force on the box, the box will start sliding on the surface and the friction between the surfaces is called sliding friction.

The force required to keep a body in motion is less than the force required to start the motion, so we can say that sliding friction is less than the static friction. **Knowledge Based Que.**

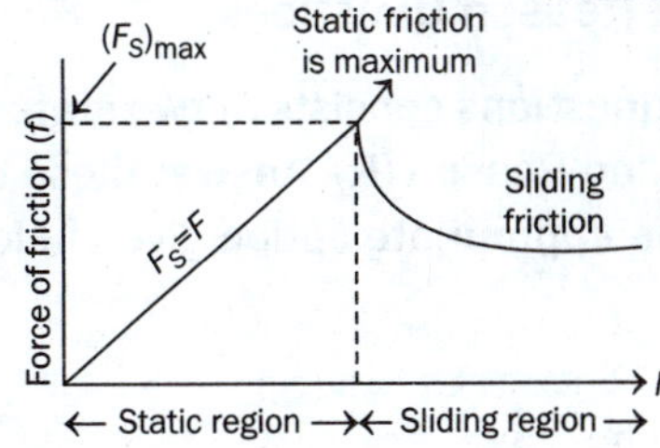

(i) Explain why the sliding friction is always greater than rolling friction?

(ii) Mention two different examples for sliding friction.

ASSESSMENT EXERCISE

Part I

Multiple Choice Questions

1. Direction of friction is always
   (a) opposes the motion
   (b) direction of motion
   (c) perpendicular to the motion
   (d) None of the above
2. Which of the following device is used to measure the force acting on an object?
   (a) Spring balance
   (b) Odometer
   (c) Both (a) and (b)
   (d) None of the above
3. Which of the following does not reduce friction?
   (a) Streamlined shape
   (b) Lubricant
   (c) Sand
   (d) Oil
4. The frictional force exerted by fluids is also known as
   (a) drag (b) static friction
   (c) rolling friction (d) sliding friction

Fill in the Blanks

5. .... kind of friction is in effect when a heavy box is pushed.
6. Friction is a ....force.
7. .... friction experienced by a body when it rolls over the surface of another body.

True/False

8. Athletes wear spikes to increase muscular force.
9. A streamlined shaped body helps in reducing drag.
10. Frictional force does not depend on the nature of the surfaces in contact.

Assertion-Reason Questions

The following questions consists of two statements -Assertion (A) and Reason (R). Answer these questions by selecting the appropriate option given below.

(a) Both A and R are true and R is the correct explanation of A.
(b) Both A and R are true but R is not the correct explanation of A.
(c) A is true but R is false.
(d) A is false but R is true.

11. **Assertion** (A) We often see that suitcase fitted with wheels are easy to pull.

    Reason (R) Rolling friction is smaller than the static and sliding friction.
12. **Assertion** (A) Rocket and aeroplane has a special body shape, i.e. streamlined shape.

    Reason (R) Streamlined shape helps object to reduces friction drag between fluid and an object moving through it.

Part II

Very Short Answer Type Questions

13. Name the force which always oppose motion.
14. The surface of matchbox should be rough. Explain why?
15. Oiling of the axles of a bicycle make the bicycle moving easily. Comment along with the reason.
16. Give the name of material which reduces the force of friction.

Short Answer Type Questions

17. We always apply powder to a carromboard. Why?
18. Explain why does a man slip when he steps on a banana peel thrown on the road?
19. Write in brief, how does a bicycle stop when its brakes are applied?
20. Some machines use streamlined shape to reduce friction. Name them.

Long Answer Type Questions

21. Explain the types of friction with examples.
22. In which ways, friction between the two surfaces can be minimised?
23. Write some disadvantages of force of friction.

Answers

1. (a) 2. (a) 3. (c) 4. (a) 5. Static 6. contact 7. Rolling 8. False 9. True 10. False 11. (a) 12. (a)

CHAPTER 10

Sound

Sound is anything that we hear, like the chirping of birds, noise of the vehicles, ringing of school bell, sound of musical instruments, etc. Sound plays an important role in our lives, it helps us to communicate with each other.

In this chapter, we will study, how sound is produced (origin), how it travels (propagates) and how we hear it.

10.1 Sound is Produced by a Vibrating Body

Sound is produced by the **to and fro motion** of an object, also known as **vibration**. It means that when any object vibrates, it produces sound.

e.g. When you strike a metal, it produces sound. Similarly, musical instruments; like manjira, ghatam, kartal, etc., produce sound due to vibration.

Manjira

Tabla

Musical instrument produces sound

Some musical instruments and their vibrating parts are given below

- In veena, sitar and guitar, plucking of strings produces sound.
- In a flute, vibrating column produces sound.
- In a tabla and mridangam, vibrating membrane produces sound.

If these objects stop vibrating, then they also stop producing sound. Even we can see and feel these vibrations.

To see these vibrations, strikes the edge of a metal dish with full of water. You will see vibrations in the water in the form of water waves.

But in some cases, the amplitude of vibrations is so small that we cannot see them.

Visualisation of sound in the form of water waves

10.2 Sound Produced by Humans

Human produces sound with the help of **voice box** also known as **larynx**. To locate voice box in your throat, put your fingers on the throat and feel a hard bump. You can feel vibration in this part while speaking.

- It is present at the **upper end of the windpipe** in the throat region.
- It contains **two vocal cords**. There is a small gap between these two vocal cords known as **slit**.

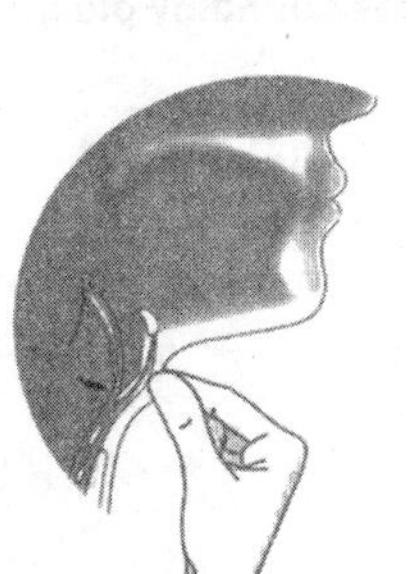

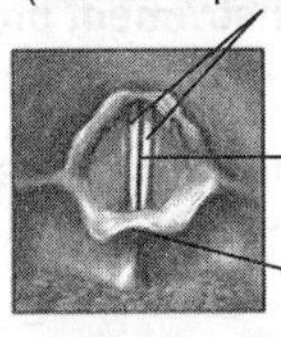

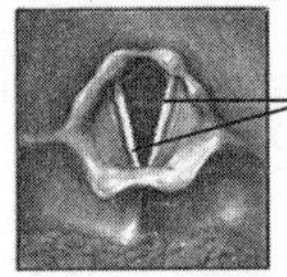

Vocal cords in larynx

Sound is produced by vibrating vocal cords

- **Muscles attached to the vocal cords** can make cords tight or loose.
- When lungs force air through the slit, then vocal cords vibrate and produce sound.
- By stretching and relaxing the vocal cord, we can change our voice. **When vocal cords are stretched, then they produce high frequency sound and when they are contracted, then they produce low frequency sound.**
- The voices of men, women and children are different because the size of vocal cords varies in them.
- Males have vocal cords about 20 mm long and have a low-pitched voice. Females have shorter vocal cords, about 15 mm long and have a high pitched voice. Children have very short vocal cords and have a different voice.

Note Vocal cords and voice box are not same. These are two different things. Vocal cords are parts of voice box. These are the pair of two bands of smooth muscle tissue.

Sound Needs a Medium for Propagation

The path through which sound travels is called **medium**, it can be solid, liquid or gas. Sound needs a medium to travel, therefore it cannot travel in vacuum.

Let us take some more examples to see the propagation of sound through medium.

- When we scratch on the table, then we hear some kind of sound. It shows sound can travel through solid.
- In the case of toy telephone, sound travels through the string.

SCIENCE INSIGHT There is no atmosphere on the moon (i.e. no medium through which sound can travel), so astronauts use special communicators on moon to talk to each other.

Try These 10.1

1. **Can we see the sound vibrations, when its amplitude is very low?**
2. **Which musical instrument produces sound by plucking of strings?**
3. **Can we notice the sound vibrations in liquid?**

We Hear Sound Through Our Ears

We hear sound through our ears. A very simple diagram of human ear is shown in the figure given below.

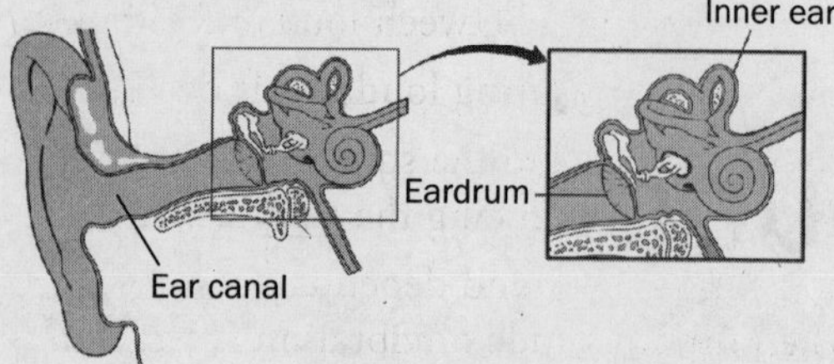

Human ear

The human ear is divided into three parts

- **Outer ear** The shape of outer ear is like a funnel. When the sound enters in it, then it travels through a canal called **ear canal**. At the end of ear canal, there is a thin elastic and stretched membrane, called **eardrum**.
- **Middle ear** It helps to pass the sound vibrations from eardrum to the inner ear.
- **Inner ear** The inner ear receives the vibrations from the middle ear and change them into signal or nerve impulses. These signal goes to the brain and we hear the sound.

10.3 Amplitude, Time Period and Frequency of Vibration

- **Oscillation** If an object moves back and forth continuously, then the object is said to be **oscillating** or **vibrating** and the motion is known as oscillation. e.g. Vibrating simple pendulum.
- **Time period** The time taken by a vibrating object to complete one vibration or oscillation is called time period. It is measured in second.
- **Frequency** The number of oscillations per second is called the frequency and it is measured in **hertz (Hz)**.

Note Frequency is the reciprocal of the time period, i.e. $f = \frac{1}{T}$.

- **Amplitude** The maximum displacement of vibrating object from its central position is called amplitude.
- Amplitude and frequency are two important properties of sound, which enables us to differentiate between two sounds.

10.4 Characteristics of Sound

There are mainly two characteristics of sound

(i) **Loudness** It is the property of sound which is used for differentiating between loud and faint sounds.

The unit of measuring loudness is decibel (dB).

It is proportional to the square of the amplitude of the vibration producing the sound. It means the loudness of sound depends upon its amplitude. When the amplitude of vibration is large, the sound produced is loud. When the amplitude is small, the sound produced is feeble.

If loudness is more than 80dB, then it becomes physically painful.

(ii) **Pitch or Shirllness** It is the property of sound that is determined by the frequency of the vibration producing it.

Pitch is proportional to the frequency of vibration. Higher the frequency, more will be pitch. Similarly lower the frequency, less will be pitch.

e.g. Frequency of drum is low, whereas the frequency of whistle is high. Similarly, a lion makes a low pitch sound, whereas a bird makes a high pitch sound.

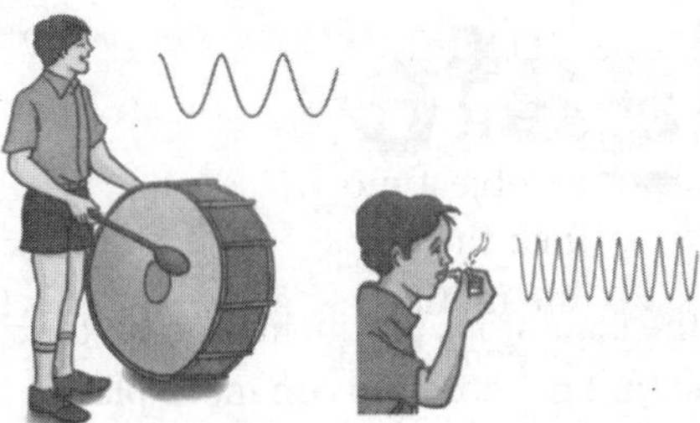

Frequency determines the pitch of a sound

Try These 10.2

1. **Mention the position of muscles of vocal cord, when we are not speaking.**
2. **Does sound need a medium to travel?**
3. **In which medium (sold, liquid or gas), sound travel fastest?**
4. **What will happen with the frequency, if we increase the time period?**
5. **Which decibel of sound makes a noise or physically painful?**

Audible and Inaudible Sounds

Every vibration produces sound but we cannot detect sound produced beyond certain limit of vibration. This limit is 20 Hz to 20 kHz.

Sound with the frequency between 20 Hz to 20 kHz is known as **audible sound.**

Sound with the frequency less than 20 Hz or more than 20 kHz is known as **inaudible sound.**

Dogs have the ability to hear sounds of higher frequency. That's why, police use high frequency whistles which dogs can hear but humans cannot.

Similarly, ultrasound equipment also works on higher frequency more than 20000 Hz.

SCIENCE INSIGHT Sound having frequency more than 20000 Hz is known as **ultrasonic waves** and sound having frequency less than 20 Hz is known as **infrasonic waves.**

10.5 Noise and Music

- Any unpleasant sound which causes discomfort to us is known as **noise**. e.g. Sound of construction work, sound of horn, etc.
- Any sound which is pleasant to your ear is known as **musical sound**. e.g. Sound produced by harmonium, sound produced by string of sitar, etc.

Noise Pollution

The presence of excessive or unwanted sounds in the environment is called noise pollution.

The sounds of vehicles, explosions including bursting of crackers, machines, loudspeakers, etc., are the major causes of noise pollution.

The major sources of noise pollution in homes are television and transistor radio at high volumes and some kitchen appliances.

Harms of Noise Pollution

Presence of excessive noise in the surroundings can cause many health related problems like, lack of sleep, hypertension (high blood pressure), anxiety, irritation and headache and many more health disorders.

A person who is exposed to a loud sound continuously may experience temporary or even permanent impairment of hearing.

Hearing Impairment

It is the inability of an individual to hear sounds properly. As some people are born with poor hearing ability, so such kind of person is said to be deaf.

Oftenly, deaf persons use a sign language with their hands to communicate with others effectively.

Partial hearing loss is generally due to ear infection, injury or old age. A person having partial hearing loss cannot hear sounds clearly.

Measures to Limit Noise Pollution

In order to control noise, we must control the sources of noise. We can control noise pollution by following points

(i) Installation of silencing devices in air craft engine, transport vehicles, industrial machines and home appliances.
(ii) The industries which produce noise should be set up away from residential areas.
(iii) Minimise the use of automobile horns.
(iv) The sound of TV and music system should be low.
(v) Plant trees along the roads and around the buildings to cut down the sounds reaching the residents.

Try These 10.3

1. **What do we call a sound with the frequency less than 20 Hz?**
2. **Which medical treatment needs the sound of higher frequency?**
3. **Is sound produced by a horn consider as a music?**

Science Glossary

Vibration To and fro motion of an object is called vibration.

Larynx It is also known as voice box. It is present in the throat region of humans and produces sound.

Vocal cords It is made of ligaments stretched across the larynx and it vibrates to create sound.

Amplitude It is the maximum displacement of a vibrating body from its mean position.

Frequency It is the number of vibrations of a vibrating body in one second.

Loudness It is the property of sound which is used for differentiating between the loud and faint sound.

Noise It refers to any unpleasant sound.

Music It refers to any pleasant sound.

ACTIVITY 1 (Page 124)

Aim To understand how sound is produced by a metal.

Material Required A metal plate (like a pan) and a stick.

Procedure

1. Take the metal plate and hang it at a convenient place in such a way that it does not touch any object.

Striking a pan

2. Now, strike it with the stick. You will hear a sound.
3. Now, touch the pan gently with your finger. You will feel some vibrations.
4. Again, strike the pan with the stick and hold the pan tightly. Now, you will not be able to hear any sound.
5. When the plate stops producing sound, touch it again. You will find no vibrations on metal plate.

Conclusion Sound is produced when the metal pan vibrates.

Viva Questions

1. Can we use a plastic plate to produce sound instead of metal plate?
2. Will you hear the sound, if you hold the pan lightly and then, strike it with the stick?

ACTIVITY 2 (Page 124)

Aim To produce sound by a rubber band.

Material Required A pencil box, a rubber band and two pencils.

Procedure

1. Take the rubber band.
2. Wrap it around the longer side of the geometry box.

3. Now, insert two pencils between the box and the stretched rubber as shown in figure.
4. Pluck the rubber band somewhere in the middle and observe the sound. You will find that band starts vibrating and gives rise to sound.

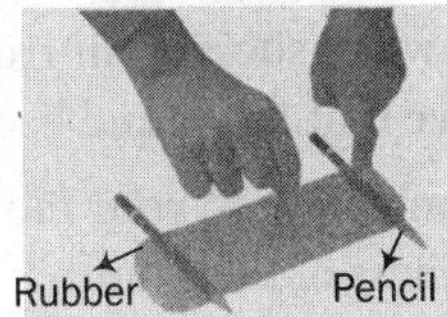

Sound created on pulling the rubber band

Conclusion Vibrating rubber band produces sound.

Viva Questions

1. Can we perform this activity with a thread instead of rubber band?
2. What will happen, if you stop the rubber band from vibrating?

ACTIVITY 3 (Page 124, 125)

Aim To find the connection between sound and vibration.

Material Required A metal dish, water and a spoon.

Procedure

1. Pour some water in the metal dish.
2. Now, strike the edge of dish with the spoon. You will hear some kind of sound.
3. Again, strike the dish and then, touch it. You will feel some vibrations.
4. Strike the dish again and observe the surface of water. You will observe waves on the surface of water.
5. Now, hold the dish and note the change in waves of the water surface. You will observe that waves become disappear.

Vibrating dish produces waves in water

Conclusion

(i) Water waves are visible until the sound is produced by the dish.

(ii) Water waves disappears when the dish stops vibrating.

Viva Questions

1. Why waves are observed on the surface of the water?
2. If the amplitude of vibrations is so small, then can we see them?

ACTIVITY 4 (Page 125)

Aim To identify the vibrating part of musical instrument ektara.

Material Required A hollow coconut shell, a thick wood strip and a strong steel string.

Procedure

1. Make musical instrument ektara as shown in the diagram.
2. Play this instrument and identify the vibrating part.

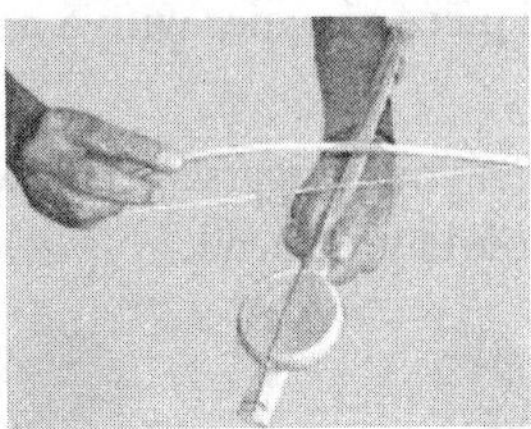
Ektara

Conclusion The vibrating part in ektara is the string.

Viva Questions

1. Can we use earthen pot instead of coconut shell?
2. Can you use any other material string instead of steel string?

ACTIVITY 5 (Page 126)

Aim To make jaltarang at home.

Material Required 6-8 bowls or tumblers, water and pencil.

Procedure

1. Fill all the tumblers with water. Water level of all tumblers should be different.
2. Now, take the pencil and strike all the tumblers one by one. You will hear different sounds.

Jaltarang

Conclusion As the amount of water in the tumbler goes on increasing, the frequency of sound produced also goes on increasing. Hence, we hear pleasant sound.

Viva Questions

1. What do you mean by jaltarang?
2. Name the vibrating part of jaltarang.

ACTIVITY 6 (Page 127)

Aim To demonstrate the working of vocal cords to produce sound.

Material Required Two rubber bands and a paper.

Procedure

1. Place the rubber strip one above the other and stretch them tight.
2. Now, blow air through the gap between them. Observe the sound produced.
3. Now, take the piece of paper with a narrow slit as shown in Fig. (b).
4. Hold it between your fingers and blow through the slit. Observe the sound produced.

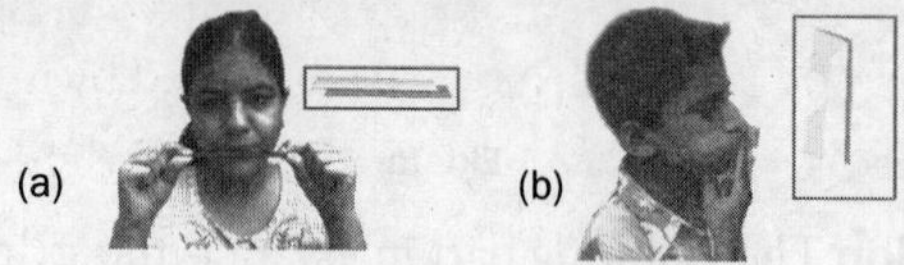

Working of vocal cords

Conclusion Vocal cords also produce sound in the same manner. When air passes through the vocal cords, it produces sound.

Viva Questions

1. Name the vibrating part of vocal cord.
2. What happens when you do not hold the rubber bands tightly?

ACTIVITY 7 (Page 127)

Aim To show that sound needs a medium to travel.

Material required Metal or glass tumbler and a cell phone.

Procedure

1. Place the cell phone into the tumbler.
2. Ask your friend to give a ring on this cell phone from another cell phone.

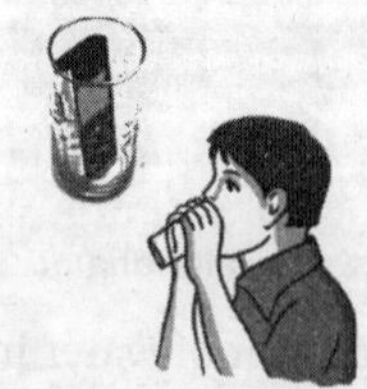
Sound needs a medium to travel

3. Listen to the ring carefully.
4. Now, surround the rim of the tumbler with your hands. Put your mouth on the opening between your hands.
5. Indicate your friend to give a ring again.
6. Listen the ring while sucking air from the tumbler. You will observe that the sound become fainter.
7. Remove the tumbler from your mouth and again notice the loudness of the sound.

Conclusion Sound requires a medium to travel.

Viva Questions

1. What is the medium in this case?
2. Why intensity of sound decreases while sucking air?

ACTIVITY 8 (Page 128)

Aim To show that sound travels through liquid.

Material required A bucket or bath tub, clean water and a small bell.

Procedure

1. Fill the bath tub with clean water.
2. Take the small bell in one hand and shake this bell inside the water.
3. Make sure that, the bell does not touch the body of the bath tub.
4. Place your ear gently on the water surface. Take care that water should not enter into the ear. Try to listen the sound of bell.

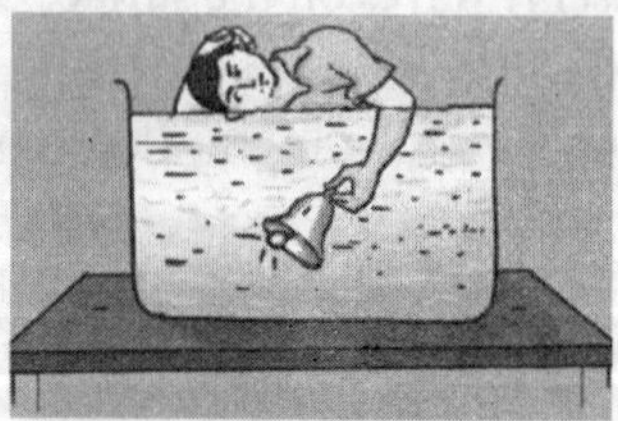
Sound travelling through water

Conclusion Sound can travel through liquid.

Viva Questions

1. What is the medium in this case?
2. Will you still hear sound, if you use oil instead of water?

ACTIVITY 9 (Page 128)

Aim To show that sound travels through solid.

Material required A meter scale.

Procedure

1. Take the meter scale and hold its one end near your ear.
2. Ask your friend to gently scratch or tap at the other end of the scale. You will hear some kind of sound.

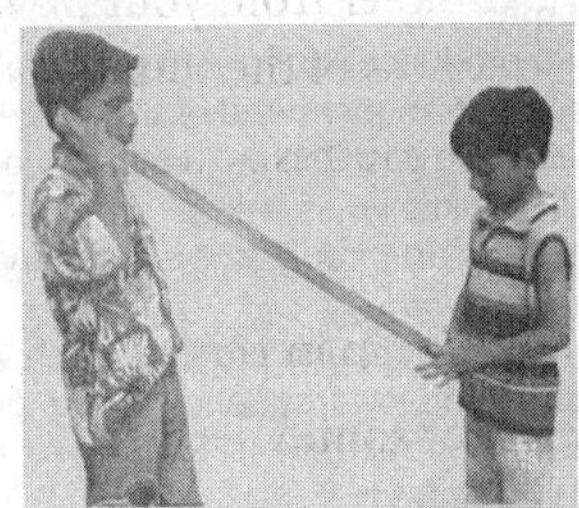

Sound travelling through a meter scale

Conclusion Sound can travel through solids.

Viva Questions

1. Do you hear the same loudness of the sound, if you move the scale for from the ear?
2. What is the medium in this case?

ACTIVITY 10 (Page 129)

Aim To demonstrate the working of eardrum.

Material required A tin can, rubber balloon, rubber band and four-five grains of dry cereal.

Procedure

1. Take the tin can and cut its ends.
2. Stretch the piece of rubber ballon across one end of the can and fasten the balloon with rubber band.

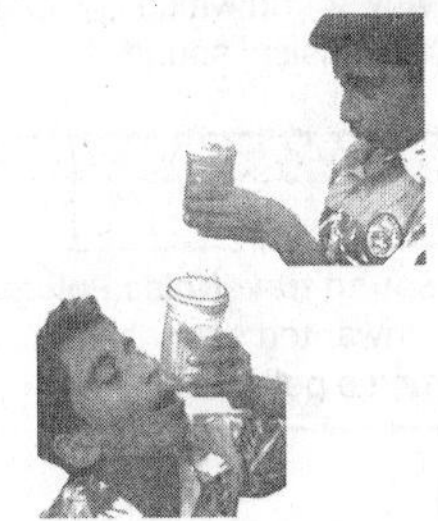

Understanding action of an eardrum

3. Now, put grains of cereal on the stretched rubber.
4. Now, ask your friend to make any strong sound.
5. Observe the movement of grains.

Conclusion When sound is made, then grains start jumping. This is due to vibrations of rubber sheet. In the same manner, the eardrum works.

Viva Questions

1. Why the rubber sheet vibrates?
2. What is the role of eardrum in hearing?

ACTIVITY 11 (Page 130, 131)

Aim To demonstrate the dependence of loudness of sound on the amplitude of vibration of sound.

Material required Metallic tumbler, tablespoon and a thermocol ball.

Procedure

1. Strike the metallic tumbler with the tablespoon gently and hear the sound produced by it.
3. Now, strike hard the tumbler with the spoon and hear the sound again.
4. Now, suspend a small thermocol ball touching the rim of the tumbler.
5. Vibrate the tumbler by striking it. Note the displacement of the ball and measure it. It will give you the amplitude of vibration of the tumbler.
6. Now, strike the tumbler gently and then a little harder. Compare the amplitude of vibrations of the tumbler in the two cases.

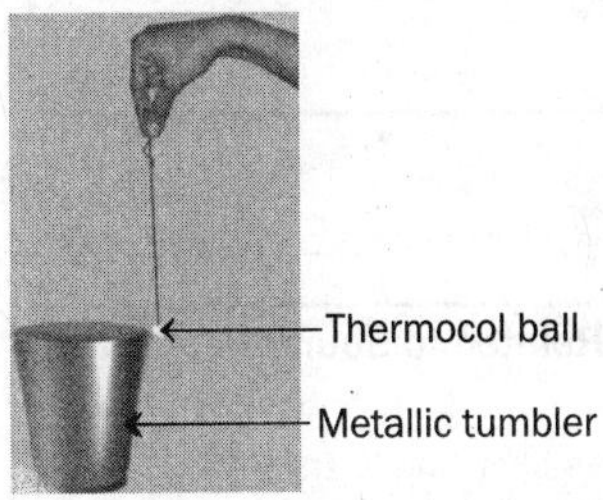

Thermocol ball touching the vibrating glass tumbler

Conclusion Amplitude of vibration is large for higher loudness and it is less for lower loudness.

Viva Questions

1. Which unit is used to measure the loudness of sound?
2. Is it correct, loudness of sound is directly proportional to the square of amplitude of vibration?

Production of Sound

- **By Human**
  - Human produces sound with the help of voice box (larynx), it is present at upper end of wind pipe.
  - Contains two vocal cords (small gap between two vocal cord known as a slit).
  - Lungs force air through the slit, then vocal cords vibrate and produce sound.
  - High frequency sound produce when vocal cords are stretched and low frequency sound produce when vocal cords are contracted.
- **By Vibrating Body**
  - To and fro motion of an object, known as vibration which produces sound.
  - If object stop vibrating, then they also stop producing sound.
  - Vibrations can be seen in the form of water waves.
- **Musical Instrument and their vibrating part**
  - Veena-strings
  - Flute-column
  - Tabla-membrane

Ear

We hear sound through our ears.

Parts of Ears

- Outer Ear
  - Shape of outer ear is like a funnel.
  - Sound enters in it and travel through ear canal.
  - At the end of ear canal, a thin elastic and stretched membrane present which is known as eardrum.
- Middle Ear
  Helps to pass sound vibrations from eardrum to the inner ear.
- Inner Ear
  Receives vibration and ch...ge them into signal.

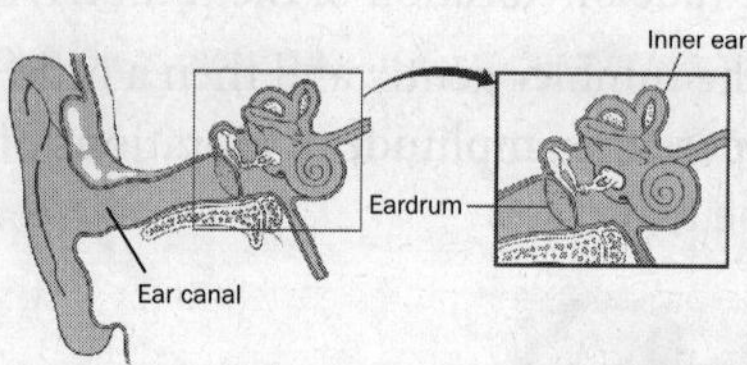

Solid | Liquid | Gas

Sound Need Medium to Travel

SOUND

Types of Sound

- **Audible sound**
  Frequency between 20 Hz to 20 kHz.
- **Inaudible sound**
  Frequency less than 20Hz or more than 20 kHz.

Noise and Music

- Any unpleasant sound which discomfort to us is known as noise.
- Any sound which is pleasant to your ear is known as musical sound.

Noise Pollution

Unwanted sounds in the environment is called noise pollution.

- **Harms of Noise Pollution**
  - Sound of vehicles, explosions including bursting of crackers, machines loudspeakers, etc., are causes of noise pollution.
  - Excessive noise in the surroundings can causes many health related problems like lack of sleep and hypertension, etc.
- **Measures to Limit Noise pollution**
  - Industries which produces noise should be setup away from residential area.
  - Minimise the use of automobile horns.

Terms Related to Sound

- **Oscillation**
  Object moves back and forth continuously.
- **Amplitude**
  Maximum displacement of vibrating object from its central position.
- **Time period**
  Time taken by vibrating body to complete one oscillation.
- **Frequency**
  Number of oscillations per second and measured in hertz.

Characteristics of Sound

- **Loudness**
  - Property of sound which is used for differentiating between loud and faint sounds.
  - Measured in decibel (dB)
- **Pitch or Shirllness**
  Property of sound that is determined by the frequency of the vibration producing it.

NCERT FOLDER

Complete Explanations of all NCERT's Questions

Intext Questions

Q 1. How is the blind folded person able to guess which player is nearer to her? **Page 123**

Ans. The vibration due to the movement of closer player is more than others and the blind folded person easily imagine in which direction a player is nearer to her.

Q 2. Briefly, mention the experience when you touch a sound producing school bell. **Page 124**

Ans. When we touch a sound producing school bell, we feel the vibration in it.

Q 3. How does the sound propagate? **Page 127**

Ans. Sound needs a medium for propagation.

Q 4. Is it possible that the decreasing amount of air in the tumbler had something to do with decreasing loudness of the ring? **Page 128**

Ans. Yes; If the amount of air starts decreasing in the tumbler, then the loudness of the ring also decreases.

Q 5. Does sound travel in liquids? **Page 128**

Ans. Yes, sound can travel through liquids.

Q 6. Can you say that sound can travel through strings? **Page 129**

Ans. Yes; Sound can travel through strings.

Q 7. How can we hear sound through solid, liquid and gases? **Page 129**

Ans. Sound travels faster in solid as compare to liquid and gases because the particles in the solid are much closer than liquids and gases.

Q 8. If an object oscillates 20 times in 1 s, what would be its frequency? **Page 130**

Ans. As we know that, the frequency is the total number of oscillations in 1 s. So, the frequency will be 20 Hz.

Q 9. How is it possible that you can recognise many familiar sounds without seeing the objects producing them? **Page 130**

Ans. We can recognise many familiar sounds of objects without seeing them because different objects produce different sounds.

Q 10. What factors make the sound differ from each other? **Page 130**

Ans. Amplitude and frequency.

Q 11. Is there any difference between the sound of a baby and the adult? **Page 131**

Ans. Yes, the frequency of the sound of a child is higher than that of an adult.

Q 12. Why your voice is different from that of your teacher? **Page 131**

Ans. This is because the sound produced by you have different amplitude and frequency as that of your teacher.

Q 13. Can we hear the sound of all vibrating bodies? **Page 132**

Ans. A sound is audible to us only if the sound produced by the vibrating body is in the audible range, i.e. 20 Hz to 20 kHz.

Q 14. Is the sound always pleasing? **Page 132**

Ans. No

Q 15. Can you list some sources of noise pollution? **Page 132**

Ans. Sounds of vehicle, bursting crackers, loudspeakers, etc.

Q 16. Name the sources in the home that may lead to noise. **Page 132**

Ans. The sources that may lead to the noise are transistor, radio at high volume, television, desert coolers, air conditioners, etc.

Q 17. How can the noise pollution be controlled in a residential area? **Page 133**

Ans. The following steps should be taken to controlled noise pollution in a residential area

(i) The television and loudspeaker should be run at the low volumes.

(ii) Silencing devices must be installed in the transport vehicles like tractor, trucks, etc.

(iii) Industries should be set up away from the residential areas.

Exercise

Q.1 Sound can travel through

(a) gases only (b) solids only
(c) liquids only (d) solids, liquids and gases

Ans. (d) Sound can travel through solids, liquids and gases but it cannot travel in vacuum.

Q.2 Voice of which of the following is likely to have minimum frequency?

(a) Baby girl (b) Baby boy
(c) A man (d) A woman

Ans. (c) Voice of a man is likely to have minimum frequency.

The frequency determines the pitch of a sound. If the frequency of vibration is higher, the sound is shrill and has a higher pitch. If the frequency of vibration is lower, the sound has a lower pitch.

Q.3 In the following statements, tick T against those which are True and F against those which are False.

(a) Sound cannot travel in vacuum.
(b) The number of oscillations per second of a vibrating object is called its time period.
(c) If the amplitude of vibration is large, sound is feeble.
(d) For human ears, the audible range is 20 Hz to 20000 Hz.
(e) The lower the frequency of vibration, the higher is the pitch.
(f) Unwanted or unpleasant sound is termed as music.
(g) Noise pollution may cause partial hearing impairment.

Ans. (a) True
(b) False; The number of oscillations per second of a vibrating object is called frequency.
(c) False; Amplitude of vibration is directly proportional to the loudness of sound.
(d) True
(e) False; The lower the frequency of vibration, the lower is the pitch.
(f) False; Unwanted or unpleasant sound is termed as noise.
(g) True

Q.4 Fill in the blanks with suitable words.

(a) Time taken by an object to complete one oscillation is called...... .
(b) Loudness is determined by the .... of vibration.
(c) The unit of frequency is ....
(d) Unwanted sound is called ....
(e) Shrillness of a sound is determined by the .... of vibration.

Ans. (a) time period (b) amplitude
(c) hertz (d) noise
(e) frequency

Q.5 A pendulum oscillates 40 times in 4 s. Find its time period and frequency.

Ans. Given, number of oscillations = 40

Time taken = 4 s

As we know, number of oscillations per second is frequency.

$$\therefore \text{ Frequency} = \frac{\text{Number of oscillations}}{\text{Time taken}}$$

$$= \frac{40}{4} = 10 \text{ Hz}$$

$$\therefore \text{ Time period} = \frac{1}{\text{Frequency}}$$

$$= \frac{1}{10} = 0.1 \text{ s}$$

Q.6 The sound from a mosquito is produced when it vibrates its wings at an average rate of 500 vibrations per second. What is the time period of the vibration?

Ans. Given, number of vibrations = 500

Time taken = 1 s

$$\therefore \text{ Time period} = \frac{\text{Time taken}}{\text{Number of vibrations}}$$

$$= \frac{1}{500} = 0.002 \text{ s}$$

Q.7 Identify the part which vibrates to produce sound in the following instruments.

(a) Dholak (b) Sitar (c) Flute

Ans.

	Instrument	Vibrating part
(a)	Dholak	Stretched membrane
(b)	Sitar	Strings
(c)	Flute	Air columns

Q.8 What is the difference between noise and music? Can music become noise sometimes?

Ans. Differences between noise and music are

Noise	Music
It is unpleasant sound.	It is pleasant sound.
It leads to noise pollution.	No such pollution takes place.
It is hazardous to health.	It is good for health.
No special instruments are required to produce noise.	Special instruments are required to play music.

Yes, music becomes noise sometimes, when it crosses the bearable range of sound for the ears.

Q.9 List the sources of noise pollution in your surroundings.

Ans. As we know that, noise pollution is caused by excessive sound in our surroundings. The sources of such excessive sound are as follow

(i) Television and transistor radio at high volume

(ii) Sounds of vehicles

(iii) Explosions including bursting of crackers, machines, loudspeakers, etc

(iv) Honking of horns

Q.10 Explain in what way noise pollution is harmful to human.

Ans. Lack of sleep, hypertension (high blood pressure) and temporary or permanent impairment of hearing are harmful effects of noise pollution.

Q.11 Your parents are going to buy a house. They have been offered one on the roadside and another three lanes away from the roadside. Which house would you suggest your parents should buy? Explain your answer.

Ans. We will suggest our parents that they should buy a house, which is three lanes away from roadside.

As taking house on roadside, means bearing a noise pollution which leads to harmful effects on health.

Therefore, to attain a piece of mind and to avoid noise pollution, it is better to buy a house three lanes away from the roadside.

Q.12 Sketch larynx and explain its functions in your own words.

Ans. In humans, the sound is produced by the voice box also called larynx. We can easily feel this part of the body by putting our fingers on the throat and find a hard bump that seems to move when we swallow.

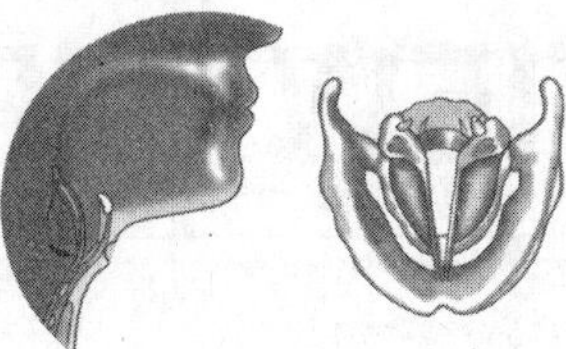

Larynx or voice box in humans

Structure

(i) It is the upper end of the wind pipe.

(ii) Two vocal cords are stretched across the voice box or larynx.

(iii) The vocal cords are stretched in such a manner that it leaves a narrow slit between them for the passage of air.

Working

(i) When the lungs force air through the slit, the vocal cords vibrate and hence, produce sound.

(ii) Muscles attached to the vocal cords can make the cords tight or loose.

(iii) When the vocal cords are tight and thin, the type or quality of voice is different from that when they are loose.

Q.13 Lightning and thunder take place in the sky at the same time and at the same distance from us. Lightning is seen earlier and thunder is heard later. Can you explain why?

Ans. Lightning is seen earlier than the sound of thunder because light travels faster than sound. Hence, it reaches us before the sound does.

REVIEW EXERCISE

Including Competency Based Questions

Part I

Multiple Choice Questions

1. What is an example of an object that works on vibrations?

(a) A spinning top
(b) A coin is tossed
(c) Marble rolling on a ramp
(d) Guitar string being plucked

2. Which of the following statements are correct? NCERT Exemplar

(i) Sound is produced by vibrations.
(ii) Sound requires a medium for propagation.
(iii) Light and sound both require a medium for propagation.
(iv) Sound travels slower than light.

(a) (i) and (ii) (b) (i), (ii) and (iii)
(c) (ii), (iii) and (iv) (d) (i), (ii) and (iv)

3. Sound cannot travel through

(a) solid (b) liquid (c) air (d) vacuum

4. A list of mediums is given below NCERT Exemplar

(i) Wood (ii) Water
(iii) Air (iv) Vacuum

In which of these mediums can sound travel?

(a) (i) and (ii) (b) (i), (ii) and (iii)
(c) (iii) and (iv) (d) (ii), (iii) and (iv)

5. Which option explains how sound is produced by the voice box in a human throat?

(a) The voice box vibrates by the air coming out from lungs
(b) The vocal cords vibrate by the air coming in through the voice box
(c) The vocal cords stretched across the voice box vibrates by air coming from lungs
(d) The stretched vocal cords across the voice box produce the air to vibrate the voice box

6. What is the structure of the eardrum?

(a) It is the stretched cord in the ear
(b) It is the stretched membrane in the ear
(c) It is the nerve which transmits a signal to the brain
(d) It is the funnel type canal of the ear through which sound enters

7. 1 Hz is equal to NCERT Exemplar

(a) 1 vibration per minute
(b) 10 vibrations per minute
(c) 60 vibrations per minute
(d) 600 vibrations per minute

8. An object is vibrating at 5 Hz. What is its time period? NCERT Exemplar

(a) 0.02 s (b) 0.2 s
(c) 2 s (d) 20.0 s

9. The loudness of sound depends on its

(a) amplitude
(b) time period
(c) frequency
(d) speed

10. In order to reduce the loudness of a sound, we have to Competency Based Que.

(a) decrease its frequency of vibration of the sound
(b) increase its frequency of vibration of the sound
(c) decrease its amplitude of vibration of the sound
(d) increase its amplitude of vibration of the sound

11. The ultrasound waves can penetrate into matter to a large extent because they have

(a) very high frequency (b) very high speed
(c) very high quality (d) very high amplitude

12. A person works in a factory where a lot of industrial machines run daily. What harmful effects he is likely to suffer from?

(a) Fever (b) Cataract
(c) Lack of vision (d) Lack of hearing

13. Loudness of sound is measured in units of NCERT Exemplar

(a) decibel (dB)
(b) hertz (Hz)
(c) metre (m)
(d) metre/second(m/s)

14. The loudness of sound is determined by its

(a) amplitude of vibration
(b) ratio of amplitude and frequency of vibration
(c) frequency of vibration
(d) product of amplitude and frequency of vibration

15. **Pitch of sound is determined by its** NCERT Exemplar

(a) frequency (b) speed
(c) amplitude (d) loudness

16. **The maximum displacement of a vibrating body from its mean position is called**

(a) frequency
(b) time period
(c) amplitude
(d) None of the above

17. **Ultrasound has frequency of vibration** NCERT Exemplar

(a) between 20 and 20000 Hz
(b) below 20 Hz
(c) above 20000 Hz
(d) between 500 and 10000 Hz

18. **Which of the following sounds can be classified as noise for humans?** Competency Based Que.

(a) Sounds that are softer than 20 dB
(b) Sounds that are in between 20 dB and 40 dB
(c) Sounds that are between 40 dB and 80 dB
(d) Sounds that are louder than 80 dB

19. **Which of the following are used to study the growth of foetus inside the mother's womb?**

(a) Radiowaves (b) X-rays
(c) Infrared waves (d) Sound waves

Answers

1. (d)	2. (d)	3. (d)	4. (b)
5. (c)	6. (b)	7. (c)	8. (a)
9. (a)	10. (c)	11. (a)	12. (d)
13. (a)	14. (a)	15. (a)	16. (c)
17. (c)	18. (d)	19. (d)	

Fill in the Blanks

1. Sound is produced by .... objects.
2. The other name of human voice box is ....
3. Sound can travel in .... , ... and ....
4. The loudness of normal breathing of human is .... dB.
5. Vibration is repeated .... and .... motion.
6. A tight membrane vibrates at a much .... frequency than a loose one.
7. Sound which is pleasing to our ears is called ....
8. A person having partial hearing loss can hear properly by using a device called .... aid.

Answers

1. vibrating	2. larynx
3. solids, liquids, gases	4. 10
5. to, fro	6. higher
7. music	8. hearing

True/False

1. The pitch of the sound depends on the frequency of the wave.
2. In human beings, the vibration of vocal cords produces sound.
3. Higher the amplitude of vibration, lesser is the pitch.
4. Regular vibrations produce musical sounds.
5. Shriller sound has more frequency.
6. Plantation along roadside can reduce noise pollution.
7. Man cannot hear the sound of bats.

Answers

1. True	2. True	3. False	4. True
5. True	6. True	7. True	

Match the Columns

1. Match the Column I with Column II.

Column I	Column II
(a) Audible frequency range	(i) More than 20 kHz
(b) Normal breathing	(ii) 20 Hz to 20 kHz
(c) Ultrasonic waves	(iii) 10 dB
(d) Length of vocal cords in man	(iv) Frequency
(e) Number of oscillations per second	(v) 20 mm long

Answer

1. (a)–(ii), (b)–(iii), (c)–(i), (d)–(v), (e)–(iv)

Assertion-Reason Questions

The following questions consist of two statements–Assertion (A) and Reason (R). Answer these questions by selecting the appropriate option given below

(a) Both A and R are true and R is the correct explanation of A.
(b) Both A and R are true but R is not the correct explanation of A.
(c) A is true but R is false.
(d) A is false but R is true.

1. **Assertion** (A) Astronauts in space can hear each other.
Reason (R) Loud sound have high amplitude.
2. **Assertion** (A) Tabla, sitar, flute and harmonium are musical instruments.
Reason (R) Sound is produced by vibrations in musical instruments.
3. **Assertion** (A) Frequency is measured in hertz (Hz).
Reason (R) Lower the frequency, higher is the pitch of the sound.

4. **Assertion** (A) Human beings cannot hear sound less than 20 Hz.
Reason (R) Audible range of human is 20 Hz to 20 kHz.

Answers

1. (d) A is false because sound needs medium to travel but there is no medium in space. R is correct. Hence, the correct option is (d).
2. (a) Both A and R are correct because without vibration, sound cannot be produced. Hence, the correct option is (a).
3. (c) R is false because for higher frequency pitch of the sound is higher. Hence, the correct option is (c).
4. (a) The audible range of sound for human being is indeed from 20 Hz and 20 kHz. So, both A and R are correct and R is the correct explanation. Hence, the correct option is (a).

Case Based Question

1. **Aditi hangs four steel dishes of the same size but different thickness.**
She hits each of them with an iron rod.
Competency Based Que.

Striking a steel dish with iron rod

	Dish 1	Dish 2	Dish 3	Dish 4
Thickness of dish	1 mm	1.5 mm	0.5 mm	2 mm

Based on the above picture, answer the following questions.

(i) The thicker the dish, the lower will be the vibration. Which dish will produce the loudest sound when hit?
(a) Dish 1 (b) Dish 2
(c) Dish 3 (d) Dish 4

(ii) Which of these statements proves that sound can travel through solids?
(a) We can hear the sound of wind.
(b) We can hear the sound of lightning.
(c) We can hear a bell ringing from a distance.
(d) We can hear heartbeats by using a stethoscope.

(iii) Which part of the human ear vibrates on receiving sound waves?
(a) Ear lobe
(b) Eardrum
(c) Inner ear
(d) Ear canal

Answer

1. (i) (c) (ii) (d) (iii) (b)

Part II

Very Short Answer Type Questions

1. **Does any part of our body vibrate when we speak? Name the part.** **NCERT Exemplar**

Ans. Yes, while speaking the part which vibrates is called vocal cords. It is below the throat and creates vibrations while speaking.

2. **Explain how can you describe vocal cords?**

Ans. The two ligaments which stretch across the larynx in such a way that it leaves a narrow slit between them for the passage of air, are known as vocal cords.

3. **Name two musical instruments which produce sound by vibrating strings.** **NCERT Exemplar**

Ans. Guitar and sitar are the two musical instruments which produce the sound by vibrating string.

4. **Why do we not hear the sound of an explosion on the surface of the moon?**

Ans. There is no atmosphere on the moon and sound waves need a medium to travel, so we cannot hear the sound on the moon.

5. **How do whales and dolphins hear the sound?**

Ans. Through water as a liquid medium, both whales and dolphins hear the sound.

6. **When we hear a sound, does any part of our body vibrate? Name the part.** **NCERT Exemplar**

Ans. It is the eardrum which vibrates and sends vibrations to the inner air, when we hear any sound.

7. **A baby recognises her mother by her voice. Name the characteristic of sound involved.**

Ans. Pitch is that characteristic of sound due to which distinction can be done between two sounds.

8. **What is the frequency of wave with time period 0.025 s?**

Ans. Given, $T = 0.025$ s,

$$\nu = \frac{1}{T} = \frac{1}{0.025} = 40 \text{ Hz}$$

9. **Different bees produce buzzing sounds of different pitches. Which affects the pitch of the bee's buzzing sound?**

Ans. The faster the bee vibrates its wings, the greater the frequency of the sound and the pitch is directly proportional to the frequency of sound. Hence, higher the frequency, the more will be the pitch.

10. Our steps do not produce loud sound, if we walk on a carpet floor. Explain with the help of a reason.

Ans. As the amplitude of vibrations of floor is reduced and the sound of our steps becomes feeble, so due to this reason, we do not produce the loud sound when we walk on the carpet floor.

11. Mention the name given to the maximum displacement of a vibrating body from its central position.

Ans. Amplitude is a name given to the maximum displacement of a vibrating body from its central position.

12. Explain why babies have feeble sound?

Ans. Due to the small amplitude of their sound, babies have feeble sound.

13. Three different vibrating objects produce three types of sounds *X*, *Y* and *Z*. The sounds *X* and *Y* cannot be heard by a man having normal range of hearing but sound *Z* can be heard easily. The sound *X* can be heard by a bat whereas sound Y can be heard by a rhinoceros. What type of sounds are *X*, *Y* and *Z*? **Competency Based Que.**

Ans. *X* is ultrasonic sound, *Y* is infrasonic sound and *Z* is audible sound.

14. Lightning can be seen at the moment when it occurs. Paheli observes lightning in her area. She hears the sound 5 s after she observed lightning. How far is she from the place where lightning occurs? (Speed of sound = 330 m/s) **NCERT Exemplar**

Ans. We know that,

Distance = Speed × Time = 330 × 5 = 1650 m

= 1.65 km (∵ 1 km = 1000 m)

So, she is standing at 1.65 km from the place where the lightning occurs.

15. A hearing aid that is attached to the ear helps people who suffer from hearing loss. What is the main function of the hearing aid?

Ans. The hearing aid amplifies the sound received from the surroundings.

Short Answer Type Questions

1. Suppose a stick is struck against a frying pan in vacuum. Will the frying pan vibrate? Will we be able to hear the sound? Explain. **NCERT Exemplar**

Ans. Yes, the frying pan will vibrate. Since, it is being hit by the stick but vibrations need a medium to travel and there is no medium in vacuum, so we cannot hear the vibrations produced.

2. A stretched string on being set into vibration, produces the audible sound. Explain how?

Ans. A stretched string on being set into vibration forces, the surrounding air to vibrate. This vibrating air in them affects our eardrum and produces an audible sound.

3. Astronauts in outer space have to use radios to communicate with one another. Why?

Ans. In outer space, there is no medium to help transmit sound. To communicate with one another, astronauts make use of electromagnetic waves such as radio waves which can travel through vacuum.

4. Two astronauts are floating close to each other in space. Can they talk to each other without using any special device? Give reasons. **NCERT Exemplar**

Ans. No, they cannot talk to each other without using any special device because there is no medium in space and sound needs medium to travel.

5. The sound produced by a mosquito is quite different from the roar of a lion. Explain the distinguishing points along with the reason.

Ans. A mosquito produces sound by the vibration of its wing, in open air while the lion roars by the vibration of its vocal cords.

Due to this, the amplitude of the sound produced by mosquito will be less than the sound produced by a lion and even the pitch and quality of the two sounds are different which make the two sounds different and distinguishable.

6. Explain the process, how bats use ultrasonic waves to catch a prey?

Ans. The ultrasonic waves produce by the bats are high pitched which are not heard by the human beings. So, these ultrasonic waves after striking the insect send back an echo which is heard by the bat and finally it gets over on the insect and catches it.

7. Last Monday, Anita and her parents were going to the market by an auto rickshaw. On her way while taking a left turn, they heard the horn of speeding truck towards the turn. Suddenly, the auto rickshaw driver stopped his vehicle by applying brake. Thus, by adopting the precautionary measure by blowing horn, the truck driver saved the lives.

(a) The loudness of horn depends on what factor?

(b) Mention the values displayed by both the drivers.

Competency Based Que.

Ans. (a) The factor on which the loudness of horn sound depends is the amplitude of vibration of horn.

(b) The values displayed by both the drivers are awareness and sensitivity.

8. We have learnt that vibration is necessary for producing sound. Explain why the sound produced by every vibrating body cannot be heard by us? NCERT Exemplar

Ans. Since, range of vibrations is different for different objects. But we can only hear the vibrations which lie between 20 Hz to 20000 Hz, so sound of every vibration cannot be heard by us.

9. We have a stringed musical instrument. The string is plucked in the middle first with a force of greater magnitude and then with a force of smaller magnitude. In which case, would the instrument produce a louder sound?

Ans. It will create more loud sound in case of string stretched with a greater force because amplitude is greater in this case and loudness depends on the amplitude. Greater will be the loudness, greater will be the amplitude.

10. A simple pendulum makes 10 oscillations in 20 s. What is the time period and frequency of its oscillations? NCERT Exemplar

Ans. Given, number of oscillations = 10

Time taken = 20 s

As we know that, the number of oscillations per second is frequency.

$$\therefore \text{Frequency} = \frac{\text{Number of oscillations}}{\text{Time taken}}$$

$$= \frac{10}{20} = 0.5 \text{ Hz}$$

$$\therefore \text{Time period} = \frac{1}{\text{Frequency}} = \frac{1}{0.5} = 2\text{s}$$

11. Boojho saw a cracker burst at night at a distance from his house. He heard the sound of the cracker a little later after seeing the cracker burst. Give reason for the delay in hearing the sound.

Ans. The light travels faster than sound, so the light from the cracker reaches faster than that of sound of the cracker.

Speed of light in air = 3×10^8 m/s

Speed of sound in air = 330 m/s

12. Explain the reason for not hearing of the screams of a bat by us.

Ans. As we know that, the audible frequency range for human being is 20 Hz to 20 kHz. So, it is an obvious thing that the frequency of bat is beyond this range due to which, we are usually unable to hear the screams of a bat.

13. Suggest three measures to limit noise pollution in your locality. NCERT Exemplar

Ans. Some measures to limit noise pollution in our locality are given as

(i) The industries which produce noise should be set up away from the residential areas.

(ii) The television and the music systems should be run at the low volumes.

(iii) The aircraft engines, transport vehicles, industrial machines and home appliances must be installed with silencing devices.

14. List three sources of noise pollution in your locality.

Ans. Sources of noise pollution are

(i) Horns of vehicles

(ii) Loudspeakers of temples

(iii) Generators running without silencers

15. Briefly explain total hearing impairment.

Ans. Hearing impairment means a person has damaged hearing ability and cannot hear properly. There are some people who born with poor hearing ability. A person with very poor hearing ability is said to be deaf, so deafness is total hearing impairment.

Long Answer Type Questions

1. The townhall building is situated close to Boojho's house. There is a clock on the top of the townhall building which rings the bell every hour. Boojho has noticed that the sound of the clock appears to be much cleared at night. Explain. Competency Based Que.

Ans. We know that speed, pitch, loudness all are initiated with a vibration. During the day, there is a number of vibrations around us. So, the sound coming from the clock gets disturbed and amplitude of vibrations becomes small. But during the night, there are not such multiple vibrations in the environment.

So, sound is more clear. Further, the dew factor at night increases the speed of sound as moisture level increases.

2. An alarm bell is kept inside a vessel as shown in figure. A person standing close to it can distinctly hear the sound of alarm. Now, if the air inside the vessel is removed completely, how will the loudness of alarm get affected for the same person? **NCERT Exemplar**

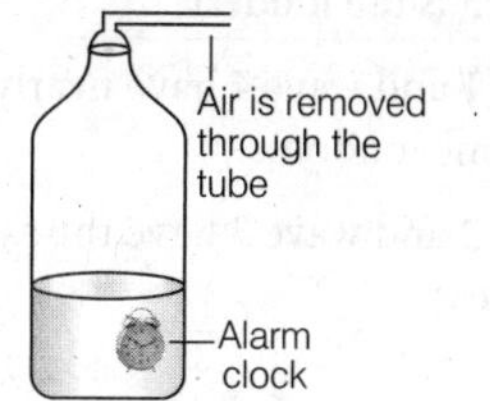

Ans. Initially, the person is able to hear the sound coming from air and from water distinctly. But after sometime, when the air is completely removed from the bottle, the sound will not pass through the vacuum in the glass. So, the man will not hear the sound which was coming through the air initially.

3. How is sound produced and how is it transmitted and heard by us? **NCERT Exemplar**

Ans. Sound is produced when any object starts vibrating by any means.

These vibrations travel from the sources all around the environment through the particles, thus it reaches to its destination, i.e. our ear. Now, it enters our ear and travels down a canal at the end of which a thin membrane is stretched tightly, known as eardrum. The eardrum sends vibrations to inner part of the ear and finally reaches to the brain and we hear the sounds.

4. Mention the property of vibrations which determine the pitch of the sound. Briefly explain along with some examples.

Ans. The property which determines the shrillness or pitch of a sound is the frequency. If the frequency of vibration is higher, then we can say that the sound has a higher pitch. If the frequency of vibration is lower, we can say that the sound has a lower pitch.

e.g. The drum vibrates with a low frequency.

Thus, it produces a low pitched sound. Besides this, a whistle has a high frequency produces a sound of higher pitch. A bird makes a high pitched sound while a lion makes a low pitched roar. However, the roar of a lion is very loud while the sound of bird is quite feeble.

5. Kanika switched ON the television to listen to her favourite music. After sometime, she heard a loudspeaker sound coming from her neighbour house. Then, she switched OFF the television and closed her ears, so that loudspeaker sound should not enter her ears.

(a) State the type of sound coming from the television.

(b) Explain how Kanika as able to distinguish between the category of sound?

(c) Mention whether the sound coming from TV and loudspeaker was audible or inaudible.

(d) Give the value displayed by Kanika here.

Ans. (a) The sound of the music was coming from the television.

(b) She realised after hearing both the sounds that the sound coming from TV is pleasant and enjoyable and that coming from outside loudspeaker is noisy and painful.

(c) The sound coming from TV and loudspeakers was in audible range, i.e. 20 Hz to 20 kHz.

(d) The value displayed by Kanika is attraction towards music and hate towards the loudspeakers.

6. Anjali's grandfather was talking to her about the quality of sound produced by different musical instruments. The instruments like sitar, harmonium, flute, etc., give us a pleasant sensation of hearing. The dholak on the other side creates a noise.

(i) Mention the name of the vibrating part of sitar.

(ii) Briefly explain how the loudness is created by dholak?

(iii) We hear a shrilling sound by flute. Explain why?

(iv) Mention the values displayed by Anjali's grandfather. **Competency Based Que.**

Ans. (i) String of sitar is a vibrating part of sitar.

(ii) Since, if we beat the dholak, then the membrane of dholak starts vibrating with high amplitude and as a fact, the loudness is directly proportional to the square of amplitude. Therefore, in the form of the loudness is created by beating dholak.

(iii) The sound wave produced by flute is regular curving, so there is no part of noise. Thus, we hear shrilling sound of flute.

(iv) The values displayed by Anjali's grandfather are scientific methods and critical thinking.

Case Based Questions

1. Raghav kept a mini sound player in each of two similar containers. He then tightly covered both the containers with stretched plastic sheets. He placed some tiny rubber beads on the surface of the sheets. The picture shows what Raghav noticed when he turned ON the sound player.

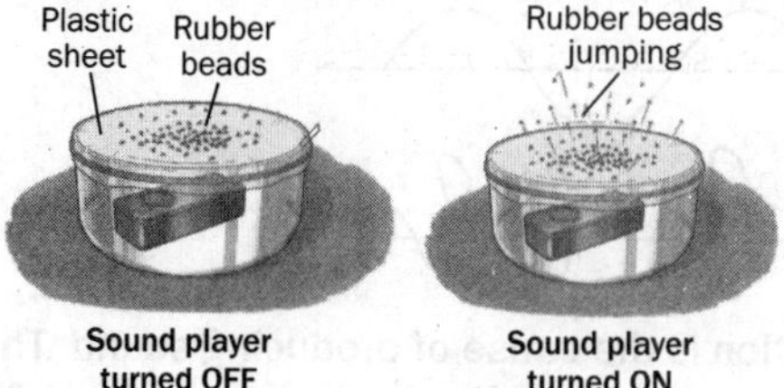

(i) Which of these questions can be answered using the result of Raghav's activity?

(a) Does sound travel as waves?

(b) Does sound produce vibration?

(c) Does sound travel through vacuum?

(d) Does sound travel faster in solids than in gases?

(ii) Would the result of Raghav's activity change, if fewer beads had been used? Explain your answer.

2. The picture shows four sound waves.

Wave 1
Wave 2
Wave 3
Wave 4

Based on the above picture, answer the following questions.

(i) Which sound wave has the highest pitch?

(ii) Which of these is true about the four sound waves?

	Is the statement true?	Yes or No
(a)	Wave 3 is the loudest	Yes/No
(b)	Wave 1 and wave 4 have nearly the same loudness	Yes/No
(c)	Wave 2 and wave 3 have the same loudness	Yes/No

Answers

1. (i) (b)

(ii) Number of beads will not change the result of activity because the vibration of plastic sheet depends on the sound.

2. (i) High frequency produces high pitch. Hence, wave 2 has highest pitch.

(ii) (a) Yes (b) Yes (c) No

Skill Based Questions as per NEP 2020

1. The figure shown in the diagram is the normal human ear. Observe the diagram carefully and answer the following questions. **Knowledge Based Que.**

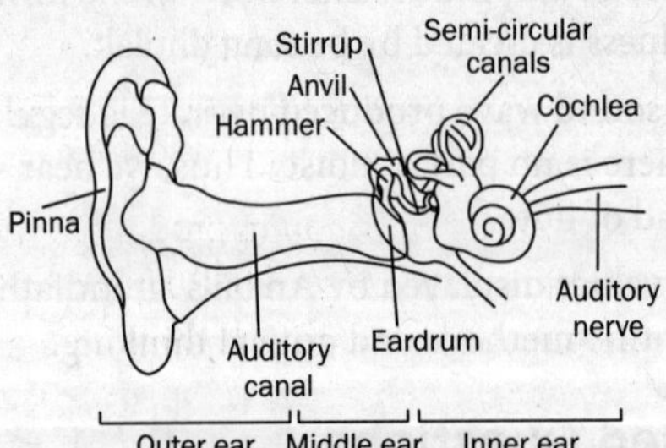

(i) Name different parts of human ear.

(ii) What passes messages from the ear to the brain ?

(iii) In which part of the ear is the eardrum located ?

2. Given below are two graphic waves, which of the two indicates the one for noise and for music ? **Thinking Based Que.**

(i)

(ii)

3. Vibration is the cause of producing sound. The fact is that sounds of frequencies less than about 20 vibrations per second cannot be detected by the human ear. Here is the table of data of some animals with their frequency range of sound waves. **Knowledge Based Que.**

Animal	Frequency range of sound waves
Elephant	15-12000 Hz
Human	20-22000 Hz
Dog	65-45000 Hz
Chicken	125-2000 Hz

(i) A cat made a purring sound that had a frequency of 35 Hz. Which of the animals mentioned in the table can hear the purring ?

(a) Only human

(b) Only elephant

(c) Dog and chicken

(d) Elephant and human

(ii) Which of these will reduce noise pollution?

(a) Regulating the use of loudspeakers

(b) Setting up more thermal power plants

(c) Using more electric vehicles

(d) (a) and (c) both

ASSESSMENT EXERCISE

Part I

Multiple Choice Questions

1. Sound can be produced by
(a) applying on object
(b) vibration of objects
(c) passing electric current through an object.
(d) effect of magnet on an object

2. Loudness of sound depends upon its
(a) frequency (b) pitch
(c) amplitude (d) shirillness

3. The human brain can sense sound frequencies
(a) less than 20 Hz (b) between 20 Hz and 20000 Hz
(c) more than 20000 Hz (d) All of the above

Fill in the Blanks

4. The speed of sound in air is ....

5. Muscles attached to the vocal cords can make the cords .... or ....

6. The pitch of the sound depends on the ....

True/False

7. The speed of sound is more than the speed of light.

8. The sound travels fastest in the solids.

9. The sound waves produced by the bats are infrasonic.

Assertion-Reason Questions

The following questions consist of two statements- Assertion (A) and Reason (R). Answer these questions by selecting the appropriate options given below.

(a) Both A and R are true and R is the correct explanation of A.
(b) Both A and R are true but R is not the correct explanation of A.
(c) A is true but R is false.
(d) A is false but R is true.

10. Assertion (A) Sound travels slower through gases than liquid.
Reason (R) The molecules in gases are farther apart from each other.

11. Assertion (A) The sound of woman is shriller than man.
Reason (R) The pitch of the sound depends on the frequency of sound.

Part II

Very Short Answer Type Questions

12. Explain how does a sound making object differ from one that is silent?

13. Mention the reason that brings the sound of fire crackers to our ears.

14. Mention the name of passage in the outer ear which carries sound waves to the eardrum.

Short Answer Type Questions

15. Cymbals (manjira) produces sound. Explain how?

16. The moment we put our ear to the railway line, we can hear the sound of an approaching train even when the train is far off but its sound cannot be heard through the air. Why?

17. How is musical sound differ from noise?

18. Write some harmful effects of noise pollution.

Long Answer Type Questions

19. Sound produced by a stretched wire is due to vibrations. Show by an activity.

20. Mention the frequency of sound produced when the vocal cords are (a) tight and thin, (b) loose and thick.

21. Draw a neat labelled diagram of human ear and explain its working.

Answers

1. (b) **2.** (c) **3.** (b) **4.** 344 m/s **5.** tight, loose
6. frequency **7.** False **8.** True **9.** False **10.** (a) **11.** (b)

CHAPTER 11

Chemical Effects of Electric Current

In earlier classes, we have learnt that the materials which allow electric current to pass through them easily are called **good conductors of electricity.** e.g.,aluminium (Al) and copper (Cu) .

On the other hand, the materials which do not allow electric current to pass through them are called **poor conductors of electricity**. e.g., rubber, plastic and wood.

We have already studied about conduction of electricity in solids. In this chapter, we will study about the conduction of electricity in liquids and the chemical effects of electricity.

11.1 Conduction of Electricity in Liquids

Like solids, liquids may also conduct electricity. **Some liquids are good conductors of electricity and some are poor conductors of electricity**.

To examine whether a liquid permits electric current to pass through it or not, we can use the tester.

When the liquid like lemon juice, vinegar etc., is between the two ends of the tester, **the bulb glows.**

On the other hand, when the liquid like distilled water is between the two ends of the tester, the **bulb does not glow.**

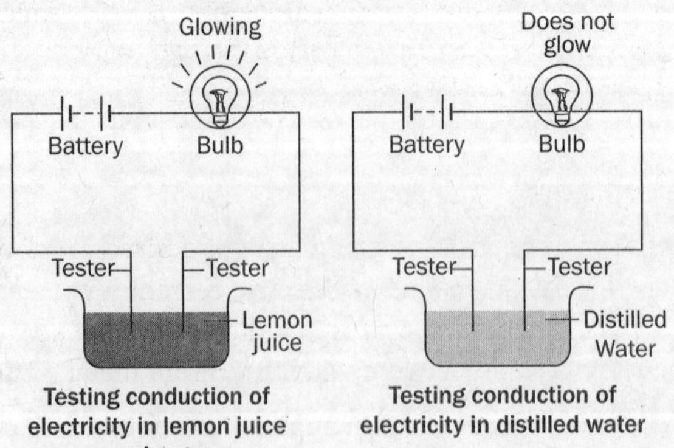

Testing conduction of electricity in lemon juice or vinegar

Testing conduction of electricity in distilled water

From above experiments, we can say that lemon juice and vinegar are the liquids that allows the electricity to pass through them. i.e. They are conducting liquids, while distilled water does not allow the electricity to pass through it, i.e. it is not a conducting liquid.

Detecting Weak Electric Current through a Liquid

In some situations, even the liquid is conducting but the bulb does not glow.

It may be due to low conductivity of liquid that it allows only a weak current to pass through it. This weak current is not sufficient to heat the filament of bulb to a high temperature.

If the electrical conductivity of liquid which we are testing, is very small, then the current in the circuit may be weak. The weak electric current flowing through liquids can be detected in two ways.

(i) With the help of LED (Light Emitting Diode)

(ii) With the help of a compass surrounded by turns of circuit wire.

By using LED LED can be used in the tester in place of bulb. It lights up even when a very weak current passes through the circuit.

LED has two wires. One wire is longer than the other. The longer wire is connected to the positive terminal and short wire is connected to the negative terminal of battery.

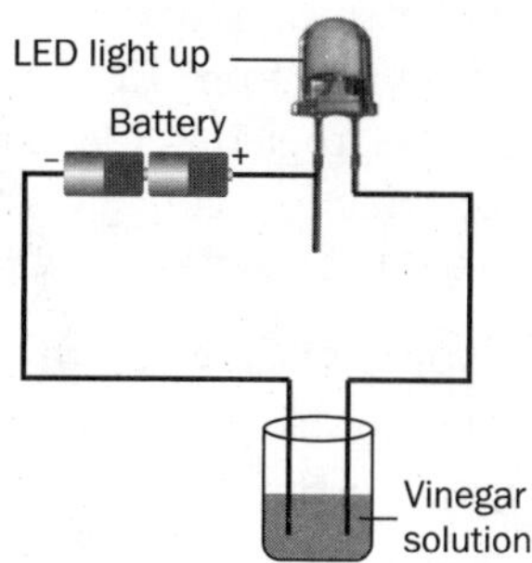

LED lights up even when weak current flows through a liquid

With the help of a compass We know that, electric current produces a magnetic effect. So, when a weak electric current flows in a wire, this produces a magnetic effect due to which a compass needle starts deflecting. So, this test circuit shows the presence of electric current.

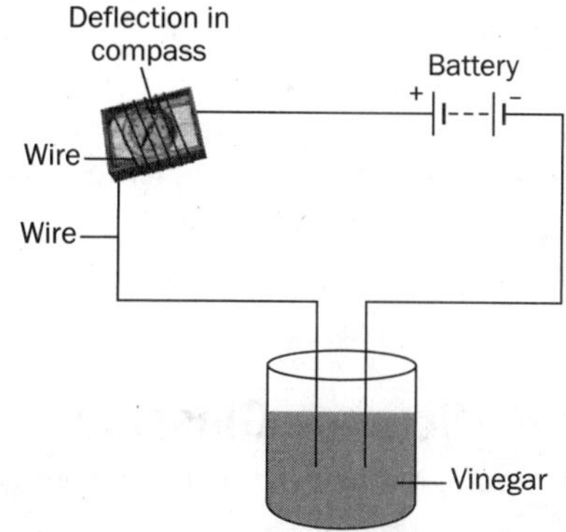

Magnetic compass shows deflection even if weak current passes through the liquid

Poor Conductors can be Good Conductors

Poor conductors are those materials which allow the electricity to pass through them under certain conditions.

As we know, **air is poor conductor of electricity** but during lightning, an electric current pass through it.

Similarly, **distilled water does not conduct electricity** but when we add some salts, acids, bases to it, this solution starts conducting electricity.

So, we can say that **liquids like solutions of acids, bases and salts are good conductors of electricity**.

The water that we get from sources like handpumps, taps, tube well, etc., contains small amount of natural salts. This natural salts make it a good conductor of electricity.

Try These 11.1

1. **Which effect of electric current is used to detect weak current in a circuit?**
2. **Can LED be used to detect strong current?**
3. **Does milk conduct electricity?**
4. **Is it true, the water which we get from sources such as taps, handpumps, wells and ponds is good conductor of electricity?**

11.2 Chemical Effects of Electric Current

When electric current is passed through conducting liquids, it causes chemical changes in the liquids. This is called chemical effect of electric current.

The passage of an electric current through a conducting solution may cause following chemical effects

(i) Change in colour of the conducting liquid.

(ii) Deposits of metal on the electrodes.

(iii) Bubbles of gas near the electrodes.

Electrodes

The conducting rods are generally made up of carbon. These rods are known as electrodes. The electrode connected to the positive terminal of battery is called **anode** while the electrode connected to the negative terminal of battery is called **cathode**.

The chemical effect produced by an electric current depends on the nature of conducting solution and on the nature of electrode used.

SCIENCE INSIGHT When electric current is passed through conducting water, it breaks the water into hydrogen gas and oxygen gas. This breaking of water through electric current is called **chemical decomposition.** Such chemical decomposition of conducting liquids through electric current is called **electrolysis.**

Electroplating

The process of depositing a thin layer of desired metal over a metal object with the help of electric current is called electroplating. e.g. Wheel rims, handle of a bicycle are made shiny by coating them with chromium metal.

It is one of the most common applications of the chemical effects of electric current.

The objective of electroplating is

(i) To protect metal from rusting or corrosion.

(ii) To make metal look more shiny and attractive.

Some electroplated objects

Note Carbon is only a non-metal, which can be electroplated with copper.

Process of Electroplating

(i) When an electric current is passed through the copper sulphate solution, then the solution dissociates into copper and sulphate.

(ii) Now, the free copper gets drawn to the electrode connected to the negative terminal of the battery and gets deposited on it.

(iii) An equal amount of copper gets dissolved into the solution from the other electrode (Copper plate).

(iv) Hence, the loss of copper from the solution is restored and the process of transferring copper from one electrode to other, continues.

(v) Here, the copper transfers from anode to cathode.

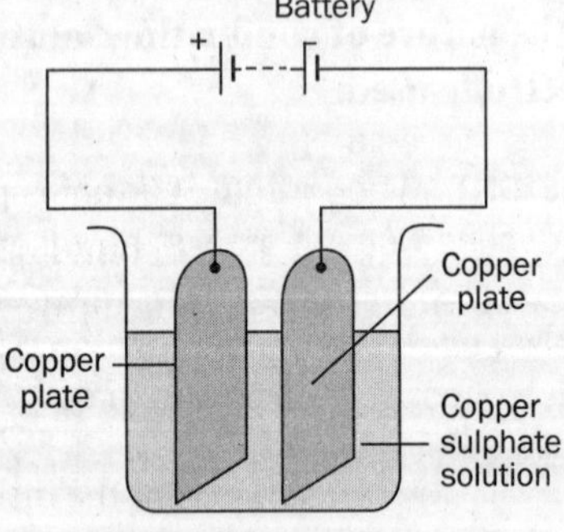

A simple circuit showing electroplating

Uses of Electroplating

As chromium has a shiny appearance and it does not corrode and resist scratches. So, the objects made from a cheaper metal get coating of chromium over it.

Following are the uses of electroplating in our day-to-day activities.

(i) The electroplating of silver and gold on the less expensive metals like iron, copper, etc is done by jewellery makers. So, these kind of ornaments have the appearance of silver or gold but are much less expensive.

(ii) Tin cans used for storing food are made by electroplating tin into iron. Tin is less reactive than iron. Thus, by electroplating the iron with tin, the food does not come into contact with iron directly, so it is protected from getting spoilt.

Some Major Concerns of Electroplating

The conducting solutions like copper sulphate in the electroplating process are the pollutants for environment.

It contains various types of salts which may be poisonous. It may affect aquatic as well as human life, so the disposal of the used conducting solution is a major concern for us.

Try These 11.2

1. Which is more reactive tin or iron?

2. During electroplating, the pure metal is deposited at?

3. Write any one harm of electroplating.

4. Name the carbon electrode which is connected to the positive terminal of the cell.

5. When electricity is passed through a conducting solution, its colour changes, what does it indicate?

(a) Heating effect of electric current

(b) Chemical effect of electric current

(c) Magnetic effect of electric current

Science Glossary

Good Conductors Materials which allow an electric current to pass through it, is known as good conductor. e.g., Salt water.

Poor Conductor Materials which allow only very small amount of current to pass through it, is known as poor conductor e.g., acetic acid /vinegar.

Electrolyte A liquid which conducts electricity is known as electrolyte.

Electrode The carbon rods whose metal caps are covered by copper wires and joined to a battery are known as electrode.

Electrolytic cell An arrangement in which a cell having two electrodes is kept in a conducting liquid in a vessel, is called electrolytic cell.

Electrolysis The chemical decomposition produced by passing an electric current through an electrolyte is called electrolysis.

Electroplating The process of depositing a thin layer of desired metal over a metal object with the help of electric current is called electroplating.

Let's Investigate

ACTIVITY 1 (Page 139)

Aim To ensure that the tester is working properly.

Material Required An electric bulb, a battery, a metal wire.

Procedure

1. Firstly, connect all the materials as shown in the figure to make a tester.
2. Join the free ends of the tester together for a moment. This completes the circuit of a tester and observe it.
3. Now, if the bulb does not glow, it means that the tester is not working.
   The reason behind this may be that the connections are loose or the bulb is fused or the battery is used up.
4. Check whether all the connections are tight or not or replace the bulb and battery with another fresh bulb and battery.
5. Now check, if the tester is working or not.

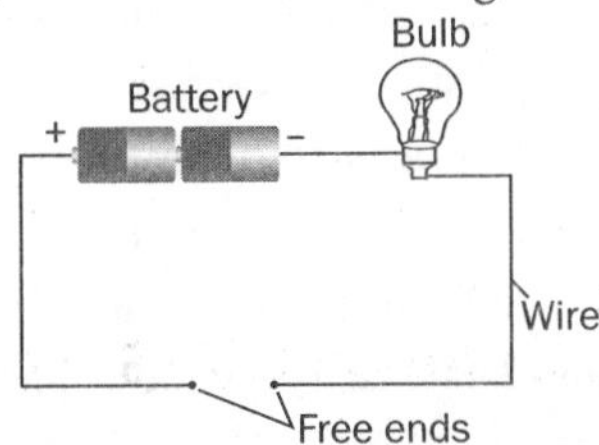

Conclusion We have come to the conclusion that our tester is working. Now, we can use it to test the various liquids conductivity.

Viva Questions

1. What things should we keep in mind while testing?
2. Name the materials required to form a tester?

ACTIVITY 2 (Page 139)

Aim To test the conduction of electricity in lemon juice or vinegar.

Material Required A tester, few caps of plastic bottles, lemon juice or vinegar.

Procedure

1. Firstly, collect few small plastic caps of discarded bottles and clean them.
2. Now, put a teaspoon of lemon juice or vinegar in a plastic cap.
3. Bring the tester over this beaker and let the ends of tester dip into the lemon Juice or vinegar.
   [Ensure that the ends should not be more than 1 cm apart]
4. Observe the bulb, you will find that bulb glows very dimly.

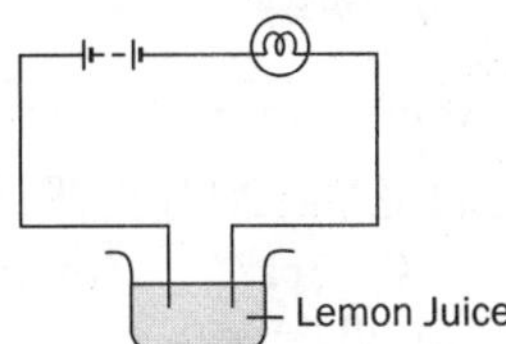

Testing conduction of electricity in lemon juice or vinegar

Conclusion We have concluded that the liquid between two ends of the tester allows the electric current to pass through it.

The dimly glowing bulb indicates that though vinegar or lemon juice conducts electricity but they are weak conductor of electricity.

Viva Questions

1. What do you mean by weak conductors?
2. What will happen, if we connect free ends of a tester for a longer time?

ACTIVITY 3 (Page 140)

Aim To observe the conduction of electricity through different liquids by using another tester.

Material Required. A compass, different liquids like lemon juice, tap water, vegetable oil etc., an empty match box, two electric wires.

Procedure

1. Firstly, take a cardboard tray from the inside of a discarded match box and place a small compass inside it.
2. Now, wrap an electric wire around the cardboard tray and connect its one free end to the terminal of a battery after leaving the other end free.
3. Take another piece of wire and connect it to the other terminal of the battery. Your tester is ready to use.
4. Now, repeat Activity 2 with the help of this tester. You will find a deflection in the compass needle when the free end of the tester is dipped in the lemon juice.

5. Repeat the activity with other liquids such as tap water, vegetable oil, milk, honey etc and observe the deflection. Remember to wash and wipe dry the ends of the tester after testing each liquid.

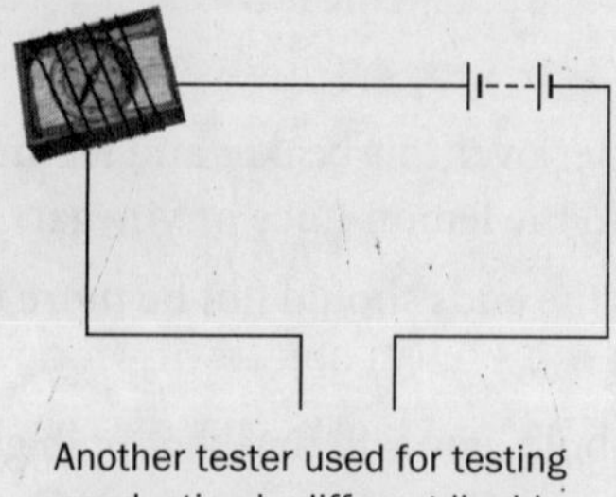

Another tester used for testing conduction in different liquids

In each case, observe whether the magnetic needle shows deflection or not. Record your observations in below table.

Material	Compass needle shows deflection Yes/No	Good / Poor Conductor
Lemon Juice	Yes	Good
Tap Water	Yes	Good
Vegetable Oil	No	Poor
Milk	No	Poor
Honey	No	Poor
Distilled Water	No	Poor

Conclusion We have concluded that some liquids are good conductors of electricity whereas, other liquids are poor conductors of electricity.

Viva Questions

1. On which effect does this tester work?
2. Is vinegar good conductor or poor conductor?

ACTIVITY 4 (Page 141)

Aim To show that a poor conductor can be a good conductor under some conditions.

Material Required Distilled water, common salt, tester, plastic cap of a discarded bottle.

Procedure

1. Firstly, take some distilled water in plastic cap.
2. Now, use the tester to check whether distilled water conducts electricity or not. You will find no electricity is conducted by the distilled water.
3. Dissolve a pinch of common salt in distilled water and test the conductivity. You will find that electricity is conducting here.

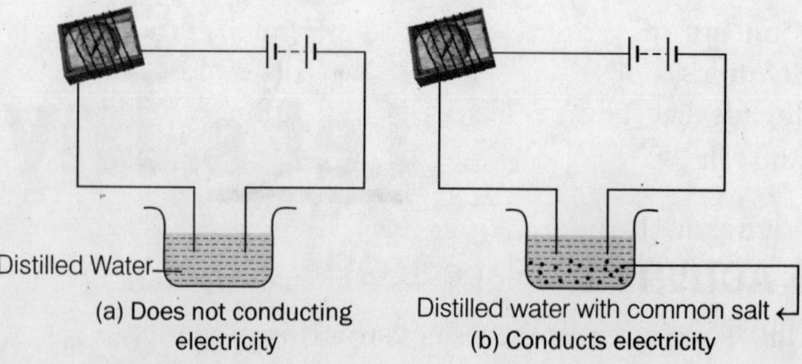

(a) Does not conducting electricity (b) Conducts electricity

Conclusion We have concluded that, under some conditions poor conductor can become good conductor of electricity.

Viva Questions

1. Why it is advisable that we should not touch the electric wire with wet hands?
2. Does the amount of salt in water affect conductivity?

ACTIVITY 5 (Page 142)

Aim To show that, acid, base and salt solutions also conduct electricity.

Material Required Three plastic caps of discarded bottles, distilled water, a tester, lemon juice, caustic soda, sugar.

Procedure

1. Take three clean plastic caps of discarded bottles and pour about two teaspoons of distilled water in each of them.
2. Add a few drops of lemon juice to distilled water in first cap. Similarly, add caustic soda and sugar to second and third cap, respectively.
3. Now, test which solution conducts electricity and which does not.

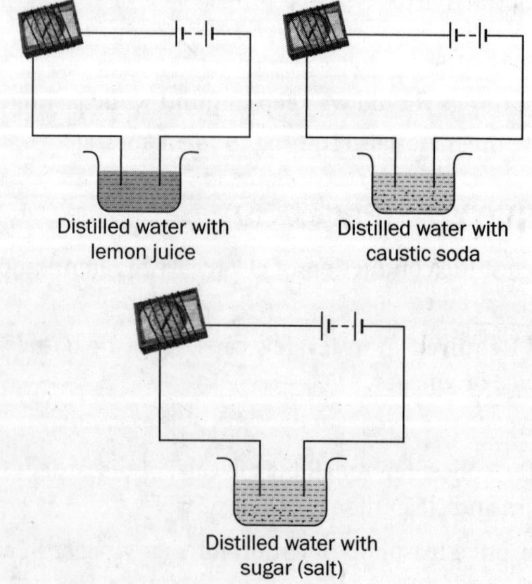

Conclusion We have concluded that, all the three solutions conduct electricity. It means that most of the liquids that conduct electricity are solutions of acids, bases and salts.

Viva Questions

1. Name the substances which, when dissolved in distilled water, make it conducting.
2. Why distilled water cannot conduct electricity?

ACTIVITY 6 (Page 142, 143)

Aim To demonstrate the chemical effects of electric current.

Material Required A battery, copper wires, carbon rods, lemon juice, water.

Procedure

1. Firstly, take out carbon rods from two discarded cells. Clean their metal caps with sand paper.
2. Now, wrap copper wires around the metal caps of the carbon rods and join them to a battery.
3. Now, put a cup of water in a beaker. Also, add a few drops of lemon juice to the water to make it more conducting.
4. Now, immerse the electrodes in this solution. Make sure that, the metal caps of carbon rods are above the level of electrolyte in a beaker.
5. Wait for 3 to 4 min. Notice the electrode carefully, we will see that the bubbles of gases are produced at the two carbon electrodes.

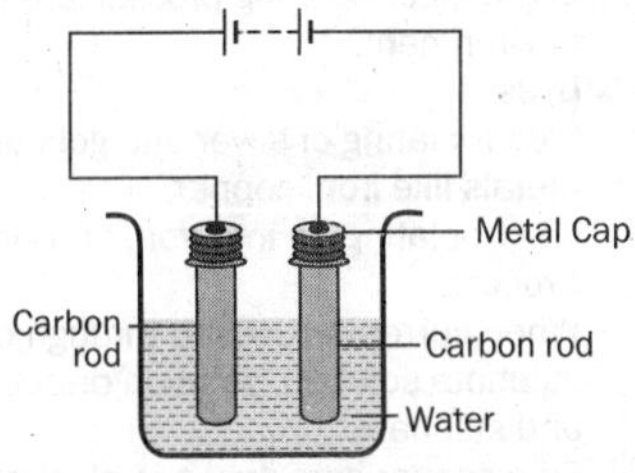

Passing current through water

Conclusion We have concluded that, the chemical reaction has taken place in the solution, when electric current is passing through it.

Viva Questions

1. Does chemical effect produced by an electric current depend on the nature of conducting solution?
2. What are the other chemical effects that can be seen due to passage of electric current through a conducting solution?

ACTIVITY 7 (Page 144)

Aim To electroplate a metal object with copper.

Material Required Copper sulphate, 250 mL distilled water, dry beaker, copper plates.

Procedure

1. Firstly, take copper sulphate and two copper plates of size around 10cm × 4cm.
2. Now, take 250 mL of distilled water in a clean and dry beaker and dissolve two teaspoons of copper sulphate in it and add a few drops of dilute sulphuric acid to this solution to make it more conducting.
3. Now, clear the copper plates with sand paper and connect it to the terminals of a battery and immerse them in copper sulphate solution.
4. Allow the current to pass for about 15 min.
5. Now, remove the electrodes from the solution and look at them carefully.

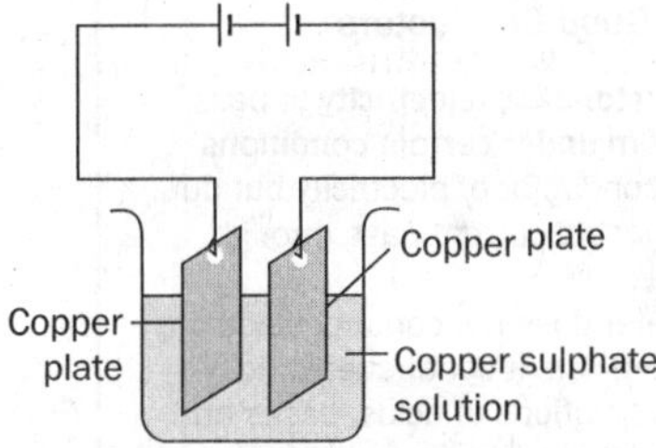

A simple circuit showing electroplating

Conclusion We have concluded that the copper metal gets transferred from the positive electrode to the negative electrode.

Viva Questions

1. Which electrode is connected to the positive terminal of cell?
2. Why electroplating is so beneficial for a metal?

Detecting Weak Electric Current

Due to low conductivity of liquid, weak current passes through it.

- **It can be detected**
  - **By Using LED**
  It lights up even when a very weak current passes through the circuit.
  - **With the Help of Compass**
  When weak electric current passes, it produces magnetic effect due to which compass needle starts deflecting.

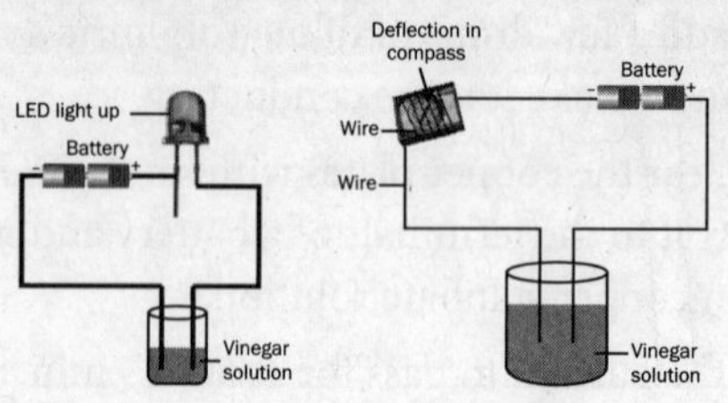

Conduction of Electricity in Liquids

Liquids may also conduct electricity.

- **On the basis of conduction, it divides into two types**
  - **Bad Conductor**
  Liquids that don't allow electricity to pass through them.
  e.g. Distilled water
  - **Good Conductor**
  Liquids that allows electricity to pass through them.
  e.g. Lemon juice, vinegar.

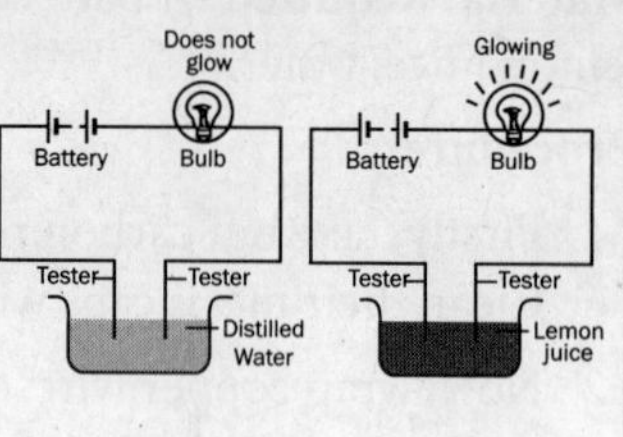

Poor Conductors can be Good Conductors

- **Poor conductor allow electricity to pass through them under certain conditions**
  - Air is poor conductor of electricity but during lightning, electric current pass through them.
  - Distilled water does not conduct electricity but by adding salt, it conduct electricity.
  - Liquids like solutions of acids, bases and salts are good conductors of electricity.

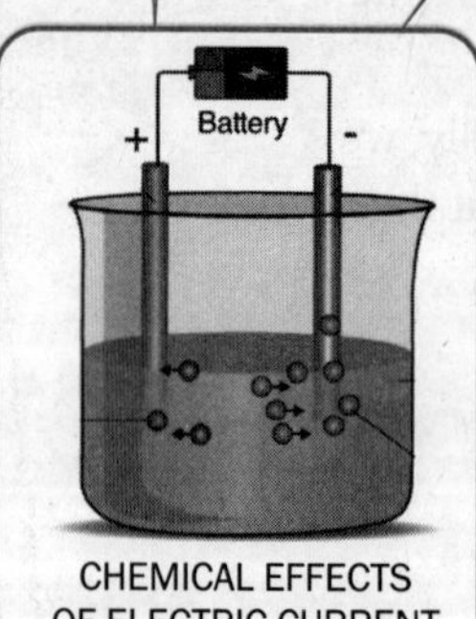

CHEMICAL EFFECTS OF ELECTRIC CURRENT

Electroplating

Process of depositing thin layer of desired metal over a metal object with the help of electric current.

- **Objective**
  - To protect metal from rusting or corrosion.
  - To make metal look more shiny and attractive.
- **Major Concerns**
  The conducting solutions like copper sulphate in the electroplating process are pollutants for environment.
- **Uses**
  Electroplating of silver and gold on less expensive metals like iron, copper,
  Electroplating tin into iron, tin is less reactive.
- **Process**
  - When current is passed through copper sulphate solution, solution dissociates into copper and sulphate.
  - Free copper gets drawn to electrode connected to negative terminal of battery and deposit on it.
  - An equal amount of copper gets dissolved into solution from other electrode (copper plate).
  - Loss of copper from solution is restored and process of transferring copper one electrode to other, continues.
  - Copper transfers from anode to cathode.

Important Points

- When electric current passes through conducting liquids, it causes chemical changes.
  - Change in colour of conducting liquid
  - Deposit of metal on electrode.
  - Bubble of gas
- Chemical effect produced by it depends on the nature of conducting solution and electrode.

NCERT FOLDER

Complete Explanations of all NCERT's Questions

Intext Questions

Q1. It is dangerous to touch an electrical appliance with wet hands. Explain why? Page 138

Ans. Wet hand acts as good conductor. So, we feel electric shock when we touch electrical appliance with wet hands.

Q2. Paheli and Boojho want to remind you that one should not experiment with the electric supply from the mains or a generator or an inverter. Why ? Page 138

Ans. The electrical supply which comes in our domestic main electrical line is about 120 V. We should not use this high voltage electricity for an experiment. This can cause serious injuries or instant death.

Q3. Sometimes we see that the liquid is conducting but the bulb may not glow. Why ? Page 139

Ans. The bulb does not glow because the current through it is too weak.

Q4. The bulb glows when the electric current passes through it. Explain why? Page 139

Ans. Due to the heating effect of current, the filament of the bulb gets heated to a high temperature and it starts glowing. However, if the current through a circuit is too weak, the filament does not get heated sufficiently and it does not glow.

Q5. When a compass needle is brought near a current carrying wire, then what happens? Page 140

Ans. When a compass needle is brought near a current carrying wire, then needle deflects.

Q6. Can we make another tester which can detect a weak current ? Page 140

Ans. Yes, we can use another effect of an electric current to make another kind of tester, i.e. magnetic effect of electric current.

Q7. Does poor conductors also allow electricity to pass under certain conditions ? Page 141

Ans. Yes, poor conductors can conduct electricity under certain conditions like wet wood.

Q8. Give the name of these substances which when added to distilled water make them good conductors of electricity. Page 142

Ans. Acids, bases and salts are those substances which when added to distilled water make them good conductors of electricity.

Q9. Give the names of the three effects of electric current. Page 142

Ans. The three effects of electric current are

(i) Heating effect of current

(ii) Magnetic effect of current

(iii) Chemical effect of current

Q10. An electric current is passed through a conducting solution. List any three possible observations. Page 143

Ans. Three possible observations are

(i) The colour of the solution may change depending upon the electrodes.

(ii) The temperature of the solution may increase.

(iii) Bubbles near the electrodes can be seen.

Q11. After doing the electroplating activity, Paheli interchanged the electrodes and repeated the activity. What do you think she would observe this time ? Page No. 144

Ans. Paheli will observe the gas bubbles.

Q12. In electroplating process, what about the loss of copper from the solution? Page No. 144, 145

Ans. An equal amount of copper gets dissolved in the solution from anode, thus the loss of copper from the solution is restored.

Exercise

Q1. Fill in the blanks.

(a) Most liquids that conduct electricity are solutions of ...., ... and ....

(b) The passage of an electric current through a solution causes .... effects.

(c) If you pass current through copper sulphate solution, copper gets deposited on the plate connected to the .... terminal of the battery.

(d) The process of depositing a layer of any desired metal on another material by means of electricity is called ....

Ans. (a) acids, bases, salts
(b) chemical
(c) negative
(d) electroplating

Q 2. When the free ends of a tester are dipped into a solution, the magnetic needle shows deflection. Can you explain the reason ?

Ans. When the free ends of a tester are dipped into a solution, then the liquid between the two ends allows the electric current to pass and the circuit of the tester becomes complete. Also, when the current passes through the tester, it establishes a magnetic effect and hence, magnetic needle shows deflection.

In other words, we can say that the solution is a good conductor of electricity, so the needle gets deflected.

Q 3. Name of three liquids which when tested in the manner shown in figure below may cause the magnetic needle to deflect.

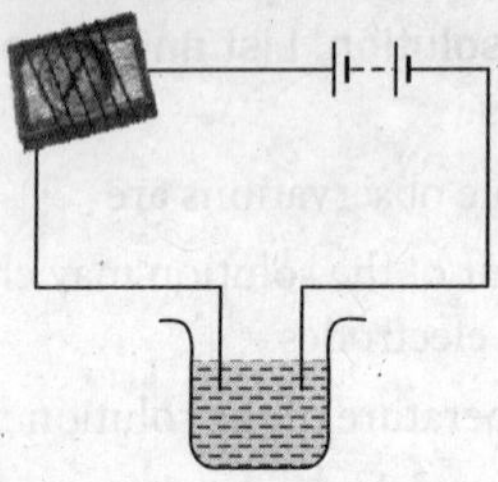

Ans. The three liquids are as follows
(i) Tapwater
(ii) HCl or hydrochloric acid
(iii) Sodium hydroxide

Q 4. The bulb does not glow in the setup shown in figure below. List the possible reasons. Explain your answer.

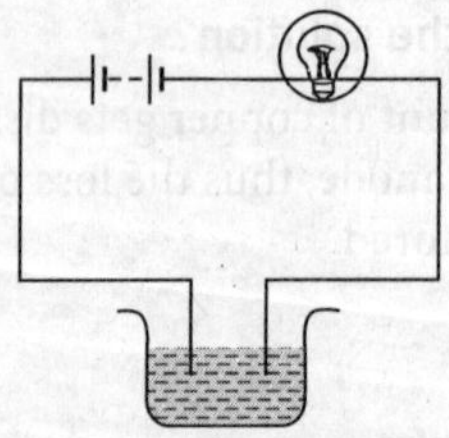

Ans. The possible reasons are as follows
(i) The current is not produced by the given liquid and hence, bulb does not glow.
(ii) Connections are loose.
(iii) Bulb is fused.
(iv) Cells are used up.

Q 5. A tester is used to check the conduction of electricity through two liquids, labelled *A* and *B*. It is found that the bulb of the tester glows brightly for liquid *A*, while it glows very dimly for liquid *B*. You would conclude that

(a) liquid *A* is a better conductor than liquid *B*
(b) liquid *B* is a better conductor than liquid *A*
(c) both liquids are equally conducting
(d) conducting properties of liquid cannot be compared in this manner

Ans. (a) We conclude that liquid *A* is a better conductor than liquid *B*.

Q 6. Does pure water conduct electricity? If not, what can we do to make it conducting?

Ans. No, pure water does not conduct electricity because it has no dissolved salt in it.

Hence, pure water can be made conducting by dissolving salt in it.

Q 7. In case of a fire, before the firemen uses the water hoses, they shut off the main electrical supply for the area. Explain why they do this?

Ans. Since, tap water is a very good conductor of electricity. So, if the main electrical supply will remain ON, it can be fatal to human life because it can lead to electrocution due to water.

Q 8. A child staying in a coastal region tests the drinking water and also the seawater with his tester. He finds that the compass needle deflects more in the case of seawater. Can you explain the reason?

Ans. As we know that the current produces the magnetic effect and causes the deflection in magnetic needle. In case of sea water, the salt content is much higher than that of drinking water. Thus, it produces more current than drinking water.

Therefore, as a result, the deflection in magnetic needle is more in case of sea water rather than drinking water.

Q 9. Is it safe for the electrician to carry out electrical repairs outdoors during heavy down pour? Explain.

Ans. No, it is not safe for the electrician to carry out electrical repairs outdoors during heavy downpour. Because rainwater is a good conductor of electricity. So, during heavy downpour, there is a huge risk of electrocution.

Q 10. Paheli had heard that rainwater is as good as distilled water. So, she collected some rainwater in a clean glass tumbler and tested it using a tester. To her surprise she found that the compass needle showed deflection. What could be the reasons?

Ans. While it rains, the rain drops get mixed with the suspended particles of the air. So, they do not remain pure. It becomes the mixture of salts and other impurities. Thus, it shows the conduction of electricity.

But in case of distilled water, no conduction of electricity takes place as distilled water do not contain salts or impurities. Thus, it becomes a bad conductor of electricity.

Q 11. Prepare a list of objects around you that are electroplated.

Ans. List of objects that are electroplated are as follows:

(i) Bath taps, kitchen gas burners.

(ii) Jewellery makers electroplate silver and gold on less expensive metals.

(iii) Electroplating iron cans with tin to store food.

(iv) Handle bar of cycles and motorcycles.

(v) Rims of cycles, buckles of clothes and belts.

Q 12. The process that you saw in Activity 7 is used for purification of copper. A thin plate of pure copper and a thick rod of impure copper are used as electrodes. Copper from impure rod is sought to be transferred to the thin copper plate. Which electrode should be attached to the positive terminal of the battery and why?

Ans. The impure rod of copper should be attached to the positive terminal of the battery and pure copper plate should be attached to the negative terminal of the battery. When electric current is passed through the copper sulphate solution, copper sulphate dissociates into copper and sulphate ions.

The free copper gets drawn to the electrode connected with negative terminal of the battery and starts depositing on it.

From the other electrode, a thick rod of impure copper, an equal amount of copper gets dissolved into the solution. Hence, the loss of copper from the solution is restored and the process continues. Thus, copper gets transferred from one electrode to the other.

REVIEW EXERCISE

Including Competency Based Questions

Part I

Multiple Choice Questions

1. Plastic wire is

(a) an insulator (b) a conductor
(c) Both (a) and (b) (d) None of these

2. Electrolytes conduct electricity due to the movement of

(a) electrodes (b) atoms
(c) electrons (d) ions

3. The solution that can conduct electricity is of

(a) pure water
(b) water and acid solution
(c) water and salt solution
(d) Both (b) and (c)

4. Which one of the following solutions will not conduct electricity? NCERT Exemplar

(a) Lemon juice (b) Vinegar
(c) Tap water (d) Vegetable oil

5. Boojho and Paheli performed experiments taking similar bulbs and cells but two different solutions *A* and *B* as shown in figure. NCERT Exemplar

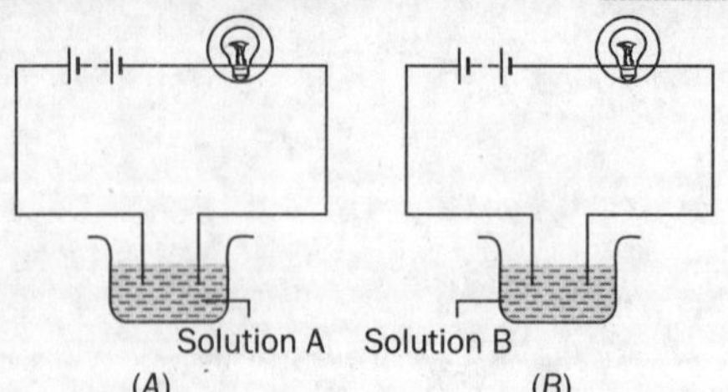

They found that the bulb in the set up *A* glows more brightly as compared to that of the set up *B*. You would conclude that

(a) higher current is flowing through the circuit in set up *A*
(b) higher current is flowing through the circuit in set up *B*
(c) equal current is flowing through both the circuits
(d) the current flowing through the circuits in the two setups cannot be compared in this manner

6. An electric current can produce NCERT Exemplar

(a) heating effect
(b) chemical effect
(c) magnetic effect
(d) chemical, heating and magnetic effects

7. When electric current is passed through a conducting solution, there is a change of colour of the solution. This indicates NCERT Exemplar

(a) the chemical effect of current
(b) the heating effect of current
(c) the magnetic effect of current
(d) the lightning effect of current

8.

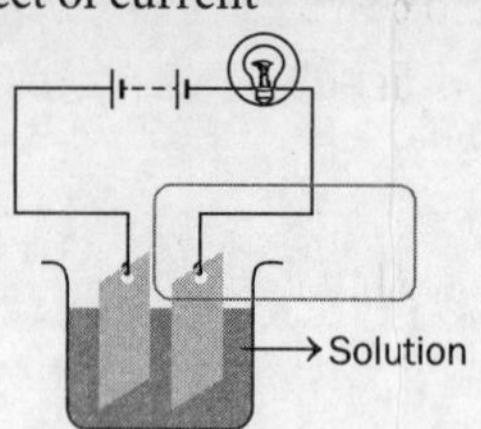

Which of the following solutions will not make the bulb glow in figure? NCERT Exemplar

(a) Sodium chloride
(b) Copper sulphate
(c) Silver nitrate
(d) Sugar solution in diluted water

9. The process of depositing a thin layer of any superior metal over an object of a cheaper metal with the help of electricity is called

(a) electro refining (b) electro-metallurgy
(c) electroplating (d) None of the above

10. Which of the following metals is used in electroplating to make objects appear shining? NCERT Exemplar

(a) Iron (b) Copper
(c) Chromium (d) Aluminium

11. Boojho's uncle has set up an electroplating factory near his village. He should dispose off the waste of the factory Competency Based Que.

(a) in the nearby river
(b) in the nearby pond
(c) in the nearby corn field
(d) according to the disposal guidelines of the local authority

Answers

1. (a)	**2.** (d)	**3.** (d)	**4.** (d)
5. (a)	**6.** (d)	**7.** (a)	**8.** (d)
9. (c)	**10.** (c)	**11.** (d)	

Fill in the Blanks

1. Materials which do not allow an electric current to pass through them are called ....
2. Small amounts of a mineral salt present naturally in water makes it a .... of electricity. **NCERT Exemplar**
3. LED glows even when a .... electric current passes through it.
4. If we pass current through a conducting solution then .... effect takes place.
5. A liquid that conducts electricity due to the presence of ions is called ....
6. The object to be electroplated is taken as .... electrode. **NCERT Exemplar**
7. One of the most common applications of chemical effect of electric current is ....
8. Electroplating is used to give more .... to the cheap objects.
9. Electroplating of .... is done on objects like water taps and cycle bell to give them a shiny appearance. **NCERT Exemplar**

Answers

1. insulator
2. good conductor
3. small
4. chemical
5. electrolyte
6. negative
7. electroplating
8. attraction/shining
9. chromium

True/False

1. Some liquids are good conductors of electricity and some are poor conductors.
2. Distilled water conducts the electric current.
3. Adding of sugar makes pure water conducting.
4. Most liquids that conduct electricity are solutions of acids, bases and salts.
5. Electric bulb glows due to chemical effect of electricity.
6. The passage of an electric current through a conducting liquid causes chemical reactions.
7. The chemical effect of electric current is used in purification of salts.
8. The chemical reaction brought about by an electric current may produce changes in the colour of solutions.
9. Electrolysis is a chemical change.
10. During the electrolysis of water, hydrogen gas is liberated at the anode.
11. During electroplating, the object to be electroplated is made anode.

Answers

1. True
2. False
3. False
4. True
5. False
6. True
7. False
8. True
9. True
10. False
11. False

Match the Columns

1. **Match the Column I with Column II.**

Column I	Column II
(a) Insulator	(i) Electric circuit
(b) Conductor	(ii) Conducts current
(c) Closed path	(iii) Prevents rusting
(d) Solution of distilled water and salt	(iv) Rubber
(e) Electroplating	(v) Copper
(f) Lemon juice	(vi) Added to water to increase the conductivity

Answer

1. (a)–(iv), (b)–(v), (c)–(i), (d)–(ii), (e)–(iii), (f)–(vi)

Assertion-Reason Questions

The following questions consist of two statements- Assertion (A) and Reason (R). Answer these questions by selecting the appropriate option given below

(a) Both A and R are true and R is the correct explanation of A.
(b) Both A and R are true but R is not the correct explanation of A.
(c) A is true but R is false.
(d) A is false but R is true.

1. **Assertion** (A) Sea water is a good conductor of electricity.
   Reason (R) Sea water contains different types of salts.
2. **Assertion** (A) Distilled water is a poor conductor of electricity.
   Reason (R) Distilled water contains small amount of mineral salt which makes it poor conductor.
3. **Assertion** (A) A magnetic compass can be used in place of electric bulb to make a tester.
   Reason (R) A compass get deflected when it is placed nearby a current carrying conductor.
4. **Assertion** (A) Materials like wheel rims, handle of bicycles etc are coated with chromium metal to make it more shiny and attractive.
   Reason (R) Chromium metal does not corrode and save materials from scratches.

Answers

1. (a) Sea water contains different types of salts and ions. These salts are responsible for conducting electricity. This is the reason that sea water is a good conductor of electricity.
2. (c) Distilled water is a poor conductor of electricity as it is free from mineral salts.
3. (a) We can detect the presence of electric current with the help of magnetic compass. A compass starts deflecting when it is placed nearby a current carrying wire.
4. (a) Chromium metal is less reactive. It does not corrode easily. That's why materials like rims, handle of bicycles etc., are coated with chromium metal.

Case Based Question

1. Tia used four different objects to fill the gap in an electric circuit, separately.
The table shows what she found. Competency Based Que.

Object in the gap	The bulb
Plastic	Does not glow
Copper wire	Glows brightly
Wooden block	Does not glow
Graphite stone	Glows dimly

(i) Which of these best conducts electricity?
(a) Wood (b) Plastic
(c) Copper (d) Graphite

(ii) Which of these is a chemical effect of electric current?
(a) Glowing of bulb
(b) Heating of water
(c) Ringing of mobile phone
(d) Chromium plating on iron.

(iii) Which of these is a correct pair of an insulator and a conductor?

	Insulator	Conductor
(a)	Aluminium	Cotton
(b)	Thermocol	Rubber
(c)	Copper	Iron
(d)	Wax	Aluminium

Answer

1. (i) (c) (ii) (d) (iii) (d)

Part II

Very Short Answer Type Questions

1. Will the solution of sugar in distilled water conduct electricity? NCERT Exemplar

Ans. The sugar solution in distilled water will make it a good conductor of electricity and current can easily pass through it.

2. The fresh fruits and vegetables conduct electricity to some extent. Explain why

Ans. Due to the presence of various salt solution in fruits and vegetables, they are able to conduct electricity to some extent.

3. State, which one is a better conductor of electricity sea water or drinking water.

Ans. As sea water contains more salt which increases conductivity. So, sea water is a good conductor of electricity.

4. Mention any one important difference in the conduction of electricity by solids over liquids.

Ans. Since, no chemical changes takes place when electricity is allowed to pass through the solids while in liquids chemical changes take place when electricity is passed through it.

5. Name the effect of current responsible for the glow of the bulb in an electric circuit. NCERT Exemplar

Ans. The heating effect of electric current is responsible for the bulb to glow in an electric circuit.

6. A chemical compound is produced by the method of electrolysis. Give an example.

Ans. Solution hydroxide or caustic soda is produced by the electrolysis of an aqueous solution (water solution) of sodium chloride.

7. Mention the place where should we dispose the waste electrolytes in electroplating.

Ans. The waste electrolytes should be disposed far away from residential areas.

8. Why is tin electroplated on iron to make cans used for storing food? **NCERT Exemplar**

Ans. Electroplating is done on the iron to prevent it from rust and corrosion. By electroplating the iron with tin, the food does not come into contact with iron directly, so it is protected from getting spoilt.

9. During the electrolysis of water, at which electrode, hydrogen gas is evolved?

Ans. During the electrolysis of water, hydrogen gas is evolved at the cathode.

10. Explain, why is a layer of zinc coated over iron? **NCERT Exemplar**

Ans. Layer of zinc is coated over iron because zinc prevents it from rust and corrosion.

Short Answer Type Questions

1. Boojho made the circuit as shown in figure. He wanted to observe what happens when an electric current is passed through water, but he forgot to add a few drops of lemon juice to water. Will it make any difference to his observations? Explain. **Competency Based Que.**

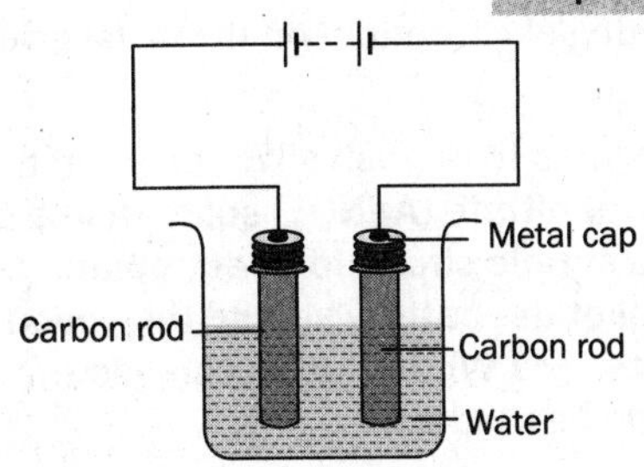

Ans. Adding few drops of lemon juice in water will increase the conductivity of the solution. The current will flow in both the cases but adding of lemon juice makes it easy for the current to flow.

2. Observe the following circuit given in figure.

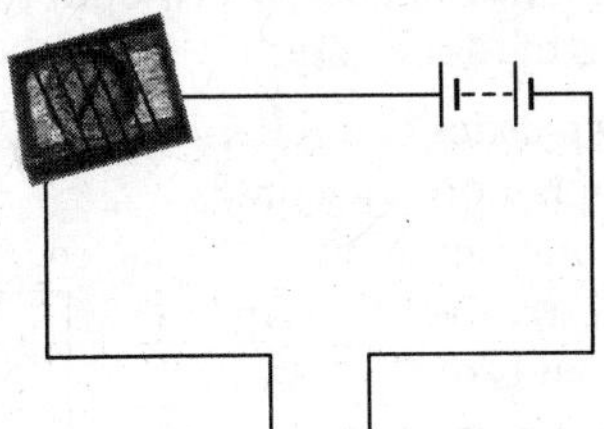

Current does not flow in the circuit, if there is a gap between the two wires. Does it indicate that air is a poor conductor of electricity? Does air never conduct electricity? Explain. **NCERT Exemplar**

Ans. Yes, if current is not flowing through the air gap between the wires, it means that air is a poor conductor of electricity.

Air conducts electricity only when there is great voltage or there is some moisture in air.

3. Boojho made the circuit given in figure and observed that the bulb did not glow. On Paheli's suggestion, he added one more cell in the circuit. The bulb now glows. Explain.

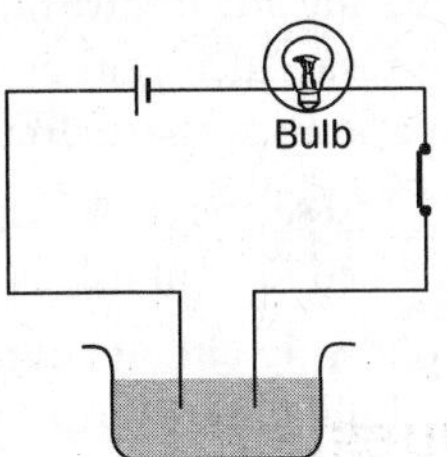

Ans. Initially, the bulb was not glowing because the voltage required to make the bulb glow was not sufficient.

When the voltage increases more than a particular value, the bulb starts glowing because it gets sufficient energy to heat its filament.

4. Paheli setup an experiment using liquid *A* in the beaker as shown in figure. She observed that the bulb glows. Then, she replaced the liquid *A* by another liquid *B*. This time the bulb did not glow. Boojho suggested replacing the bulb by an LED. They observed that the LED glows. Explain. **Competency Based Que.**

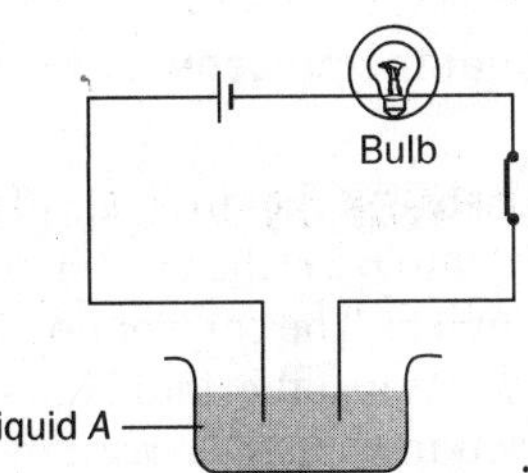

Ans. Liquid *A* is a good conductor of electricity and it allows the maximum current to pass through it which is sufficient to glow the bulb.
But when it is replaced by another liquid *B*, bulb does not glow because liquid *B* is not a good conductor of electricity.
But the small current which is passing through *B* is sufficient to glow a low voltage LED, so it glows.

5. Last Monday, Ankush woke up late in the morning. So, he saw the time and suddenly realised that he had got late for an interview, which he was supposed to give after reaching the venue by the right time. Immediately, he turned ON the geyser but it did not work. He got more tensed, then he used an electric iron rod through which he could get some boiled water for his bath. Actually, there was an earthing problem in the switch board which he was unaware

of. He was barefoot and was just about to switch ON the electric iron rod but at the same he was stopped from doing so by one of his room partner living with him. It could be dangerous for Ankush.

(i) Explain in brief that what could be happened with Ankush, if he switched ON the electric iron rod (without wearing any slippers in his foot).

(ii) Mention the values showed by Ankush's friend.

Ans. (i) If Ankush switched ON the electric iron rod and (without wearing any footwears), then he could have met with some accident, either in the form of electrical sparking or short circuit of switch board.

(ii) Ankush's friend seems to be very intelligent and very much concerned for Ankush as well.

6. Observe the following circuits carefully. In which circuit, will the bulb glow? Write 'Yes' or 'No' in the blank space provided alongwith each of the circuit given in figure. NCERT Exemplar

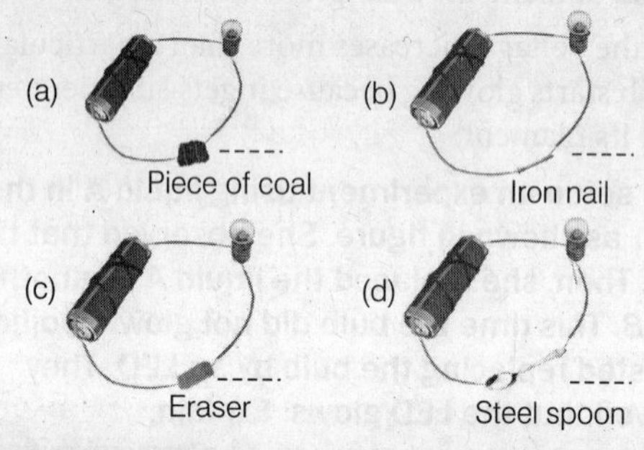

Ans. (a) No (b) Yes (c) No (d) Yes

7. Explain in brief the procedure of glowing of bulb in a liquid.

Ans. If the liquid between the two ends of a tester allows the electric current to pass, then the circuit of the tester becomes complete. The current flows in the circuit and the bulb glows. When the liquid does not allow the electric current to pass, the circuit of the tester is not complete and the bulb does not glow.

8. State the reason, why do we need magnetic compass to test the conduction of electric current.

Ans. Sometimes the bulb does not glow on passing electric current. This is because the electric current flowing through a conductor is so small .So, in case of small current, we need magnetic compass to test the conduction.

9. Observe figure.

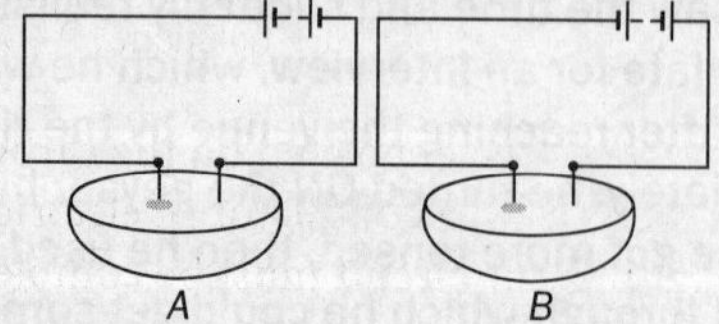

Which of these two circuits *A* or *B* shows the correct observation? NCERT Exemplar

Ans. It is not clear from the diagram that what is *A* and *B*. So, we cannot predict the actual solution. But if we compare with NCERT activity, this seems to be a potato and correct diagram is *A* because positive terminal makes the green spot on the potato.

10. Explain how can we purify the impure metals? HOTS

Ans. By an electrolysis process, we use a thick rod of impure metal as anode and thin strip of pure metal as cathode. A water soluble salt of the metal is taken as electrolyte. On passing electric current, the metal dissolves from the impure anode and goes into electrolyte solution which is then deposited on the cathode in pure form.

11. We should throw conducting materials used in electroplating far away from residential areas. Explain why?

Ans. As the conducting solutions or electrolytes contain various types of salts which may be poisonous and also usually acidic in nature. So, in electroplating factories, the disposal of used conducting materials is a major problem and it should be disposed off in a proper way far away from the human population.

12. State some advantages of electroplating.

Ans. The advantages of electroplating are given below

(i) It protects the metal from corrosion and rusting.

(ii) It is used to coat desired metals on other objects.

(iii) It can make more reactive metals like iron.

(iv) Coating of chromium on the metal gives luster to the objects.

13. Paheli wants to deposit silver on an iron spoon. She took silver nitrate ($AgNO_3$) solution in a beaker and set up a simple circuit for electroplating. Which terminal of the battery should the spoon be connected to? What material should the other electrode be made of? NCERT Exemplar

Ans. The spoon should be connected to the negative terminal of the battery. The other electrode should be of silver, so that silver ions get deposited on an iron spoon.

Long Answer Type Questions

1. Prove that lemon juice and vinegar are good conductors of electricity.

Ans. Take a few plastics or rubber caps of bottles. Put one teaspoon of lemon juice or vinegar in one cap. Now, bring the tester over the cap and let the ends of the tester dip into lemon juice or vinegar. So, we can see that, bulb starts to glow. It indicates that lemon juice and vinegar are good conductors of electricity.

Battery Bulb

2. You are provided with a magnetic compass, an empty matchbox, a battery of two cells and connecting wires. Using these objects, how will you make a tester for testing an electric circuit? Draw the necessary circuit diagram and explain. **Competency Based Que.**

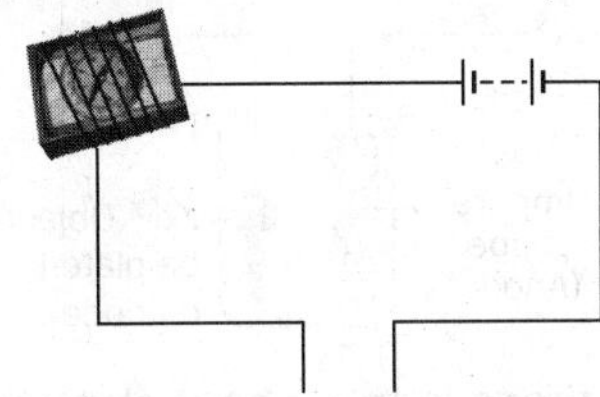

Ans. Take the tray from the inside of a discarded matchbox. Wrap an electric wire a few times around the tray. Place a small compass needle inside it. Now connect one free end of the wire to the one terminal of a battery. Leave the other end free.

Take another piece of wire and connect it to the other terminal of the battery. Join the free ends of two wires momentarily.

The compass needle should show deflection. Your tester with two free ends of the wire is ready.

3. Observing that the bulb does not glow in the circuit shown in Fig. (a) Boojho changed the circuit as shown in Fig. (b). He observed deflection in the magnetic compass. **NCERT Exemplar**

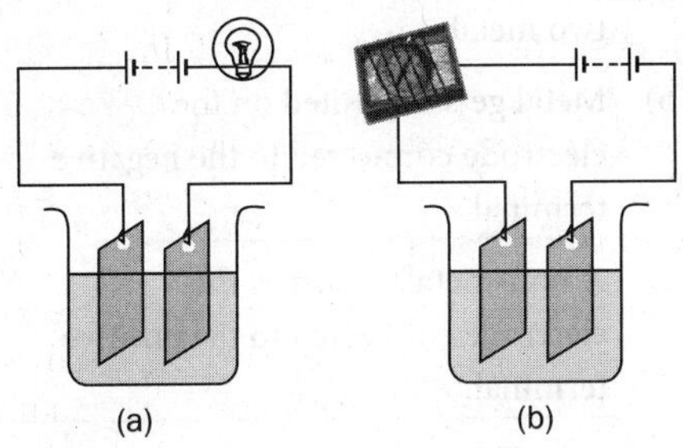

(i) What does the deflection in magnetic compass indicate?

(ii) Why did the bulb not glow in Fig. (a)?

(iii) What would be the effect of increase in the number of turns in the coil wound around the magnetic compass in Fig. (b)?

Ans. (i) The deflection in the magnetic compass shows that the current is flowing in the circuit.

(ii) The bulb did not glow, it may be because of the current passing through the circuit could be weak. Also, it may happen because of other reasons like due to bulb fused or the connections may be loose.

(iii) An increase in the number of turns in the coil wound around the magnetic compass would increase the magnetic field around the magnetic compass which will result in the increase in the deflection in the magnetic compass.

4. One day Ram was performing an experiment. He was trying to design an electric circuit in which he included tester, bulb and a battery. He had so much eagerness regarding this experiment that in so much hurry, he forgot to take the connecting wires of aluminium. He took the wires without any coating of PVC on them, so it could be dangerous for him. Any how, he managed to design an electric circuit but the moment, he switched ON the circuit, a spark was produced and bulb got fused with a small sound. He was about to touch those wires and heated bulb with his bare hands, at the same time, his teacher suggested him to perform the experiment by taking precautions.

(i) Explain what could have happened, if Ram would touched the electric bulb with his bare hands.

(ii) Mention why should he use the aluminium wires in his experiment?

(iii) State the values shown by Ram's teacher here.

Competency Based Que.

Ans. (i) If Ram touched the heated electric bulb, then his hands could get a severe burn and he would not be able to perform the experiment again with the same desire.

(ii) He use the aluminium wires in his experiment because, aluminium is a good conductor of electricity.

(iii) Ram's teacher has a great concern towards Ram, so that he can perform the experiment carefully and can get to its fruitful conclusion.

5. In the circuit given in the figure, Boojho observed that copper is deposited on the electrode connected to the negative terminal of the battery. Paheli tried to repeat the same experiment but she could find only one copper plate. Therefore, she took a carbon rod as negative electrode. Will copper be still deposited on the carbon rod? Explain your answer. **NCERT Exemplar**

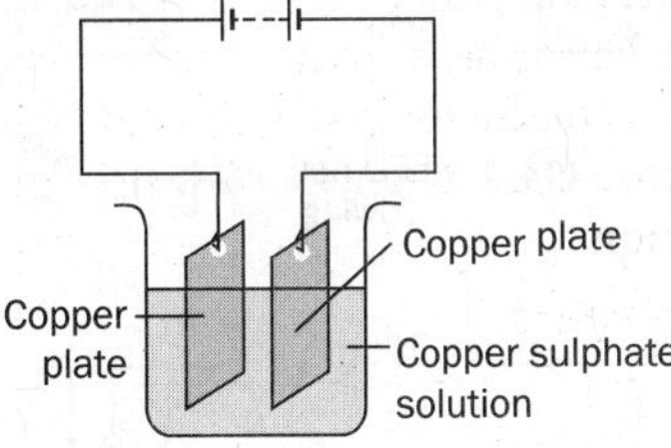

Ans. Copper will not be deposited on the carbon rod because, carbon rod is a poor conductor of electricity. For electroplating, the circuit must be completed and that can be completed only by using the conducting material. Instead of carbon rod, it should be any metal, then only it can be electroplated.

6. Observe the circuit given in figure.

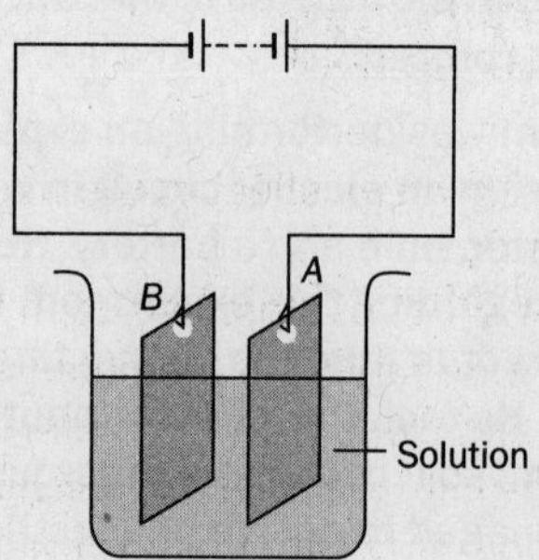

Boojho set up this circuit for purification of copper. What will be the nature of (a) plate *A*, (b) plate *B* (c) and the solution.
Explain the process of purification. **NCERT Exemplar**

Ans.

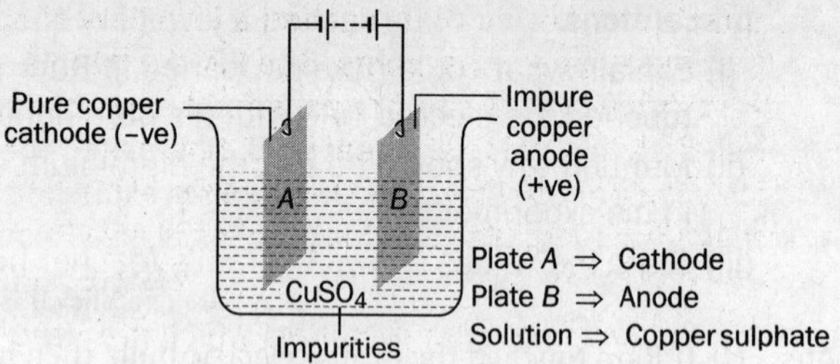

We take $CuSO_4$ solution and dip a pure copper plate as cathode (–ve) and impure copper plate as anode (+ve). Due to voltage of battery, the impurities from the impure sample slowly deposit at the bottom and the copper plate becomes purified.

Case Based Questions

1. Rashmi made separate electric circuits with four different solutions. **Competency Based Que.**

The pictures show what she found.

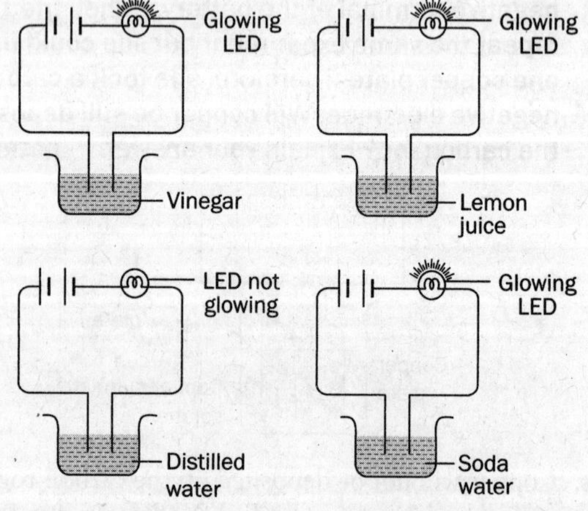

(i) What can be concluded from her activity?
(a) LED glows only in solutions
(b) All four solutions are insulators of electricity
(c) All four solutions are good conductors of electricity
(d) Acids and bases are good conductors of electricity

(ii) Which safety precaution must Rashmi follow while doing this activity?
(a) Wear boots (b) Wear goggles
(c) Wear headphones (d) Wear rubber gloves

(iii) Will an electric device work, if we place the positive terminal of a battery towards the negative point of the device? Explain your answer.

2. Electroplating is the process of adding a surface layer of metal on another metal.

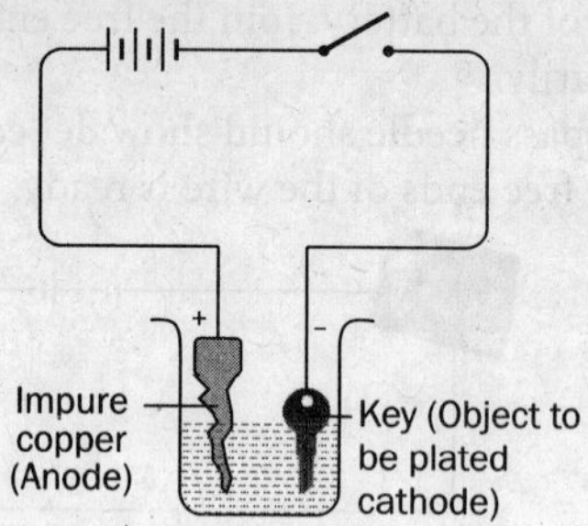

(i) Which of these is true about electroplating? Choose 'Yes' or 'No' for the correct response.

	Is the statement true?	Yes or No
(a)	The solution used contains ions of two metals.	Yes / No
(b)	Metal gets deposited on the electrode connected to the negative terminal.	Yes / No
(c)	A non-metal is used as the electrode connected to the positive terminal.	Yes / No

(ii) Which of these is an example of electroplating?
(a) Colouring of jeans
(b) Painting of a wall
(c) Lamination of a photograph
(d) Gold plating of imitation jewelleries

Ans. 1. (i) (d) (ii) (d)
(iii) The electric device will not work as there will be insufficient amount of electric current flowing from a battery to a device.

2. (i) (a) No (b) Yes (c) No (ii) (d)

Skill Based Questions as per NEP 2020

1. Dharma want to test whether lemon juice is a good conductor of electricity or poor conductor. For this purpose, she made following circuit She observed that bulb does not glow, then she reported to her teacher that lemon juice is an insulator. Her teacher asked her to replace the bulb with any LED and repeat. **Experimental Skill Que.**

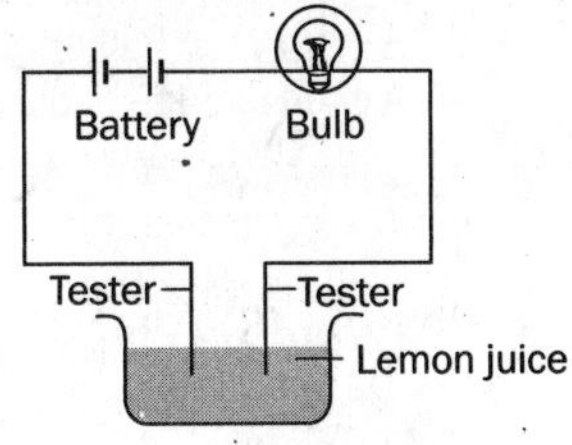

(i) Will the LED glow ?

(ii) What will happen, if she decreases the distance between the two rods of tester ?

2. **Activity : To make an electric pen.**

Materials required : Potassium iodide salt, water, metal sheet, starch solution, paper napkin, copper wire, battery. **Experimental Skill Que.**

Procedure

1. Take potassium iodide salt solution in a beaker, battery and a metal sheet.
2. Connect the metal sheet to the negative terminal of the battery.
3. Add a few drops of starch solution to it.
4. Soak a paper napkin in the potassium iodide solution and place it on the metal sheet.
5. Connect another wire to the positive terminal of the battery. Write with the positive terminal on the paper napkin.

Answers the following questions.

(i) Are you able to write?

(ii) Why is it possible?

3. Sakshi and her mother reached a jewellery shop to purchase some ornaments. She liked a bangle set very much but her mother asked not to purchase that because that was not a real gold. She asked the shopkeeper about it. The shopkeeper explained the process of gold plating, this process is also known as electroplating. **Research Based Que.**

(i) Name some other materials which are used for electroplating.

(ii) What is the need of electroplating in the above case? Give one more use of electroplating.

ASSESSMENT EXERCISE

Part I

Multiple Choice Questions

1. Which of the following metals is used in electroplating to make object more shiny and attractive?
(a) Graphite (b) Zinc
(c) Chromium (d) Iron

2. The object to be electroplated is taken as
(a) cathode
(b) anode
(c) Both can be taken
(d) None of these

3. Water can be dissociated into its components by the process of
(a) electroplating
(b) electrolysis
(c) evaporation
(d) All of these

Fill in the Blanks

4. LEDs glow if longer lead is connected to .... terminal of the battery and shorter lead is connected to ....terminal of the battery.

5. The depositing a layer of gold on silver ornaments is known as ....

True/False

6. Due to heating effect of current, bulb produces light.

7. LEDs are not better options than electric bulb in tester.

8. Vegetable oil mixed in distilled water is a good conductor of electricity.

Assertion-Reason Questions

The following questions consist of two statements-Assertion (A) and Reason (R). Answer these questions by selecting the appropriate option given below.

(a) Both A and R are true and R is the correct explanation of A.
(b) Both A and R are true but R is not the correct explanation of A.
(c) A is true but R is false
(d) A is false but R is true.

9. Assertion (A) Pure water is a poor conductor of electricity.

Reason (R) Pure water contains many minerals which are beneficial for human health.

10. Assertion (A) Water decomposes into hydrogen and oxygen on heating at high temperature.

Reason (R) Chemical effect of current is used to decompose chemical compounds into their elemental form.

Part II

Very Short Answer Type Questions

11. Give two examples of conductor.

12. Name the metal which is usually electroplated on car parts such as bumpers and bicycle handle bars made of steel.

13. Acidified water is electrolysed by using carbon electrodes. What is produced at cathode and at anode?

Short Answer Type Questions

14. Are lemon juice, vinegar and tap water, conductors or insulators?

15. All liquids conduct electricity. Comment.

16. Define cathode and anode.

17. Why chromium is used for electroplating?

Long Answer Type Question

18. A strip of impure copper metal is given to you. Describe briefly, how you will purify it by using the chemical effects of electric current?

Answers

1. (b) 2. (a) 3. (b) 4. positive, negative 5. electroplating
6. True 7. False 8. False 9. (c) 10. (b)

CHAPTER 12

Some Natural Phenomena

Anything that occurs on its own in nature without any kind of human intervention is called a **natural phenomenon**. It may include the weather of a place, fog, storms, winds, tides, volcanic eruptions and cyclones, etc.

In this chapter, we will discuss about two destructive natural phenomena which are **lightning** and **earthquakes** and also discuss about the various steps which can be taken to reduce the destruction caused by these.

12.1 Lightning

A short burst of fire which occurs due to the sudden flow of electric current between two objects is known as an **electric spark**.

It can be observed in our daily life in many situations like, when a plug is loose in its socket, when the wires become loose on an electric pole, etc.

In nature, lightning is caused by the accumulation of charges in the clouds. Initially, people are afraid of lightning and consider it as wrath of God. But we need not to be afraid of lightning, but we should take precautions to protect ourselves from the sparks.

Charging by Rubbing

When an object is rubbed with an appropriate object (like polythene, dry hair), it acquires a small electric charge and it is said to be a **charged object**. So, we can say that an electric charge can be produced by rubbing one object with another object of a specific kind. An object with no electric charge on it, said to be an **uncharged object**.

Some common examples of charging by rubbing are

(i) **When a plastic refill is rubbed with polythene**, it acquires a small electric charge.

(ii) **When a plastic comb is rubbed with dry hair**, it acquires a small electric charge.

Try These 12.1

1. **Which scientist shows the lightning and spark are the same phenomena?**
2. **Can separation of electric charge create a spark?**
3. **Can our body acquire electric charges by rubbing it with some material?**

12.2 Types of Charges and their Interaction

- When two objects are rubbed together, then both the objects get charged with opposite charges. i.e. **positive charge** (+ sign) and **negative charge** (– sign).

  e.g. When we rub a glass rod with a silk cloth, then the charge acquired by a glass rod is positive and silk cloth gets a negative charge.
- Nature of the object determines which object gets a positive charge and which one gets a negative charge.
- Depending upon the type of electric charge on the objects, they will either attract or repel each other.

  (i) **Like charges repel each other** It means, if both the bodies have same type of charges, they will repel each other.

  (ii) **Unlike charges attract each other** It means, if both the bodies have different types of charges, they will attract each other.

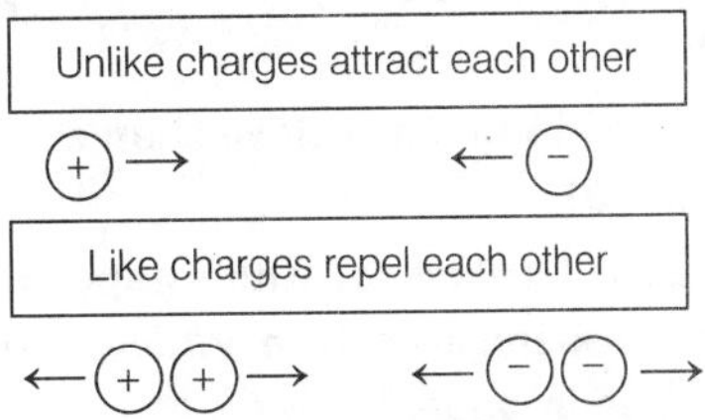

- The electrical charges generated by rubbing are known as **static charges**, e.g. by rubbing plastic comb with dry hair. Static charges do not move themselves. If these charges move, then they constitute electric current.

Transfer of Charges

Electric charge can be transferred from a charged object to an uncharged object, it is called transfer of charge.

On the basis of transfer of charges, we can construct a device called an **electroscope**. It is a device which is used to test whether an object is carrying a charge or not.

Detection of Charge with Electroscope

In order to detect the electric charge on a body, we touch the metal top of electroscope with it and notice the aluminium leaves.

(i) **If the body is electrically charged**, then the leaves diverge out.

(ii) **If the body is electrically uncharged**, then the leaves do not diverge.

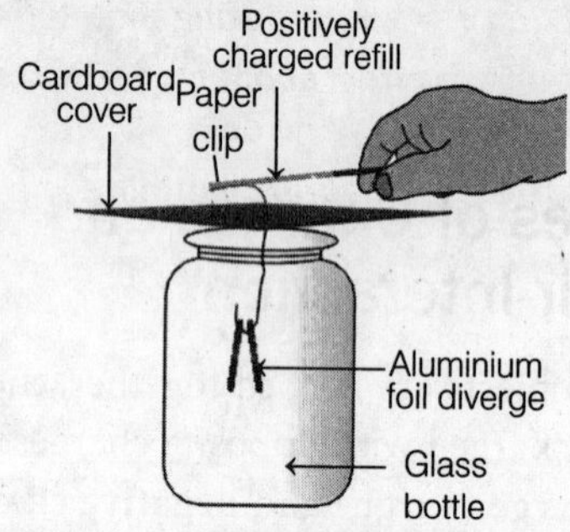

A simple electroscope

An electroscope proves that electric charge can be transferred from a charged object to another through a metal conductor.

Earthing

The process of transferring an electric charge from a charged object to the earth is known as earthing.

When a body losses charge to the earth or any other body, then it is said to be **discharged**.

Note Earthing is provided in buildings to protect us from electrical shocks due to any leakage of electric current.

Try These 12.2

1. **What will happen when a positive charge is kept near a negative charge?**
2. **A student rubbed a glass rod with a paper, the charge acquired by glass rod is positive. Which type of charge will be acquired by paper?**
3. **Name the process of transferring an electric charge from charged object to the earth.**

12.3 Story of Lightning

- Lightning is bright streaks or flashes of light seen in the dark cloud sky, due to transfer of charges from cloud to cloud or from cloud to the earth. It is usually followed by loud cracking sound known as **thunder**.
- During the development of thunderstorm, there is always an upward movement of air while the water droplets move downward.
- These vigorous movements cause separation of charges. Therefore, the top of the cloud becomes positively charged while the bottom of the cloud becomes negatively charged.
- The quantity of opposite electric charges on the top and bottom of storm clouds become very large, so the air which is normally a poor conductor of electricity will remain no longer able to resist their flow. Therefore, the electric charges start flowing with high speed.
- When both the positive and negative charges of cloud meet, then they produce an intense spark of electricity. We observe this electric spark as the flash of lightning in the sky. This process is also called an **electric discharge**.
- The process of electric discharge can occur between two or more clouds or between clouds and the earth.

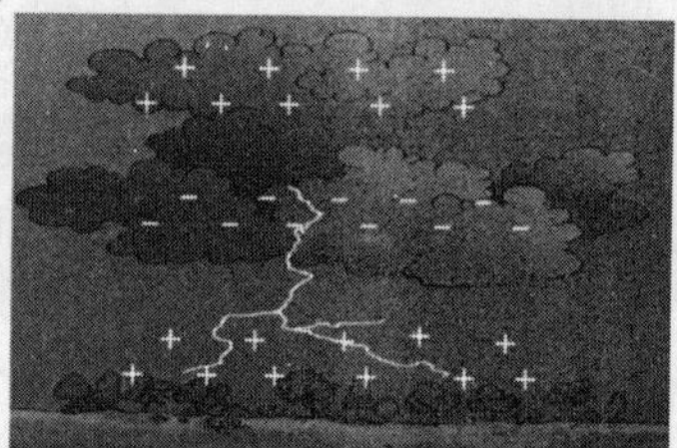

Accumulation of charges leading to lightning

Lightning Safety

During thunderstorms and lightning, a house or a building is always a safe place to be in. Any open place is not a safe place. If you are travelling by car or by bus, then you are safe inside with windows shut.

The following precautionary measures should be taken to protect ourselves from lightning strikes during a thunderstorm.

Lightning safeties Outside the House

- **Do's During a Thunderstorm**

(i) We should stay away from tall trees.

(ii) If we are in a park or forest, we should take shelter under shorter trees.

(iii) If we are in a closed car, we should stay inside with windows and doors closed.

(iv) Squat on the floor. This position makes us the smallest target to be struck.

Safe position during lightning

- **Don'ts During a Thunderstorm**
  - (i) Do not stand in open ground during a thunderstorm.
  - (ii) Do not carry an umbrella as its metal rod is a good conductor of electric charge.
  - (iii) Always stay away from poles or other metallic objects.

Lightning Safeties Inside the House

- **Do's During a Thunderstorm**
  - (i) We should switch OFF the TV as antennas fixed on the roof of a building are prone to lightning strike.
  - (ii) We should avoid touching the metallic pipes and electric equipment connected by electric wires in the house.
  - (iii) We should unplug electrical appliances like refrigerator, computers, etc.
- **Don'ts During a Thunderstorm**
  - (i) We should not use a wired telephone.
  - (ii) We should not take bath as water is a good conductor of electricity.

Lightning Conductor

A device which is used to protect buildings from the effects of lightning is known as lightning conductor.

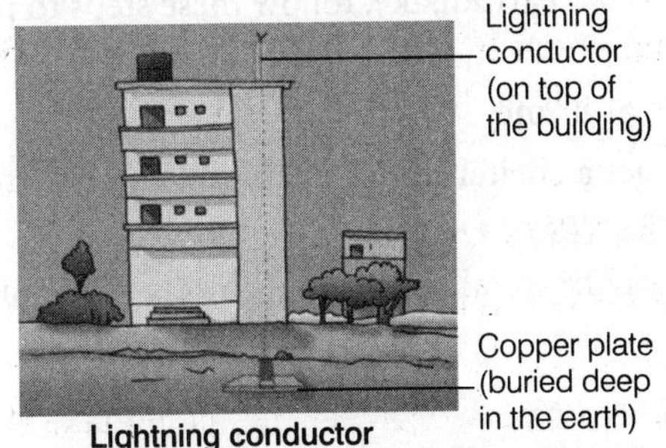

Lightning conductor

The top end of lightning conductor is pointed which is fixed above the highest point of the building. The lower end of the lightning conductor is fixed to a metal plate, buried deep into the ground as shown in figure.

Lightning Conductor Protects the Building from Thunderstorms

- If the lightning strikes on a building, it will firstly strike the top end of lightning conductor.
- The lightning conductor provides an easy route for the transfer of electric charge to the ground.
- The electrical energy of lightning which passes through the metal strip get discharge safely in the ground through the buried metal plate.

  Since, the lightning charges do not pass through the building, no damage is caused.

Try These 12.3

1. **Is it safe to talk on cell phone during thunderstorm?**
2. **A traveller sits under a tree, suddenly he hears thunderstorm. What should he do?**
3. **What is the safe position during lightning?**

12.4 Earthquake

A sudden shaking or trembling of the earth which lasts for a very short time is an earthquake. It can cause an immense damage to buildings, bridges, dams and people.

A sudden shaking of the earth causes tremors and these tremors produce waves on the surface of the earth. Tremors can be caused due to volcano eruption or a meteor hitting the earth.

Causes of Earthquake

The tremors are caused by the disturbances inside the earth. Before learning about the causes, we should know that the earth consists of three layers.

(i) **Core** The innermost part of the earth is called its core.

(ii) **Mantle** The central region of the earth is called mantle.

(iii) **Crust** The outermost layer of the earth is called crust.

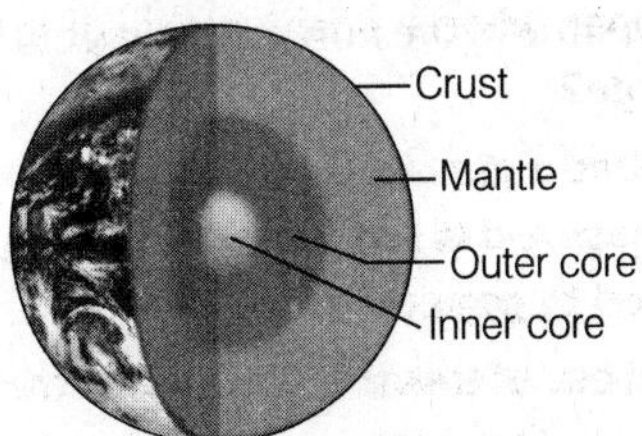

Structure of the Earth

The outermost layer of the earth is fragmented due to which the earth crust is divided into many plates. These plates are in continuous motion.

When these plates collide with one another or brush past one another, then they cause disturbance in the earth's crust. **This disturbance results as an earthquake on the earth surface.**

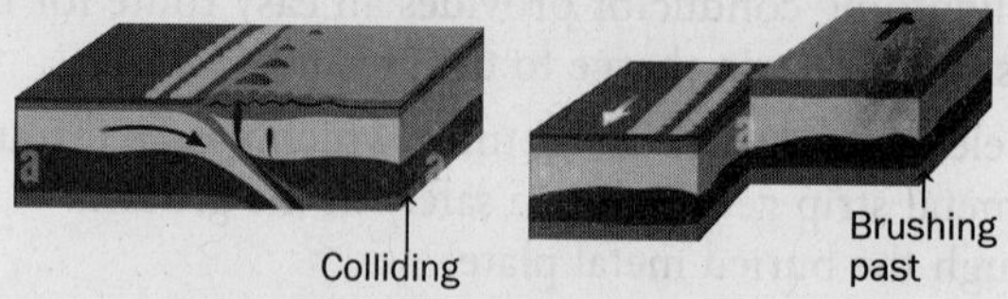

Movements of the earth's plates

SCIENCE INSIGHT The place inside the earth's crust where the earthquake is generated is called **focus of the earthquake.**

Seismic or Fault Zones

As earthquakes are caused by the movement of plates, the boundaries of the plates are the weak-zones where earthquakes are more likely to occur. These weak zones are also known as **seismic** or **fault zones.**

In India, Kashmir, Western and Central Himalayas, the whole of North-East, Rann of Kutch, Rajasthan and the Indo-Gangetic plain are the most threatened areas.

Richter Scale

It is a scale which is used to measure the intensity or magnitude of an earthquake.

Destructive earthquakes have magnitudes higher than 7 on the richter scale.

Seismograph

The seismic waves are those waves which are produced by tremors on the earth surface. These waves are recorded by an instrument called the **seismograph.**

- This instrument is simply a vibrating rod or a pendulum which starts vibrating when tremors occur.
- A pen is attached to the vibrating system and this pen records the seismic waves on a paper which moves under it.
- By studying these waves, scientists can construct a complete map of the earthquake, as shown in figure. They can also calculate its power to cause destruction.

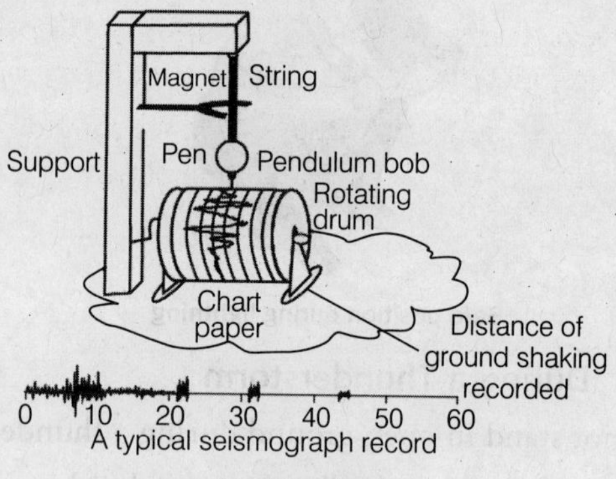

A seismograph

Protections Against Earthquake

Some of the important precautions which can be taken by the people living in seismic zones are as follows

(i) All the quake-proof houses should be constructed by using modern building technology. For which, we should consult a qualified architects and structural engineers.

(ii) Even in highly seismic areas, it is advisable to use mud or timber for building houses, as these are better than heavy material which keep roofs as light as possible.

(iii) There should be the tight fixation of cupboards and shelves to the wall, so that they do not fall when shaking occurs.

(iv) The heavy mirrors, photo frames, water heaters, etc., should be mounted to the wall at low levels, so that in the event of an earthquake, they do not fall on the people.

(v) Since, some buildings may catch fire due to an earthquake, it is necessary that all buildings, especially tall buildings, have fire fighting equipment in working order.

In the event of an earthquake, follow these steps to protect yourself.

- **If you are at home**

(i) Try to get a shelter under a table and stay there till the shaking stops.

(ii) Stay away from tall and heavy objects as they may fall on you.

(iii) If you are on bed, then do not get up. Immediately, protect your head with a pillow.

- **If you are outside your home**
  (i) Observe a clear spot away from buildings, trees and overhead power lines. Drop to the ground.
  (ii) Besides this, if we are in car or bus, we should not come out. The car should be driven slowly to a clear spot.

Try These 12.4

1. The outer most layer of the earth is
   (a) core (b) mantle (c) crust
2. Nepal recorded the magnitude of earthquake as more than 7. Is it destructive or non-destructive earthquake?
3. Which device is used to measure the magnitude of earthquake?

Science Glossary

Electric spark A short burst of fire which occurs due to the sudden flow of electric current between two objects.

Lightning Lightning is an electric spark but on a huge scale.

Electroscope A device which is used to test whether an object is carrying charge or not.

Earthing The process of transferring an electric charge from a charged object to the earth.

Lightning conductor A device which is used to protect buildings from the effects of lightning.

Earthquake A sudden shaking or trembling of the earth which lasts for a very short time.

Richter scale A scale which is used to measure the intensity or magnitude of an earthquake.

Let's Investigate

ACTIVITY 1 (Page 151)

Aim To prove that an object gets electrically charged by rubbing.

Material Required A ball pen refill, a small piece of paper, dry leaf, polythene, etc.

Procedure

1. Firstly, take a ball pen refill and rub it vigorously with a piece of polythene.
2. Now, bring it close to a piece of paper. Be ensure that the rubbed part of refill should not be touched by our hand. We will find that the refill attracts the tiny pieces of paper.
3. Repeat the activity with small pieces of dry leaf, husk and mustard seeds and note down the observation. We will find that the refill attracts the tiny pieces in each case.

Conclusion We can conclude that when the plastic refill is rubbed with polythene, dry leaf or mustard seeds etc., it acquires a small electric charge.

Viva Questions

1. Which type of charges are generated by rubbing?
2. Can you charge an object by rubbing it with an object of the same material?

ACTIVITY 2 (Page 151)

Aim To record that different objects get electrically charged when rubbed with different materials.

Material Required Refill, balloon, eraser, steel spoon, polythene, dry hair, silk cloth.

Procedure

1. Collect the objects given in the table and rub them against the materials listed next to it in the table.
2. Bring the charged object (rubbed object) close to tiny pieces of paper and observe, it attracts or not.

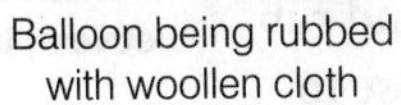
Balloon being rubbed with woollen cloth

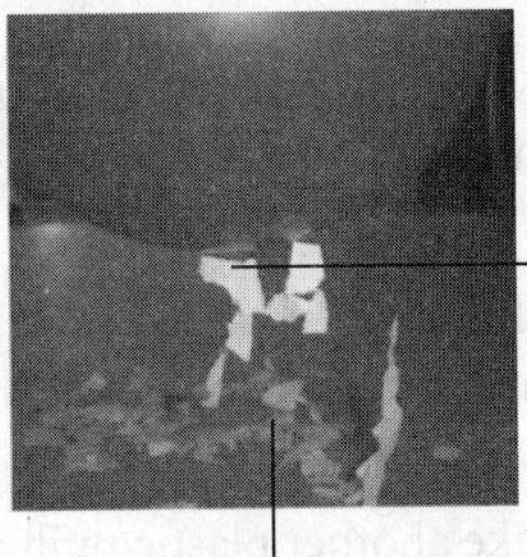

Object gets electrically charged by rubbing

3. Record your observations in the table.

Objects rubbed	Materials used for rubbing	Attracts / does not attracts pieces of paper	Charged /not charged
Refill	Polythene, woolen cloth	Yes	Charged
Balloon	Dry hair	Yes	Charged
Eraser	Wool	Yes	Charged
Steel spoon	Woolen cloth	No	Not charged

Conclusion We have concluded from observation table that the objects rubbed with different materials get charged and attracts a tiny pieces of paper except steel spoon because it is a good conductor.

Viva Questions

1. Does a charged refill attract tiny piece of paper?
2. Can we charge a steel spoon by rubbing it with a silk cloth?

ACTIVITY 3 (Page 152)

Aim To understand the interaction between two types of electric charges.

Material Required Two inflated balloons, two refill, woollen cloth, polythene.

Procedure

1. Firstly, hang two inflated balloons in such a way that they do not touch each other.
2. Now, rub both the balloons with a woollen cloth and release them.

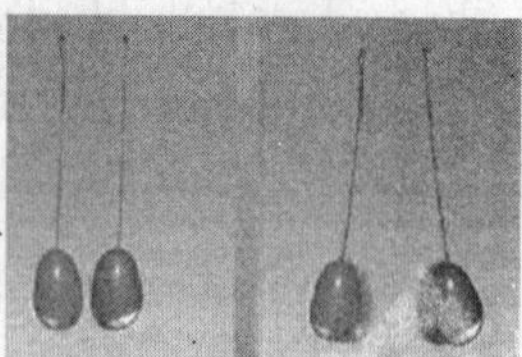

Like charges repel each other

We will observe that both the balloons start repelling each other. They both acquire same charge that is negative charge.

3. Now, bring a plastic refill and rub it with polythene. It will acquire some charge.
4. Place this charged plastic refill in a glass tumbler using the tumbler as a stand.

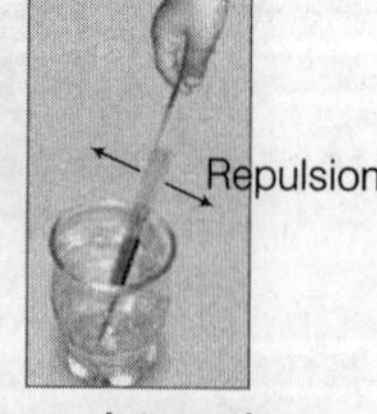

Interaction between like

5. Now, take another plastic refill and rub it with polythene and bring it close to the charged refill which is already placed in glass tumbler.

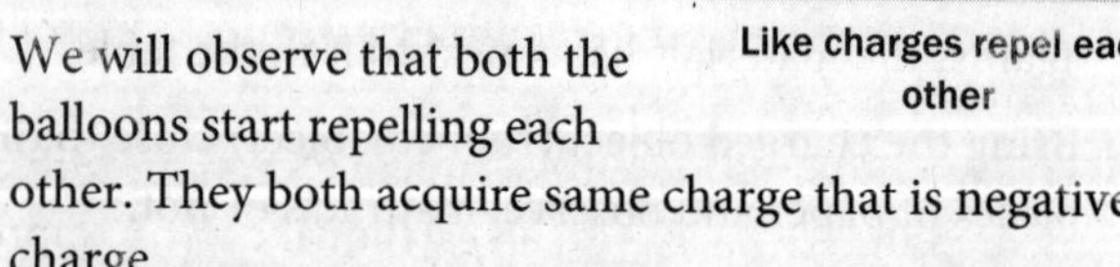

We will find that the charged refill in the tumbler moves away. It means both the refills repel each other, as they acquire same charges that is positive charge.

6. Again, rub a refill with polythene and place it gently in a glass tumbler as before.
7. Now, bring an inflated charged balloon near the refill.

We will observe that the charged refill moves towards the charged balloon. As, they both acquire different charges.

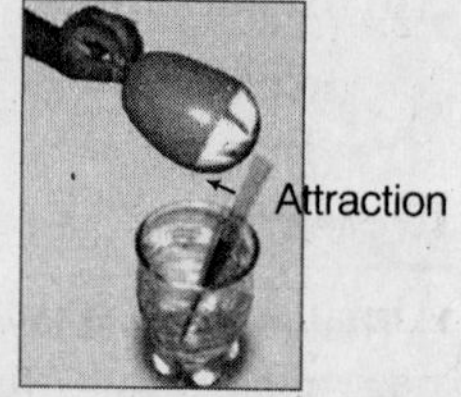

Unlike charges attract each other

Conclusion We have concluded from the activity that like charges repel each other and unlike charges attract each other.

Viva Questions

1. What are the two properties of electric charges?
2. What do you observe when two charged plastic refill come close to each other?

ACTIVITY 4 (Page 153)

Aim To understand the working of an electroscope.

Material Required An empty jam bottle, a cardboard, a metal paper clip, two small pieces of aluminium foil, a refill.

Procedure

1. Choose an empty jam bottle and take a piece of cardboard slightly bigger in size than the mouth of the bottle.
2. Now, pierce a hole in the cardboard, so that a metal paper clip can be inserted.
3. Cut two strips of aluminium foil about 4cm × 1 cm each. Hang them on the paper clip as shown in the figure.
4. Now, fix the paper clip in the cardboard lid, so that it gets perpendicular to it as shown in the figure.
5. Now, charge a refill and make it touch with the end of the paper clip. We can see that the two aluminium foils move away from each other.
6. Gently, touch the other charged bodies with the ends of paper clip. Here, we find no differences in the working of foil strips.

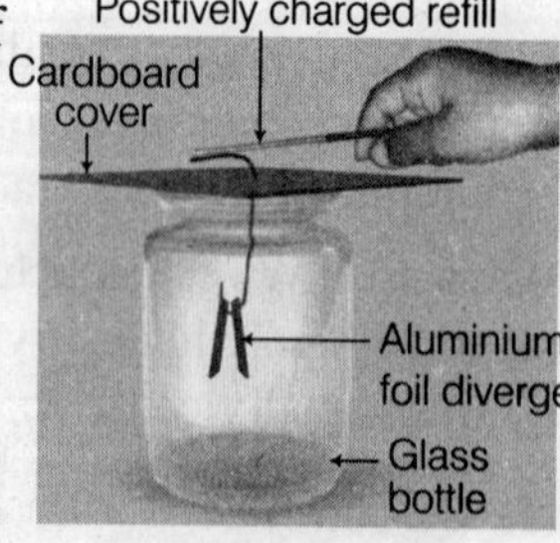

A simple electroscope

Conclusion We have concluded that a charged body transfers all its charges to aluminium foil through paper clip which causes the aluminium leaves to diverge. Therefore, greater the amount of electric charge on a body, greater the aluminium leaves will diverge.

Viva Questions

1. What is the working principle of electroscope ?
2. Which device is used to detect the presence of charges on a body?

ACTIVITY 5 (Page 157)

Aim To prepare a short report on the suffering of the people during and after the earthquakes.

Material Required Newspapers, magazines.

Procedure

1. Collect some newspapers and magazines of different publishers.
2. Read the articles carefully based on the earthquakes.
3. Now, collect some pictures showing the damage caused by these earthquakes from these newspapers and magazines.
4. Make a short report on the destruction caused by earthquakes.

Ground water pipes breakdown

Building collapse

Tsunami in coastal areas

Bridge breakdown

Damaging effects of earthquake

Conclusion Earthquake is a natural calamity. It is a sudden shaking or trembling of the earth which lasts for a short time. Some of the damaging effects of an earthquake are as follows

(i) Earthquake may cause landslides and tsunami in hilly and coastal areas.

(ii) Earthquake may break ground water pipe which disrupts the water supply system.

(iii) Earthquake brings destruction of buildings, dams, railway tracks, roads, etc.

(iv) Earthquake may cut-off the communication system and the affected areas get totally disconnected from the rest of world.

Viva Questions

1. Which device is used to measure the intensity of an earthquake?
2. Name some other calamities caused by an earthquake.

ACTIVITY 6 (Page 158)

Aim To make a report of some devastation caused by the tsunami in India.

Material Required A political world map.

Procedure

1. Firstly, take a world map.
2. Now, locate the eastern coast and Andaman and Nicobar islands in India. Mark other countries around the Indian ocean which could have suffered damage from tsunami.
3. Now, collect some information from your parents or other elders to make a report of some devastation caused by tsunami in India.
4. Prepare a report in neat and clean handwriting.

Conclusion We have located the eastern coast of India, Andaman and Nicobar island and other countries around the Indian ocean.

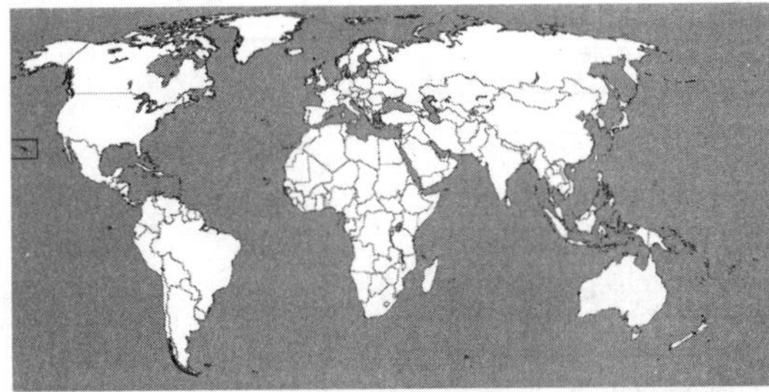

1. Bangladesh	5. Malaysia	9. Madagascar
2. Myanmar	6. Somalia	10. South Africa
3. Thailand	7. Kenya	11. Seychelles
4. Indonesia	8. Tanzania	12. Maldives

Some information of the devastation caused by tsunami in India is given above.

A major tsunami occurred in the Indian Ocean on 26th December 2004. At 8 : 38 AM, an earthquake of 6.1 approx magnitudes was felt in Andaman island. At 9 : 00 AM, this affected India's South-Eastern coast.

Thousands of people died, many people lost their families. The coastal area destroyed completely. Many fisherman and their community were ruined by the tsunami.

It was one of the most devastating natural calamities, people have ever witnessed.

Viva Questions

1. What are the safety measures that should be taken by government during the tsunami?
2. Does tectonic plate movement cause tsunami ?

Earthquake

A sudden shaking or trembling of earth which lasts for a very short time.

- **Cause**
  When the plates of crust collide with one another.
- **Seismic or Fault Zones**
  Boundaries of plates where earthquakes are more likely to occur.
- **Richter Scale**
  Used to measure the intensity/magnitude of earthquake.
- **Seismograph**
  Instrument used to record the motion of ground during earthquake.
- **Protections against Earthquake**
  - Quake-proof houses should be constructed.
  - Tight fixation of cupboards shalves to wall.
  - Use mud/timber for building houses.

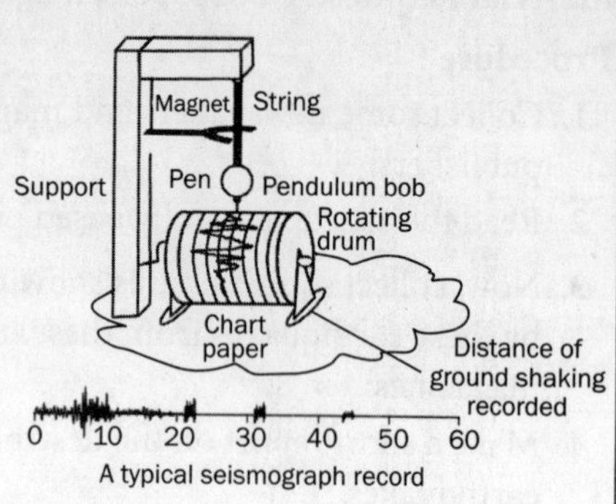

A typical seismograph record

Electric Spark

Short burst of fire which occur due to sudden flow of electric current between two objects.

Charges

When two objects are rubbed together, then both the object get charged with opposite charges, i.e.

- Positive charge (+ve sign)
- Negative charge (–ve sign)

- **Charging by Rubbing**
  When an object is rubbed with an appropriate object, it acquires a small electric charge.
- **Interaction of Charges**
  - Like charges repel each other.

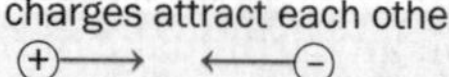

  - Unlike charges attract each other.

Lightning

Bright streaks of light seen in dark cloud sky, followed by thunder (loud sound).

- **Lightning Conductor**
  Device used to protect buildings from the effects of lightning.
- **Lightning Safety Inside the House**
  - Switch OFF TV
  - Avoid touching metallic and electric things
  - Avoid using a wired telephones
  - Avoid taking bath
- **Lightning Safety Outside the House**
  - Stay away from tall trees.
  - Take shelter under shorter tree.
  - Stay inside closed car with windows and door closed.
  - Don't stand in open ground.
  - Don't carry umbrella.
  - Stay away from metallic objects.

Transfer of Charges

Electric charges can be transferred from charged object to an uncharged object.

- **Earthing**
  Process of transferring an electric charge from a charged object to the earth.
- **Electroscope**
  An electroscope proves that electrical charge can be transferred from a charged object to another through a metallic conductor.

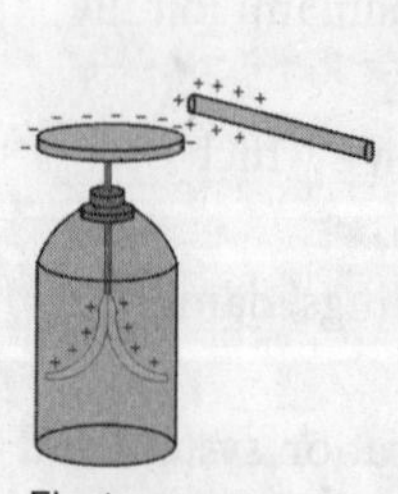
Electroscope

NCERT FOLDER

Complete Explanations of all NCERT's Questions

Intext Questions

Q1. What is an earthquake? **Page 157**

Ans. An earthquake is a sudden shaking or trembling of the earth which lasts for a very short time.

Q2. What causes an earthquake? **Page 158**

Ans. The outermost layer of the earth is fragmented. Each fragment is known as plates. These plates are in continuous motion. When these plates collide with one another, then they cause disturbance in the earth's crust. This disturbance shows up as an earthquake on the earth surface.

Q3. What could cause a disturbance inside the earth? **Page 158**

Ans. The movement of tectonic plates, when it collide with one another, then it cause a disturbance inside the earth.

Q4. If scientists know so much about earthquakes, can they also predict when and where next one will strike? **Page 159**

Ans. No, it is not yet possible to predict when and where the next earthquake might occur because they cause disturbance in the earth's crust.

Exercise

Q1. Which of the following cannot be charged easily by friction?

(a) A plastic scale
(b) A copper rod
(c) An inflated balloon
(d) A woollen cloth

Ans. (b) As copper is a conductor, so on rubbing it, the charges start flowing across the length of copper rod which constitute electric current. So, copper cannot be charged easily by friction.

Q2. When a glass rod is rubbed with a piece of silk cloth, the rod

(a) and the cloth both acquire positive charge
(b) becomes positively charged, while the cloth has a negative charge
(c) and the cloth both acquire negative charge
(d) becomes negatively charged, while the cloth has a positive charge

Ans. (b) becomes positively charged, while the cloth has a negative charge.

Q3. Write T against True and F against False in the following statements.

(i) Like charges attracts each other.
(ii) A charged glass rod attracts a charged plastic straw.
(iii) Lightning conductor cannot protect a building from lightning.
(iv) Earthquakes can be predicted in advance.

Ans. (i) F, as like charges repel each other and unlike charges attract each other.

(ii) T, but it may repel also if charges are similar.

(iii) F, as lightning conductor can protect a building from lightning.

(iv) F, as it is not possible to predict the occurrence of earthquakes.

Q4. Sometimes, a crackling sound is heard while taking off a sweater during winters. Explain.

Ans. The crackling sound heard, while taking off a sweater during winters is due to rubbing of two objects, i.e. body and the wool. The rubbing of the static charges produces lightning or the spark in our clothes that produces a crackling sound. The electric charges produced by rubbing are called static charges.

Q5. Explain, why a charged body losses its charge, if we touch it with our hand?

Ans. When we touch a charged body, it losses its charge due to the process of earthing. As our body is a good conductor of electricity and transfers the charge to the earth.

Q6. Name the scale, on which the destructive energy of an earthquake is measured. An earthquake measures 3 on this scale. Would it be recorded by a seismograph? Is it likely to cause much damage?

Ans. Destructive energy of an earthquake is measured on Richter scale.
Yes, the earthquake will be recorded by a seismograph in the form of seismic waves.
The earthquake measuring 3 on Richter scale cannot cause much damage.

Q7. Suggest three measures to protect ourselves from lightning.

Ans. Lightning is an electric spark on huge scale which is caused by the accumulation of charges in clouds.

Some measures to protect ourselves from lightning are as follows

(i) We should stay under covered area or inside the room.

(ii) We should not take bath during lightning.

(iii) We should not use TV, phone, computers during lightning.

Q 8. Explain, why a charged balloon is repelled by another charged balloon, whereas an uncharged balloon is attracted by another charged balloon?

Ans. Since, both the balloons acquire the same charges when being charged upon rubbing. Thus, they repel each other.

On the other hand, one charged and the other uncharged balloon attract each other. This is due to the property of charges that unlike charges attract each other. The uncharged balloon having opposite charge is attracted by the other charged balloon.

Q 9. Describe with the help of a diagram, an instrument which can be used to detect a charged body.

Ans. The instrument which is used to detect a charged body is an electroscope.

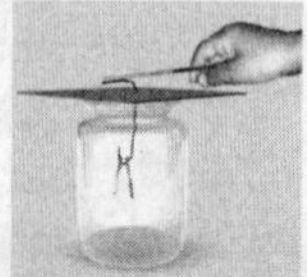

A simple electroscope

Construction

(i) Take an empty jam bottle.

(ii) Take a piece of cardboard slightly bigger in size than the mouth of the bottle.

(iii) Pierce a hole in it, so that a metal paper clip can be inserted.

(iv) Open out the paper clip.

(v) Cut two strips of aluminium foil about 4×1 cm each. Hang them on paper clip.

(vi) Insert the paper clip in the cardboard, so that it remains perpendicular to it.

(vii) Charge a refill and touch it with the end of the paper clip.

Working

(i) The aluminium foil strips receive the same charge from the charged refill through the paper clip. The strips carrying the same charge repel each other, they become wide open.

(ii) Touch the end of paper clip gently with hand and we will find a change in the foil strip. Repetition gives the same result.

Q 10. List three states in India where earthquakes are more likely to strike.

Ans. Some earthquake prone states of India are as follows

(i) Kashmir (ii) Gujarat

(iii) Rajasthan

Q 11. Suppose you are outside your home and an earthquake strikes. What precautions would you take to protect yourself?

Ans. The precautions are as follows

(i) We should move to an open space, where trees and buildings are not available.

(ii) If we are driving, we should not come out. We should slow down the vehicle and move slowly away from that area to a safe spot.

Q 12. The weather department has predicted that a thunderstorm is likely to occur on a certain day. Suppose you have to go out on that day. Would you carry an umbrella? Explain.

Ans. Carrying an umbrella is not advisable during thunderstorm. As the rod of umbrella and its supporting wires are made up of metals. Thus, during thunderstorm, the conducting objects should be avoided.

REVIEW EXERCISE

Including Competency Based Questions

Part I

Multiple Choice Questions

1. Lightning occurs due to
(a) rain (b) wind
(c) electric discharge (d) None of these

2. Sparks can be seen on the electric poles, due to which wire becomes
(a) loose (b) tight
(c) wrinkle (d) None of these

3. The like charges
(a) repel each other
(b) attract each other
(c) no interaction takes place
(d) All of the above

4. The charge acquired by glass rod when it is rubbed with a silk is
(a) positive (b) negative
(c) Both (a) and (b) (d) None of these

5. Two charged objects are brought close to each other. Choose the most appropriate statement from the following options. NCERT Exemplar
(a) They may attract.
(b) They may repel.
(c) They may attract or repel depending on the type of charges they carry.
(d) There will be no effect.

6. Which of the following can be charged with static electricity?
(a) Alloy (b) Metal
(c) Insulator (d) Semiconductor

7. Electric current is to be passed from one body to another. For this purpose, the two bodies must be joined by
(a) cotton thread (b) plastic string
(c) copper wire (d) rubber band

8. An electroscope is a device which is used to find, if an object is NCERT Exemplar
(a) charged (b) magnetic
(c) free of cracks (d) hot

9. Lightning conductor
(a) destroys the building
(b) protects the building
(c) does not effect the building
(d) None of the above

10. Where is the lightning rod attached to protect the building from lightning?
(a) On the top of building
(b) In the middle of building
(c) On the bottom of building
(d) All of the above

11. Which of the following is not likely to cause tsunami? NCERT Exemplar
(a) A major nuclear explosion under sea
(b) Earthquake
(c) Volcanic eruption
(d) Lightning

12. The movement of the earth's plates causes
(a) cyclones (b) lightning
(c) earthquake (d) thunderstorms

13. The earth's plate responsible for causing earthquake is
(a) the crust of the earth
(b) the mantle of the earth
(c) the inner core of the earth
(d) the outer core of the earth

14. Consider the list of terms given below Competency Based Que.

(i) Seismic (ii) Mantle
(iii) Fault zone (iv) Inner core

The boundaries of the earth's plate are known as
(a) (i) and (ii) (b) (i) and (iii)
(c) (iii) and (iv) (d) (ii), (iii) and (iv)

15. The waves produced on the earth's surface is called
(a) radio waves
(b) longitudinal waves
(c) microwaves
(d) seismic waves

16. Tsunami means
(a) earthquake
(b) flood
(c) earthquake under sea
(d) eruption of volcano is sea

17. The outermost layer of the earth is called Competency Based Que.
(a) mantle (b) outer core
(c) crust (d) inner core

18. **Major earthquakes are less likely to occur in** NCERT Exemplar

(a) North-East India (b) Rajasthan
(c) Rann of Kutch (d) Orissa

19. **Which instrument is used to measure earthquake?**

(a) Polygraph (b) Seismograph
(c) Biometer (d) Thermometer

20. **Consider the list of terms given below** NCERT Exemplar

(i) Tsunami (ii) Landslide
(iii) Floods (iv) Lightning

Earthquakes can cause

(a) (i), (ii) and (iii) (b) (ii) and (iv)
(c) (ii), (iii) and (iv) (d) (iii) and (iv)

Answers

1. (c)	**2.** (a)	**3.** (a)	**4.** (a)
5. (c)	**6.** (c)	**7.** (c)	**8.** (a)
9. (b)	**10.** (a)	**11.** (d)	**12.** (c)
13. (d)	**14.** (b)	**15.** (d)	**16.** (c)
17. (c)	**18.** (d)	**19.** (b)	**20.** (a)

Fill in the Blanks

1. When charges move, they constitute an ...... current.

2. ...... types of charges are gained by rubbing objects.

3. The process of transfer of charge from a charged object to the earth is called ....

4. Lightning strike could destroy ...... and ....

5. Lightning conductor can ...... buildings from the effect of lightning.

6. Earthquake is caused by a ...... deep inside the earth's crust.

Answers

1. electric	**2.** Two	**3.** earthing
4. life, property	**5.** protect	**6.** disturbance

True/False

1. The process of electric discharge cannot occur between clouds and the earth. NCERT Exemplar

2. Bathing outdoors should be avoided during thunderstorm.

3. Earthquakes can occur anytime all over the world.

4. The plates of the outermost layer of the earth are always in continuous motion. NCERT Exemplar

5. Tremors on the earth can also be caused by the eruption of a volcano. NCERT Exemplar

Answers

1. False **2.** True **3.** True **4.** True **5.** True

Match the Columns

1. **Match the Column I with Column II.**

	Column I		Column II
(a)	Richter scale	(i)	Sudden shaking of the earth
(b)	Waves recorder	(ii)	Conductor
(c)	Earthquake	(iii)	Earthing
(d)	Copper	(iv)	Earthquake under sea
(e)	Transfer of charge to the earth	(v)	Lightning
(f)	Tsunami	(vi)	Seismograph
(g)	Sudden discharge of charges	(vii)	Intensity of earthquake

Answer

1. (a)–(vii), (b)–(vi), (c)–(i), (d)–(ii), (e)–(iii), (f)–(iv), (g)–(v)

Assertion-Reason Questions

The following questions consist of two statements - Assertion (A) and Reason (R). Answer these questions by selecting the appropriate option given below.

(a) Both A and R are true and R is the correct explanation of A.
(b) Both A and R are true but R is not the correct explanation of A.
(c) A is true but R is false.
(d) A is false but R is true.

1. **Assertion** (A) The most destructive earthquakes have magnitude more than 7 on richter scale.
Reason (R) We should move inside our houses or tall buildings during earthquakes.

2. **Assertion** (A) A charged body repels an uncharged body.
Reason (R) Like charges repel each other while unlike charges attract each other.

3. **Assertion** (A) An earthquake is a sudden shaking or trembling of the earth which lasts for a short time.
Reason (R) The plates inside the earth crust collide with one another which causes earthquake.

4. **Assertion** (A) An electroscope is a device which is used to test whether an object is carrying charge or not.
Reason (R) Electroscope is based on the transfer of charges.

Answers

1. (c) We should not move inside our house or tall buildings during an earthquake because tall buildings may collapse and cause accident.
2. (d) A charged body always attracts an uncharged body.
3. (a) Earthquake are caused by sudden shaking colliding of plates inside earth's crust.
4. (a) Electroscope determines whether any object is charged or not by the transfer to charges.

Case Based Questions

1. Amit was travelling in a taxi when he saw lightning at some distance. He heard a loud thunder after a few seconds. **Competency Based Qus.**

(i) What should Amit do immediately to remain safe?

(a) Increase the speed of the car

(b) Stop the car and remain seated inside

(c) Stop the car and take shelter inside a building

(d) Turn the car and travel in the opposite direction

(ii) Which of these conditions results in lightning?

(a) Negative and positive charges meeting

(b) The number of negative charges increasing

(c) The number of positive charges increasing

(d) Negative and positive charges moving away from each other.

(iii) A lightning conductor protects a building from lightning. What is a lightning conductor made of?

(a) Glass (b) Metal

(c) Wood (d) Plastic

2. The diagram shows the focus of an earthquake. Focus is the point inside the earth's crust where the earthquake originates. 1, 2, 3 and 4 are four locations on the earth's surface.

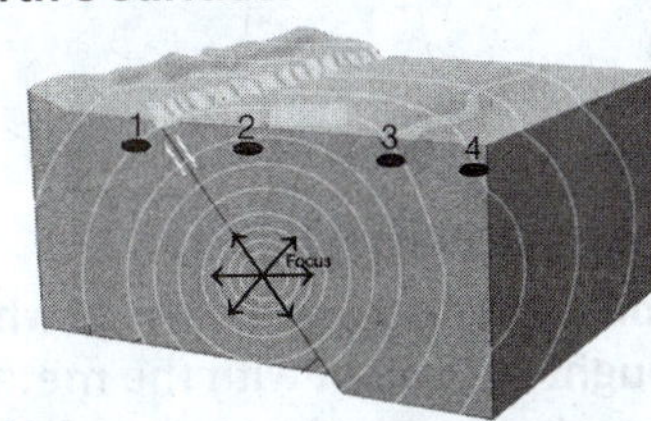

(i) In which location will the effect of the earthquake be maximum?

(a) Location 1 (b) Location 2

(c) Location 3 (d) Location 4

(ii) Raju was in his garden when an earthquake hit the place. What should Raju do to remain safe?

(a) Move to an open space

(b) Run away from the place

(c) Take shelter under a staircase

(d) Take shelter under a large tree

3. Richter scale measures the strength of earthquakes.

Richter scale measurement of the earthquake	Example of damages due to the earthquake
3.0-3.9	No damages but some vibrations felt
4.0-4.9	Cracks in windows, some unstable objects fall
5.0-5.9	Building walls may collapse, movement of furniture
6.0-6.9	Building roofs may collapse, loss of few lives
7.0-79	Cracks on ground, underground pipes broken, loss of many lives

(i) The damages from an earthquake are listed below.

2 people died

5 building roofs collapsed

12 building walls collapsed

What could be the likely reading on the richter scale for the earthquake?

(a) 4.8 (b) 5.4

(c) 6.5 (d) 7.3

(ii) Which of these statements is true about earthquake?

(a) Earthquakes can cause soil erosion.

(b) Most of the earthquakes occur in mountain regions.

(c) The location and duration of earthquakes can be predicted.

(d) Earthquakes are caused by the movement of underground plates.

Answers

1. (i) (b), (ii) (a), (iii) (b)
2. (i) (b), (ii) (a)
3. (i) (c), (ii) (d)

Part II

Very Short Answer Type Questions

1. If a charged plastic straw is brought near another uncharged plastic straw, what will happen? **NCERT Exemplar**

Ans. Any charged plastic straw will attract another uncharged plastic straw, when brought near to it.

2. Mention the name of the nature of charges on a glass rod and silk cloth when both of them are rubbed with each other.

Ans. When a glass rod and silk cloth are rubbed with each other, then the positive charge gets induced on glass rod and negative charge on silk clothes.

3. Plastic straws *A* and *B* are rubbed with dry cotton cloth. What will happen, if they are brought near each other? **NCERT Exemplar**

Ans. The rods will acquire the similar charge and hence they will repel each other.

4. If a charged plastic straw is brought near another uncharged plastic straw, then what actually happens?

Ans. If a charged plastic straw is brought near the uncharged plastic straw, then they will attract each other.

5. The aluminium strips in an electroscope as shown in figure are replaced by plastic strips and a charged body is brought in contact with the metal clip. What will happen? **Competency Based Que.**

Ans. If aluminium strips are replaced by plastic strips, we cannot predict whether the object is charged or not.

6. If an object is touched with the metal top of an electroscope its aluminium leaves diverge, then what conclusion do we get from this observation?

Ans. We get conclude from this observation that the object has an electric charge on it.

7. How earthing helps to protect buildings?

Ans. Earthing helps to transfer unwanted electric charges in electrical circuits to flow to earth and in such a way it prevents electrical equipments from damage.

8. Briefly, explain what did the people think the cause of lightnings in the ancient time?

Ans. In ancient times, people were scared of lightning and thought that the wrath of god was visiting to them.

9. During thunderstorm, when we are in an open place away from home, then where should we take shelter?

Ans. We should take shelter under small trees.

10. In order to protect the building from lightning, briefly mention the place, where should the lightning rod be attached?

Ans. The lightning rod should be attached on the top of the building.

Short Answer Type Questions

1. You might have observed on a dry day that when you touch the screen of a television or computer monitor (with picture tube), you get a slight shock. Why does it happen? **NCERT Exemplar**

Ans. It happens because the television screen or computer monitor are charged and have static charges. When we touch them with our hands which are uncharged, the charges attract our hands and transfer through our hands and we get a small shock.

2. In an electroscope, if a negatively charged body is brought in contact with the metal clip, the strips of the electroscope diverge. If now another charged object carrying equal amount of positive charge is brought in contact with the clip, what will happen? **NCERT Exemplar**

Ans. As, it is clear from the figure whether we bring a positive or negative rod, the strips will repel always because equal amount of charges are transferred to the strips and like charges always repel each other.

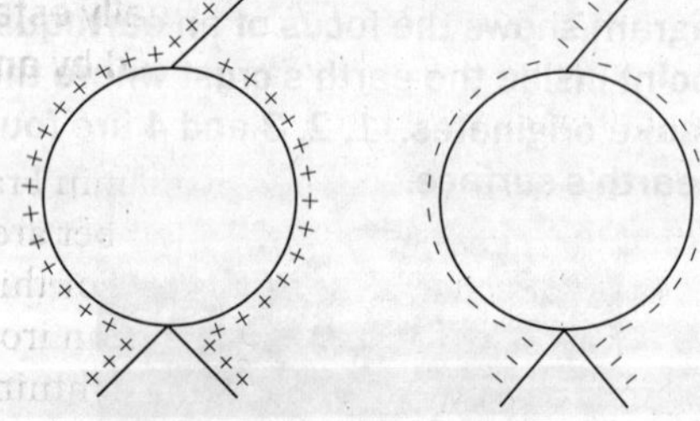

3. The strips of an electroscope diverge when a charged body is brought in contact with the metal clip. Now the clip is touched gently by our hand. What will happen to the strips? Explain. **Competency Based Que.**

Ans. If we touch the strip while standing on ground (not on any insulating base), the charges will pass through our hand to the ground because they will get the path to flow and strips will not diverge.

4. During the construction of a building, the lightning conductor was left hanging in the air by mistake. Would the lightning conductor be still effective? Explain. **NCERT Exemplar**

Ans. Lightning conductor will not work, if left hanging in the air because in order to work, it must be installed properly and grounded using any metal (copper) plate.

5. Explain the concept of lightning rod. Also, explain how it protects the buildings?

Ans. The device which is used to protect tall buildings from the effect of lightning is called lightning conductor. Also, metallic rod is installed in the walls of the buildings during its construction and one end of the rod is kept out in air and the other end is fixed in the ground.

So, it provides an easy route for transfer of electric discharge to the earth.

6. Identify the lightning conductor and the copper plate in figure. NCERT Exemplar

Ans.

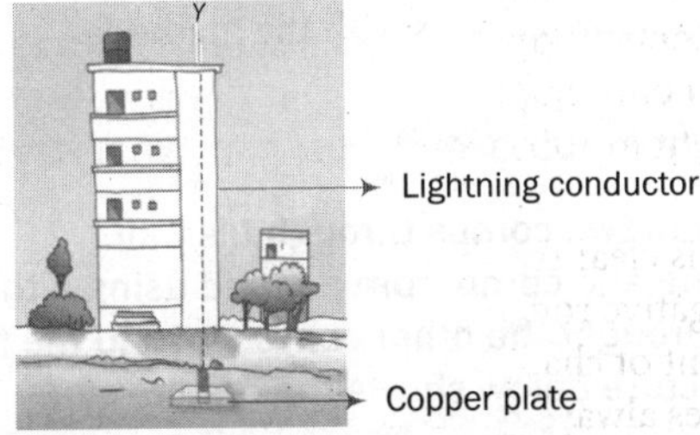

7. Give the name of scientist who actually established the relation between sparks produced by amber and thunderstorms. Explain in brief.

Ans. There was an American scientist Benjamin Franklin who established that sparks produced by amber are similar to the sparks produced by thunderstorm. For this, he flew a kite tied with a silken thread which had an iron key attached to it on rainy day. So, during lightning, he experienced the shock through iron key, which proved that clouds also carried charges.

8. If air and cloud are good conductors of electricity, do you think lightning could occur? Explain. NCERT Exemplar

Ans. No, there will not be lightning at all because all the charges collected at the clouds will continuously transfer through air and there will be no lightning.

9. Explain the electric discharge that occurs in clouds.

Ans. During thundering, negative charges get accumulated near the clouds and positive charges accumulate near the ground. So, when these charges meet, then electric discharge takes place between ground and clouds. So, a large amount of energy is released in the form of thunder and lightning.

10. If the materials used for constructing a building were good conductors, do you think lightning will strike the building? Will the lightning conductor be still required to be installed in the building? Competency Based Que.

Ans. Lightning will not strike the building in such a case because all the lightning striking the building will reside on the surface of the building. Now, there is no need of installing any lightning conductor because all the work of lightning conductor is done by the conducting material itself.

11. Mention three precautions that you will take to protect yourself, if earthquake strikes when you are inside the house. NCERT Exemplar

Ans. Three precautions during earthquake inside the house are as follows

(a) Instead of running away, we should get under a desk, table or bench.

(b) Pick a safe place where things will not fall on you, away from windows, bookcases or tall heavy furnitures.

(c) Wait at your safe place until the shaking stops.

12. Is it possible to predict the occurrence of an earthquake?

Ans. No, scientists have tried lots of different ways of predicting earthquake but none have been successful so far. They have a pretty good idea of where an earthquake is most likely to hit but they still cannot tell exactly when it will happen.

Long Answer Type Questions

1. If the metal clip used in the electroscope is replaced by an ebonite rod and a charged body is brought in contact with it, will there be any effect on the aluminium strips? Explain. NCERT Exemplar

Ans. The ebonite rod acquires charge when rubbed. So, the charge transfer will be either too less or there will be no transfer of charges, so the strips of aluminium will not diverge and we will not be able to predict the object whether it is charged or not.

2. Explain how lightning takes place ?

Ans. Clouds having water droplets, coming from different directions, strike each other and due to striking, a friction force is created when they rub each other and during rubbing, the charges appear on clouds (static charges).

They grow in number due to continuous charging and finally discharge when any region of moisture is found on the earth because they get the path of discharge due to this place.

3. Explain why it is safer to use a wireless telephone instead of a landline telephone during lightning ? NCERT Exemplar

Ans. It is not safer to use a wired telephone during lightning because at that time lightning can enter the wire of telephone, if it is open somewhere, that is if there is any cut in the wire. On the other hand, there cannot be any possibility of this type in wireless telephone.

4. During lightning, if you are outside the house, then what precautions would you take?

Ans. Precautions during lightning while we are outside are as follows

(a) Do not stand underneath a natural lightning rod such as a tall and isolated tree.

(b) Stand away from any fountain or any water body.

(c) Get away from tractors and other metal equipments like wire fences, metal pipes, rails and another metallic paths.

5. Priya went to the school with umbrella on rainy season. One day, while returning from the school the rain started on the way. Priya opened her umbrella and saved herself from rainwater. After sometime, she observed some lightning sparks in the sky. Suddenly, she folded her umbrella and went to a shelter under a closed building.

(i) State the cause of lightning.

(ii) Priya folded her umbrella. Explain why?

(iii) Mention the method opted by Priya here.

Competency Based Que.

Ans. (i) In the clouds, accumulation of charges causes lightning.

(ii) As we know that the top end of stretched umbrella is a metal part. Since, the metal is a good conductor of electricity, so if lightning strikes to the ground, then it can take the path towards umbrella. Therefore, to avoid herself from danger, Priya folded the umbrella and went to a closed building.

(iii) The immediate response and the scientific method is opted by Priya here.

6. Mention the name of those regions of the earth that are more prone to earthquake.

Ans. Earthquakes are usually caused by the movement of plates on the outer layer of earth. So, the regions which fall on the boundaries of these plates are called danger zones. In India, the most dangerous zones which are prone to earthquakes are Kashmir, western and central himalyas, the whole of North-East, Rann of Kutch, Rajasthan and the Indo-Gangetic plains.

7. In year 2013, there was a showcase in IIT Hyderabad. All the students from different schools and colleges were invited on that occasion. Naveen with his friends went to see the projects made by M.Tech students. He found a project based on the construction of anti-earthquake buildings in which the small houses of iron rods were constructed. One house was with a hose containing water and the other was without hose. They were shocked on shaking of both the houses.

(i) Describe an earthquake.

(ii) Explain the meaning of quake-resist building.

(iii) Mention which force reduces the shaking in a building with hose.

(iv) State the feeling about the students who showed their project.

Ans. (i) A sudden shaking of the earth which lasts for very short time is called an earthquake.

(ii) Quake-resist building means that the buildings should be constructed in such a way that it can withstand for more time even on shaking of the earth.

(iii) The viscous force of water resists the oscillation or vibration of building caused by shaking of the earth and ultimately reduces the shaking in building with hose.

(iv) They used applications of science and technology and were more curious with the methods.

Case Based Question

1. Ryan ran two combs through his hair. He hung one comb from a stand using a thread. Ryan brought the other comb close to the first comb. The picture below shows the result.

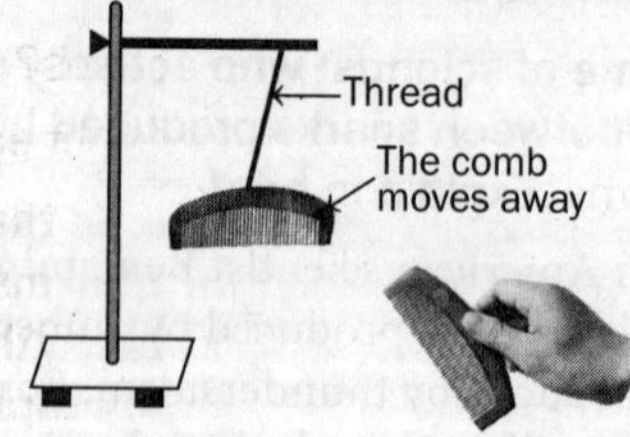

(i) Why did the comb move away from the other?

(ii) Ryan repeats the activity using a pair of glass rods in place of the combs. What is most likely to happen in this case?

(a) The hanging rod will move away

(b) The hanging rod will come closer

(c) The hanging rod will show no change

(d) The hanging rod will start spinning.

Answer

1. (i) The comb moved away from the other because both the combs acquired same or like charges when they were run through hair and, like charges repel each other.

(ii) (a)

Skill Based Questions as per NEP 2020

1. Activity : Creating a charge detector.

Research Skill

Material Required : A plastic cup, 2 strips of aluminium foil (3 cm × 1 cm), a piece of copper wire.

Procedure

1. Take an empty transparent plastic glass and keep it upside down.
2. Pierce a hole at the bottom of the glass, so that copper wire can be inserted as shown in figure.
3. Twist one end of wire in the shape of coil and bend another end to hang aluminium foil.
4. Cut 2 strips of aluminum foil about 3 cm × 1 cm and hang them as shown in figure.
5. Bring a charged body near it.

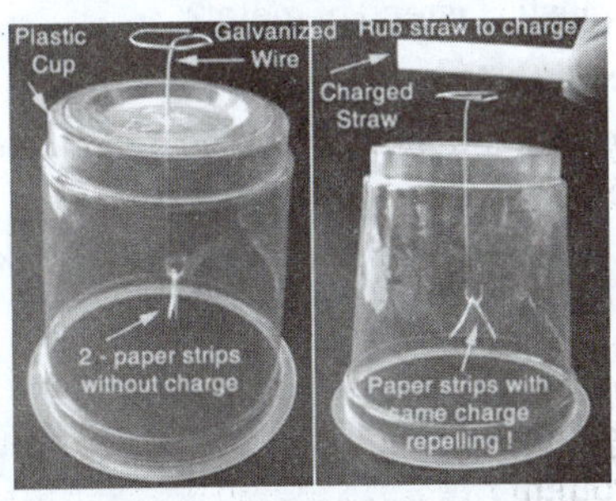

Answer the following questions.

(i) Is there any effect on the foil strips?

(ii) Do they repel each other or attract each other?

2. Earthquakes produce seismic waves that reach the Earth's surface. A seismograph is an instrument that records the seismic waves. The strength of the earthquake is calculated from the graph recorded.

Knowledge Based Que.

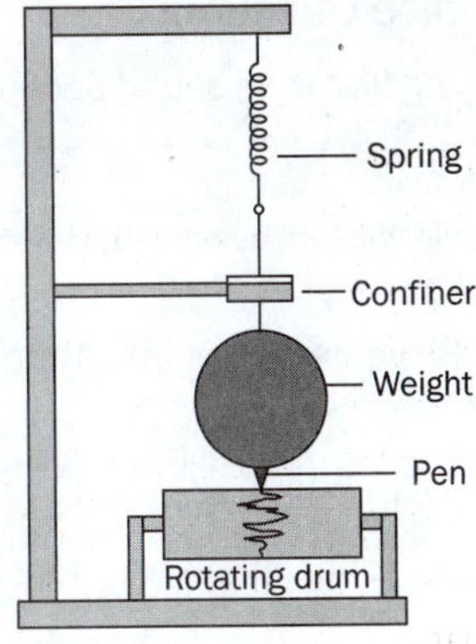

Which of these graphs shows the strongest earthquake?

(a) 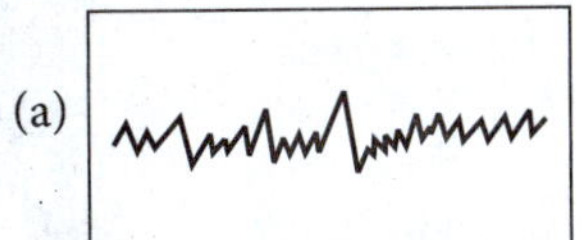

(b) 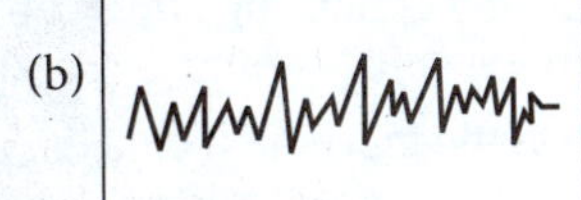

(c) 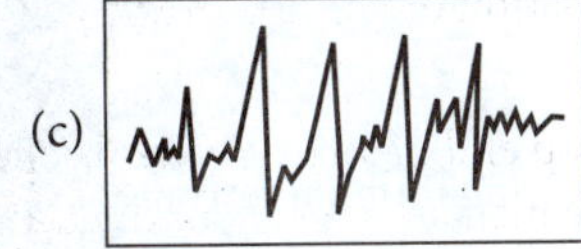

(d) 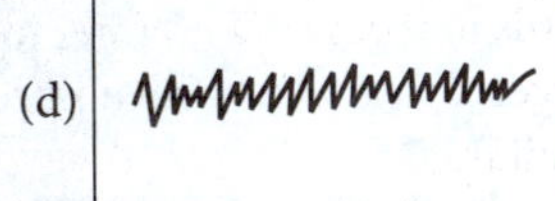

ASSESSMENT EXERCISE

Part I

Multiple Choice Questions

1. We see lightning first than sound because
(a) sound travels faster than light
(b) light travels faster than sound
(c) light travels in vacuum but sound does not
(d) None of the above

2. The magnitude or intensity of an earthquake can be measured by
(a) electroscope (b) richter scale
(c) Both (a) and (b) (d) None of these

3. The continuous motion of the plates inside earth crust causes
(a) cyclone (b) rain
(c) earthquake (d) thunderstorm

4. The innermost layer of earth is called
(a) crust (b) mantle
(c) core (d) None of these

Fill in the Blanks

5. Static charges can be induced by ....

6. .... is a device used to protect buildings from the effect of lightning.

7. Earthquake is caused due to the movement of .... plates in the earth crust.

True/False

8. Unlike charges repel each other.

9. We should not take bath during thunderstorm.

10. Seismograph is used to detect the presence of electric charge in a body.

Assertion-Reason Questions

The following questions consists of two statements -Assertion (A) and Reason (R). Answer these questions by selection the appropriate option given below.

(a) Both A and R are true and R is the correct explanation of A.
(b) Both A and R are true but R is not the correct explanation of A.
(c) A is true but R is false.
(d) A is false but R is true.

11. Assertion (A) Maximum damage occurs at epicentre.
Reason (R) Destructive energy of an earthquake is measured on richter scale.

12. Assertion (A) We should not use an umbrella while crossing an open field during a thunderstorm.
Reason (R) As the rod of umbrella and its supporting wires are made up of metals, it may affect the person who holds the umbrella.

Part II

Very Short Answer Type Questions

13. Plastic straws *A* and *B* are rubbed with dry cotton cloth. What will happen, if they are brought near each other?

14. Will the lightning conductor still working, if it was made out of plastic instead of metal?

15. Define earthing.

16. Explain why should a person not stand under a tree during a thunderstorm?

17. Write the range of a very strong earthquake on Richter scale.

Short Answer Type Questions

18. State what will actually happen, when we touch the metal top of a charged electroscope with our fingers? What is this process known as?

19. How does lightning take place in the clouds?

20. What do you understand by the process of electric discharge?

21. What precautions should we take during an earthquake, if we are outside?

Long Answer Type Questions

22. Name the three layers of earth. Draw a labelled diagram to show the structure of the earth.

23. We should use mobile phones rather than landline phones during thunderstorm. Give reasons.

Answer

1. (b) **2.** (b) **3.** (c) **4.** (c) **5.** rubbing **6.** Lightning conductor **7.** tectonic **8.** False **9.** True False **11.** (b) **12.** (a)

Light

CHAPTER 13

In the world, we usually see a variety of objects. Sometimes, we are unable to see anything in a dark room, but on lighting up the room, we are able to see the things in the room. So, it is obvious that light is a form of energy which enables us to see objects.

Light Makes Things Visible

We can see objects when light emitted from them reaches to our eyes. Those objects which emit their own lights are known as **luminous objects**. e.g. Sun, light bulb, etc.

However, some objects like table or books do not have their own light, these are known as **non-luminous objects**. We can see these non-luminous objects, if light rays get reflected from their surfaces and reaches to our eyes.

13.1 Reflection of Light

When a ray of light falls on any smooth surface or mirror, then the direction of light changes. This phenomenon is known as reflection of light.

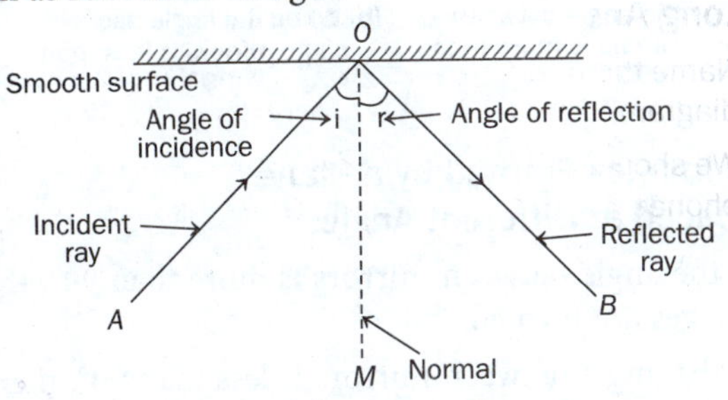

Some important terms related to reflection of light

- **Incident ray** The light ray which strikes the surface is known as incident ray. In figure, *AO* is the incident ray.
- **Reflected ray** The light ray which comes back from the surface after reflection is known as reflected ray. In figure, *OB* is the reflected ray.
- **Normal** It is an imaginary line which is perpendicular to the mirror at the point of incident. In figure, *OM* is the normal ray.
- **Angle of incidence** The angle between incident ray and the normal is known as angle of incidence. In figure, $\angle AOM$ is the angle of incidence.
- **Angle of reflection** The angle between reflected ray and the normal is known as angle of reflection. In figure, $\angle BOM$ is the angle of reflection.

Laws of Reflection

Reflection of light follows certain laws known as laws of reflection. There are two laws of reflection as given below

(i) **First Law of Reflection** The angle of reflection is always equal to the angle of incidence ($\angle i = \angle r$).

(ii) **Second Law of Reflection** The incident ray, the normal at the point of incidence and the reflected ray, all lie in the same plane.

SCIENCE INSIGHT The study of light and its behaviour while interacting with other objects is known as optics. Euclid studied the reflection and proposed the laws of reflection.

13.2 Types of Reflection

There are two types of reflection

- **Regular reflection** When a beam of parallel light rays is incident on a smooth plane surface, then the reflected rays will also be parallel. This type of reflection is called regular reflection. e.g. Reflection from plane mirror.

Since, plane mirror shows regular reflection, so we can see clear images of objects in a plane mirror.

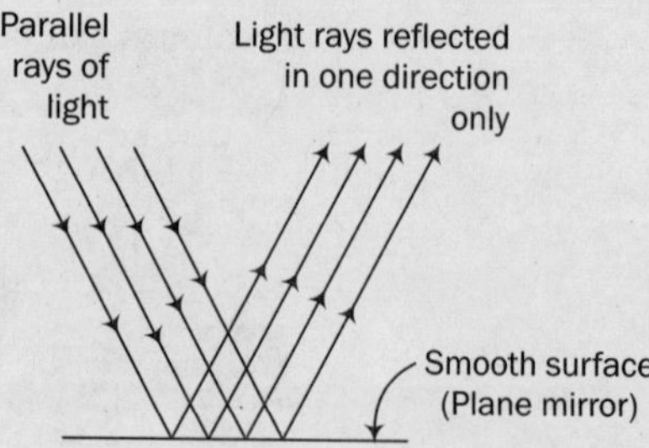

Incident light is reflected in only one direction

- **Diffused or irregular reflection** When a beam of parallel light rays is incident on a rough surface, the reflected rays scatter in different direction. This type of reflection is called diffused or irregular reflection. e.g. Reflection from rough wall.

  The first law of reflection is also followed by irregular reflectlion. Irregular reflection forms a blurry image because reflected rays scatter in different direction.

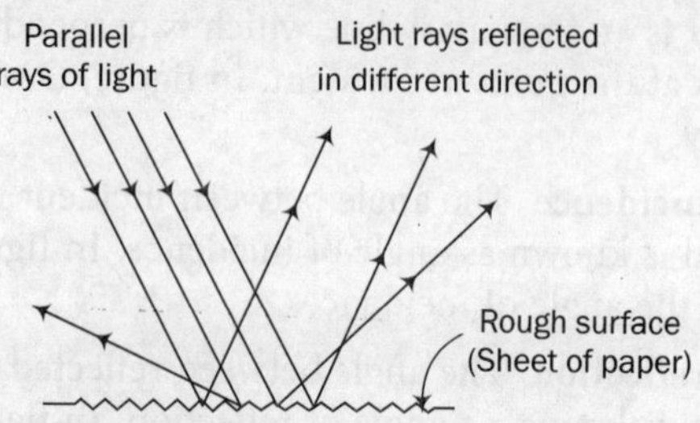

Incident light is reflected in different direction

Image Formation by a Plane Mirror

There are some characteristics of image formed by a plane mirror

(i) The image formed by a plane mirror is **erect.**

(ii) The image formed by the plane mirror is of the **same size as the object.**

(iii) The image formed by a plane mirror is at the same distance behind the mirror as the object is in front of it.

(iv) The image formed by a plane mirror is behind the mirror.

(v) The image formed by plane mirrors are **laterally inverted,** i.e. **the left side comes to the right** and **the right side comes to left.**

13.3 Reflected Light can be Reflected Again

When a reflected light falls on a plane mirror, then it gets reflected again. It also follows the law of reflection.
e.g. In a barber's shop, we see the back of the head using multiple reflection of two mirrors.
Similarly, a periscope works on principle of the multiple reflection of two mirrors, where the beam of light from the object is reflected twice by the two mirror surfaces.

Multiple Images

We know that, a plane mirror forms only a single image of an object but when two plane mirrors are placed at some angle, the light rays reflected by the first mirror strike the second mirror and get reflected again. This results in the formation of multiple images.

This shows that the image of the object formed in the first plane mirror acts as an object for the second plane mirror.

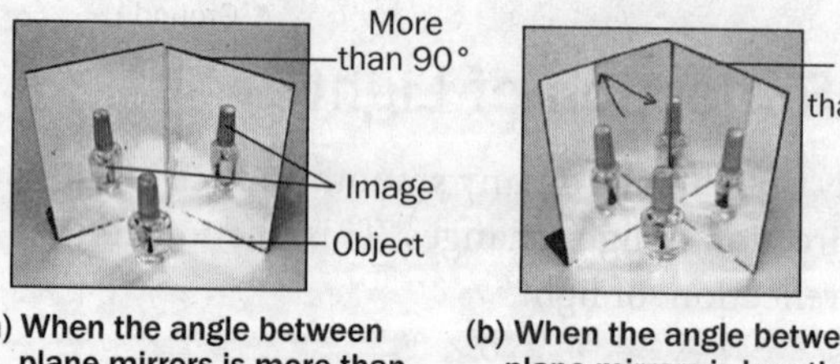

(a) When the angle between plane mirrors is more than 90° (b) When the angle between plane mirrors is less than 90°

Multiple Images Formed by a Plane Mirror Placed at Different Angles

- When the angle between mirrors is more than 90°, then two images are formed.
- When the angle between mirrors is less than 90°, then number of images increases.

- When the object is kept between two parallel plane mirrors, then infinite images are formed.

Note Number of images of an object formed when two plane mirrors are inclined at an angle is given by

$$\frac{360°}{\theta \text{ (given angle)}} - 1$$

Kaleidoscope

A kaleidoscope is an optical instrument with two or more reflecting surfaces tilted to each other at an angle.

It is used by designer of wallpapers and fabrics artists to get idea for new patterns.

An interesting feature of a kaleidoscope is that you will never see the same pattern again.

It is based on the principle of multiple reflections of light.

Construction

- It contains three plane mirrors inclined at an angle of 60° to each other in a tube.
- One end of tube is closed with two circular glass discs, the inner one is transparent glass and the outer one is ground glass. The other end of tube is closed by a cardboard disc with the small hole in the centre.
- Glass pieces and bangle pieces of various colours are kept between the two discs.

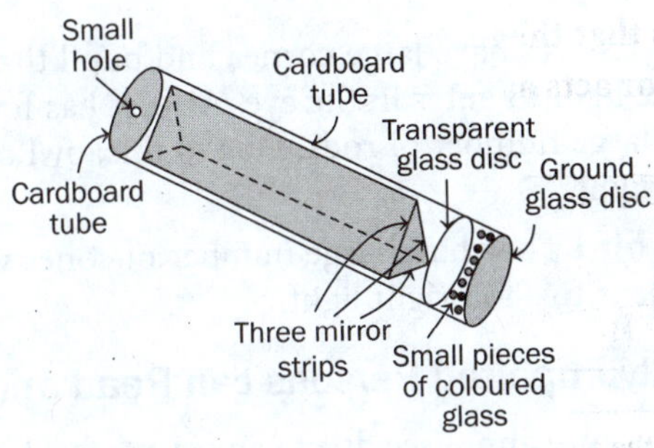

Note Ground glass is a type of glass which is partially transparent.

Try These 13.1

1. **Mention the type of reflection of light that takes place from (a) a rough surface and (b) a smooth surface.**
2. **Are laws of reflections valid for irregular reflection?**
3. **Determine the number of images formed when an object is placed between two parallel plane mirrors facing each other.**
4. **Mention the name of a phenomenon which takes place when patterns are formed in a kaleidoscope.**

13.4 Sunlight : White or Coloured

The sunlight is considered as white light but actually it contains seven colours. These seven colours can be seen by passing sunlight through a prism.

When this sunlight or white light passes through the prism, it splits into seven different colours and this process is called **dispersion of light**. One of the best example of dispersion of light is **formation of rainbow**.

13.5 Human Eye

Eye is a very important sense organ which is used to see objects around us.

Structure of the Eye

The shape of eye is roughly spherical, it contains following parts

- The outer coat of eye is white in colour. It is tough, so that it can protect the interior parts of eye from any accident.

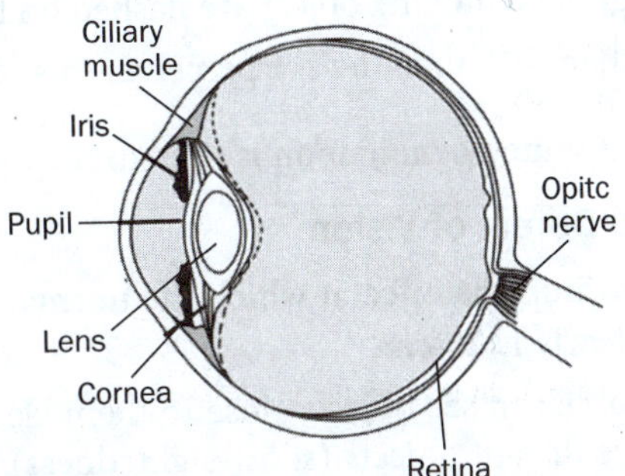

- **Cornea** The transparent part of the outermost layer is cornea. The main function of cornea is to protect the eye but it also helps in focusing light due to its shape.
- **Iris** It is coloured part of eye situated just behind the cornea. The colour of iris can be brown, green or blue. It controls the amount of light entering in the eye.
- **Pupil** The small black opening in the iris is pupil. The size of pupil is controlled by iris.

Note In dim light, our pupil expands to allow more light to enter into our eyes while in bright light, it contracts.

- **Lens** Just behind the pupil, a transparent and elastic structure is present. It is thicker in the centre just like a convex lens. It focuses the light on the retina.
- **Ciliary muscles** The lens is attached to ciliary muscles. These muscles are used to change the shape of eye lens to focus image on the retina.

- **Retina** A screen on which the image is formed in the eye is known as retina. The retina contains many optic nerves. These optic nerves carry image in the form of electrical signal to the brain.
- **Optic nerves** There are two types of cells in optic nerve
  (i) **Cones** These are sensitive to bright light. It is responsible for colour vision.
  (ii) **Rods** These are sensitive to dim light. It is responsible for vision in dim light.

Blind spot At the junction of optic nerve and the retina , there are no sensory cells. The brain cannot sense image formed at this spot. Hence, it is named as blind spot.

Eyelids The part of an eye which prevents any object from entering the eye are known as eyelids. It also shut out if light is not required.

Persistence of Vision

Any image formed on retina does not vanish immediately. It persists there about $\frac{1}{16}$ th of a second. Due to this fact, if steady images of a moving object are flashed on the eye at a rate faster than $\frac{1}{16}$ s, then the eye perceives this object as moving. The same phenomenon is used in movies.

Range and Defect of Vision

- The **minimum distance** at which the normal eye can see objects clearly is **25 cm**.
- Some people can see objects close to them clearly but cannot see distant objects (short-sightedness). On the other hand, some can see distant objects clearly but are unable to see nearby objects (long-sightedness).

These eye defects can be corrected by using proper power of lens.

- In old age, the eye sight becomes foggy due to cloudy eye lens, which is known as **cataract**. This defect can be corrected by getting proper surgery.

SCIENCE INSIGHT Short-sightedness is known as **myopia**, whereas long-sightedness is known as **hypermetropia**.

Care of Eyes

To avoid above defects, take care of your eyes by following below steps.

(i) Do not rub your eyes. If dust particles go into your eyes, then wash it gently. If there is no improvement, then go to a doctor.

(ii) Do not look at powerful source of light like sun or laser.

(iii) Insuffcent light can cause eye strain, headaches or injury to retina.

(iv) Always read at the normal distance of vision.

(v) If advised by eye specialist, then use spectacles.

(vi) Take a proper balance diet in your meal, especially vitamin A which cures the problem of night blindness.

Try These 13.2

1 Which type of lens is present in human eye ?
2 What is the name of the point inside the human eye where the image is not visible ?
3 Which part of our eye gives it a distinctive colour?

13.6 Eyes of Other Animals

Different animals have different eye shape, some of them are given as follows

- **Crab** Its eyes are very small and present on stalk, so crab can see enemy even if it approaches from behind.
- **Butterfly** They have large compound eyes made up of thousands of little eyes. They can see in all directions. It can sense even small movement in an object.
- **Owl** Its eyes have large cornea and pupil that allows more light to enter in the eye. Also, it has few cones and large number of rods. Due to this, owl can see in the night.
- **Day bird** They have large number of cones which are sensitive to bright light.

Visually Impaired Persons can Read and Write

Some people cannot see due to any eye defect but they can identify things using other senses like touching and listening.

Based on these senses, some **optical aids** and **non-optical aids** are used to improve the life of visually impaired person.

(i) **Non-Optical aid** It includes following aids
- **Visual aids** These aids can magnify words and provide suitable intensity of light and material at proper distances.
- **Tactual aids** These aids are based on sense of touch. e.g. Braille writer state and stylus.

- **Auditory aids** These aids are based on hearing. e.g. Cassettes, talking books, etc.
- **Electronic aids** These aids are based on electronic devices. e.g. Talking calculators and computers.

(ii) **Optical aids** These are optical devices like bifocal lenses, contact lenses, telescopic aids, etc.

Braille System

Braille is a written language for visually challenged person. This system was adopted in 1932. It has series of patterns of raised dots. These dots represent **specific alphabets** and **numbers.** There are 63 dot patterns. Combination of these patterns produces words and grammatical sign. Visually challenged people can recognise these words by touching them.

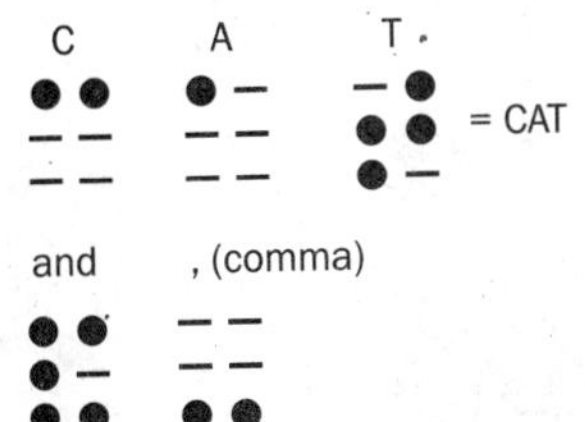

Example of dot patterns used in braille system

Try These 13.3

1. **What happens to the size of the pupil of our eye in presence of bright light?**
2. **Which non-optical aid is based on hearing?**
3. **What is the most popular resource for visually challenged persons which can make them read and write ?**

Science Glossary

Laws of reflection These are sets of two universal laws which are followed by any light rays during reflection.

Angle of incidence The angle between incident ray and normal is known as angle of incidence.

Angle of reflection The angle between reflected ray and normal is known as angle of reflection.

Cornea It is the transparent front part which helps in focusing light on retina.

Iris Coloured part of eye situated just behind the cornea.

Pupil The small opening in the middle of iris through which light enters in the eye.

Lens A transparent and elastic structure present behind the pupil. It is thicker in the centre.

Rods These cells are present in retina and are sensitive to dim light.

Cones These cells are sensitive to bright light.

Retina It is a part of eye which acts as a screen.

Cataract It is a defect of eye in which eye lens becomes cloudy and eyesight becomes hazy.

Braille It is a written language for visually challenged person.

Let's Investigate

ACTIVITY 1 (Page 165)

Aim To understand the reflection by a plane mirror.

Material Required Drawing board, white sheet, comb, plane mirror, black paper and a torch.

Procedure

1. Fix the white sheet of paper on the drawing board.
2. Take the comb and close all its holes except one present in the middle with the help of black paper.
3. Hold the comb perpendicular to the drawing board.
4. Now, take the torch and throw light on the comb. Light must fall on the opening of the comb.
5. You will see a ray of light falling on the drawing board. Place a plane mirror in the path of light and observe what happens to the ray coming from the comb.

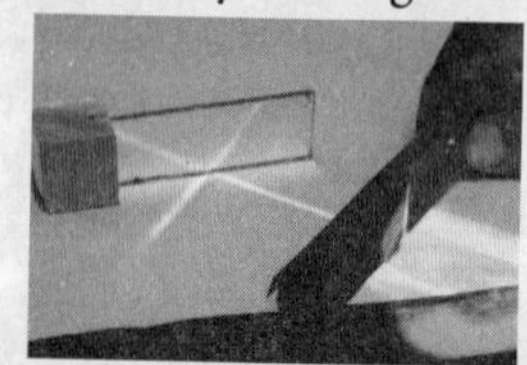

Arrangement for showing reflection

Conclusion The light ray strikes with the mirror and changes its path. The ray coming from the comb is incident ray and the ray going after striking the mirror is reflected ray.

Viva Questions

1. What is the need of closing all the holes of the comb except one?
2. What other thing can you use instead of torch?

ACTIVITY 2 (Page 166, 167)

Aim To understand the second law of reflection.

Material Required A chart paper (white) , a plane mirror, a comb, black paper and a torch.

Procedure

1. Spread the white chart paper on the table such that it extends little beyond the edge of the table.
2. Close all the holes of the comb with black paper, except one at the middle.
3. Place plane mirror and comb perpendicular to the table as shown in figure.
4. You will see the incident ray and reflected ray on the white chart paper. Now, bend the chart paper at the end of the table.
5. You will not see the reflected ray on the bended portion of the chart paper. Now, bring the paper back to its original position. You will again see the reflected ray.

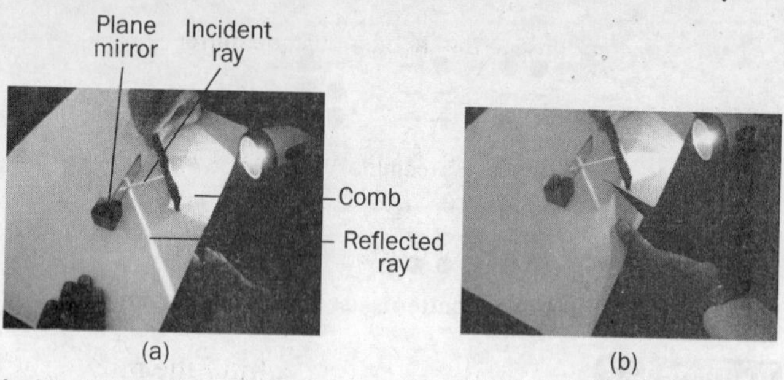

Incident ray, reflected ray and the normal at the point of incidence lie in the same plane

Conclusion We have concluded that the incident ray, reflected ray and the normal all lie in the same plane.

Viva Questions

1. State second law of reflection.
2. What will happen, if you paint the mirror black?

ACTIVITY 3 (Page 167, 168)

Aim To study the formation of image by a plane mirror.

Material Required Drawing board, a white paper, a plane mirror, a pencil and a ruler.

Procedure

1. Paste the white paper on the drawing board.
2. Consider that an object is at *O*. Now, draw two rays *OM* and *OH* incident on the mirror.
3. Draw two reflected rays *MN* and *HG* by making angle of reflection equal to angle of incidence.

   Extend these reflected rays further. You will find that they do not meet.
4. Now, extend the two reflected rays using a pencil and ruler behind the mirror (dotted lines). Mark the point *I* where they meet.

Since, the reflected rays do not actually meet at I, we say that it is a virtual image.

5. Measure the distance of object (PO) and distance of image (PI) from the mirror (PQ).

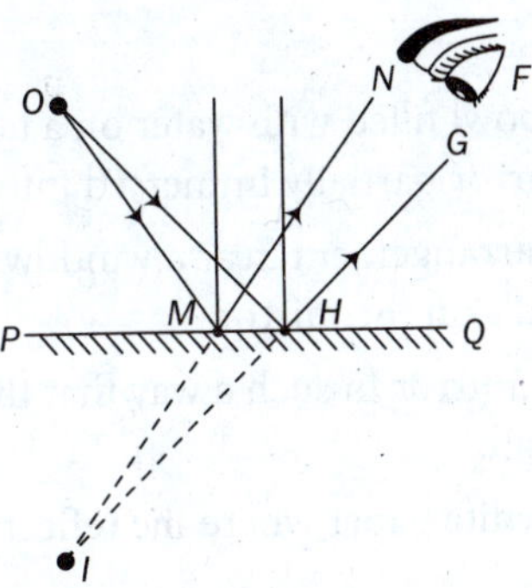

Image formation in a plane mirror

Conclusion

(i) The distance of object from the mirror is same as the distance of the image from the mirror i.e. $PO = PI$.

(ii) The image formed by plane mirror is virtual.

Viva Questions

1. Which type of image is formed behind the mirror?
2. Can you form the image with the help of only one ray?
3. Where do the two reflected rays meet to form an image?

ACTIVITY 4 (Page 168)

Aim To study the properties of reflection from an irregular surface using laws of reflection.

Material Required White sheet, ruler, protractor and a pencil.

Procedure

1. Draw a rough surface on the white sheet as shown in figure (a).

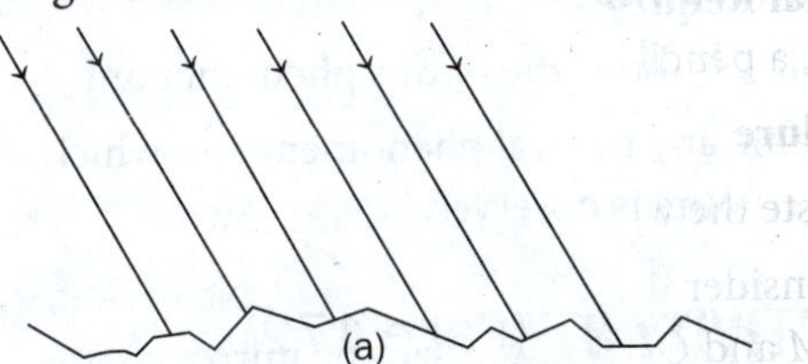

Parallel rays incident on an irregular surface

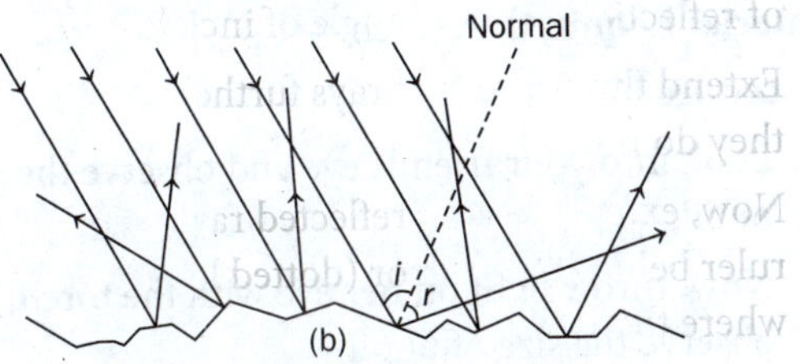

Rays reflected from irregular surface

2. Draw parallel rays which fall on this surface. These rays are incident rays.
3. Draw perpendicular line at every point of incident on the surface.
4. Now, measure the angle between normal and incident ray for every ray. This is angle of incidence.
5. Draw angle of reflection which is equal to the angle of incidence as shown in figure (b), then draw reflected rays.

Conclusion Incident rays are parallel but reflected rays are not parallel. Hence, irregular surfaces produce irregular or diffused reflection.

Viva Questions

1. Is angle of incidence always equal to angle of reflection?
2. Is first law of reflection valid for rough surfaces?

ACTIVITY 5 (Page 170)

Aim To study the number of images formed by two mirrors inclined at some angle.

Material Required Two mirrors, any small object like pen, pencil or rubber.

Procedure

1. Place two mirrors at right angles to each other with their edges touching.
2. Place the object in between the mirrors. We can see two images in the mirrors.

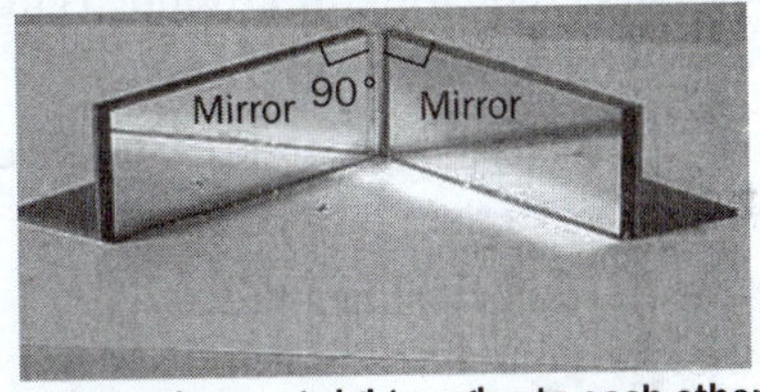

(a) Two mirrors at right angles to each other

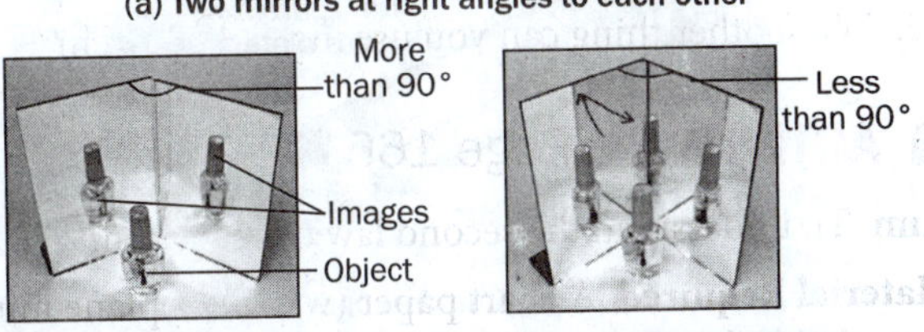

(b) When the angle between plane mirrors is greater than 90°

(c) When the angle between plane mirrors is less than 90°

3. Now, change the angle between mirrors (like 45°,60°,120°,180°). You can set angles with the help of a protractor.
4. Note down the number of images formed in each case.

Conclusion

1. When angle between mirrors is greater than 90°, then two images are formed.
2. When the angle between mirrors is less than 90°, then number of images increases.

Viva Questions

1. How many images are formed, if the two mirrors are parallel to each other?
2. For which angle of mirrors, you will get only one image?

ACTIVITY 6 (Page 170, 171)

Aim To build a kaleidoscope.

Material Required Three rectangular mirror stripes (15 cm × 4 cm), circular cardboard tube, cardboard disc, a circular transparent glass plate, a circular grounded glass plate and several small pieces of coloured glass or bangles.

Procedure

1. Take the three rectangular mirror strips and join them to form a hollow prism with their reflecting surface facing each other.
2. Fix this prism in a circular cardboard tube and close one end of the tube by a cardboard disc. Make a small hole in this disc.
3. Close the other end of prism with the circular glass plate.
4. Put several pieces of coloured bangles on this plate.
5. Close the end of tube with the grounded circular glass plate. Now, your kaleidoscope is ready.
6. Now, see through the hole and rotate the cardboard.

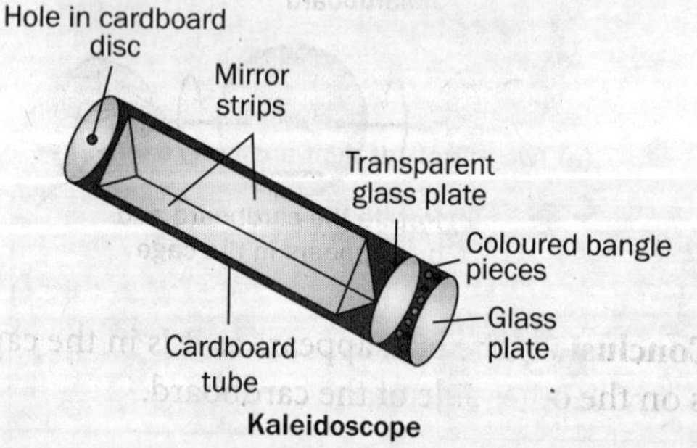

Kaleidoscope

Conclusion We observed different patterns in the kaleidoscope every time. These patterns are visible due to multiple reflection by glass strips.

Viva Questions

1. On which principle, a kaleidoscope works?
2. What is the angle between three mirrors in Kaleidoscope?

ACTIVITY 7 (Page 171)

Aim To show that sunlight is made up of seven colours.

Material Required A bowl filled with water, a plane strip of mirror, white paper.

Procedure

1. Place the bowl filled with water on a table. Now, place a strip of mirror partially immersed into the water.
2. Place this arrangement near a window such that direct sunlight falls on the mirror.
3. Adjust the mirror in such a way that the reflected light fall on a wall.
4. Place the white paper where the reflected light fall on the wall.
5. Observe the colours of reflected light.

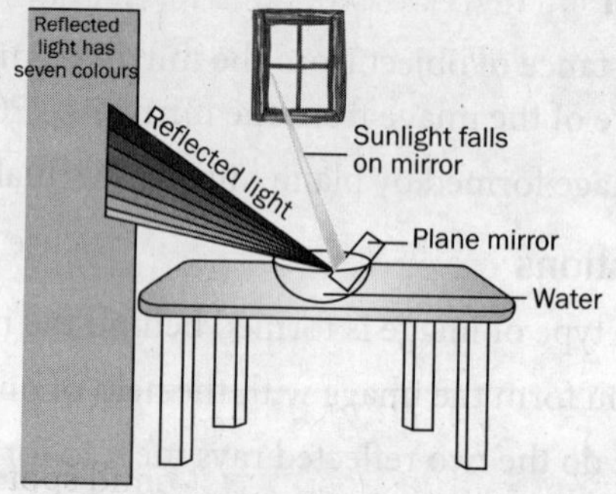

Dispersion of light

Conclusion Sunlight is made up of seven colours named as violet,indigo, blue, green, yellow, orange and red.
In short form, it is known as VIBGYOR (first letter of every colour) and the splitting of light into its constituent colours is known as dispersion of light.

Viva Questions

1. What is the name of this phenomenon?
2. Name any natural phenomenon in which this pattern of colours is observed.

ACTIVITY 8 (Page 172)

Aim To observe the effect of light on the size of pupil.

Material Required A torch.

Procedure

1. Look into your friends eye and observe the size of pupil.
2. Now, throw light on her eye with the torch. Now, observe the size of pupil.

3. Now, switch OFF the light and observe the size of pupil once again.

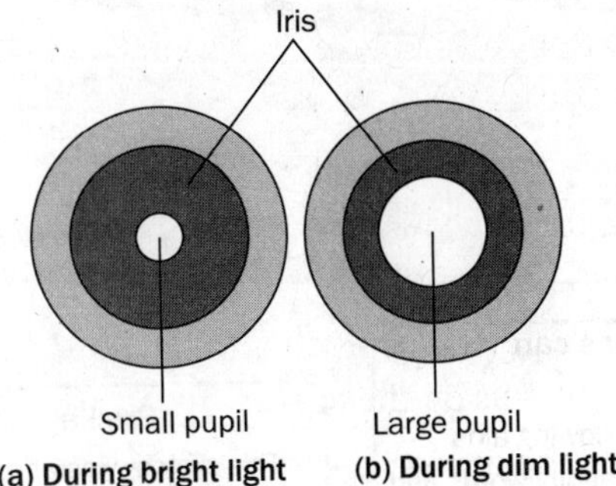

(a) During bright light (b) During dim light

Conclusion

1. Size of pupil is small when the torch is ON. This happens to protect eye from intense light.
2. Size of pupil increases when the torch is switched off. This happens to gather more light to see objects clearly.

Viva Questions

1. Who controls the size of pupil?
2. What happens to the size of pupil if you use dim light source instead of bright light source?

ACTIVITY 9 (Page 172)

Aim To demonstrate the existence of blind spot in the eye.

Material Required A white paper strip and a marker.

Procedure

1. Make a round mark and a cross mark on a sheet of paper with the help of marker. The round mark should be on the right side of the cross mark.
2. Distance between the two marks should be 6-8 cm.
3. Now, hold this paper at an arm's length from the eye.
4. Close your left eye and look continuously on the cross mark.
5. Move the sheet slowly towards your eye and keep your eye on the cross.
6. Move the sheet towards your eye until the round mark disappears.
7. Now, close your right eye and look at the round mark, then repeat step 5 and 6.

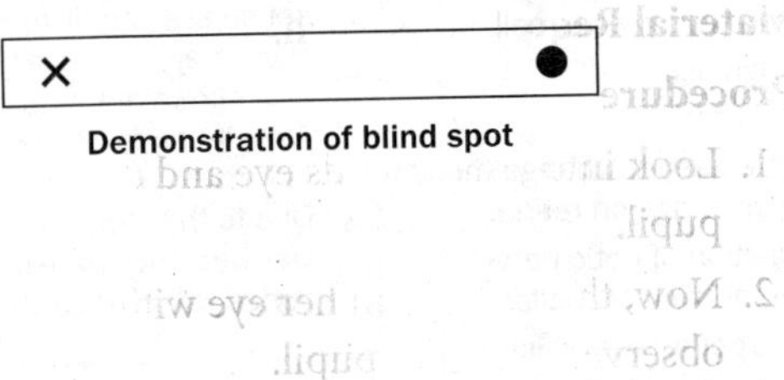
Demonstration of blind spot

Conclusion While bringing the strip towards the eye at some point, one mark disappears.

Viva Questions

1. Where is the blind spot located in the eye?
2. What is blind spot?

ACTIVITY 10 (Page 173)

Aim To understand the persistence of vision.

Material Required A square piece of cardboard, a long thread and a pencil.

Procedure

1. Make two holes in the cardboard as shown in figure.
2. Draw a cage on one side of the cardboard and a bird on the other side of the cardboard.
3. Now, insert the string in the hole as shown in the diagram.
4. Now, hold the free ends of the thread on both sides and twist it in such a way that the cardboard rotates very fast. Now, write your observation.

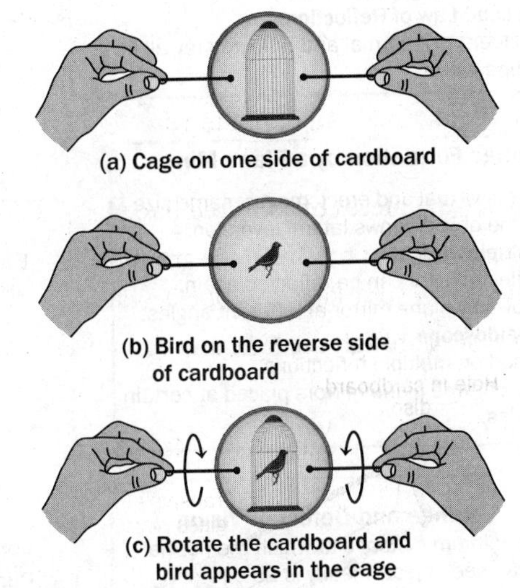
(a) Cage on one side of cardboard

(b) Bird on the reverse side of cardboard

(c) Rotate the cardboard and bird appears in the cage

Conclusion The bird appears as it is in the cage but it is on the other side of the cardboard.

Viva Questions

1. What is the minimum distance for eyesight?
2. For how long, a picture can persist on the retina?

Reflection of Light

Ray of light falls on any smooth surface or mirror, then the direction of light changes. This phenomenon is known as reflection of light.

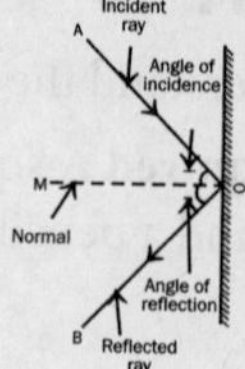

Types of Reflection

- **Regular Reflection**
  - Parallel incident rays emerge out as parallel reflected rays.
  - Seen in plane mirror.

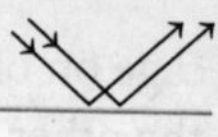

- **Diffused Reflection**
  - Parallel incident rays are
  - reflected in various direction.

Laws of Reflection

- **First Law of Reflection**
  Angle of incidence is always equal to angle of reflection ($\angle i = \angle r$).
- **Second Law of Reflection**
  Incident ray, normal and reflected ray all lie in same plane.

Visually Impaired Persons can Read and Write

1. **Non-Optical aids** It includes following aids
   - **Visual aids** These aids can magnify words and provide suitable intensity of light.
   - **Tactual aids** These aids are based on sense of touch, e.g. braille writer state and stylus.
   - **Auditory aids** These aids are based on hearing, e.g. cassettes, talking books, etc.
   - **Electronic aids** These aids are based on electronic devices. e.g. Talking calculators and computers.
2. **Optical aids** These are optical devices like bifocal lenses, contact lenses, telescopic aids, etc.

Braille system

- This system was adopted in 1932.
- It has series of patterns of raised dots.
- These dots represent specific alphabets and numbers.
- There are 63 dot patterns.
- Combination of these patterns produces words and grammatical sign.

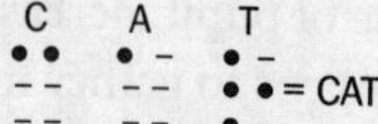

LIGHT

Types of Objects

- **Luminous objects**
  Those objects which emit their own light, e.g. sun, light bulb, etc.
- **Non-Luminous objects**
  Those objects which do not have their own light, e.g. table, book etc.

Image Formation by a Plane Mirror

Forms virtual and erect images, same size as the object shows lateral inversion.

- **Multiple Images**
  - Reflected light can be reflected again.
  - Shows by plane mirror at different angles.
- **Kaleidoscope**
  - Based on multiple reflections.
  - Two or more plane mirrors placed at certain angles.

Human Eye and its Parts

Eye is a very important sense organ which is used to see object around us.

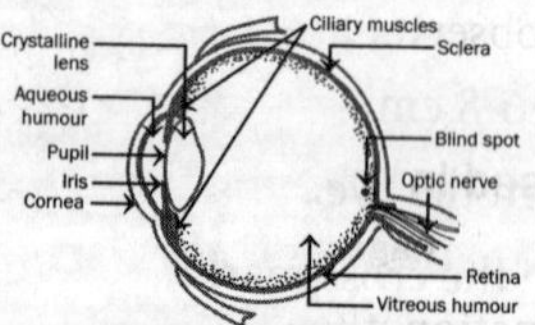

Parts of Eyes

- **Cornea** It is transparent part.
- **Pupil** It is small opening in cornea.
- **Iris** It is located behind cornea. It give eyes their colour.
- **Lens** It is transparent structure focuses light on retina.
- **Retina** It is light sensitive layer.
- **Optic nerves** These are in two types of cell
  (i) Cones Sensitive to bright light.
  (ii) Rods Sensitive to dim light.
- **Ciliary muscles** These are used to change the shape of eye lens to focus image on retina.
- **Blind spot** It is at the junction of optic nerve and the retina, there are no sensory cells.
- **Eyelids** These are the part of an eye which prevent any object from entering the eye.

Sunlight : White or Coloured

- The sunlight is considered as white light but actually it contains seven colours. These seven colours can be seen by passing sunlight through a prism.
- When this sunlight or white light passes through the prism, it splits into seven different colours and this process is called dispersion of light. One of the best example of **dispersion of light** is **formation of rainbow.**

Range and Defect of Vision

- The minimum distance at which the normal eye can see objects clearly is 25 cm.
- Some people can see objects close to them clearly but cannot see distant objects is called **short-sightedness.**
- Some people can see distant objects clearly but are unable to see nearby objects is called **long-sightedness.**
- In old age, the eye sight becomes foggy due to cloudy eye lens, which is known as **cataract.**

Care of Eyes

- Do not rub your eyes, if dust particles go into your eyes.
- Do not look at powerful source of light like sun or laser.

Eyes of Animals

- **Crab** Its eyes are very small and present on stalk, so crab can see enemy even if it approaches from behind.
- **Butterfly** They have large compound eyes made up of thousands of little eyes. It can sense even small movement in an object.
- **Owl** Its eyes have large cornea and pupil that allows more light to enter in the eye. Also, it has few cones and large number of rods.
  Due to this, owl can see in the night.
- **Day bird** They have large number of cones which are sensitive to bright light.

NCERT FOLDER

Complete Explanations of all NCERT's Questions

Intext Questions

Q.1 Do you see any relation between the angle of incidence and the angle of reflection? Page 166

Ans. The angle of incidence is always equal to the angle of reflection.

Q.2 What would happen if we threw the light on the mirror along the normal? Page 166

Ans. If we throw the light on the mirror along the normal, the light ray will be reflected back in opposite direction.

Q.3 Can the reflected rays be further reflected, if incident on another mirror? Page 169

Ans. Yes, the reflected rays can be further reflected, if incident on another mirror.

Q.4 Do you know, how you could see the hair at the back of your head? Page 169

Ans. The reflection of our hair falls onto the mirror at the back and that reflection gets reflected onto the mirror infront of us, whose virtual image again gets reflected into our eyes and we can see the back of our hair.

Q.5 Can you explain, how reflection from the two mirrors enables us to see objects which are not visible directly? Page 169

Ans. When light falls on one mirror, it is reflected back and falls on the mirror and gets reflected to the observer's eyes.

Q.6 What happens if two plane mirrors are used in combination? Page 169

Ans. When two plane mirrors are used in combination, then they will form multiple images for an object.

Q.7 Do we see all objects due to reflected light? Page 169

Ans. Yes, nearly everything we see around us is due to reflected light, e.g. moon receives light from the sun and reflects it.

Q.8 What kind of lens is thicker at the centre? Page 172

Ans. Convex lens is thicker in centre.

Exercise

Q.1 Suppose you are in a dark room. Can you see objects in the room? Can you see objects outside the room? Explain.

Ans. In the dark room, we cannot see objects because the objects are visible only when light from an object enters in our eyes.

We can see the objects outside the room, if there is light outside. If there is no light outside the room again, we cannot see the object.

Q.2 Differentiate between regular and diffused reflection. Does diffused reflection mean the failure of the laws of reflection?

Ans. Differences between regular and diffused reflection are

Regular reflection	Diffused reflection
It is caused by the reflection from smooth and shiny surfaces.	It is caused by reflection from unpolished and rough surfaces.
Reflected rays are parallel to each other.	Reflected rays are not parallel to each other.

No, the diffused reflection does not mean the failure of the laws of reflection.

Q.3 Mention against each of the following whether regular or diffused reflection will take place when a beam of light strikes. Justify your answer in each case.

(a) Polished wooden table
(b) Chalk powder
(c) Cardboard surface
(d) Marble floor with water spread over it
(e) Mirror
(f) Piece of paper

Ans. (a) **Polished wooden table** As the surface is smooth, so there is a regular reflection through it.

(b) **Chalk powder** Since, the surface is not smooth or it is uneven, thus there is a diffused reflection through it.

(c) **Cardboard surface** As its surface is uneven, so it will produce a diffused reflection.

(d) **Marble floor with water spread over it** As marble floor itself is very smooth, besides this there is a layer of water on it which makes the surface regular for reflection.

(e) **Mirror** Since, the surface of mirror is smooth, thus it will produce a regular reflection.

(f) **Piece of paper** Since, the surface is uneven, thus it will produce a diffused reflection.

Q.4 State the laws of reflection.

Ans. There are two laws of reflection as below

(i) The angle of incidence is equal to the angle of reflection.

(ii) Incident ray, reflected ray and the normal drawn at the point of incidence to the reflecting surface, all lie in the same plane.

Q.5 Describe an activity to show that the incident ray, the reflected ray and the normal at the point of incidence, all lie in the same plane.

Ans. Refer to Activity 2 on page 230.

Q.6 Fill in the blanks in the following.

(a) A person 1 m in front of a plane mirror seems to be .... m away from his image.

(b) If you touch your .... ear with right hand in front of a plane mirror, it will be seen in the mirror that your right ear is touched with ....

(c) The size of the pupil becomes ....when you see in dim light.

(d) Night birds have .... cones than rods in their eyes.

Ans. (a) 2 (b) left, left hand

(c) large (d) lesser

Q.7 Angle of incidence is equal to the angle of reflection.

(a) Always

(b) Sometimes

(c) Under special conditions

(d) Never

Ans. (a) Always

Q.8 Image formed by a plane mirror is

(a) virtual, behind the mirror and enlarged

(b) virtual, behind the mirror and of the same size as the object

(c) real at the surface of the mirror and enlarged

(d) real, behind the mirror and of the same size as the object

Ans. (b) Virtual, behind the mirror and of the same size as the object

Q.9 Describe the construction of a kaleidoscope.

Ans. Refer to text on page 227.

Q.10 Draw a labelled sketch of the human eye.

Ans. Refer to figure in text on page 227.

Q.11 Gurmit wanted to perform an activity using a laser torch. Here, teacher advised her not to do so. Can you explain the basis of the teacher's advise?

Ans. Laser light comes from a very small hole and the lens of the laser light is also very small, so the light will penetrate into one part of the eye and it can injure the retina, whereas the normal torch spreads out the light which does not cause any harm to our eyes.
So, the beam of laser light should not be used to perform an activity.

Q.12 Explain how you can take care of your eyes?

Ans. We can take care of our eyes in the following manner

(i) If advised, use suitable spectacles.

(ii) Too little or too much light is bad for eyes. Insufficient light can cause eye strain and headache.

(iii) Too much light like that of the sun, a powerful lamp or a laser torch can injure the retina.

(iv) Wash the eyes frequently with clean water.

(v) Always read at normal distance for vision.

(vi) Never rub your eyes.

Q.13 What is the angle of incidence of a ray, if the reflected ray is at an angle of 90° to the incident ray?

Ans. We know that, the angle of incidence is equal to the angle of reflection and the reflected ray is at an angle of 90° to the incident ray.

$\therefore \quad \angle i = \angle r = 45°$

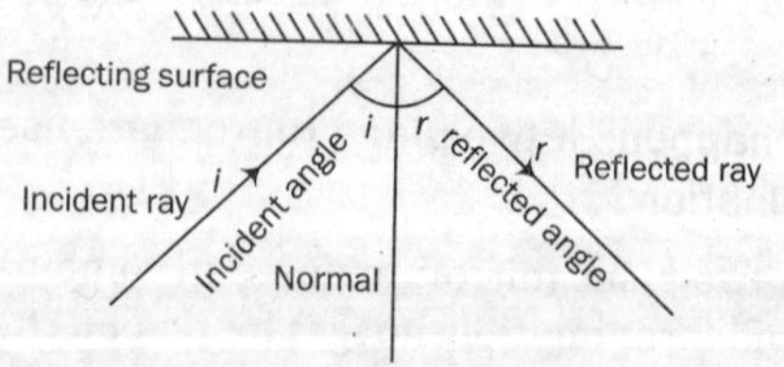

Q.14 How many images of a candle will be formed, if it is placed between two parallel plane mirrors separated by 40 cm?

Ans. Infinite number of images will be formed due to multiple reflections of light.

Q.15 **Two mirrors meet at right angles. A ray of light is incident on one at an angle of 30° as shown in figure. Draw the reflected ray from the second mirror.**

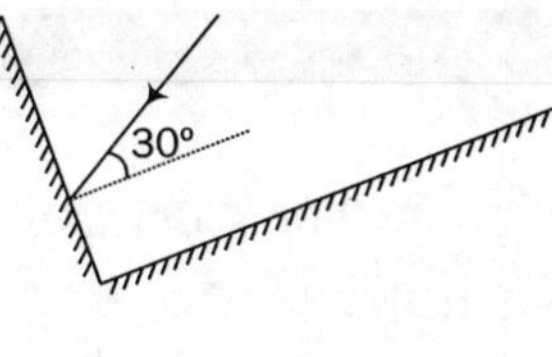

Ans. The diagram will be as follows

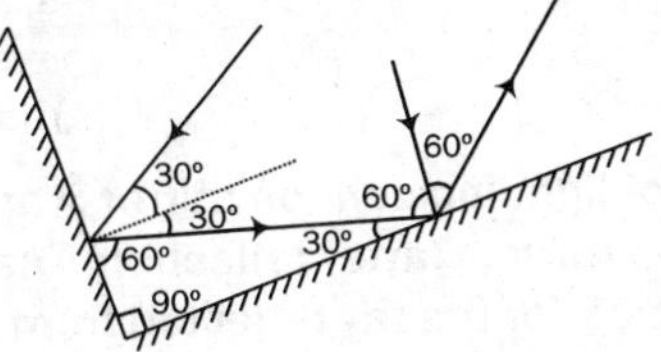

Q.16 **Boojho stands at *A* just on the side of a plane mirror as shown in figure. Can he see himself in the mirror ? Also, can he see the image of objects situated at *P*, *Q* and *R* ?**

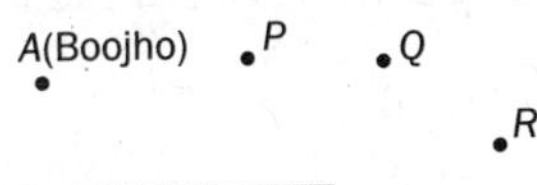

Ans. As Boojho is not in the range of reflecting surface rather, he is standing away from the mirror, so he cannot see himself in the mirror. But he can see the image of *P* which is in the reflecting area but not of *Q* and *R*.

Q.17 **(i) Find out the position of the image of an object situated at *A* in the plane mirror.**

(ii) Can Paheli at *B* see this image?

(iii) Can Boojho at *C* see this image?

(iv) When Paheli moves from *B* to *C*, where does the image of *A* move?

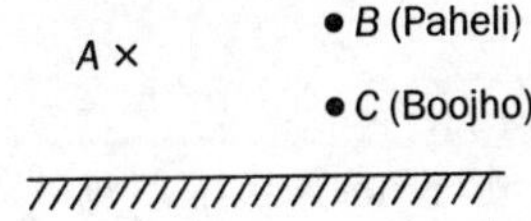

Ans. (i) Since, it is plane mirror, so the image is formed behind the mirror and there is a lateral inversion in it.

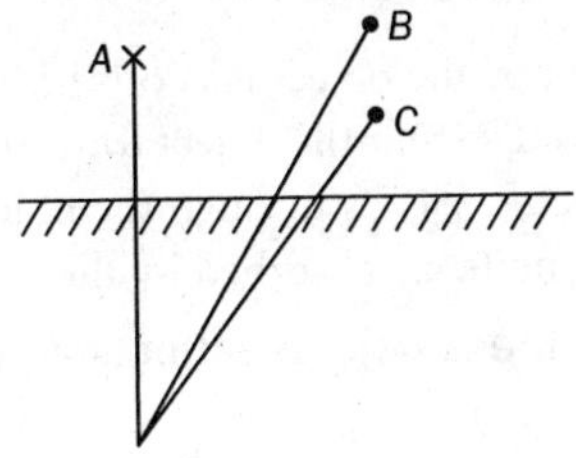

(ii) Yes, Paheli can see the image of object *A*.

(iii) Yes, Boojho can also see the image of object *A*.

(iv) No change in the position of the image of *A*.

REVIEW EXERCISE

Including Competency Based Questions

Part I

Multiple Choice Questions

1. We can see a non-luminous object when light **NCERT Exemplar**

(a) emitted by the object falls on the eye
(b) is reflected from the object towards our eye
(c) completely passes through the object
(d) gets completely absorbed by the object

2. Which of these objects reflects light? **Competency Based Que.**

(a) The sun (b) The moon
(c) A glowing bulb (d) Burning wood

3. A tiny mirror *M* is fixed on a piece of cardboard placed on a table. The cardboard is illuminated by light from a bulb. The position of eye with respect to position of bulb is shown in figure as *A, B, C* and *D*. In which position, mirror will be visible? **NCERT Exemplar**

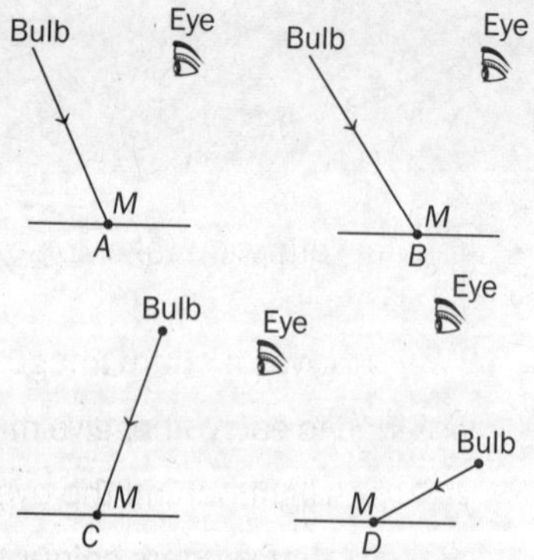

(a) *A* (b) *C*
(c) *B* (d) *D*

4. Two mirrors *A* and *B* are placed at right angles to each other as shown in figure.

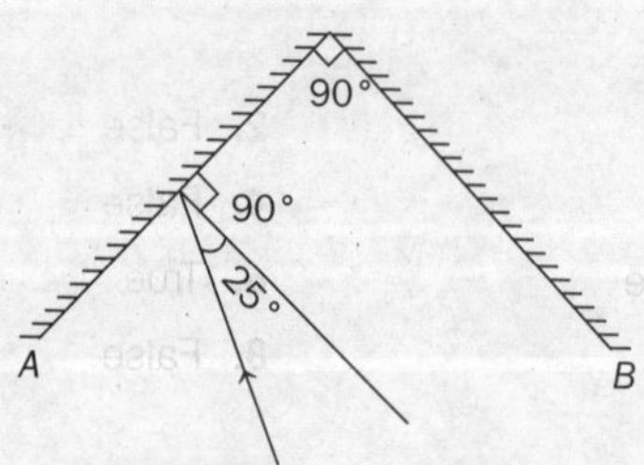

A ray of light incident on mirror *A* at an angle of 20° falls on mirror *B* after reflection. The angle of reflection for the ray reflected from mirror *B* would be

(a) 25° (b) 70°
(c) 50° (d) 115°

5. A small hole *P* is made in a piece of cardboard. The hole is illuminated by a torch as shown in figure. The pencil of light coming out of the hole falls on a mirror.

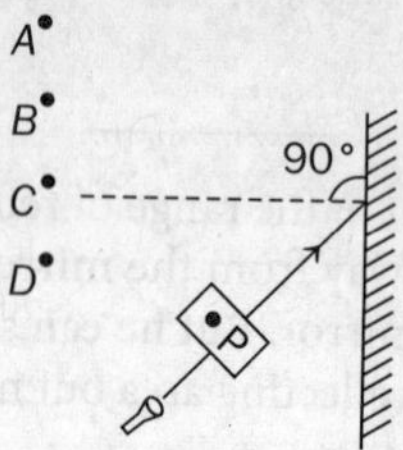

At which point should the eye be placed so that the hole can be seen? **Competency Based Que.**

(a) *A* (b) *B*
(c) *C* (d) *D*

6. Light is falling on surfaces S_1, S_2, S_3 as shown in figure. **NCERT Exemplar**

Surface S_1
Surface S_2
Surface S_3

Surfaces on which the angle of incidence is equal to the angle of reflection is/are

(a) Only S_1 (b) S_1 and S_2
(c) S_2 and S_3 (d) All the three surfaces

7. As the angle between two plane mirrors is decreasing gradually, the number of images of an object placed between them

(a) first increases then decreases
(b) first decreases then increases
(c) increases
(d) decreases

8. How does the eye change in order to focus on near or distant objects?

(a) The eye lens moves in or out
(b) The retina moves in or out
(c) The eye lens becomes thicker or thinner
(d) The pupil becomes larger or smaller

9. In the figure of the human eye, the cornea is represented by the letter NCERT Exemplar, CBSE Question Bank

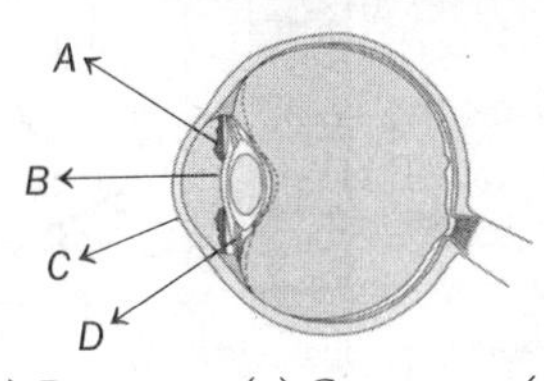

(a) *A* (b) *B* (c) *C* (d) *D*

10. The change in converging power of an eye lens is caused by the action of CBSE Question Bank

(a) retina (b) optic nerve
(c) ciliary muscles (d) iris

11. Which of the following statements is correct regarding rods and cones in the human eye?

(a) Cones are sensitive to dim light.
(b) Cones are sensitive to bright light.
(c) Rods are sensitive to bright light.
(d) Rods can sense colour.

12. Part of the eye which controls the entering of light is called NCERT Exemplar

(a) iris (b) cornea (c) lens (d) retina

13. A person cannot see the distant objects clearly, (though) he can see the nearby object clearly. He is suffering from the defect of vision called

(a) myopia (b) hypermetropia
(c) cataract (d) night blindness

14. The picture shows a candle in front of two plane mirrors joined at their sides. Competency Based Que.

What will increase the number of images formed in the mirrors?

(a) Decrease in the size of the object
(b) Increase in the size of the mirrors
(c) Decrease in the angle between the two mirrors
(d) Increase in the distance between the object and the mirrors

Answers

1. (b)	2. (b)	3. (a)	4. (b)
5. (a)	6. (d)	7. (c)	8. (c)
9. (c)	10. (c)	11. (b)	12. (a)
13. (a)	14. (c)		

Fill in the Blanks

1. .... reflection takes place from smooth surface.
2. .... is the defect in which a person can see nearby object very clearly but cannot see distant objects.
3. The minimum distant at which the eye can see objects distinctly is .... for a normal person.
4. The image of an object persists on the retina of an eye for about.........second even after the object has disappeared.
5. If the still pictures of a moving object are flashed on our eyes at a rate faster than.......pictures per second, the eye perceives the object as moving.
6. In a movie, the still pictures in proper sequence are projected on the screen usually at the rate of .... pictures per second.

Answers

1. Regular	2. Myopia	3. 25 cm
4. 1/16	5. 16	6. 24

True/False

1. Diffused/Irregular reflection takes place from rough surfaces.
2. Diffused reflection gives a sharp image.
3. Two mirrors inclined to each other give multiple images.
4. An eye lens focuses light behind the eye at cornea.
5. The part of the eye that renders colour to it is cornea.
6. Cones and rods are the light sensitive cells.
7. Sunlight, called white light consists of seven colours.
8. Visually challenged people can read and write with hearing aid.

Answers

1. True	2. False
3. True	4. False
5. False	6. True
7. True	8. False

Match the Columns

1. Match the Column I with Column II.

	Column I		Column II
(a)	Cones	(i)	Spectrum
(b)	Iris	(ii)	Sensitive for bright light
(c)	Retina	(iii)	Dispersion of light
(d)	Rainbow	(iv)	Controls the size of pupil
(e)	Band of seven colours	(v)	Image formed

Answer

1. (a)-(ii), (b)-(iv), (c)-(v), (d)-(iii), (e)-(i)

Assertion-Reason Questions

The following question consists of two statements - Assertion (A) and Reason (R). Answer these questions by selecting the appropriate option given below.

(a) Both A and R are true and R is the correct explanation of A.
(b) Both A and R are true but R is not the correct explanation of A.
(c) A is true but R is false.
(d) A is false but R is true.

1. Assertion (A) Irregular surfaces produce diffused reflection.
Reason (R) Due to failure of law of reflection, diffused reflection is produced.

2. Assertion (A) Night birds have more rods than cones.
Reason (R) Rods are more sensitive for dim light than cones.

3. Assertion (A) Iris controls the size of lens.
Reason (R) Iris controls the amount of light entering in the eye.

4. Assertion (A) Eye sight becomes foggy in old ages.
Reason (R) Crystalline lens becomes milky and cloudy in old ages.

Answers

1. (c) The law of reflection is followed by every surface but due to irregularities, some surfaces produce diffused reflection. Hence, A is true but R is false.
2. (a) Night birds have more rods than cones because they are designed by nature to see in night. Hence, both A and R are true and R is the correct explanation of A.
3. (d) Iris controls the size of pupil. Hence, A is false but R is true.
4. (a) Both A and R are true and R is the correct explanation of A.

Case Based Questions

1. The diagram shows how an object is seen through a periscope. x and y are two angles on the path of the light ray. **Competency Based Que.**

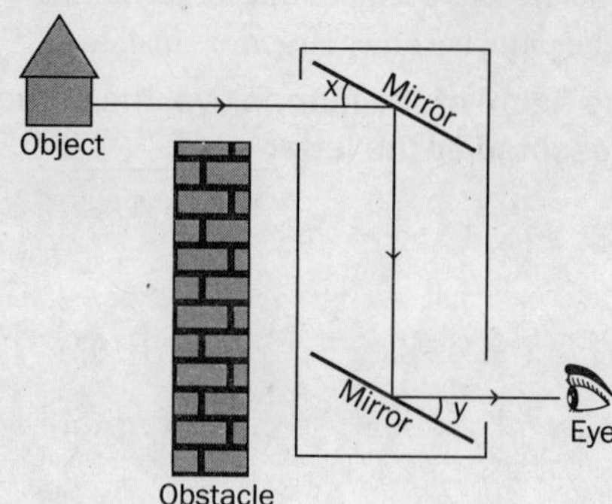

(i) Which condition is required for the periscope to work properly?

	Is the statement true?	Yes or No
(a)	Angle x should be equal to angle y.	Yes/No
(b)	Object to be viewed should be within 5 m of the periscope.	Yes/No
(c)	Top of the periscope should be higher than the top of the obstacle.	Yes/No

(ii) How many times is a light ray is reflected in the periscope ?

(a) Once (b) Twice
(c) Thrice (d) Four time

2 Reema has a multi-coloured disc. She finds that the disc appears white when she spins it rapidly.

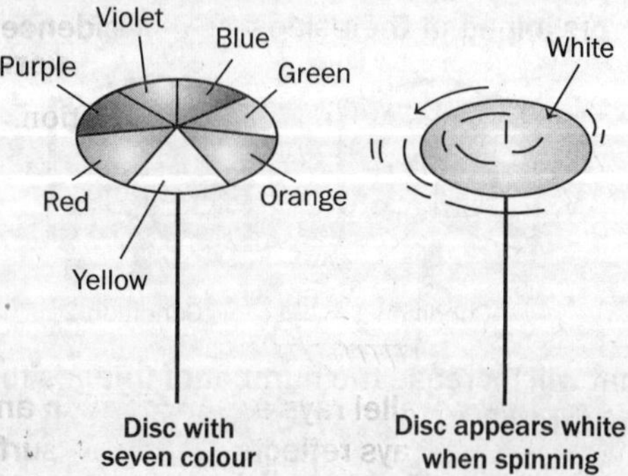

(i) What can be concluded from the picture?

(a) All discs are multi-coloured
(b) All spinning objects appear white
(c) Objects lose its colour on spinning
(d) White is a mixture of seven different colours

(ii) Splitting of white light into seven colours is called

(a) spectrum (b) rainbow

(c) dispersion (d) repulsion

(iii) White light is made up of

(a) 1 colour

(b) 3 colours

(c) 5 colours

(d) 7 colours

(iv) The band of seven colours that constitute white light is called as

(a) rainbow (b) pallete

(c) spectrum (d) wave

Answer

1. (i) (a) Yes, (b) No, (c) Yes (ii) (b)

2. (i) (d), (ii) (c), (iii) (d), (iv) (c)

Part II

Very Short Answer Type Questions

1. Why are we able to see the tap water in the glass even though it is colourless?

Ans. Tap water reflects the light into our eyes. As long as an object reflects light into our eyes, we can see it.

2. Light travels fastest in vacuum. Why?

Ans. Light travels fastest in vacuum than any other medium because there is no obstruction to the passage of light in vacuum.

3. Mention the five English letters that do not show lateral inversion on suffering reflection from a plane mirror.

Ans. The five English letters which do not show the lateral inversion on suffering reflection are A, H, O, T, U.

4. How many times a ray of light is reflected by two plane mirrors placed parallel and facing each other? NCERT Exemplar

Ans.

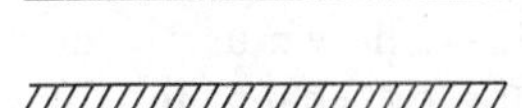

The ray is reflected infinite times between the two plane mirrors placed parallel to each other.

5. The angle between incident ray and reflected ray is 60°. What is the value of angle of incidence? NCERT Exemplar

Ans. Since, angle of incidence = angle of reflection.
So, angle of incidence = 30°

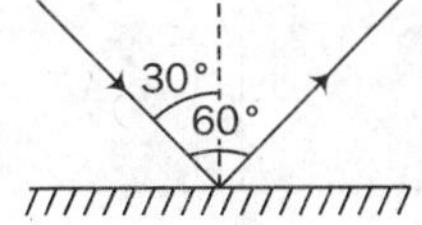

6. Imagine that parallel rays are incident on an irregular surface. Are the rays reflected from this surface parallel to each other?

Ans. No, the reflected rays from irregular surface are in different directions.

7. When a parallel beam of light hits an uneven surface, then predict the nature of reflected beam.

Ans. When light hits an uneven surface, there are many angles of incidence. Hence, the parallel beam of light rays will be reflected off the surface at different angles.

8. State the size of image formed by a plane mirror.

Ans. The size of image formed by a plane mirror is same as that of the object in front of the mirror.

9. Mention the name of device that is generally used by the designers of wallpapers and fabrics.

Ans. Kaleidoscope is a device that is generally used by the designers of wallpapers and fabrics.

10. White light is a combination of which colours?

Ans. White light is a combination of seven colours, which are Violet, Indigo, Blue, Green, Yellow, Orange, Red.

11. A safety vest helps to keep the workers who are working by the roadside safely. This especially so during the night. Why?

Ans. The reflectors on the safety vest reflect light into the motorists eyes. This helps to alert the motorists of the wearer's presence on the road.

12. State the functions of rods and cones in our eye.

Ans. Cones are responsible for colour vision, whereas rods are responsible for vision in dim light.

13. Boojho while waving his hand very fast in front of his eyes, observes that his fingers appear blurred. What could be the reason for it? NCERT Exemplar

Ans. Our eyes are not so sensitive for a large speed and when any object is very near, the ciliary muscles cannot focus the object so early.

14. Name the part of the eye which gives colour to the eyes. NCERT Exemplar

Ans. Iris has different colours, so the iris gives to its colour the eyes.

Short Answer Type Questions

1. Look at figure. Can the image of the child in it be obtained on a screen? **Competency Based Que.**

Ans. The image of the child cannot be obtained on the screen because the image is not real. The images formed by plane mirror are virtual, so these virtual images cannot be seen on the screen.

2. What is the difference between the surfaces of a sheet of sandpaper and a mirror ?

Ans. The sandpaper has a rough surface causing light that is reflected on it to be scattered at different angles. The mirror however, allows regular reflection.
Sandpaper cannot produce any image, unlike the mirror due to diffused (irregular) reflection.

3. Explain how do we see various objects?

Ans. Due to reflection, we can see various objects. Since, we know that, all surfaces reflect light. So when light falls on them (any objects), it reflects the light. In this way, this reflected light enters our eyes and due to this, we can see the object.

4. Draw figure showing the position of the plane mirror. Also, label the angle of incidence and angle of reflection on it. **NCERT Exemplar**

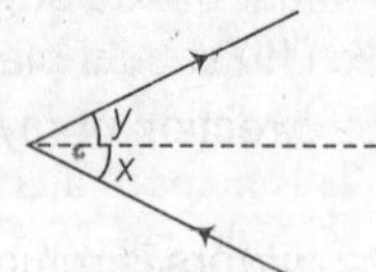

Ans.

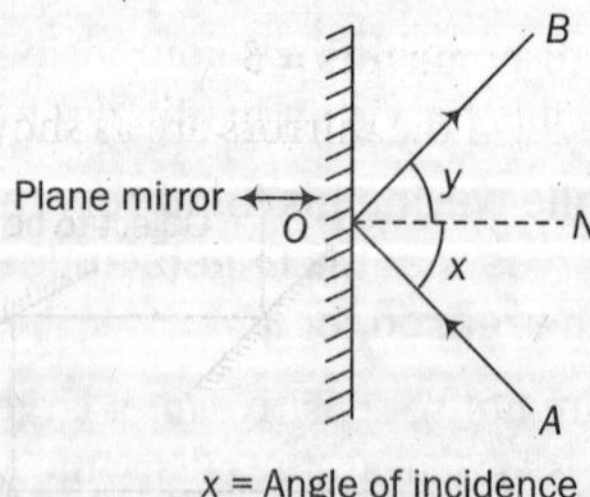

x = Angle of incidence
y = Angle of reflection

5. "The laws of reflection only holds true for regular reflection". Is this statement true or false? Explain your answer.

Ans. False, the laws of reflection holds for both regular and diffused reflection. In a diffused reflection, the reflecting surface being rough and uneven, the parallel beam of light is reflected in different directions and angles.

6. Explain what happens to light when it gets dispersed? Also, give an example. **NCERT Exemplar**

Ans. Light is splitted into its constituent colours (7 colours) when it gets dispersed, e.g. rainbow formation is due to the dispersion of white light after passing through water droplets.

7. Which part of the eye gets affected, if someone is suffering from cataract? How is it treated?

Ans. In people suffering from cataract, the eye lens becomes cloudy.
Cataract is treated by replacing the convex lens with a new artificial lens.

8. Eyes of the nocturnal birds have large cornea and a large pupil. How does this structure help them? **NCERT Exemplar**

Ans. The size of the eyes of nocturnal bird is large. Large eyes with a wider pupil, larger lens and increased retinal surface can collect more ambient light which help them to see the objects even at night easily.

9. "Though the image formation on retina is inverted but still we are able to see the erect objects". Explain how?

Ans. Yes, it is very true to say because the formation of image on the retina is conveyed to brain in the form of electrical impulses with the help of optical nerves. So, brain is able to perceive an erect image of object with the help of electrical impulses.

10. Explain in brief, how do ciliary muscles affect the functioning of eye?

Ans. As we know that, ciliary muscles can contract and relax, because of it, this can change the shape of eye lens which results in change in its focal length. So, eye lens can make image of nearby objects and also far off objects on retina.

11 The picture shows the size of the pupil under two different conditions.

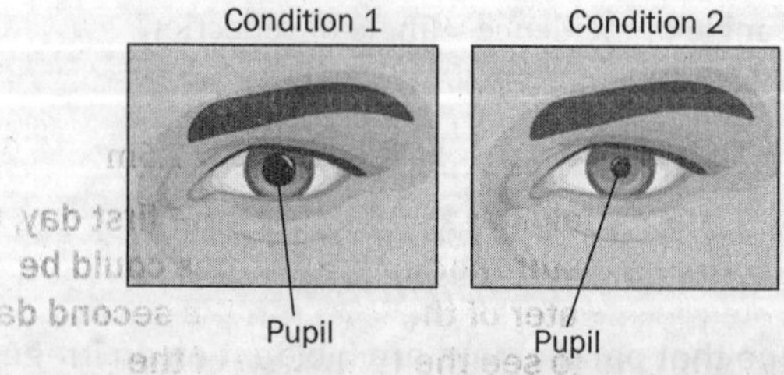

What makes the pupil change size between conditions 1 and 2?

Ans. In condition 1, eyes get insufficient amount of light. That's why, the pupil expands but in condition 2, eyes get large amount of light that's why pupil contract.

Long Answer Type Questions

1. There is a mistake in each of the following ray diagrams given as figure (a), (b), and (c). Make the necessary correction(s). **Competency Based Que.**

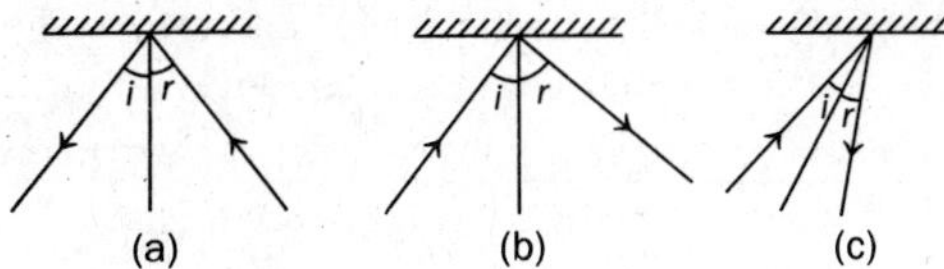

Ans. The correct diagrams are as below

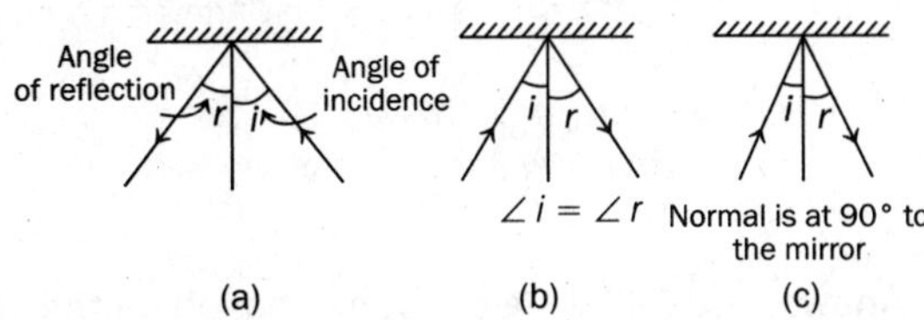

2. A man stands 10 m in front of a large plane mirror, so how far must he walk before he is 5 m away from his image?

Ans. As, per the given information, point O is initial position of the man and I is initial position of the image of the man can be show with the help of a figure.

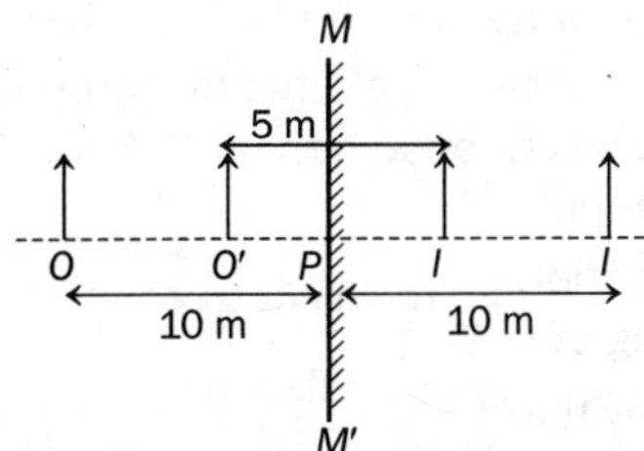

Point O' is final position of the man and I' is final position of the image of the man. From the figure,

$$O'P + PI' = 5\text{ m} \qquad [O'P = PI']$$

$$\Rightarrow \quad O'P + O'P = 5\text{ m}$$

$$\Rightarrow \quad O'P = 2.5\text{ m}$$

Distance walked by the man $= OP - O'P$

$= 10 - 2.5 = 7.5\text{m}$

3. Aditya visited a lake on two days. On the first day, the reflection of the surrounding mountains could be seen clearly in water of the lake. On the second day, he was not able to see the reflection of the mountains clearly. Give one possible reason for this phenomenon and explain your answer clearly.

Ans. The unclear image of the mountains on the second day is probably due to wind blowing across the lake causing it to lose its calmness. When the lake is calm, the surface of the lake is smooth and regular reflection occurs, allowing a clear image of the mountains to be formed. When the wind blows across the lake, the surface of the lake becomes rough and uneven causing a diffused reflection. Hence, the image formed of the mountains will be unclear and blurred.

4. Figure shows the word REST written in two ways in front of a mirror. Show how the word would appear in the mirror ? **Competency Based Que.**

R
E
S
T

REST

Ans. According to reflection properties of plane mirror, it forms same size, laterally inverted images of the object infront of them.

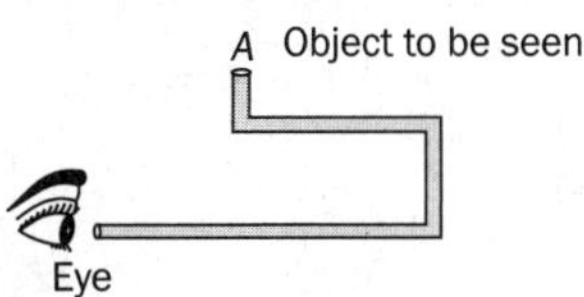

5. Boojho planned an activity to observe an object *A* through pipes as shown in figure, so that he could see objects which he could not directly see.

A Object to be seen

Eye

(i) Mention how many mirrors should he use to see the objects?
(ii) Indicate the positions of the mirrors in the figure.
(iii) State what must be the angle w.r.t. the incident light at which he should place the mirrors?
(iv) Indicate the direction of rays in the figure of (ii) Part.
(v) If any of the mirrors is removed, will he be able to see the objects? **NCERT Exemplar**

Ans. (i) Number of mirrors = 3

(ii) Positions of the mirrors are as shown in figure

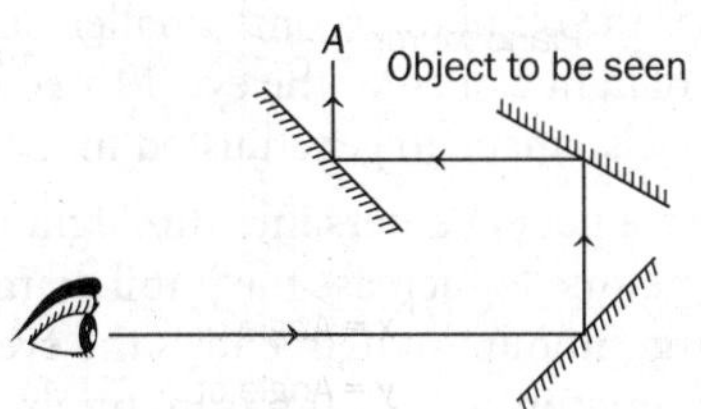

(iii) Mirrors should be placed at 45° w.r.t. the incident light, so that ray can move forward.

(iv) Direction of rays is shown in figure.

(v) He will not be able to see the objects if any of the mirrors is removed, since he will not get the rays after that removed mirror.

6. How is the phenomenon of reflection used in making a kaleidoscope. What are the applications of a kaleidoscope? NCERT Exemplar

Ans. Kaleidoscope is a cylinder with three mirrors containing loose, coloured objects such as beads or pebbles and bits of glass. As the viewer looks into one end, light entering the other creates a colourful pattern due to reflection. Its applications are given below

(i) It works on the principle of multiple reflection, where several mirrors are placed at an angle (usually 60°) to one another. Typically, these are three rectangular mirrors set at 60° to each other, so that they form an equilateral triangle.

(ii) The 60° angle creates seven duplicate images of the objects, 5 at 60° and 2 at 90°. As the tube is rotated, the tumbling of the coloured objects present varying colours and patterns.

(iii) It is used in decoration purposes, attractive toys, etc.

7. Write down the names of parts of the eye in the blank spaces shown in figure.

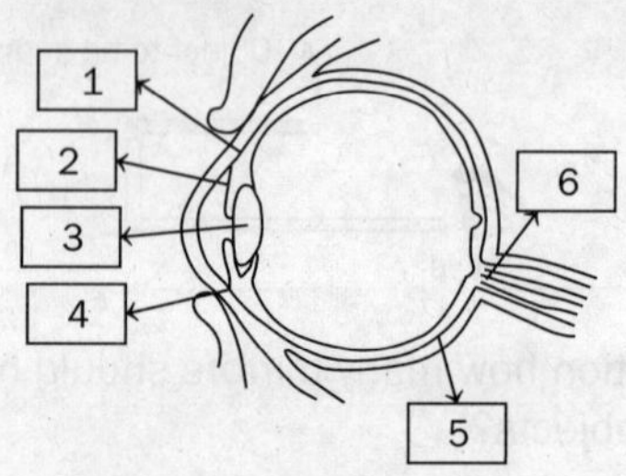

Ans. 1. Ciliary muscles 2. Iris
3. Lens 4. Cornea
5. Retina 6. Optic nerves

8. Explain the reason for the following statement "we usually take sometime to see the objects in a dim light room, when we enter into the room from bright sunlight outside".

Ans. Since, when we are in the bright sunlight at that moment iris causes the pupil to become smaller, so that a little amount of light can enter the eye. Moreover, the rods of retina are also made to get adjusted in the same manner. And when a person enters into dim light room, then iris takes sometime to increase the pupil diameter, due to which large amount of light enters the eye, so that's why when we enter into the room from bright sunlight outside, then we usually take sometime to see the objects in a dim room.

Case Based Question

1. The picture shows a light ray from a candle falling on a mirror. *P, Q, R, S* and *T* are five points behind the mirror.

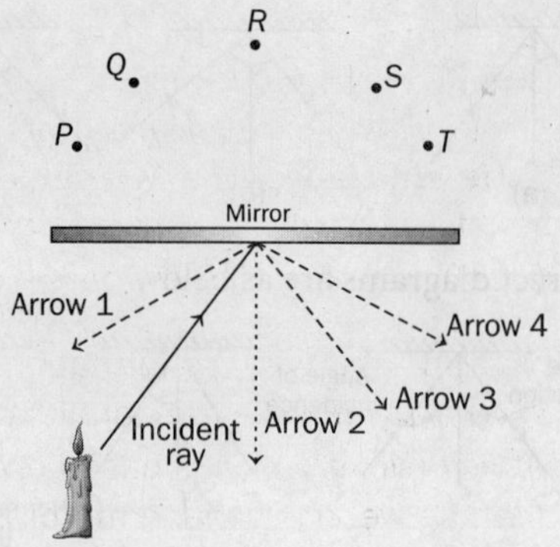

Answer the following questions based on the above information.

(i) Which arrow represents the light ray reflected by the mirror?

(a) Arrow 1 (b) Arrow 2
(c) Arrow 3 (d) Arrow 4

(ii) At which point, will the image of the candle form? Will the image be erect or inverted ?

(iii) Which of these statements is true for reflection of light rays? Choose 'Yes' or 'No' for the correct response.

	Is the statement true?	Yes or No
(a)	Light rays are reflected by plane surfaces only.	Yes/No
(b)	Angle of incidence is equal to the angle of reflection	Yes/No
(c)	Incident ray and reflected ray meet at the same point.	Yes/No

Ans. (i) (c) Arrow 2 is normal to the mirror. Hence, by measuring angle between incident ray and arrow 2, the reflected ray will be arrow 3. Option (c) is correct.

(ii) Extend the arrow 3 behind the mirror. It will meet to *Q*. Hence, image will be formed at *Q*. Plane mirror always forms the image in the same orientation as the object. Since, the object is erect, hence the image will also be erect.

(iii) (a) No, (b) Yes, (c) Yes.

Skill Based Questions as per NEP 2020

1. Sunita is a science student. She performs an activity to obtain multiple images of an object by two plane mirrors. She starts placing these mirrors at different-different angles. She was surprised to see the number of images started increasing as she decreases the angle between two plane mirrors. **Activity Based Que.**

(i) Draw a ray diagram for the formation of images when two plane mirrors are parallel to each other.

(ii) Name two devices which is based on the multiple reflection between two plane mirrors.

(iii) How do we determine the number of images formed by two plane mirrors at a certain angle?

2. Two mirrors *A* and *B* are placed at right angles to each other as shown in figure. A ray of light incident on mirror *A* at an angle of 25° falls on mirror *B* after reflection.

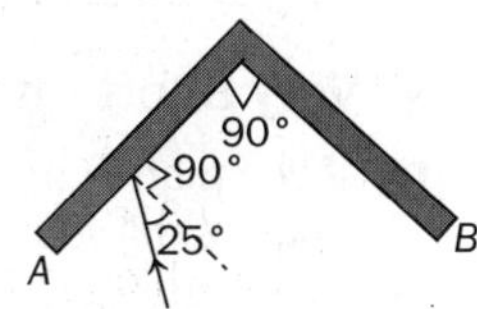

The angle of reflection for the ray reflected from mirror *B* would be **Knowledge Based Que.**

(a) 25° (b) 50°

(c) 65° (d) 115°

3. A student studies that a plane mirror results in a laterally inverted image after reflecting. Which of these represents the image likely to be formed by a plane mirror? **Thinking Based Que.**

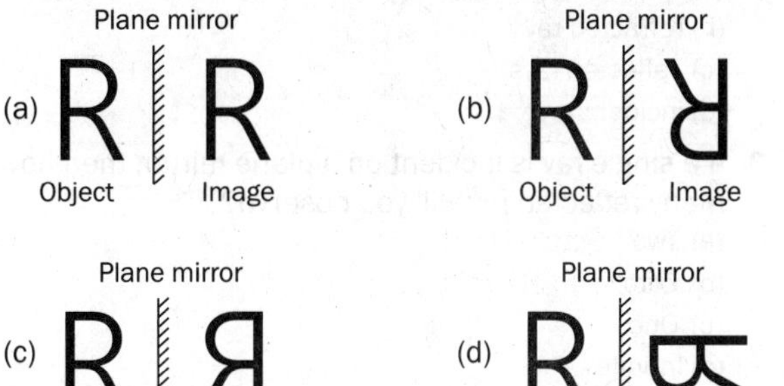

ASSESSMENT EXERCISE

Part I

Multiple Choice Questions

1. The nature of image formed by a plane mirror is
   (a) always virtual
   (b) always inverted
   (c) always real
   (d) real and virtual
2. The light ray after reflection from a surface is known as
   (a) normal ray
   (b) refracted ray
   (c) reflected rays
   (d) incident ray
3. If a single ray is incident on a plane mirror, then how many reflected ray will you observe?
   (a) Two
   (b) Zero
   (c) One
   (d) Infinite

Fill in the Blanks

4. The incident ray, the normal ray and the reflected ray, all lie in the .... plane.
5. When the angle between plane mirrors is more than 90°, it forms ...... images.
6. .... is the transparent part of the outermost layer of eye.

True/False

7. The law of reflection is not valid for rough surfaces.
8. Periscope works on the multiple reflection by plane mirror.
9. Sunlight is a mixture of eight different colours.

Assertion-Reason Questions

The following questions consists of two statements-Assertion (A) and Reason (R). Answer these questions by selecting the appropriate option given below.

(a) Both A and R are true and R is the correct explanation of A.
(b) Both A and R are true but R is not the correct explanation of A.
(c) A is true but R is false.
(d) A is false but R is true.

10. **Assertion** (A) Owl can see very well in the night.
    Reason (R) Owl has a large cornea and a large pupil to allow more light in its eye.
11. **Assertion** (A) Rainbow is the natural phenomenon of multiple reflection.
    Reason (R) Rainbow forms when sunlight falls on the rainwater droplets.

Part II

Very Short Answer Type Questions

12. If two plane mirrors make an angle of 60°. How many images will you found?
13. Give any one precaution to take care of eyes.
14. Name the part of eye
    (a) which controls the amount of light entering the eye.
    (b) which converges light rays to form the image.
15. State the information that you get about sunlight from the formation of a rainbow.

Short Answer Type Questions

16. Explain lateral inversion with an example.
17. Briefly explain the term persistence of vision.
18. Name any one defect of the eye. How is it corrected?
19. What are the functions of optic nerve and retina?

Long Answer Type Questions

20. Explain the laws of reflection with the help of diagram.
21. Draw a labelled diagram showing how a plane mirror forms an image of a point placed in front of it.

Answers

1. (a) 2. (c) 3. (c) 4. same 5. two 6. cornea 7. False 8. True 9. False 10. (a) 11. (d)

Explanations of Skill Based Questions

Chapter 1 Crop Production and Management

1. The possible reasons behind the variability in the production of cotton in state C from year 2020 to 2021 are as follows
   (i) Cotton is a kharif crop, i.e. it requires sufficient amount of rain. In the year 2020 state 'C' might have faced drought conditions which further reduced the productivity of cotton.
   (ii) Proper manuring and weeding was not done.
2. Seed treated with insecticide contain a precise amount of insecticide that protects crops from insects infestation and diseases during germination and early development. It also increases root growth and seedling height. In the given setup, treated seed (set A) show early germination of seeds and better growth of seedlings whereas seeds of set B show poor germination. These seeds damaged in soil due to insect infestation.
3. (i) He was spraying weedicides on crop to kill weeds.
   (ii) Farmer cover their mouth and nose while spraying weedicides because they can be lethal if they get inside the body.
4. (i) The grains were kept on terrace for the purpose of drying them before storage.
   (ii) Yes, it is necessary to dry freshly harvested grains in the sun to reduce the moisture in them. This prevents the attack by insects, pests, bacteria and fungi.

Chapter 2 Microorganisms : Friend and Foe

1. (i) The given microorganism is bread mould (*Rhizopus*). Which is grows on bread. It belongs to fungi.
   (ii) It grows well in moist conditions because moist condition provides moisture and nutrients for the mould to grow.
   (iii) If it is not safe to eat infected bread because it can produce toxins which is harmful to human health.
2. (i) Microbes are minute organisms that are invisible to the naked eye. These are classfied into four major groups, i.e. bacteria, fungi, protozoa and some algae.
   (ii) Microorganisms are used for various purposes. They are used in the preparation of curd, bread, cake, alcohol, vaccine, antibiotics, etc.
3. (i) Prakhar could be affected by food poisoning.
   (ii) Cooked rice left out at room temperature can lead to bacterial growth and foodborne illness.
4. (i) A vaccine is a substance that stimulates the body's immune system to produce antibodies and provide immunity against diseases.
   (ii) Vaccines are made from dead or inactive microbes that are unable to cause disease.

Chapter 3 Coal and Petroleum

1. Some major thermal plants in India are
   - Vindhyachal thermal plants in MP
   - Mundra Thermal Power station in Gujrat.
   - Ultra Mega Power plant in MP.
   - Tiroda Power plant in Maharashtra.

   The reason of these power plants are located at the respective places is the availability of coal for them. Each power plant have such mines around them.
2. (i) Diesel car is less economical in comparison to electric car.
   (ii) The increase in carbon dioxide is causing the earth's atmosphere to warm.
   (iii) The values possessed by Sohan are knowledgeable and good friend.
3. (i) In thermal power plant, the coal is broken into pieces for easy combustion to heat the water in the boilor. Water is then turned into steam with high pressure and temperature.
   (ii) The values possessed by Nikita are aware, and vignant towards environmental issue.

Chapter 4 Combustion and Flame

1. (i) (a) Oxygen (b) Fuel
   (ii) Ramya's mother should switched off the gas first and cover the container with a plate so that oxygen supply get cut off from the fire.
2. If pepsi is poured into the bowl, the candle flame will be put out. As soft drinks like pepsi contains water and carbon dioxide.
3. (i) When wood burns, the carbon present in it is oxidised to carbon dioxide (CO_2) which is a non-poisonous gas. When the windows are closed, fresh air or oxygen cannot enter the room. Due to the insufficient supply of oxygen, carbon is oxidised to carbon monoxide (CO) which is a highly poisonous gas. It causes suffocation in a closed room. On opening the windows, the poisonous gas slowly diffused out of the room and fresh air came inside due to which the feeling of suffocation reduced gradually.
   (ii) Mohan is quite intelligent, quick in decisions and caring about his family.
4. (i) The symptoms observed in the villagers show that oxides of nitrogen and sulphur must be coming out of the chimney. This is due to combustion of fossil fuels like coal, oil, natural gas, gasoline, etc., to produce high temperatures at which oxidation of

atmospheric nitrogen takes place forming NO and NO_2. SO is produced due to combustion of sulphur containing coal and fuel oil.

(ii) Mr. Lalit Jain was intelligent, social and caring about villages.

Chapter 5 Conservation of Plants and Animals

1. The graph above shown clearly that the population of American Bison has grown exponentially between 1902 and 1912. The threatened species such as black buck, white eyed, duck, elephant golden, cat, etc. are protected and prevented in the wildlife sancturies.

2. (i) Preventing cutting of trees.
(ii) Putting a ban on hunting of animals.
(iii) Efficient utilisation of natural resources.
(iv) The reserves and protected areas should be developed carefully.

3. (i) The construction of highway passing through the middle of forest may lead to
- The loss of natural habitats for many plants, animals and birds which eventually leads to the decrease in biodiversity of that area.
- Significant increase in the level of air pollution.
- Decrease in the number of trees that eventually causes shortage of useful products we obtain from trees.
- Will also increase the number of vehicles on the roads which will further contribute to noise pollution.

(ii) Forests are helpful to mankind in many ways out as given below
- They provide us with variety of useful products such as honey, wood, timber, medicinal plants, firewood, etc.
- Helps in promoting rainfall.
- Provides balance of carbon dioxide and oxygen in nature.
- Prevents soil erosion.
- Maintain global temperatrue.

4. (i) The animals whose numbers are diminishing to the level that they might face extinction are known as endangered animals. These are on the verge of getting diminished from the earth and if appropriate actions are not taken to save them they will soon becomes extinct.
(ii) Yes, it is wrong to harm animals because each and every animal whether small or large has its own importance in balancing the ecosystem. Every animal forms a part of a food chain and food webs which are essential in maintaining balance in nature. For instance, we are indirectly harming ourselves if we cause harm to them.
(iii) Flora-Sal, wild mango, etc.
Fauna-Giant squirrel, flying squirrel, bison, etc.

5. 1. Endangered, 2. Red Data Book, 5. Deserts
1. Extinct, 3. Endemic, 4. Biodiversity

Chapter 6 Reproduction in Animals

1. (i) Yes, a female hen (or chicken) lays unfertilised eggs.
(ii) The eggs we get in the stores are unfertilised because they are produced by the female hen without undergoing fertilisation.

2. (i) *In vitro* fertilisation is a technique which is used to over care the problems related to infertility in couples to have baby of their own.
(ii) Some women are unable to conceive or have babies of their own because their oviducts or Fallopian tubes are blocked and the sperms cannot reach the egg for fertilisation. Hence, preventing the ova from being fertilised.

3. Gametes are the cells that has sex-chromosomes, i.e. XX in female and XY in male that combines together during sexual reproduction. During fertilisation, the two gametes one from the mother and other from the father fuses together to form a zygote. Therefore, the baby born bears characters of both parents though mother gives birth to a baby.

Chapter 7 Reaching the Age of Adolescence

1. People in our society are unaware about the causes and transmission of AIDS and show distracted behaviour towards the patient. This is due to the following misconceptions. People contact with virus through touching, kissing, blood transfusion and mosquito bites. It can be transmitted by sharing food, clothes, etc.

2. The low sex ratio in a country is due to the desire of having a male child. The common believe that boys brings economic stability to the family and girls are burden for them. Thus, the girl child is more likely to be killed at birth.

3. (i) Some of the changes may includes increase in height, growth of facial hairs, broadness of shoulders, acne and pimples on face, development of sex organ, growth of pubic hair, etc.
(ii) This special period is called as puberty.
(iii) Amit is attaining the age of puberty in which the body undergoes certain changes by which the adolescents becomes capable of undergoing reproduction.

4. (i) Sex chromosome is the 23rd pair in human beings out of the 46 pairs) chromosomes that determine the sex of the individual (i.e. either male or female).
(ii) No, it is not right to blame mother for the sex of a child because it is the father who decides the sex of the child as the male gamete (sperm) bears two chromosomes, i.e. X and Y.

5. Across

3. Adam's apple, 4. Endocrine, 7. Pituitary

8. Hormone, 9. Insulin, 10. Oestrogen

Down

1. Testosterone, 2. Thyroid, 3. Adolescence,

5. Target site, 6. Larynx, 7. Puberty

Chapter 8 Force and Pressure

1. Resultant force on the left hand side,

F_{net} (left) $= 15\text{ N} + 30\text{ N} = 45\text{ N}$

Force on the right hand side, F_{net} (right) = 35 N

So, $F_{net} = F_{net}$ (left) $- F_{net}$ (right) $= (45 - 35)\text{ N} = 10\text{ N}$

∴ Direction will be from left to right.

2. (i) (a), (ii) (d), (iii) (d), (iv) (b)

Chapter 9 Friction

1. (b)

2. (i) The two factor are as follows

(a) The nature of two surfaces in contact.

(b) The force with which two surfaces are pressed together.

(ii) This pencil cell travelled the fastest on silk cloth as it faces, the least amount of time in this case.

$$\text{Average time taken} = \frac{4.20 + 4.20 + 425}{3} = 4.225$$

(iii) The friction force enables us to walk and roam this world around us, which is obviously a great positive part. But at the same time, friction is also cause for the wear and tear of our shoes. The sole of our shoes gets damaged after sometimes due to the friction between the sole and the ground.

3. (i) We know that the force of friction directly depends upon the area of contact between two surfaces. Since, the area of contact between surfaces is lies in case of rolling as compared to sliding, the sliding friction always greater than the rolling friction.

(ii) Two examples of sliding friction are

(a) Rubbing of palms together to produce heat.

(b) Children sliding down through slides in playground.

Chapter 10 Sound

1. (i) The human ear is divided into three parts

(a) Outer ear (b) Middle ear

(c) Inner ear

(ii) The inner ear passes the messages from ear to the brain in form of impulses.

(iii) The eardrum is located within the outer ear.

2. (i) Represents music as it is composed by regular vibrations of constant amplitude.

(ii) Represents noise as it is composed of irregular vibrations of low and high amplitudes.

3. (i) (d) Elephant and human.

(ii) (a) Regulating the use of loudspeaker.

Chapter 11 Chemical Effects of Electric Current

1. (i) Yes, the LED will glow as it requires very small amount of current to do so.

(ii) The LED will glow brighter than before as decreasing the distance between the rods allows more current to flow through the circuit.

2. (i) Yes, we are able to write.

(ii) It is possible due to the electrolysis of potassium iodide solution which produces iodine. This iodine reacts with starch to produce blue colour ink.

3. (i) Chromium, zinc and copper are used for electroplating.

(ii) Electroplating is mainly done for avioding corrosion of metals and for decorative purposes.

The most familiar uses of electroplating are used in jewellery and purification of metals.

Chapter 12 Some Natural Phenomena

1. (i) The foil strips move away when the charged body is brought near the detector.

(ii) The foil strips repel each other as they become charged with the charge of same type.

2. (i) (b) In a seismograph, large deviations means more stronger earthquake, hence (b) shows the strongest earthquake.

Chapter 13 Light

1. (i)

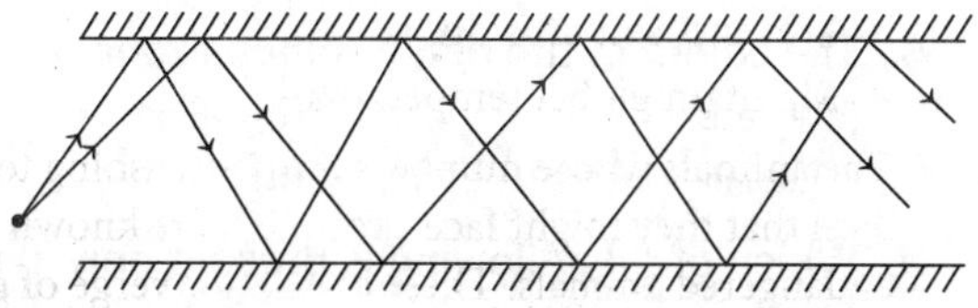

In such case, the ray will be reflect infinite times.

(ii) Kaleidoscope and the mirror setting used by hair salons.

(iii) Number of images formed by two plane mirrors at a certain angle are given by

$$\Rightarrow \frac{360°}{\theta \text{ (given angle)}} - 1$$

2. (c)

3. (c)

Sample Question Paper 1 (Solved)
Science

Time : 3 hrs	M.M. : 80

General Instructions

1 This question paper comprises 39 questions. All questions are compulsory.
2 This question paper is divided into five sections - A, B, C, D and E.
3 **Section A** - Question Nos. 1 to 20 are multiple choice questions. Each question carries 1 mark.
4 **Section B** - Question Nos. 21 to 25 are very short answer type questions. Each question carries 2 marks.
5 **Section C** - Question Nos. 26 to 34 are short answer type questions. Each question carries 3 marks.
6 **Section D** - Question Nos. 35 to 38 are long answer type questions. Each question carries 5 marks.
7 **Section E** - Question No. 39 is source-based/case-based question which carry 3 marks.

Section A

1. Which of the following shows internal fertilisation?
(a) Humans (b) Cows
(c) Hens (d) All of these

2. Which of the following fuels is expected to leave a residue upon burning?
(a) Coal (b) Petrol
(c) Natural gas (d) LPG

3. The strength of force expressed by its
(a) weight
(b) mass
(c) magnitude
(d) longitudinal force

4. The colour of the non-luminous zone is
(a) white (b) yellow
(c) blue (d) black

5. Which of the following is present only in plants?
(a) Plasma membrane (b) Cell wall
(c) Nuclear membrane (d) Cytoplasm

6. When electric current is passed through the copper sulphate solution, copper sulphate dissociates into
(a) copper and sulphate
(b) copper and sulphur
(c) copper and oxygen
(d) None of the above

7. Which of the following is best fuel for automobiles?
(a) Petrol (b) CNG
(c) Diesel (d) Kerosene

8. Thyroxin is produced by
(a) pituitary gland
(b) adrenal gland
(c) thyroid gland
(d) testes

9. Which of the following is true about friction?
(a) Friction can only slow things down
(b) Friction is a force that only occurs on rough surfaces
(c) Friction is a force that occurs only between solids
(d) Friction is a force that only occurs when an object moves

10. The lowest temperature at which a substance catches its fire is called
(a) moderate temperature
(b) ignition temperature
(c) minimum temperature
(d) extreme temperature

11. In which of the following states is an earthquake most likely to occur?
(a) Gujarat
(b) Kerala
(c) Chhattisgarh
(d) Karnataka

12. Yeast is used in the production of

(a) sugar (b) alcohol
(c) hydrochloric acid (d) oxygen

13. Which of the following gas is used to extinguish fire?

(a) Oxygen (b) Hydrogen
(c) Carbon dioxide (d) Nitrogen

14. Voice box has stretched string like part which vibrate to produce sound are called

(a) larynx (b) vocal cords
(c) nerves (d) arteries

15. Which of the following are male reproductive organs?

(a) Ovary, testis, penis
(b) Ovary, uterus, testis
(c) Uterus, testis, penis
(d) Testis, penis, sperm duct

Direction (Q. Nos. 16-20) *The following questions consist of two statements **Assertion** (A) and **Reason** (R). Answer these questions by selecting the appropriate option given below.*

(a) Both A and R are true and R is the correct explanation of A
(b) Both A and R are true, but R is not the correct explanation of A
(c) A is true, but R is false
(d) A is false, but R is true

16. Assertion (A) Magnesium and charcoal are combustible substances.
Reason (R) A chemical process in which a substance reacts with oxygen to give off heat is called combustion.

17. Assertion (A) In bright light, the size of the pupil is small.
Reason (R) Pupil controls the amount of light entering to the eye.

18. Assertion (A) In summer, the frequency of watering the plants is lower.
Reason (R) It may be due to the increased rate of evaporation of water from the soil and the leaves.

19. Assertion (A) Copper sulphate solution dissociates into copper and sulphate ions by passing electric current.
Reason (R) Copper sulphate solution is a poor conductor of electricity.

20. Assertion (A) Endemic species of plants and animals are found easily.
Reason (R) Indian giant squirrel and flying squirrel are endemic species.

Section B

21. How does a sound producing object differ from silent?

22. Give two examples of any two exhaustible resources.

23. What do you mean by flora and fauna?

Or **What do you mean by biosphere reserves ?**

24. Give two uses of petroleum

Or **What are petrochemicals?**

25. Define national park.

Section C

26. Give two examples of each solid, liquid and gaseous fuels.

Or **What is the difference between coal gas and coke?**

27. Define asexual reproduction. Describe any two methods of asexual reproduction in animals.

28. Can sound travel through a vacuum? Why or why not?

29. Explain the changes that occur in puberty stage.

Or **In humans, sex of a child is determined by male gamete. Comment.**

30. How does a matchstick catch fire?

31. Explain the difference between static friction and sliding friction.

Or **Why do sea divers wear specially designed suit?**

32. How does deforestation lead to a decrease in the water holding capacity of the soil?

33. Mention any three characteristics of a good fuel.

Or **Why should the fossil fuels be used with care ?**

34. Why porters wear turbans when they have to carry heavy loads on their heads?

Section D

35. Why should we use some resources like coal and petrol in limit?

Or **Why is natural gas considered as cleaner fuel and how is it transported.**

36. What is irrigation? Describe two methods of irrigation which conserve water.

Or **(i) Why organic manure is considered better than fertilisers?**

(ii) What are weeds ? What is weeding and why it is necessary?

37. How would you use an electroscope to determine the nature of charge of a charged body?

38. What are the changes in males at puberty?

Section E

39. During a class discussion on fuels used for household, Anu had suggested a fuel called petrol, but her teacher said that it is not a safe fuel for the household activity. Anu wanted to know the reasons why petrol cannot be used as a fuel for household activity even though its efficiency is high and it is widely used in vehicles.

(i) Why petrol is not a safe fuel for household activity?

(ii) What fuels do we uses in our houses?

(iii) What value of Anu is shown here?

Answers

1. (*d*) Humans, cows and hens all are show internal fertilisation. This is because fertilisation takes place inside the body of an individual (female).

2. (*a*) Among the given options, coal is expected to leave a residue upon burning.

3. (*c*) The strength of a force is expressed by its magnitude. The magnitude of a force is expressed in the SI unit of force called newton.

4. (*c*) The colour of the non-luminous zone is blue.

5. (*b*) Cell wall is present only in plants. It is not present in animal cell.

6. (*a*) On passing electric current through the copper sulphate solution, copper sulphate dissociates into copper and sulphate.

7. (*b*) CNG is best fuel for automobiles as it produces pollutants in very small amounts.

8. (*c*) Thyroid gland is to produced thyroxin hormones that help to regulate the body's metabolism.

9. (*d*) Friction is a force that only occurs when an object moves.

10. (*b*) The lowest temperature at which a substance catches its fire is called ignition temperature.

11. (*a*) In India earthquakes most likely occurs in Gujarat.

12. (*b*) Yeast is used in the production of alcohol, which convert sugar into ethanol and carbon dioxide.

13. (*c*) Carbon dioxide gas does not support combustion and acts as extinguisher of fire.

14. (*b*) Voice box has stretched string like parts, which vibrate to produce sound are called vocal cords.

15. (*d*) Male reproductive organs include testis, penis and sperm duct.

16. (*a*) Both A and R are true and R is the correct explanation of A.

17. (*a*) Both A and R are true and R is the correct explanation A.

In bright light, the size of the pupil is small, pupil controls the amount of light entering to the eyes.

18. (*d*) A is false, but R is true. A can be corrected as In summer the frequency of watering the plants is higher. This is because of the increased rate of evaporation.

19. (*c*) A is true, but R is false. R can be corrected as Copper sulphate solution is a good conductor of electricity as by passing electric current, it can dissociate into its ions copper and sulphate, that are responsible for flow of current.

20. (*d*) A is false, but R is true. A can be corrected as Endemic species are those species of plants and animals which are found exclusively in a particular areas.

21. A sound producing object vibrates, while a silent does not. We can feel the vibration by touching them.

22. Two examples of exhaustible resources are coal petroleum, etc.

23. The plants and animals found in a particular area are termed flora and fauna respectively of that area.

Or

Biosphere reserves are the large areas of protected and meant for conservation of wildlife, plants and animals resources and traditional life of the tribal recycling in that area. It helps to maintain biodiversity and culture of that area.

24. Two uses of petroleum are as follows

(i) It is used to run vehicles.

(ii) It is used in petroleum products like vaseline.

Or

Petrochemicals are chemical products derived from petroleum. These are used in the manufacture of detergents, fibres. etc.

25. A national park is an area reserved for wildlife where they can freely use the habitats and natural resources.

26. Solid fuels — Wood, cow dung.

Liquid fuels — Kerosene, petrol.

Gaseous fuels — Hydrogen, natural gas.

Or

Coke is a tough, porous and black substance and almost pure form of carbon. While coal gas is obtained during the processing of coal to get coke. Coke is used in the manufacture of steel while coal gas is used as a fuel in many industries.

27. Asexual reproduction is defined as the production of a new organism from a single parent without the involvement of sex cells.

The two methods of asexual reproduction are

(i) **Budding** In this, a part of the organism starts bulging out. It grows slowly and develops into a separate individual. It occurs in *Hydra*.

(ii) **Binary fission** In this, a single organism is divided into two. It occurs in *Amoeba*.

28. Sound cannot travel through a vacuum. A vacuum is an area without any air, like space. So, sound cannot travel through space because there is no matter for the vibrations to work in.

29. The changes that occur during the puberty stage are

(i) **Increase in height** The most common change during puberty is the sudden increase in the height of boys and girls. The rate of growth in height varies in different persons.

(ii) **Change in body shape and appearance** When puberty sets in, rapid changes in the body shape and appearance starts in boys and girls which make them look different from one another.

(iii) **Change in voice** At puberty, the voice box begins to grow in boys as well as in girls.

(iv) **Increased activity of sweat and sebaceous glands** During puberty, the secretion of sweat gland and sebaceous gland increases.

(v) **Development of sex organs** The onset of puberty brings about complete growth and development of sex organs in boys and girls due to which their reproductive systems start functioning at this stage.

Or

A female has two X-chromosomes while a male has one X and one Y-chromosomes. When a sperm containing X-chromosome fertilises the egg. The zygote would have two X-chromosomes and develops into a female child. If the sperm contributes a Y-chromosome to the egg at fertilisation, the zygote would develop into a male child. Hence, the sex of a child is determined by a male gamete.

30. By rubbing a matchstick against a rough surface, it attains its ignition temperature and thus, catches fire.

31. Static friction that acts between two surfaces when the object starts moving from its state of rest, while sliding friction that acts between two surfaces when the object is already in motion or sliding over another surface.

Or

Since the pressure of liquid increase with the increasing depth of sea. Specially designed suits protect Scuba divers from the huge pressure of the water underneath.

32. Deforestation also leads to a decrease in the water holding capacity of the soil. The movement of water from the soil into the ground is reduced. The rainwater gets collected on soil's surface which results in floods. The other properties of the soil like nutrient, content texture also changes because of deforestation.

33. Three characteristics of a good fuel are as follows
(i) It has high calorific value.
(ii) It is very easy to transport.
(iii) It is cheap, affordable and economic.

Or

If we use fossil fuels carefully, it will result in better environment, less risk of global warming and they will be available for a longer period.

34. Porters wear turbans when they have to carry heavy loads on their heads to increase the area of contact. This reduces the pressure on the head.

35. Resources like coal and petroleum are exhaustable natural resources.
They are formed by the decomposition of dead organisms that lived millions of years ago. Their replenishment rate is very harmful to our environment causing air pollution as well as global warming. Hence, we should use coal and petroleum in limited amounts.

Or

Natural gas is considered as a cleaner fuel be cause it produces fewer pollutants when burned.
It is transported under high pressure as compressed natural gas (CNG) and can be used directly in homes and factories through pipelines.

36. The supply of water to crops at different intervals is called irrigation.
The time and frequency of irrigation varies from crop to crop, soil to soil and season to season. In summer the frequency of watering is higher.
The two methods of irrigation which conserve water are
(i) **Sprinkler irrigation system** This irrigation system has perpendicular pipes having rotating nozzles on top, are joined to the main pipeline at regular intervals. It is more useful in the uneven land where sufficient water is not available. Sprinkler irrigation system is very useful for sandy soil.
(ii) **Drip irrigation system** This irrigation system has an arrangement of pipes with very small holes in them to water plants drop by drop just at the position of the roots. It is the best technique for watering fruit plants, gardens and trees. Water is not wasted in this type of irrigation system.

Or

(i) The organic manure is considered better than fertiliser. This is because
(a) It enhances the water holding capacity of the soil.
(b) It makes the soil porous due to which exchange of gases becomes easy.
(c) It increases the number of friendly microbes.
(d) It improves the texture of the soil.

(ii) The undesirable plants that grow naturally along with the crops are called weeds. The removal of weeds is called weeding. It is necessary since weeds compete with the crop plants for water, nutrients, space and light. Thus, they affect the growth of the crop. Some weeds interfere even in harvesting and may be poisonous for humans and animals.

37. Let the electroscope get charged with the negative charge, by touching a negatively charged ebonite rod to the metal disc of the electroscope. By doing this, the leaves of the electroscope will get open up (diverge). Now touch the body to be tested with the metal disc of charge electroscope. Either of the two things will happen.
(i) If the divergence of the leaves increase, the body has similar charge or the given body is also negatively charged.
(ii) If the divergence of the leaves decrease, the body has unlike charge or the given body is positively charged.

38. The human body undergoes several changes during adolescence. The most important change which marks puberty is that boys and girls become capable of reproduction. Several changes that occur in males during puberty are
(i) sudden increase in height.
(ii) development of long bones.
(iii) bones of the arms and the legs elongate.
(iv) growth of hair at different parts of body like facial hair, development of moustaches and beard.
(v) development of sex organs like penis, testes begin to produce sperms, etc.

39. (i) Petrol vapourises easily, so it can lead to rapid combustion. Hence, it is not safe as household fuel.
(ii) We use fuel such as kerosene and wax in our houses.
(iii) Anu has knowledge of fuel, but she is little bit confused.

Sample Question Paper 2 (Solved)

Science

Time : 3 hrs	M.M. : 80

General Instructions

1 This question paper comprises 39 questions. All questions are compulsory.
2 This question paper is divided into five sections - A, B, C, D and E.
3 **Section A** - Question Nos. 1 to 20 are multiple choice questions. Each question carries 1 mark.
4 **Section B** - Question Nos. 21 to 25 are very short answer type questions. Each question carries 2 marks.
5 **Section C** - Question Nos. 26 to 34 are short answer type questions. Each question carries 3 marks.
6 **Section D** - Question Nos. 35 to 38 are long answer type questions. Each question carries 5 marks.
7 **Section E** - Question No. 39 is source-based/case-based question which carry 3 marks.

Section A

1. Which of the following fuels is not formed from the remains of plants and animals?

(a) Coal (b) Petroleum
(c) Natural gas (d) Wood

2. If we apply the force along the right, the friction acts along the

(a) right direction
(b) left direction
(c) Both right and left directions
(d) None of the above

3. The process of conversion of sugar into alcohol is called

(a) nitrogen fixation (b) moulding
(c) fermentation (d) infection

4. Where does natural gas occur?

(a) Above petroleum oil
(b) Below petroleum oil
(c) Along with petroleum oil
(d) Inside volcanic mountains

5. The epicentre of an earthquake is

(a) deep under the crust of earth
(b) in the mantle of earth
(c) on the surface of earth
(d) in the core of earth

6. The most common carrier of communicable disease is

(a) ant (b) housefly
(c) dragonfly (d) spider

7. Which one of the following is not a fossil fuel?

(a) Petrol (b) Wood
(c) Diesel (d) Coal

8. Angle of incidence is equal to the .... angle of reflection.

(a) always (b) sometimes
(c) under special conditions (d) never

9. Out of the following groups of crops, which group is included in kharif crops?

(a) Rice, wheat, cotton (b) Rice, maize, soybean
(c) Maize, soybean, mustard (d) Rice, mustard, cotton

10. What are the most common sources of energy used in automobiles?

(a) Wood and coal (b) Petroleum and diesel
(c) Natural gas and coal (d) LPG and cow dung

11. Number of vocal cords in human is

(a) one (b) two (c) four (d) six

12. Which of the following does not represent a microorganism?

(a) Protozoa (b) Fungi
(c) Bacteria (d) Insect

13. Which of the following is not a product of petroleum?

(a) Diesel (b) Kerosene
(c) Natural gas (d) Plastic

14. Which one of the following forces is a contact force?

(a) Force of gravity (b) Magnetic force
(c) Force of friction (d) Electrostatic force

15. The number of nuclei present in a zygote is
(a) one (b) two (c) four (d) None of the above

Direction (Q. Nos. 16-20) *The following questions consist of two statements* ***Assertion*** *(A) and* ***Reason*** *(R). Answer these questions by selecting the appropriate option given below.*

(a) Both A and R are true and R is the correct explanation of A
(b) Both A and R are true, but R is not the correct explanation of A
(c) A is true, but R is false
(d) A is false, but R is true

16. Assertion (A) There will be no action of external force on an object moving with uniform velocity.
Reason (R) The force acting on an object need not cause motion. It may deform its dimension.

17. Assertion (A) Matchstick does not catch fire on its own at room temperature.
Reason (R) The head of the safety match contains only antimony trisulphide and potassium chlorate.

18. Assertion (A) Farmer have to add manure to the fields to replenish the soil with nutrients.
Reason (R) Continuous cultivation of crops makes the soil rich in nutrients.

19. Assertion (A) Water can be used to control fire on electrical equipment or oil.
Reason (R) Water is commonly used to control fire.

20. Assertion (A) Plants must be planted along the roads and around buildings.
Reason (R) Plant help to maximise the harmful effects of noise pollution.

Section B

21. What are the differences between multicellular and unicellular organisms?

22. What is range of audible sound?

23. What do you mean by the term agricultural practices?

Or What do you understand by manures?

24. How are heat and light produced in the Sun?

25. When does the net force become zero?

Or Give two examples each of situations in which you push or pull to change the state of motion of objects.

Section C

26. Sunlight and air are inexhaustible natural resources. Comment.

Or What tips are given by PCRA to save petrol and diesel?

27. State one observation from everyday life which shows that sound travels slower than light.

28. Explain how many types of fertilisations are there?

29. Why is natural gas a very important fossil fuels?

30. Give an example of chemical effect of the electric current.

Or Which metal is electroplated on iron for makings cans and why?

31. What do you mean by migration? Write the causes of migration of birds.

Or (i) What is reforestation ?
(ii) What is the aim of the forest (conservation) act ?

32. Write two important uses of coke.

33. What are the uses of an electroscope?

34. What do you mean by health? What are the factors which help to keep a good health?

Or What are carriers? How does husefly acts as a carrier?

Section D

35. A wave with a frequency of 500 Hz is traveling at a speed of 200 ms^{-1}. What is the wavelength?

36. Water gets boiled in paper cup without burning the paper. Explain.

Or Carbon dioxide is the most commonly used gas for extinguishing a fire, which properties of carbon dioxide are used here?

37. (i) What do you mean by irrigation? And write sources of irrigation.
(ii) What are the differences between fertiliser and manure?

Or Describe various tools that are used to break soil to the size of grains to get better yield.

38. **Explain why an owl can see well in the night, but not during the day whereas an eagle can see well during day, but not in the night?**

Section E

39. **One evening while playing in the ground, A man was bite by a mosquito. The next day his health started getting affected. He rushed the doctor. The doctor prescribed some medicines and some medical tests. The doctor diagnosed him with dengue fever as the reports suggested low platelets count.**

(i) How does dengue virus spread?

(ii) Write any two preventive measures for dengue fever.

(iii) How does dengue differ from malaria?

Answers

1. (*d*) Among the given fuels, wood is not formed from the remains of plants and animals.

2. (*b*) If we apply the force along the right, the friction acts along the left direction.

3. (*c*) The process of conversion of sugar into alcohol is called fermentation.

4. (*a*) Usually petroleum and natural gas occur at the same place. Petroleum occurs as liquid, whereas natural gas is in the gaseous state above petroleum.

5. (*c*) The epicentre is the point on the "earth's surface" vertically above the hypocentre (or focus), point in the crust where a seismic rupture begins.

6. (*b*) Houseflies are the most common carrier of communicable diseases.
Ant, dragon flies and spiders do not carry any diseases.

7. (*b*) Fossil fuels are energy resources formed under the Earth's surface. Hence, among the given options, wood is not the fossil fuels.

8. (*a*) Angle of incidence is always equal to the angle of reflection.

9. (*b*) Rice, maize, soybean are included in Kharif crops. These crops grown in the rainy season.

10. (*b*) The most common sources of energy used in automobiles are petroleum and diesel.

11. (*b*) Number of vocal cords in human is two.

12. (*d*) Protozoa, fungi and bacteria are microorganisms, but insect is not a microorganism.

13. (*c*) Natural gas is a separate fossil fuel that is often found along with a petroleum, but it is not a product of petroleum.

14. (*c*) Friction is a surface phenomenon. When two surfaces have irregularities. That come in contact they get interlocked preventing them from sliding against each other. So, the frictional force is a contact force dependent on the surface.

15. (*a*) Number of nuclei present in a zygote is one.

16. (*c*) A is true, but R is false. R can be corrected as
The force acting on an object can cause motion and it may deform the dimension of it.

17. (*a*) Both A and R are true and R is the correct explanation of A.

18. (*c*) A is true, but R is false. R can be corrected as
Continuous growing of crops makes the soil poorer in certain nutrients. Thus, farmers add manure to the fields to replenish the soil with nutrients.

19. (*d*) A is false, but R is true. A can be corrected as
Water is not used to control fire on electrical equipment or oil, but fire exhauster like CO_2 is used.

20. (*c*) A is true, but R is false. R can be corrected as
Plants help to minimise the harmful effects of noise pollution.

21. Organisms made of more than one cell are called multicellular, whereas organisms made up of single cell are called unicellular.

22. Range of sound between 20 Hz to 20000 Hz is called audible sound as sound between these frequencies is easily audible to human beings.

23. Agricultural practices are those practices which involve the necessary steps to be taken during production of crops.

Or Manures are organic substances obtained from the decomposition of plants and animal wastes which provide lot of humus to the soil. It is very important for the healthy growth of plants.

24. In the sun, heat and light are produced by nuclear reactions.

25. When two forces acting on an object in opposite direction are equal, then the net force becomes zero.

*Or*The two examples are as follows:

(i) **Spring** When we compress or stretch the spring, it changes its shape.

(ii) **Foam** When we compress the foam or sponge, it changes its shape.

26. Inexhaustible natural resources are those whose quantity is not based on consumption. The amount of Sunlight and air are available in unlimited quantity and cannot be exhausted by human. Hence, these are inexhaustible natural resources.

Or In India, PCRA advises people how to save petrol/diesel while driving. Their tips are

- Drive at a constant and moderate speed
- Switch off the engine at traffic lights.
- Ensure correct tyre pressure.
- Ensure regular maintenance of the vehicle.

27. Lightning and thunder take place in the sky at the same time and at the same distance from us. Lightning is seen earlier and thunder is heard later. This shows that sound travels slower than light.

28. There are two types of fertilisations

(i) **Internal fertilisation** The fertilisation which takes place inside the female body is called internal fertilisation. The male animal puts his sperms into the female animal's body and these sperms fertilise the eggs inside her body. e.g. human being.

(ii) **External fertilisation** The fertilisation which takes place outside the female body is called external fertilisation, e.g. frog and fish.

29. Natural gas is an important fossil fuel because it mainly constitutes methane and does not produce much pollution. It is a clean gas. Natural gas compressed under high pressure forms CNG which we use in our cars as fuel.

30. The passage of an electric current through a conducting solution causes chemical reaction as a result, bubbles of a gas are formed or deposits of metal are seen on electrodes or changes in colour of solution, may occur. These are some of the chemical effects of electric current.

Or It is electroplated on iron for making cans because tin is less reactive than iron. Thus, food does not come into contact with iron and is protected from getting spoilt.

31. Some species of birds fly to far away areas every year in a particular season. This phenomenon is called migration.

The causes of migration of birds are

(i) in search of food.

(ii) due to climatic changes.

(iii) for laying eggs.

(iv) to enjoy long summer days.

Or

(i) Reforestation is restocking of the destroyed forests by planting new trees.

(ii) Forest (conservation) Act is aimed at preservation and conservation of natural forests and meeting the basic needs of the people living in or near the forest.

32. Two important uses of coke are as follows.

(i) It is used in the process of metal extraction.

(ii) Steel and a variety of other products are made from coke.

33. An electroscope can be used for following purposes

(i) To detect and measure the charge on a body.

(ii) To determine the nature of charge on a body.

34. The physical and mental well-being of an individual is regarded as health.

The factors that helps to keep a good health are as follows

(i) One should eat a balanced diet.

(ii) To take care and keep personal hygiene.

(iii) Playing and walking in fresh air keep the body fit and healthy.

(iv) Avoid the alcohol and tobacco.

(v) Drink clean water, breathe in clean air and eat clean food.

Or

Some insects and animals carries diseases causing microbes and hence, act as a carriers. Housefly is one such carriers. It sit on the garbage and animal excreta and pathogens stick to their bodies. When these flies sit on uncovered food they may transfer the pathogens. Whoever eats the contaminated food is likely to get sick.

35. Given,

Frequency $(n) = 500$ Hz

Speed $(v) = 200 \text{ ms}^{-1}$

Wavelength $(\lambda) = ?$

Now,

$$\text{Wavelength } (\lambda) = \frac{\text{Speed } (v)}{\text{Frequency } (n)}$$

$$\lambda = \frac{200}{500} = 0.4 \text{ m}$$

36. When we heat the paper cup containing water, the heat given to it is rapidly transferred to water from the paper cup. The temperature of water goes on increasing until it attains its boiling point and starts boiling. As during this process, the heat is continuously being transferred to water, the paper cup does not attain its ignition temperature.

Hence, it does not burn.

Or Carbon dioxide is heavier than air and it settles down and cuts the supply of oxygen, which extinguishes the air.

37. (i) The supply of water to crops at different intervals is called irrigation. The time and frequency of irrigation varies from crop to crop, soil to soil and season to season.

In summer, the frequency of watering is higher.

The sources of irrigation are wells, tubewells, ponds, lakes, rivers, dams and canals.

(ii) The differences between fertiliser and manure are as follows

Fertiliser	Manure
A fertiliser is an inorganic salt.	It is a natural substance obtaining by the decomposition of cattle dung, human waste and plant residues.
A fertiliser is prepared in factories.	Manure can be prepared in the field.
A fertiliser does not provide any humus to the soil.	Manure provides a lot of humus to the soil.

Or

The main tool used to break soil to the size of grains are

- **Plough** It is generally made of wood. It contains a strong triangular iron strip called ploughshare and a long part of wood called plough shaft. There is a handle at one end of the shaft. The other end is attached to a beam which is placed on the bull's necks. One pair of bulls and a man can easily operate the plough.
  Wooden plough is being replace by iron plough.
- **HOE** It has a long rod of wood or iron. A strong, broad and bent plate of iron is fixed to one of its ends and works like a blade. It is pulled by animals.
- **Cultivators** Ploughing is done by tractor driven cultivator. It saves labour and time.

38. A night bird (owl) can see very well in the night, but not during the day. On the other hand, day light birds (kite, eagle) can see well during the day, but not in the night.
The owl has a large cornea and a large pupil to allow more light in its eye. Also, it has on its retina a large number of rods and only a few cones. The day birds on the other hand, have more cones and fewer rods.

39. (i) Dengue is a viral infection transmitted to humans through the bite of *Aedes* mosquitoes. The mosquito becomes infected when it takes the blood of a person infected with the virus.

(ii) The two preventive measures for dengue fever are

(a) Use mosquito repellents and wear long sleeved clothes and full pants before going outside the house.

(b) Do not let water stagnate any where, reduce the mosquito habitat.

(iii) Dengue is caused by *Aedes* mosquito, whereas malaria is caused by *Anopheles* mosquito.

Sample Question Paper 3 (Unsolved)
Science

Time : 3 hrs	M.M. : 80

General Instructions

1 This question paper comprises 39 questions. All questions are compulsory.
2 This question paper is divided into five sections - A, B, C, D and E.
3 **Section A** - Question Nos. 1 to 20 are multiple choice questions. Each question carries 1 mark.
4 **Section B** - Question Nos. 21 to 25 are very short answer type questions. Each question carries 2 marks.
5 **Section C** - Question Nos. 26 to 34 are short answer type questions. Each question carries 3 marks.
6 **Section D** - Question Nos. 35 to 38 are long answer type questions. Each question carries 5 marks.
7 **Section E** - Question No. 39 is source-based/case-based question which carry 3 marks.

Section A

1. When two objects are already moving, the friction between them is called

(a) static (b) rolling (c) sliding (d) drag

2. The coldest zone of candle flame is

(a) the middle zone
(b) the innermost zone
(c) blue zone
(d) zone of partial combustion

3. Reproduction by budding takes place in

(a) *Amoeba* (b) bacteria
(c) *Hydra* (d) *Paramecium*

4. Which of the following set of substances contains acids?

(a) Grapes, lime water (b) Vinegar, soap
(c) Curd, milk of magnesia (d) Curd, vinegar

5. The main products of combustion are

(a) Carbon dioxide and water
(b) Oxygen and water
(c) Only carbon dioxide
(d) Only oxygen

6. The first antibiotic called penicillin was extracted from

(a) bacterium (b) protozoan
(c) fungus (d) algae

7. The waves produced on the earth's surface is called

(a) seismic wave (b) longitudinal wave
(c) microwave (d) radiowave

8. Which of the following properties is not a characteristic of a good fuel?

(a) High ignition temperature
(b) Low cost
(c) Causes minimum pollution
(d) Readily available

9. Antibiotics are prepared by the microorganisms, i.e.

(a) bacteria and virus
(b) virus and fungus
(c) bacteria and fungus
(d) Protozoa and fungus

10. Which type of mirror is used to obtain a virtual, laterally inverted image and equal size of an object?

(a) Plane mirror (b) Concave mirror
(c) Convex mirror (d) All of these

11. Ignition temperature is the

(a) temperature at which a substance catches fire
(b) highest temperature at which a substance catches fire
(c) lowest temperature at which a substance does not catches fire
(d) lowest temperature at which a substance catches fire

12. Which of the following cannot be provided to the soil by a chemical fertiliser?

(a) Nitrogen (b) Humus
(c) Potassium (d) Phosphorus

13. Sound does not travel in

(a) vacuum (b) gases
(c) solids (d) liquids

14. Which one of the following is not a petroleum product?

(a) Coal

(b) Gasoline

(c) Diesel

(d) Petroleum gas

15. The carrier of malaria-causing protozoan is

(a) cockroach

(b) housefly

(c) butterfly

(d) female *Anopheles* mosquito

Direction (Q. Nos. 16-20) *The following questions consist of two statements* ***Assertion*** *(A) and* ***Reason*** *(R). Answer these questions by selecting the appropriate option given below.*

(a) Both A and R are true and R is the correct explanation of A

(b) Both A and R are true, but R is not the correct explanation of A

(c) A is true, but R is false

(d) A is false, but R is true

16. Assertion (A) A moving toy car stops after a little distance.

Reason (R) Friction opposes the motion.

17. Assertion (A) A single-celled organism perform all the necessary functions that multicellular organisms perform.

Reason (R) The size of the cells in living organisms may be as large as a million of a metre or may be as small as a few centimetres.

18. Assertion (A) Fossil fuels are an important source of energy.

Reason (R) Fossil fuels provide energy to different industries.

19. Assertion (A) The zygote develops into a new individual in sexual reproduction.

Reason (R) Embryo gets embedded in the wall of uterus.

20. Assertion (A) Alcohol and petrol can be used as household fuels for cooking.

Reason (R) They are highly inflammable substances.

Section B

21. Draw a diagram showing angle of incidence and angle of reflection.

22. What is the role of PCRA ?

23. Differentiate between contact and non-contact forces.

24. Name the scientist who discovered penicillin.

Or

Name some organisms which act as carriers of disease causing microbes.

25. Name the petroleum product. What is used for surfacing roads?

Or

Write the two uses of coke.

Section C

26. How many images will be formed when the angle between two plane mirror is

(i) 90°? (ii) 60°?

27. What are the advantages of using natural gas as a fuel?

Or **In which form, CO_2 can be stored in cylinders?**

28. How does recycling and saving of papers related to deforestation?

Or

What is the reason behind migration behaviour shown by some birds?

29. How do irregularities on the surface contribute to the force of friction?

Or

We observe the wheels of buses and trucks are broader than the wheels of car or scooters. Why?

30. State two uses of each kerosene and paraffin wax.

Or

What is CNG? What are its uses?

31. What do you mean by species? Explain some of its features.

32. Explain why lateral inversion occurs in a mirror image?

33. Write the various tips for minimising the wastage of petrol/diesel while driving vehicles.

34. What are root nodules? How are they helpful?

Section D

35. Do liquid and gases exert pressure on the walls of container in all direction? Give example to justify your statement.

36. What do you mean by ignition temperature? Why a matchstick does not catch fire on its own at room temperature?

Or

The burning of fossil fuels causes air pollution. Explain.

37. (i) How is an embryo developed?
(ii) How embryo is different from foetus?
(iii) What are test-tube babies?

Or

(i) How reproduction in hen is different from that in *Amoeba*?
(ii) Draw a well-labelled diagram of female reproductive organ in humans.
(iii) When and where the matured egg is released by the human ovaries?

38. On putting glass over a lighted candle, the candle flame flickers and produce smoke, why so?

Section E

39. Friction is a force between two surfaces that are sliding or trying to slide across each other. Friction always works in the direction opposite to the direction in which the object is moving or trying to move. It always slows a moving object down. Why you walk, friction is caused between tread on shoes and the ground. This friction acts to grip the ground and prevent sliding.
(i) When does friction arise?
(ii) Why should we apply oil in the hinges of the door?
(iii) Gymnasts apply some coarse substance on their hands. Why?
(iv) Explain why sportsmen use shoes with spikes.
(v) To slide a sledge we should increase or decrease the friction. Why?

Answers

1	(c)	2	(b)	3	(c)	4	(d)	5	(a)	6	(c)	7	(a)	8	(a)	9	(c)	10	(a)
11	(d)	12	(b)	13	(a)	14	(a)	15	(d)	16	(a)	17	(c)	18	(a)	19	(b)	20	(d)